Praise for the a

'O'Toole is Ireland's best interviewer.' – *Irish Mail on Sunday*

'O'Toole specializes in in-your-face interviews.' – *Sunday Independent*

'Jason O'Toole is the journalistic equivalent of a hangman. Cleverly giving some of his notorious subjects just enough rope to do the job themselves.' – Olaf Tyaransen, *Evening Herald*

'Indisputably Ireland's most talented and prolific interviewer.' – *Irish Daily Mail*

'O'Toole's skill is getting access to important figures and being a good listener.' – *Metro*

'Jason O'Toole, a man with a renowned skill for convincing famous people to betray secrets they would rather not have.' – John Lee, *Irish Mail on Sunday*

'When it comes to making people talk he's the best in the business.' – Pat Flanagan, *Irish Daily Mirror*

'O'Toole has developed a reputation as a journalist who gets the scoop. How does he manage to get the stars to say such revealing things?' – *Dublin Live*

'He has a reputation for hard-hitting interviews.' – Richie Taylor, *Irish Independent*

'Jason O'Toole has an extraordinary skill when it comes to Q&A interviews. He has a knack for getting the very best from his subjects; often eliciting unexpectedly candid responses to the most probing of questions.' – Sylvia Pownall, *Irish Sunday Mirror*

'O'Toole's clear talent at making his interviewees feel comfortable in sharing makes for a highly interesting read.' – *Irish Central*

Jason O'Toole is a well-known journalist and best-selling author. He has worked as a senior editor at *Hot Press* magazine, a columnist for the *Irish Sunday Mirror*, and a features writer with the *Irish Daily Mail*. He has now branched out into filmmaking with a three-part documentary on John Gilligan. This is his tenth book.

THE GILLIGAN TAPES

IRELAND'S MOST NOTORIOUS CRIME BOSS IN HIS OWN WORDS

JASON O'TOOLE

MERRION
PRESS

First published in 2023 by
Merrion Press
10 George's Street
Newbridge
Co. Kildare
Ireland
www.merrionpress.ie

© Jason O'Toole, 2023

978 1 78537 467 8 (Paperback)
978 1 78537 468 5 (Ebook)

A CIP catalogue record for this book is
available from the British Library.

All rights reserved. No part of this publication may be reproduced, stored in
a retrieval system, or transmitted, in any form or by any means (electronic,
mechanical, photocopying, recording or otherwise), without the prior written
permission of both the copyright owner and the publisher of this book.

Typeset in Calluna 12/17.5 pt

Cover design by Fiachra McCarthy

Front cover © Independent News and Media / Getty
Back cover image courtesy of the author

Unless otherwise stated, all internal images courtesy of the author

Merrion Press is a member of Publishing Ireland.

Dedicated to the memory of Paul Drury, an
old school newspaperman who really appreciated
a good old-fashioned journalistic scoop.

Contents

INTRODUCTION

JACKIE KENNEDY WAS STILL WEARING her bloodstained Chanel dress on the emergency flight back to Washington, as Lyndon B. Johnson was sworn into office mid-air. She resisted all requests from the presidential aides to change her clothes. 'Let them see what they've done,' the First Lady famously whispered.

Emotive words. But the concealed bloodshed was even more haunting when we in the Irish Republic had our very own 'Where were you when JFK was killed?' moment on 26 June 1996. The heinous murder crime scene at the Naas Road traffic lights will live on in our collective memories: ticker tape wrapped around Veronica Guerin's red Opel Calibra car with the windows shrouded. It left little to the imagination.

The wheels of justice don't necessarily turn slowly – occasionally they'll come to a screeching halt. There's never been closure in either of these two assassinations, because the mysterious gunmen were not properly identified and charged. It's impossible to maintain that justice was served in Veronica Guerin's cruel death when the only culprit convicted was the motorcyclist, Brian Meehan, who ferried the unidentified pillion passenger with a concealed Magnum on that fateful afternoon.

There were echoes of the iconic photograph of Lee Harvey Oswald getting arrested for the JFK murder when the drug baron John Gilligan, dressed in a jumpsuit, was frogmarched off the plane following his extradition back to Ireland to face trial for allegedly ordering the assassination. The diminutive figure had emerged from the shadows to become Ireland's answer to O.J. 'absolutely, 100 per cent not guilty' Simpson when he was unexpectedly acquitted of the murder. He was guilty as sin in the court of public opinion, but guilt by association was not enough to convict him.

As Judge O'Donovan pointed out in the murder trial: 'While this court has grave suspicions that John Gilligan was complicit in the murder of the late Veronica Guerin, the court has not been persuaded beyond all reasonable doubt by the evidence which has been adduced by the prosecution that that is so and, therefore, the court is required by law to acquit the accused on that charge.'

It's unusual for such shadowy figures to put their heads above the parapet – even if acquitted. But Gilligan has always maintained his innocence and didn't want to shuffle off this mortal coil without telling his side of the story. He wanted to settle old scores in the process.

Soon after his release from prison in October 2013, Gilligan mulled over the idea of doing a book. He approached me first, but I soon went cold on the idea when he was reluctant to detail his drug empire while the legal battle with the Criminal Assets Bureau (CAB) was still ongoing. Mob bosses are hubristic beasts at the best of times, but the cagey Gilligan was not complacent enough to write a book like Simpson's *If I Did It: Confessions of the Killer*.

Gilligan had much more pressing concerns when he was shot six times the following March. The book idea went out the window.

He clearly knew where all the bodies were buried, so to speak, when it came to Ireland's volcanic gangland history. However, it appeared that the old man would go to his own cold grave without shedding any further light on his turbulent life and heinous crimes.

Then, in more recent times, Gilligan once again warmed to the idea of going on record. It had finally dawned on him that there was not much time left in his own sand clock. He attempted to write a memoir at first, but quickly abandoned the idea. He might have been able to steal a work of art, but he was never going to write one. He'd be the first to admit it.

One morning in April 2022, I fired up my laptop and noticed an email from my old employer, *Hot Press* magazine, with the subject heading: 'Voice Mail from John Gilligan!' It arrived in my inbox without the exclamation mark, but my overactive imagination added in a few expletives, too. Why would one of Ireland's most notorious criminals suddenly want to reach out to me?

We hadn't spoken in almost a decade. Our paths first crossed when I conducted an interview with him for the magazine at Portlaoise Prison in 2008. It had been arranged by the convicted fraudster Giovanni Di Stefano, who was granted early release from jail in England in April 2023. He received a fourteen-year prison sentence for fraud, theft and money laundering in 2014. The British judge ordered an additional eight-and-a-half-years be later added to the sentence if he refused to compensate his victims to the tune of £1.4 million. Di Stefano gave the judge a proverbial two-finger salute and refused in colourful language.

It was a dramatic fall for this Walter Mitty chancer. Di Stefano had hoodwinked the world into believing he was a qualified legal eagle. He revelled in his moniker, The Devil's Advocate, which was bestowed upon him because he'd represented the bad, the ugly, and the downright evil. He'd even appeared on CNN to discuss his 'clients' Saddam Hussein and Slobodan Milošević. He'd also claimed to represent serial killer Dr Harold Shipman, which was subsequently denied by his actual legal representative. Other clients he boasted about representing included British gangster John Palmer, disgraced businessman Nicholas van Hoogstraten, the Great Train Robbery gang member Ronald Biggs, and mass murderer Jeremy Bamber.

Di Stefano duped the Irish establishment too when he appeared on *The Late Late Show* to discuss his representation of Paddy Holland and other notorious local criminals. He even claimed Gilligan was one of them. 'He never represented me,' Gilligan later told me. But he acknowledged that they did meet in Portlaoise Prison.

Di Stefano was nothing more than a modern-day version of the con artist Frank Abagnale Jr, the fake doctor, airline pilot and solicitor. He was portrayed by Leonardo DiCaprio in Steven Spielberg's *Catch Me If You Can.* However, Di Stefano was still the best contact to ask when I first sought interviews with Gilligan and Holland in the late noughties.

I had a date with The Devil's Advocate in late 2007. I jetted out to Rome on *Hot Press* magazine's dime to interview him. The then 52-year-old Di Stefano ran his international law practice, Studio Legale Internazionale, from his plush apartment in an affluent part of central Rome. He was in the headlines at the time for supposedly 'representing' Chemical Ali in Iraq and the serial liar and fantasist Ian Strachan, the now deceased blackmailer of a minor British Royal Family member.

'I am generally very weary of journalists because, like hookers, they generally only want something and give very little. It's really a question of supply and demand. But Jason, you seem somewhat different,' Di Stefano told me in a funny hybrid Cockney-Italian accent, which felt almost put on for show. He was a British citizen but was born in southern Italy and raised by his parents in England.

'Why am I different?' I asked.

'I pay a lot of attention to my dog, Rufus,' the affable character replied somewhat cryptically, as he stroked his dog's stomach. 'You see, young children and animals have no prejudices in life. They have no axes to grind, and they are, to coin a phrase, "mentally, socially and philosophically innocent", so I pay a lot of attention to the conduct of my young son and my dog to outsiders.'

'Your dog!'

'Let me give you an example. You never see a miserable dog in a happy family, and you never see a happy, joyful dog in an unhappy family. An animal or young child is like a kind of thermometer measuring 'the intruder'. Now, Rufus nearly always barks at almost everything. First, he barks, then he sizes up the person, and then decides what action, if any, he will take. When you came in, no bark from Rufus. No aggression. No warning. Rufus just lay near my feet or near your feet, Jason. Since Rufus approved of you, there was no reason why I could not be more open than usual.'

I wasn't going to argue with such outlandish logic. I later had to stop myself from sniggering when Di Stefano produced his certificate for the New York State Bar without any prompting. It looked just about as convincing as a teenager's forged sick note for school.

I merely nodded my head and handed the obvious fake copy back to him. My main goal here had been to cajole him into getting me access to his two most famous Irish 'clients'. Afterwards, as we both walked out of his apartment complex on that warm early summer day, I asked if he could arrange an interview with Gilligan.

'Leave it with me. I'll see what I can do,' said this small and bald rogue, as he threw a suitcase into the boot of his BMW.

Di Stefano declared he had to catch a late flight to Baghdad to meet with Chemical Ali and Tariq Aziz. As he dashed off at breakneck speed, I wondered if he was merely going around the block a few times until I'd left.

I doubted that I would ever hear from Di Stefano again, but some months later I received an unexpected call from him.

'Would you like to meet my client John Gilligan for an interview?' His voice crackled down the phone. He said he was making a long distance call from Baghdad. In light of this con artist's future jail sentence, it is entirely plausible that he was buzzing me from the comfort of his home and crunching newspaper for special effects.

'This interview is my idea. John Gilligan says he's doing this against his better judgement, but he also says you can ask any question and he'll give you an honest answer – or a "no comment" if he won't answer it. That's the deal. But he won't tell you a lie,' Di Stefano told me.

A few days later, I was sitting eyeball-to-eyeball with Gilligan at the visitors' centre in Portlaoise Prison. I was unable to bring in even a pen and paper for the visit, but soon I started receiving late night phone calls from Gilligan, repeating what he'd told me that day we'd met.

The subsequent 13,000-word interview ran over two parts in *Hot Press*. There was praise and hysteria in equal measure. It resulted in the then Minister for Justice, Dermot Ahern, ordering an investigation into how I managed to obtain a prison visit with the country's most infamous inmate. According to the prison authorities, new airport-style security measures have been implemented as a result, but they were already in place when I visited Gilligan in Portlaoise. The magazine itself was banned from prisons.

I next interviewed Gilligan when he called me a few weeks after his prison release in 2013. I printed some of our extensive conversations in a 2,000-word piece in the *Irish Daily Mail*. But our paths hadn't crossed in the ensuing eight long years, and I had felt it was not likely to occur in this lifetime – until Gilligan left that voice message.

I was in two minds about calling him back, but after a few hours I purposely picked up a new burner phone to call him. For obvious reasons, I shuddered at the prospect of Gilligan having my personal phone number. Like Gilligan, I too was now residing in Spain, and the last thing I wanted was for the local authorities to see my number flashing up on the screen of a well-known drug dealer. They could've erroneously branded me as an underworld associate.

Gilligan picked up on the fourth ring. He sounded surprised at the Spanish code +34 popping up on his screen, and cackled with laughter down the phone when he learned that I was also over there. The man dubbed 'evil personified' made his best efforts to come across as charm personified. Once the obligatory small talk was out of the way, he got down to brass tacks. Even before Gilligan launched into his sales pitch, I'd already read between the lines and sensed he wanted me to do a book on him. He'd singled me out because I was the only journalist with whom he had spoken at length on the record in the past twenty-five years and hadn't 'twisted' his words.

'I'm running out of time. I've nothing to lose,' Gilligan told me.

It was undoubtedly a journalistic scoop, but he could sense my hesitancy and gave me a week to mull it over. I spent the next few days asking myself: Was it really an offer I couldn't refuse? I lead a relatively quiet life these days and was unsure if I wanted to weather another media storm.

There has always been a peculiar propensity in some quarters in Ireland to shoot the messenger, or rather, the interviewer. In 2006, RTÉ bosses refused Pat Kenny permission to interview Paddy Holland on *The Late Late Show*. In 1997 the television host was allowed to conduct a pre-recorded radio interview with Holland, but even that never aired when the management at RTÉ felt it could prejudice any future court trials.

It seemed like we had moved with the times when Gerry 'The Monk' Hutch was permitted TV airtime by the national broadcaster on *Prime Time* in 2008, and we don't know how many his gang killed. 'The Hutch organised crime gang is in the frame for at least nine murders,' according to the *Irish Mirror* in May 2023. For years The Monk was erroneously perceived as a Robin Hood criminal and it was rarely mentioned in the press that his gang members imported drugs into the country.

I would imagine Irish TV stations would still jump at the chance to interview The Monk even now, and gory documentaries like *Serial Killer with Piers Morgan* are a big hit in Ireland. But John Gilligan is a different kettle of fish, it seems. I was a little taken aback when a prominent politician who introduced me to the producer that agreed to help turn *The Gilligan Tapes* into a documentary forewarned me: 'They always shoot the messenger. Sour grapes, and all that. Be prepared.' I don't necessarily agree. Why should there be a big media storm when the self-confessed double killer Malcolm Macarthur conducted interviews for a book earlier this year without much, if any, controversy?

The Irish public might have an insatiable thirst for true crime, but they rarely get to hear both sides of the story, as they often do in England. There have been numerous crime memoirs published over there, such as the ones by Charlie Richardson and 'Mad' Frankie Fraser.

It's peculiar that no book has ever been published by a prominent Irish gangster. But it's not from a lack of trying. Christopher 'Bronco' Dunne wrote a memoir titled *Wildfire* in his formative years, in which the iconoclastic criminal attacked the Christian Brothers for their handling of the reform schools, but was unable to find a publisher at the time, which was understandable because Ireland was still under the dark cloak of the Catholic Church.

What excuse would Bronco be met with now if he tried in vain to shop it around town? There would undoubtedly be more than one. I'd be astonished if any major Irish publisher would print John Gilligan's autobiography if he had written one, but their British counterparts would be falling over themselves if he happened to be from there.

Ireland is much more conservative than we like to pretend, with such self-imposed censorship. We're light years behind our American counterparts when it comes to their liberal libel laws. The late Cormac McCarthy, who borrowed one of his most famous book titles from W.B. Yeats's poem 'Sailing to Byzantium', would be bewildered by how Ireland is no place for old criminals longing to tell their stories.

As Anne Harris, former deputy editor of the *Sunday Independent*, once said, in a different context, everybody should be entitled to tell their side of the story. That paper's current editor, Alan English, clearly agreed with this sentiment because, when he was in charge of the *Limerick Leader*, he bravely interviewed Wayne Dundon in 2010. Here was a bloodthirsty crime boss whose gang was linked to the murders of several innocent individuals, including Roy Collins and Shane Geoghegan. The provocative headline on the inside two-page spread read: 'Why should I be sorry for Steve Collins [Ray Collins' father]? says Dundon.'

As headlines go, this one certainly didn't mince its words, but it also didn't glorify crime. Nor does this book. Sure, the main objective of my interviews with Gilligan was to get as much information as possible directly from the horse's mouth, but I also warmed to the idea because there would be great value in the exercise if it included obvious moral lessons for younger readers.

According to one of Britain's best-known crime correspondents, Duncan Campbell, there has always been an appetite for criminals' gory memoirs, but the 'most successful are those that include self-reflection'. Similar sentiments were echoed by the Glaswegian hardman-turned-artist Jimmy Boyle, who wrote his autobiography, *A Sense of Freedom*, at Barlinnie Prison in 1997. Could Gilligan be on the same page as them?

Boyle articulated very well why such books are valuable exercises when he noted: 'In writing the book in a manner that expresses all the hatred and rage that I felt at the time ... I have been told that I lose the sympathy of the reader and that this isn't wise for someone who is still owned by the state and dependent on the authorities for a parole date ... The book is a genuine attempt to warn young people that there is nothing glamorous about getting involved in crime and violence.'

As I mulled over Gilligan's offer to be interviewed, it also hit me that the Irish public would be curious to hear him in his own words, not just on the page, but also on camera. It had been a real 'water cooler moment' when The Monk appeared on RTÉ's *Prime Time* in 2008.

Yet, apart from the aforementioned interview with The Monk, I couldn't recall any other major Irish criminal willingly captured on film – excluding Martin 'The General' Cahill's childish striptease down to a pair of Mickey Mouse boxing shorts outside the Four Courts. For that matter, I couldn't even recall any English-speaking mafia boss in modern times who had spoken on camera at length for a major documentary. It would be a bit of history in the making, which was enough motivation for me.

I called Gilligan back and told him that I would be happy to write a book on him, not with him. There was a big difference. I wasn't going to be his mouthpiece and I would not pull any punches in the book. Gilligan accepted that he would not be given an easy ride. It was a risky move on his behalf because he'd be hoisted by his own petard if the veracity of his version of events was shown up as lies.

I forewarned him that he wouldn't be able to seek final approval of whatever I decided to print. He would have to buy a copy like everyone else. He understood and was still happy to conduct the series of interviews. When I said that I wanted to video record our interviews for a potential documentary, it was now his turn to ponder it all.

A book was one thing ... but a tell-all documentary, Gilligan was probably thinking, was a different matter. For him, there was the criminal underworld's unwritten code of silence. The omertà, as the Italian and American Mafia called their twisted version of honour among thieves. 'I don't want to be seen as a rat,' he said.

Gilligan seemed reassured when I said that I was only interested in hearing about his backstory and version of events surrounding the murder on the Naas Road. He didn't have to proffer views on any topic that didn't personally concern him, such as the Hutch–Kinahan feud. I wasn't asking him to do punditry.

Meanwhile, I felt the book would be best suited to the Q&A format. A straightforward biography would result in much fewer direct quotes on the page, which would be a defeat of the entire exercise: the main reason anybody would want to crack open this book would be to read Gilligan in his own words. My task as an interviewer was to be 'curious, not judgemental', to quote Walt

Whitman, to coax him to open up as much as possible – leaving it to others to look for any holes in Gilligan's words.

Fortunately, I was at ease with the Q&A style of journalism because I had done, on average, two such in-depth interviews a month for a total of six years with 'The Hot Press Interview'. The magazine's in-depth interview has long been considered an institution in itself, ever since Charles Haughey famously told John Waters in 1984: 'I could instance a load of fuckers whose throats I'd cut, and push over the nearest cliff.'

The key to Q&A interviews is to ensure they flow almost as if they were first-person prose at times, or even a play. It's a format that requires its own editing skills, which are almost second nature to me after conducting approximately 120 of them for *Hot Press*. It helped that Gilligan was a born raconteur.

There was precedent for a Q&A book on criminality. The famous British gangster John McVicar, played by The Who's Roger Daltrey in a movie, did interviews for such a book with university lecturer Laurie Taylor. Entitled *In the Underworld* (1984), it was 'written in dialogue format and offered a rare insight into organised crime in Britain', according to his obituary in the *Sunday Independent*.

McVicar, once described in the British press as 'public enemy No. 1', would later embark on a relatively successful journalism career. It's hard to imagine an Irish gangster, even if he could string a proper sentence together, sneaking into print, even on the letters pages. But Gilligan could definitely offer that same rare insight into the Irish underworld in an extended Q&A format.

However, Gilligan was apprehensive about implicating himself in various unsolved crimes. 'Because now I'm a free man and I'm going straight,' he claimed on our first day recording these interviews. 'The police and the media would say, "Make sure you charge him with them admissions that he's making now." So I'll be as honest as possible, but don't want to incriminate myself. I'm not going to tell a lie. But I can't answer every question on criminality. I can answer every question [on a crime] that I was before the court on, when found guilty or acquitted. So, when you ask me questions about that, I will not be lying. There's no double jeopardy from that period ... if I done anything wrong and I got found not guilty, I could say to you, "Yes, I did, I did it." So I'm not afraid to admit anything I did, because nothing can happen to me.'

In the end, I would present to Gilligan every serious allegation made against him in countless newspaper clippings and the half dozen books written on Veronica Guerin and him.

We agreed to start recording interviews for five days straight in early May 2022. I told him that my goal was to record at least twenty hours on tape. I assumed, incorrectly, that the book could be turned around quickly enough. Some nine months later, I was still meeting with Gilligan in an effort to probe deeper and deeper for both book and documentary. I wanted to get under the skin of this complex character, who comes across like a mixture between The General and Robert De Niro's character in *Heat*, and, in the process, help shine a light on Ireland's underworld in a way that has never been done before.

In total, we would meet on five different occasions for twenty-odd days of extensive face-to-face interviews, recording approximately thirty-five hours on film, plus many more hours of phone conversations. There are more than fifty hours of tapes there. I transcribed some 250,000 words of direct quotes; enough to fill up the pages of this book many times over.

The long-term goal here was to produce a book that would be one of the first sources future historians would turn to and heavily reference when writing about the emergence of the criminal underworld in twentieth-century Ireland. I suppose only time will tell if that will be realised, but, if nothing else, any impressionable young person will almost certainly walk away from this book with a valuable lesson if they read Gilligan's closing reflections in the last chapter.

'Crime', Gilligan repeatedly told me, 'doesn't pay.'

TAPE ONE

THE RISE OF THE STREET URCHIN

'As far back as I can remember, I always
wanted to be a gangster.'

– HENRY HILL, *GOODFELLAS*

It felt like the calm before the storm on a balmy Monday morning in early May 2022 in Torrevieja, a dreary seaside city on the Costa Blanca coastline in Spain. It was weather for suncream and baseball hats, but there was a far more pressing concern to avoid getting burned, in mafia parlance, as I waited, with some apprehension, for a face-to-face meeting with one of Ireland's most notorious figures.

To the minute, John Gilligan strode into the hotel lobby, dressed as if he had a court appearance, with a folder tucked under his arm. He might have been through the wars, but he looked relatively youngish, even with his trademark shock of grey hair. He also seemed physically strong for someone in their twilight years. It was obvious that he used to lift weights in prison from the way he pumped my hand. The only real sign of old age was his small hearing aids, but they clearly worked their magic because he never told me to speak up or to repeat a question.

He asked if we could first have a coffee or tea at a nearby outdoor café, before we got down to business. We strolled around the corner to a place facing the unruffled waters of the harbour, with the glaring sunbeams flickering around the expensive yachts.

As I sipped my sparkling water, Charles Haughey's famous GUBU acronym came to mind, but for a slightly different reason. Gilligan's proposition seemed unbelievable, bizarre and unprecedented. However, there was certainly no grotesque lifestyle on display.

*There used to be a time when this small septuagenarian was the type of big shot who could have put his hands into his deep pockets and paid cash for one of those luxury 85-foot vessels bobbing up and down in the harbour, but those halcyon days were nothing but faded memories, according to Gilligan. He talked a good game about being poor.****

The Irish expat is now supposedly living a lavish lifestyle in a plush rented villa with a swimming pool. But, on closer inspection, it's hardly a luxurious one in an opulent neighbourhood, as some in the Fourth Estate might like to spin it. It needs more than a lick of paint and there are no air cons installed to help abate the sweltering heat in the long summer. Poor Gilligan cannot even enjoy the tranquillity of lounging out on the patio area because it is swarming with ants. He complained that in winter months his old bones were freezing without an electric blanket.

But Gilligan knows he shouldn't grumble. It's a miracle he's not rotting away in a six by eight prison cell ... or worse. Gilligan only needs to look in the mirror at the bullet scar on his chest if he wants a reason to snap out of any negative train of thought.

---

* In January 2023 it was claimed that Gilligan had €100,000 stolen from him by a close associate. He denied the story was true when I called him that same morning.

How can he even afford a villa? Well, it's surprisingly cheap to live out in this neck of the woods; you can get a long-term lease for €550 a month, making it a magnet for ex-cons down on their heels. Even a box room in a Dublin council house would set you back far more these days.

You'd imagine that people like Gilligan are one of the reasons why property prices in Torrevieja are less than half of those in other popular tourist destinations in Spain, like the Canaries and Valencia, where they not only demand far better creature comforts, but also pay for the privilege of not having to live beside a gangster, who could have the police, armed with a warrant and an enforcer, at their front door at any time. That's exactly what happened to Gilligan in 2020. He was awaiting trial for possession of a gun, prescription drugs and for being a member of a criminal gang when we met.

Also, Torrevieja is not exactly the safest travel destination in Spain. The seaside city is flooded with petty thieves, drugs, prostitution and illegal immigrants out to make a fast buck. During our first meeting, Gilligan and I were sitting only a stone's throw away from the seedy back streets running behind the picturesque seafront promenade, where you'll find mostly young North African Muslims openly selling cocaine on the street corners. They will point to their nostrils and make an irritating snorting sound at every potential customer walking across their path.

It can be easy to buy into the hype about Gilligan being akin to one of those pirates in a Robert Louis Stevenson novel, with buried treasure squirrelled away in the Wicklow Mountains, or bogus bank accounts on the continent.

At first glance, you'd be forgiven for thinking that a crooked man like Gilligan must be lying through his perfectly straight but slightly yellow teeth about his penury status. Surely it was all mendacious propaganda? After all, he was suited and booted in designer gear when he turned up for our appointment. On closer inspection, it turned out to be the exclusive Canali brand, no less. One of these fine Italian-made suits would easily set you back at least €1,400. But, look a little closer and you'll notice that one of its front buttons is broken into a half-moon shape, and the lightweight wool fabric is fairly worn on the sleeves and knees. The suit was clearly a dozen seasons out of date.

You won't find a picture of Gilligan in any other suit when going in and out of courthouses, both in Ireland and Spain.

It is, in fact, the same one Gilligan had on him on a foggy early morning in October 2013 when he was finally released from Portlaoise Prison. He had originally been handed down twenty-eight years for illegally smuggling huge amounts of cannabis resin into Ireland, which was reduced to twenty years on appeal. He would clock up more convictions while incarcerated for assaulting a prison guard and being in possession of illegal contraband. But he still somehow walked free after serving only seventeen years.

The cheap white cotton shirt on him was another dead giveaway. He either didn't care about his image or was frugal to the extreme, perhaps out of necessity. I very much doubt he was dressing down on purpose, but rather was really trying his best to look good on camera.

The clothes certainly don't make the man, but Gilligan had the genuine appearance of someone who had fallen on hard times. He no longer looked like the dapper criminal under the pretence of being a legitimate businessman, one who used to enjoy all the benefits of an Aer Lingus Gold Card and stayed in five-star hotels on the continent.

I'd met Gilligan before, but it was still a surreal situation to be in his company there. You'd naturally feel uneasy seated in a public place with such a disreputable, tough-as-nails mob boss. The intensity shot up a few notches when that kingpin was someone who had once been pumped full of lead at close range and received the last rites at the hospital, but somehow miraculously survived to tell the tale.

My jumpiness somewhat subsided when Gilligan reassured me that he no longer had any enemies out to kill him. But I won't lie: there was still that nagging fear that if someone fired a shot at him while we sat in that café, I'd be caught in the crossfire.

As we finished our coffees, I was relieved when we stood up and decided to start recording some interviews, while the natural light was still good. We walked around the corner to the three-star Hotel Fontana Plaza, where I had everything set up in my modest room. As the hotel lift doors opened, a half-inebriated Irish OAP stumbled out and took a curious sideways glance. Such instances best demonstrate the stark distinction between the famous and the infamous. One gets asked for a selfie, while the other gets a horrified look.

Gilligan seemed impressed when he saw that I had set up two 4K cameras on tripods in my room. He cracked a joke about how he wished he still had it in him to steal such items. Now I started to feel much more comfortable, being in my natural element, as I switched on both of my digital tape recorders. I reassured myself that you don't usually get a hitman kicking in hotel room doors while the cameras are rolling.

So far, on my first morning there, I'd only observed the affable and jokey side of Gilligan's personality, but all that would soon change. Obviously, there was a much more cunning and darker side to his complex character. But I wouldn't fret if he took offence to any legitimate question.

I wasn't going to worry that Gilligan might take umbrage and rip off the microphone and storm out of the room in a fit of pique. I forewarned Gilligan that it was my journalistic duty to ask all the tough questions in a firm but polite manner.

Gilligan agreed, but he had two provisos: he didn't want to speak about the present circumstances of his ex-wife and two children. And he wouldn't discuss his ongoing court case in Spain as he didn't want to incriminate himself. But I wasn't going to lose any sleep if Gilligan somehow did incriminate himself on tape.

So why would he be crazy enough to unexpectedly hurl such explosive material into the public arena? Was it simply to set the record straight? Was it ego-driven? Was it to settle old scores? It was probably all of the above. Whatever the reasons, it was a bold move for someone who had already been shot six times and who, by rights, shouldn't raise their head above the parapet.

The plan was to record as many hours as possible between Monday and Friday in early May.[*]

I hooked a microphone up to Gilligan's shirt and focused the camera lenses on him. As I hit the record buttons, Gilligan leaned back in his chair and waited for the Spanish Inquisition to begin ...

JASON O'TOOLE: You must obviously feel a need to alter public opinion by conducting these interviews with me, but I hope you're not looking for a miracle.

JOHN GILLIGAN: I don't believe in God, but I know I'm going to hell. I'm no saint. I've been committing crime since the age of eight. I wanted to do the interviews for the sake of my family. They've all said, 'John, you should say something. We know you didn't do this; you didn't do that. But we're not stupid. We know you're no saint, because you always had plenty of money.'

I said, 'There's a time and place for everything.' I waited for the

---

[*]   I would eventually need to return on a further four occasions between May 2022 and February 2023, in order to get through all of my countless questions.

right time. I waited until the CAB cases were over. I waited until Brian Meehan got through the system.

And by the way, none of this can reverse what happened. None of this can ever bring back that lady, Veronica Guerin. She's dead no matter what. You can't bring back yesterdays, but people are entitled to know the truth. It's time for me to give my side of the story, because the papers have written about me for years and years and years and it's just lies after lies after lies. I'm 70 years of age. I don't know how long more I'm going to live.

Let's start at the very beginning.

I was born in 1952. We moved out from a tenement home on Prussia Street in the North Inner City to a three-bedroom terraced house in Ballyfermot when I was five or six years of age. We were a big family, thirteen of us. My mother and father had eleven children. One child died at birth. I was the oldest boy. I had three older sisters. There were two or three years in the age difference of all the children; one was a set of twins, two girls. Two sisters and two brothers are now dead.

You once told me your father John Snr 'was a very violent man, especially if he was drinking', and not only violent to you but to others. You said he never made money and, if he did, he gambled or drank it. How old were you when you first got involved in crime and was your father's lack of responsibility to his family a major factor in this?

I was only eight years of age. My brothers and sisters were starving because my father didn't provide nothing. So, I used to sell kindle all around the streets. I'd get wood, chop it up. The best place to sell it was across the field in the posh houses.

You'd knock at the hall door and you said: 'You want to buy any kindles, a penny a bundle?'

I had an old baby's pram full of kindle. You'd be wheeling it up and down the road as you knocked at the houses. I'd leave the pram outside the gate because the gardens were very long in them private houses. I'd have maybe ten bundles in my hands.

So, I go to this house one time and the woman said, 'Give us six bundles there, please.'

And then she comes out with a five-pound note. Now, this must be 1960 and she has a brown £5 note in her hand!

'Have you got change of that?' she said.

'Yeah, me father will have change,' I said.

She was waiting at the door for her change. I walked down her path and as soon as I got out of the gate, I ran. I left the pram there.

I flew over to Ballyfermot.

'Mam, look what I'm after finding,' I'd go after robbing the woman's fiver.

'God, you're very lucky, son. Where's the pram?'

'Ah, I lost it, Mam. I'll get another one.'

'It doesn't matter. You'll probably find a pram anyway.'

Anytime I robbed anything I used to say, 'Mam, I'm after finding that.'

'You're always finding things,' she said.

So that was my first crime, and I never stopped.

In 1966, you left school at only 14. Did you go straight to work?

I didn't go to school an awful lot for the last two years. I have no real education. I couldn't even pronounce some words and there are loads of words I can't even spell or read. But I can read and write normal.

I was working in a place down the Docks called Magic Polish, beside the Guinness boats. All my family used to work on the ships. My father sent down a friend to the factory where I worked with a telegram [of the job offer]. I had to give it to the captain of a cargo boat from Dublin to Liverpool.

After being six months on that I got a job on the old Munster and Leinster cattle and passenger boat, which went down from Butt Bridge. There were no trucks on that boat. It was very rare cars went on it either. It was mostly cattle and passengers, plus dogs. I was on that for five or six months.

Then I went away on British ships. Somebody wrote that I was robbing containers on the ferries: I was never on the B&I Ferries, other than that Munster and Leinster boat. The car ferries came out years later, maybe in the seventies; I was on the English ships by then. In total, I was [on and off] eleven years at sea, until 1982.

Little is known about your criminal activities in your teens, except that you were first arrested for stealing a chicken aged 11, but you didn't end up in front of a judge over that particular crime until you were 15 in 1967. What would've been your biggest caper back then?

This story sticks out in my mind: I was only maybe 16, in 1967/68. I had gambling in my blood. I was a merchant seaman. I'd left the ship when it docked in Liverpool and the money I had [earned] after eight months on the ship, I'd gambled it all in an hour in the bookies.

I was registered on what's called a pool [rotary system for the merchant navy] at The Royal Liver Buildings, at Pier Head in Liverpool. You'd get a day's leave for every week you do on a ship. So, if you're away for six months you'd get twenty-six days leave.

Then you'd have to report again for duty to go away on another ship.

I couldn't go home without giving me mother money; I'd be ashamed. So I went into the Pool again.

I said, 'Will you give me another ship?'

'Sure, you have a month's leave! Why don't you take your month's leave?' they said.

'Listen, I'm after losing my wallet. I've no money to go home to Ireland.'

So, they gave me another ship. I went away on another ship for ten months. I came back and I'd done the exact same thing: I gambled everything in my pocket!

Now, I had two brothers and my father down on the ferry. I could have gone down and got home, but I wouldn't go home without any money. I was trying to get back on the Pool. I'd go back in every day.

I was sleeping on the bench at Pier Head. One night the police woke me up at about 2 a.m.

'You can't sleep there. Move along, move along,' they said.

I walked around the town and I heard windows getting broke. I said to myself, 'Somebody's robbing something up there.'

I went up [to two young men] and I said, 'Are youse robbing?'

'Yeah.'

'I'll give youse a hand,' I said.

So, I took up with this crowd in Liverpool.

What was your first big crime with them?

We broke into a jewellery shop. I went around the back and climbed up the drainpipe to the top window and got in. I opened the back door of the jewellers.

'Jaysus, Paddy, fair play,' they'd go.

They only knew me as Paddy. They didn't know me as John. They were Scousers and I was a Paddy.

We cleaned the jewellers out. So, we had a big bag of all sorts of cheap jewellery and good jewellery. They'd be going here, there, selling, selling. I was their bagman carrying their swag. But they never gave me any money. They'd just bring me to the pub. They weren't buying any food. It was just drink, drink, drink. I didn't drink, but they'd get me a raw Bacardi.

I was with them for about three or four weeks. One day, they were leaving me standing outside the pub, while they were going in. I was starving.

I said, 'Can we get fish and chips?'

'Ah, we'll get something to eat after, Paddy.'

They went into the pub. I looked through the golden leaf design on the door window and two of them were sitting with two pies and two pints!

I had the bag of swag. I looked up and down [the street] and I seen the bus coming. I had sixpence in me pocket. I knew the bus route that would lead to the car ferry. I ran and I jumped on the bus, and I went onto the ferry. My father and two brothers were there.

I said, 'Will you sell that for me?'

'Yeah, no problem,' they said.

So, they went around and sold it real quick.

How much did you get?

They got me 700 quid. I got home and I was able to give me ma 300 quid.

The next day, my brother came home and he gives me £2,000.

'Jaysus!' I said.

'There's more coming. There was an awful lot of jewellery in that.'

I must've got about eight or nine grand for the thing. Every three or four days, one brother would come home and give me money.

And then me father came home and gives me money.

'By the way, I took £500 out of that,' my father goes, because he'd always take my money.

But them fellas [in Liverpool] couldn't ring any police station ... they were probably looking to see was there anybody charged with robbed jewellery. I never saw them again. I always used to laugh. I said, 'Youse used me, but you didn't get away with it.'

You've insisted that your father wasn't the type of petty thief who would kick in the neighbours' back door, as has been claimed. Yet it seems your father, who would eventually be thrown out of the family home, had no real qualms about stealing from his own flesh and blood.

When I was a seaman I was saving up to buy a corner shop and then a pub. But my father – his name is John Joseph Gilligan and I'm John Joseph Gilligan – knew I was getting money from the shipping company sent to the bank and he used to go into the bank and use his seaman's identification book and withdraw £200, £300 or £400. He gambled every penny I was saving. So that idea went out the window.

But then I started robbing and getting massive amounts of money – thousands upon thousands. I couldn't count what I had sometimes. Then, I was going to buy a pub and a solicitor put me off it and a pub manager pulled me aside and said, 'If you're not in the pub game, you'll be robbed blind.' I wouldn't even know how to pull the pint.

Were you ever arrested overseas while working on the boats?

Yes, in New Zealand, I was on a ship called the *New Zealand Star*. I was about 19 years of age. The women, they were called Sheilas, used to come down to the ship – ten, fifteen or twenty of them – and pick the man they wanted.

My friend had a girl and she actually climbed down a rope on the ship to get into his porthole. So, we nicknamed her Monkey. After two or three days, a couple of the girls came down and said, 'Monkey is in jail.'

I said, 'For what?'

'When she was coming in the other night the policeman on the gate wouldn't allow her in and she had an argument with him. He got her taken away and she was given three months in prison, there and then.'

Her fella said, 'John, will you come up and have a word with that policeman?'

I said, 'What do you want to do?'

'We'll give him a hiding.'

'Sure, you just go up and give him a hiding.'

And he said, 'But, you can fight better than me.'

I went up and seen him. 'What did you get her locked up for?'

'Sheilas are not supposed to be on the ships,' he said.

'But she's only a young woman. You don't abuse a woman, or give out to a woman, or be awkward with a woman.'

'Fuck off! I don't care,' he said.

So I punched the head off him. I went out the gate, not to let him know that I was on the ship. But I didn't realise I was more or less after saying what ship I was on. I went up the dock road and around the next road and I'm not joking you, there must have been about ten police cars with sirens going up and down.

I got away from them and boarded another ship. So the police was coming on board and this big giant of a policeman sees me and he says, 'Come out here.'

And his colleague said, 'Do you need a hand?'

And he said, 'I don't think so, this is only a little fella.'

But I knew I'd knock him out if I had to. So, I got brought to the police station. I had no experience really in police stations, but I'd never seen anything like it. It was just strange. I went into this room and there was like about five lights blinding me.

And they're saying, 'Why did you rob the television?'

'I didn't.' I was talking into the lights. I couldn't even see, with the big bright white lights.

And he said, 'Why did you hit the policeman?'

'He got a woman three months in jail. He shouldn't pick on a woman, you know.'

I went before the court and I was to be held in custody until the ship left. An hour before the ship sailed, they took me out of prison and put me back on the ship. But I didn't realise that they were after asking what wages I was on a month and the first officer told them what I was earning – with overtime! The week's wage was the forty hours like everybody else, but we used to work eighty to eighty-six hours. So they fined me a month's wages and the captain had to pay it.

You once told me you smuggled a gun for a mate into Ireland from South America. What else did you smuggle on the boats?

Any time the political people [Provisional IRA] needed a hand to get somebody that was wanted out of Ireland, I could get them onto a ship and across to England, or the continent. I'd done that many times. So did my father. So, I always got a little bit of respect from them.

What other type of strokes did you get up to on the boats?

Here's a good one. We were loading crates of whiskey and when they broke for dinner time, I had to batten down the hatch. I must've taken 300 cases of whiskey. I just kept taking them in. Nobody said anything to me.

I said to one of the catering guys, 'Have you any way of getting this whiskey home?'

'Me ma's partner,' he said. 'Me ma and da's divorced, but she has a partner and he's an ambulance driver. He'll come down in the ambulance and take them out, because the ship is gonna be there for three or four days.'

He came in the dock gates with the sirens on the ambulance. Me and the catering guy were filling the ambulance up with whiskey. The ambulance kept coming in and out, three or four times. I made thousands out of that whiskey.

Did you never feel any guilt?

I didn't rob small factories. Even when I used to do [big] factories I'd say to myself, 'Ah, they're insured anyway, so not to worry, they'll get paid. Sure when I clear a factory out and take everything the man has in it, it's like he's after having a Beano – a one-day sale – because of the insurance.' It was like they sold everything to one customer. I'd be after robbing it, but the customer would be the insurance [company] paying up their insurance.

I often sent people back to the factory asking, 'Do you want to buy back your stuff at a third of the price?'

They'd say, 'No! Jaysus, keep it. I'm delighted you robbed it. I couldn't sell some of that stuff. I don't know how you're gonna sell it.'

But I could sell anything. Anytime I was broke, I went down and robbed a factory and then when I sold the goods I went to the bookies. And if I came out of the bookies broke, I went off and robbed a factory that night.

So, they were my happier times.

But doesn't the cost of insurance then increase because of such crimes?

I'm not a bad person. I could see people classing me as a bad person because I robbed. If you look at it from a proper person's point of view, yeah, I would be a bad person. But how I justify that is: I'm fussy who I rob. I never broke into a house. I never robbed somebody's car, or robbed a handbag, or done silly things like that. I always felt that I didn't leave somebody high and dry, skint – they'd get the insurance. And they can afford that. And nine times out of ten, I'd say most of the stuff at these factories is on credit from a bigger manufacturer. So, it didn't concern me. Of course I was wrong, but I didn't feel the guilt.

What other criminal codes did you have?

You must wear gloves! And if you're doing something more serious, put a balaclava on. Them's the rules. And do you know what the number one rule is? It's very, very important for every criminal – don't get caught, and get what you went in for.

Despite being involved in a huge amount of crime, you spent relatively little time in prison before your marriage. You only really started to become something of a jailbird after you settled down.[*]

When my trial would be coming up, I'd go away on a ship and my solicitor would go to the court and the prosecution and say, 'Mr Gilligan, a registered seaman, has gone away. He's signed on a ship for two years.'

So, they put the case back for mention in six months' time; not a trial, just for mention. And then I'd leave the ship and come home. I'd do another few strokes and, if I got charged again, I'd do the same again.

Why did you give up your life at sea?

I'd be gone for four or five or six or seven months. So Geraldine was getting fed up not seeing me. I know I was getting fed up not seeing her. I went away at 14 years of age and I was, more or less, still working on ships when I was 21.

And then I went back to sea after I was married. I worked until 1981 or 1982 on the passenger liner *St Patrick* from Cork to Le Havre. I also worked on the *Lady Gwendolen* and the *Lady Patricia*. I worked on the Guinness boat for close to a year. I was making 400 quid a week, sometimes 500 quid a week. It was great money. I also worked in the B&I Shore Gang workers. Plus, I drove a lorry in 1974, delivering bricks and cement to building sites.

---

[*]   Gilligan married the then 17-year-old Geraldine Dunne, two days shy of his 22nd birthday in March 1974. She was already pregnant with their first child, Tracey, who was born five months later in September.

Yet, despite the great pay from an honest day's work, you continued to steal?

I don't know what it was – a light went on in my head when I robbed that fiver when I was selling the kindles and I never stopped thinking about taking stuff. I just robbed and robbed and robbed. Like, if I seen it I used to think it was mine. I used to take it. I was always at it. I got involved in crime through stupidness, like anybody else. But I didn't see it as stupid at the time.

How did you first meet Geraldine, who was also from Ballyfermot?

When I got home from sea I regularly called to see a friend of mine that I grew up with, Tommy Gore. The ship docked and you could go home at six o'clock. You had to be back at eight o'clock the next morning.

So, one time in 1970 I came up to see Tommy and I was told he was down in his girlfriend's house. And on the way down to his girlfriend's house, I saw the sister of Tommy's girlfriend. She was with another girl called Geraldine.

'Is Tommy down with Anne, ya?' I said.

'Yeah. We'll walk you down,' they said.

And then I started chatting Geraldine up. Tommy was after saying to me he'll get me a date with a girl across the road and the four of us will go out.

But when I got down to Tommy, I said: 'That girl that's with Anne's sister, I'd like to go out with her instead.'

He fixed it for me. I started dating her. And then I had to go back to sea and every time I come back, I'd go out with her.

Geraldine was considerably younger than you. She was what the Americans would class as jailbait, i.e., under age.

I was with Geraldine since she was 14. She told me she was 16! But she was tall for her age. She was taller than me, but I think kids in schools were taller than me. She was a well-developed female.

She was working in a factory called Textiles in Chapelizod. Geraldine came from a very respectable family. They all have their own businesses. They're a lovely family. You wouldn't get a better mother-in-law or a father-in-law on this planet. They were beautiful people. I loved them.

I was with her for a few months and then she said it was her 16th birthday next week, and then a year later, she said, 'I'm only 16 now.'

'For fuck sake! How old are you?' I said.

'I'm 16.'

'Never tell lies.'

How did you get involved in more serious crime, such as armed robbery?

It was in 1971 or 1972. I stopped working on the boats and I came home and I met some people. They asked, 'Would you like to come on a blag?'

And I said, 'What's a blag?'

'To rob a bank or building society or a post office,' one of them said.

'What would I get?' I asked.

'You get £4,000–£5,000,' he said.

'Yeah, I'll have a bit of that. What would I have to do?'

And he said, 'Just run in with the gun and tell them to get on the ground and scream, "If you move, I'll shoot", you know.'

'I don't know if I'd be any good at that,' I said.

'Just practise in a mirror, because we're going to do it tomorrow,' he said.

So, I was practising in the mirror all night: 'Get on the ground, move and I'll shoot. Get on the ground, move and I'll shoot.'

I was very nervous now, because I'd never done that before. So when I ran into the place to rob it, what did I say? I went in and screamed in an aggressive tone to the people, 'Shoot and I'll move!'

I made a total hames of it. I felt really stupid after.

But it is totally wrong to put the fear of God into somebody by pointing a gun in their face. Would you not agree?

No, it wouldn't be right. And that's if I done that. I never seen an armed robber sticking a gun in anybody's face – they point the gun or shotgun only, as far I know.

Even pointing a gun is unacceptable ...

Terrifying people is wrong. But like in that film *Heat*, Robert De Niro said, 'Stay on the ground. It's not your money, you won't get hurt.'

So ninety-nine out of a hundred robbers that use a gun have no intention to hurt somebody. Some of them go wrong; somebody in the public jumps up and tries to grab one and somebody gets shot. They should have stayed on the ground.

I don't know why you actually need a gun loaded if you're going in just to terrify people. A lot of robbers want the gun loaded in case the police come to shoot. But I would think that'd be wrong. I wouldn't go in with a loaded gun.

Like, the police would have the right to shoot you if their life is in danger. You'd put the gun down real fast. You're not gonna shoot somebody. So why would you want to put bullets in it?

I suppose some people got away in a car chase from the police in them days. I don't think you'd get away now. Sure, there's very little armed robberies now because there are cameras everywhere. I think them days are gone.

You said the first time you robbed the bank you were nervous. Did such jumpiness soon disappear?

You're trying to get me to incriminate myself, that I done more than one [*laughs*]. I wasn't nervous, to answer your question.

You boasted in our *Hot Press* interview about carrying out two or three armed robberies in a day. Was there ever an occasion when you fired a gun?

Yeah, but I can't go into details on that, because I'd be incriminating myself. Make no mistake about it, the police and the Director of Public Prosecutions would be looking at this tape to see is there any way they can charge me with things I said – that's why I can't go into details about a lot of the robberies I done. They'd go: 'He's after giving us something. We can nick him.'

I can say I done robberies because I got convicted of robberies. But they could charge me if I said something specific and I've no doubt in me mind they would get me two years in custody, like they did in Belfast with the five-and-a-half months on remand [in 2019], and turn around and say: 'We're dropping the case. There's no evidence.'

Did you ever carry a gun when not robbing banks?

There was a time when I carried a gun. I used to have a gun in a holster. I was after bringing back a gun from South America. My best friend was Brendan King. I often left the ship to come home to get him out on bail because he'd after been arrested on an armed robbery.

So, I'd have it [the gun] Monday, he'd have it Tuesday, I'd have it Wednesday ... but for no reason at all, it was just silly. I think I was 17 at the time.

The police was looking for us, because we were robbing places. They raided my mother's house and took a photograph out of my seaman's book. I only looked like a 12-year-old kid in it, because I was 14 when I got the seaman's book. I had a baby face. The people they were showing my photograph to were saying, 'No, that's not him.'

Why did you stop robbing banks?

The banks were getting sophisticated – they could press a button and the doors would lock and you'd be locked inside.

Plus, a policeman told me: 'If we get an opportunity, because you're dangerous, we're gonna put one in your head.'

And he named ten people that they were gonna kill. He said, 'Tell them to stop or we'll kill them. Once we get an opportunity – that you've had a gun in your hand – we'll just put you down.'

I said, 'These guys aren't messing.'

And one of the men was killed – they shot him when he was on the ground. One got shot in the head; he's still alive, but there's a bullet in his head.

I don't blame them because they're out there protecting the public and putting their life on the line. And fuckers like us wouldn't hesitate to shoot them to get away from an armed robbery with the money.

Were you prepared to shoot a guard?

Yes, of course. You wouldn't go out and say, 'I'm going to shoot these cops,' because I'd never have any intention in my head to do it. But I'm answering you very honest – not actually shoot him dead, but shoot at them to stop them, to get away. If one of them got hit and did die, well, you wouldn't plead guilty to that. You'd say, 'I didn't do it.'

But would you not feel any remorse?

Of course you would, yeah. That's not right, killing anybody. Even if you killed somebody in a road accident, I don't think you can live with yourself. You'd be a very sad man or woman. I think a lot of people that happens to become alcoholics, or even commit suicide. They wouldn't be able to live with themselves.

As we wrapped up filming for the first day, Gilligan's candid answers left me wondering how any of the spineless individuals involved in Veronica Guerin's murder could even look at themselves in the mirror. It's a question I'd eventually put to Gilligan. I was left deflated at the thought of how the Guerin family never received proper justice. Only Brian Meehan, the driver of the motorbike, was ever convicted for his role in the journalist's murder.

But who was the cold-blooded pillion passenger who ruthlessly fired six shots from a Magnum gun through the driver's window of Veronica's red Opel Calibra on that fateful day in 1996? I figured it was only a matter of time before Gilligan confided in me.

As I stood there on the fourth-floor balcony at the end of that first day and watched the diminutive Gilligan exit the hotel and saunter off, it dawned on me that he probably wouldn't be walking off into any proverbial sunset. He had an impending court date and any sizeable jail sentence in your seventies is a bit like dog years: one human year behind bars would feel like seven in dog years. There were no guarantees that he wouldn't be carried out in a wooden box. Gilligan sounded upbeat about his chances of getting a suspended sentence, but I suspected he privately feared the worst.

I put on my earphones and checked the sound. Gilligan's voice was crystal clear. 'I don't believe in God, but I know I'm going to hell. I'm no saint.'

It didn't sound like Gilligan was about to suddenly become repentant like the good thief, Dismas, on the cross beside Jesus Christ on Calvary. But Gilligan knew he was in the last chance saloon. It was his final opportunity to tell his side of the story and hopefully clear up a lot of the confusion, myths and 'downright lies'. But I forewarned him: he'd be quickly found out and made to look very foolish if he spoon-fed me horse manure.

As Gilligan melted into the crowd down below, I thought about Dante when he passed through the gate of hell with its inscription, 'Abandon all hope, ye who enter here.'

TAPE TWO

THE APPRENTICESHIP
OF FACTORY JOHN

'I used to think that all those factories were mine. If
I wanted to take anything out of those factories, I'd
just go and do it. It wasn't a case of, "Will I be able to
do it?" They were mine. In my head, I owned them.'

– JOHN GILLIGAN, SPEAKING TO THE AUTHOR IN 2008

*On the second day, I immediately pegged Gilligan as a gambling
addict when I went down to the hotel lobby and discovered him glued
to horse racing on his low-cost phone. He had the look of someone
who would probably bet on cockroach races.*

*Gilligan was still in the same suit, but he was carrying a plastic
bag with a couple of new short-sleeved shirts he had picked up in one
of the nearby El Chino stores, as Spaniards refer to popular Chinese
bazaar shops that have sprung up like mushrooms across the country.*

*Gilligan thought it would be a good idea if he wore a fresh shirt
each day we filmed, to show on screen how many days he had spent*

recording these interviews. I cannot decide if he was purposely putting on a big show about being penniless, or if he was genuinely trying to put his best foot forward. Perhaps it was a bit of both. Before his whole world came crashing down around him, Gilligan could've walked into an upmarket men's tailors and paid top dollar for a designer label shirt, but something tells me he probably would've got more of a kick out of wearing one that fell off the back of a lorry.

I looked away when Gilligan pulled off the shirt from yesterday and ripped open the plastic wrapping on one of the fresh ones, but not before I got a glimpse of the scars from the bullet holes. Such a sight is enough to send a shiver down anybody's spine.

When he buttoned up the fresh beach shirt and was suddenly transformed into a harmless-looking pensioner, the phrase 'looks can be deceiving' took on a whole new meaning. He could've just been another guiri – the Spanish version of the Mexican word gringo – living out his final days on the cheap in the Mediterranean.

Except Gilligan was refused a State pension and claimed he survived merely by gambling on horses at the local bookies or on a phone app, which he was always keeping an eye on. He talked about needing to win a modest quota every day in order to put food on the table. No doubt sceptics will find that hard to swallow.

But during the first week of filming, he seemed to be regularly winning small amounts. He clearly got a kick out of calling himself a professional gambler, even if he could no longer bet in an entire year the same amount that he would've nonchalantly put down on one single horse in the mid-nineties.

He claimed he had not been involved in criminal activity since his last arrest in 2020. One thing was for sure, it would be a kamikaze move for him to get back into the drug trade then. He was too well known to the local police, who no doubt had been keeping a watchful eye on him. But Gilligan's always been a loose cannon, which means all bets are off when it comes to predicting what his next move might be.

He certainly couldn't fall back on his old trade. Gilligan was then clearly too old to break into factories and probably didn't have the wherewithal to crack modern alarm systems. A leopard's spots might not change, but the day always comes when they can no longer outrun and outfox the law.

When setting up the camera for our second day of filming, I wondered if he received compensation from the culprit who had ordered the hit on him? I made a note to ask him when we reached the attempt on his life.

I was determined to keep the interviews in chronological order, so I focused on the period when he became known as 'Factory John', going down in folklore as the mastermind of the vast majority of the major warehouse heists – not just in Dublin, but throughout the country – with his crew, dubbed 'The Hole in the Wall Gang', between the mid-seventies and 1994. It was another sketchy period of his life that needed fleshing out.

Did you get a thrill out of committing crime?

I didn't do it for a buzz. Some people commit crime for a buzz. I committed crime for money. I mostly did it to look after my family.

After you stopped carrying out armed robberies because of a fear of getting shot, as you claimed earlier, you next began to break into factories. You once told me, 'I used to think that all those factories were mine. If I wanted to take anything out of those factories, I'd just

go and do it. It wasn't a case of, "Will I be able to do it?" They were mine. In my head, I owned them.'

I learnt how to do the alarms. I was breaking into a factory when it was closed and all the workers went home. I turned the alarms off and I'd go in and I would clean them out. I'd leave nothing. Part of my joke was: when the lorry, or lorries, was loaded, I used to get the kettle out of the factory kitchen and sometimes the toilet brush and leave it at the loading bay, as much to say, 'If I had room I'd have put these on the lorry.'

It probably sounds bizarre but that was the banter I used to have. I suppose when the police came they'd go, 'It's that little fucker again.'

It earned you the moniker 'Factory John'.

I think that was in the later years. It appeared in the paper one day. They were naming up to ten or twenty criminals and then somebody went, 'And now we'll come to Factory John ...' And it kinda stuck.

The journalists, they're always looking for a one-liner. I remember one paper referring to me as the leader of the Robin Hood Gang because I was robbing the factories in the Robinhood Industrial Estate.

You were also known as the Hole in the Wall Gang, because you'd burn openings in the side of the factory walls and chisel your way inside.

But most of the factories in the end got the alarm company to put in what we'd call 'thumpers', because of the holes being put in their walls. A thumper is an electrical wire going all around the wall, and every six feet there'd be a little junction box with a thumper. If you gave the wall a thump of a sledgehammer it would vibrate, and the alarm went off. I used to go around to all the tyre companies and get the scrap tyres for cars and lorries. I'd put all the tyres up against the back of the factory wall. I'd have a pack of firelighters and set fire to the tyres. I'd throw empty Guinness bottles around to make it look like there was fellas having a drink at the back wall, and that they had set the tyres on fire.

The tyres used to bake the wall. You could come up four or five days later with a screwdriver and pick the wall out – like picking clay out. It didn't set off the thumpers. Once you got a hole in the wall for the size of the articles you'd be taking, you could creep through the hole and hand out what you wanted.

Did you have any other techniques to break into buildings?

I used to go into a hardware shop and buy a window cleaner with magnets to go on both sides of the window and they'd stick together.

I used to break them open and take the magnets out. The magnets would be about the same size as a box of matches. I used to put a football lace on it and it would be about four foot long.

And I used to go around the factories in the industrial estates and look for lorries backed up to the wall. Usually the driver was after coming back [too] late if the lorry was backed up to the wall. I'd see if there was pressure on the tyres – it was a good sign that it was loaded.

I'd put a magnet in the letter box of the factory and I could hear the lorry keys clicking to the magnet. I'd pull it back up and sometimes three or four set of lorry keys would be on it. So, I'd open the lorry and drive it forward, to have a look at it. If there was good stuff in it that I could sell I'd drive it off, and if it didn't I'd just put it back and put the keys back.

Any time the police [would] stop me they'd always see the magnet in my car and they used to say, 'What's that for?'

'That's just for when I buy a bit of scrap.'

A magnet won't stick to stainless steel. Some sink units aren't stainless steel. You get better money for stainless steel. So that's what I used to say it was for. I was using the magnet for twenty years and this is the first time they'll ever hear about that.

Did you use these magnets for any other scams?

At the nearest post box beside top solicitors that deal in settlements, I would put a square piece of steel into the bottom of the post box seconds after the postman emptied it. It had to be a nice clean bit of steel to let the post guy think a workman left it there.

I'd drop the magnet into the post box and then pull up the post, which would come up on top of the steel plate. I'd take all the letters out and open them nicely, not rip them. If there were no large cheques inside I'd Sellotape it back and put it in another post box. I'd give the ones with large cheques to John Traynor and he [would] get them cashed. There'd be no panic, as people would phone the solicitor asking if the cheque [was] coming and they say, 'It's in the post.' True story.

How did you plan your factory heists?

I had to use my wits. I would always get my transport and I'd park it offside, mostly outside the pub. And then I'd go up to the factory in a car and I'd do the alarm system.

One time I went up to this factory that had your top of the

range stereos worth £250 each. That was a good bit of money in the eighties. It's more than a thousand quid now. I knew they had a full stock.

I'd bring two fellas with me. I would leave a man watching the place to see if anybody came. I used to get walkie-talkies they used in the ESB because you could talk under the ground on them. We could say, 'The police is here,' and so on.

I opened the place up. I had all the stereos ready to take – 700 of them. But I goes down to my truck and I see the police were parked alongside it. I waited a half an hour and they were still there.

I said, 'Jesus! I have no way of getting that truck because they're gonna follow me.'

So, I came up with a good idea. I went across the road from the pub where there was two telephone boxes. I got Ballyfermot Garda Station in the telephone book and I rang them up. When they said hello I said, 'There's an armed robbery ... an armed robbery in RT Rentals on Ballyfermot Rd ... an armed robbery there. I have to go now ... an armed robbery there.'

And I hung up.

By the time I walked across the road the police car was flying down the road with the sirens on. I jumped into my truck and I went up to the factory and I filled it up. I'd done three or four trips out of the factory.

Now, they knew it was me in the end, but they'd no proof. They just knew I took the truck.

We were doing a factory in the country. We were using walkie-talkies.* The driver was called Mick and one of the fellas on the stroke was called Mick.

---

*   In 2008 Gilligan cracked up when he told me this story about using walkie-talkies on a heist.

I used to have the lorry driver parked down the town, until we got everything into the loading bay of the factory. There was no point in having the lorry outside for three or four hours and then somebody would come along and you'd have to run away and you'd lose the lorry and the whole lot.

I was just putting everything into the loading bay. Say, I'd have three fellas with me and the fella down in the truck in the town would be watching for any police activity and he'd tell me if the police was coming up that road.

So, we got everything into the loading bay and I said to one of the fellas who was called Mick, funny enough, 'Will you tell Mick to come up with the truck?' Now, the town would be a mile away. He said, 'Okay.'

So, the next thing I'm looking around and saying, 'Where's Mick? I can't find him.' I looked around for the walkie-talkie and I found it up on top of some boxes we were getting ready to load. I picked it up and I said, 'Mick?'

And he said, 'Yeah.'

And I said, 'Who's with you?'

He said, 'Mick?'

I said, 'The other Mick? Put him on,' and then I said, 'What are you doing down with him?'

He says, 'John, you told me to go down and get him!'

I said, 'What do you think the fuckin' walkie-talkie is for?' May my mother turn in her grave – that happened.

Knowing you, you probably didn't even have a licence to drive a truck.

I never had a full licence in my life, and nine times out of ten I wouldn't have insurance. And the reason why I never bothered getting tax and insurance is because I always had [ongoing] criminal charges and if convicted I'd just plead guilty to the summons for tax and insurance and you'd get six months run into your sentence. I used to always be getting summons for driving with no tax, no insurance and no licence. I'd be always in court.

But that little trick obviously wouldn't work if you had no other outstanding criminal charges.

You'd only get six months if you're convicted, but it'd be an inconvenience to me if you were taken out of circulation for that [long]. So I came up with an idea. I used to wait 'til the day before I was due in court and I would ring up the Garda station and I'd say, 'Is Garda Bowden on duty today?'

And he'd go, 'He's not on 'til tomorrow.'

I'd ring up later on. I'd go, 'Could I speak to the sergeant? This is Mr Nolan out of the High Court.'

And they go, 'Yeah, hang on ... coming.'

'This is Sergeant Smith.'

And I'd say, 'This is the register of the High Court, Mr Nolan. John Gilligan has taken an application before the High Court to get the case put off tomorrow. That case won't be going ahead in the District Court tomorrow. So, you can tell that guard he doesn't need to turn up in court. The case will be pulled back until the outcome of the High Court case.'

'Okay.'

And I'd say, 'Make sure you put a notice on the board. There's no point in him wasting his time coming down to court, sitting all day, when the case is not gonna get called.'

And he'd say, 'Okay, I'll do that.'

I'd just hang up then.

So, the guard wouldn't turn up in court. But I would turn up.

So when the case gets called, my solicitor would say, 'There's no guard here!'

The judge would say, 'I'll put it back for a second call.'

And a half an hour later the solicitor would say, 'Can you get that case recalled again?'

So, they'd strike out the charge. I'd be free to go, too. They couldn't come back again because the statute of limitation on summons was six months and by the time the policeman was coming back at you again it would be over a year. I outfoxed the police that way maybe twenty or thirty times.

Did the penny finally drop?

I think somebody started talking and then the next time I done it the guard turned up in court and I got six months. But I appealed and then when I went to jail for a serious crime, I just dropped the appeal and the six months ran in [to another sentence].

Had you no qualms about swearing on the Bible and not telling the truth?

I did this a couple times, and in all my years before the courts, only one solicitor ever realised what I had said. You know, when you get into the witness box to give evidence they get you to stand up and state your name and put your left hand on the Bible, and your right up in the air?

'State your name.'

'John Joseph Gilligan.'

Then the register would say, 'Repeat after me ...'

And he'd say, 'I swear to tell the truth, and you go 'I swear to tell the truth.'

And he said, 'The whole truth ...'

And I say, 'The whole truth ...'

And he says, 'And nothing but the truth.'

And I would say, 'And anything but the truth!'

And they wouldn't cop it because they'd be just so used to people saying the same thing all the time. But I'd always say, 'Anything but the truth.'

In one case the solicitor said, 'Did I hear you right saying, "and anything but the truth?"'

I said, 'You did.'

The two of us broke our heart laughing.

'You're lucky you weren't caught,' he said.

'I just do it for a buzz.'

Did you ever tamper with court evidence?

I had a criminal trial in the eighties: I was accused of breaking into a big factory and clearing it out. There was a big safe in the factory and I was tipped off that it had a lot of money in it.

So, I brought along my burner gas bottles and the set of gauges and steel-burning cutters. But before I finally had the safe fully cut, I ran out of gas!

Luckily, though, in that industrial estate there was a big steel factory. I only had to break into it in order to get full bottles of gas, which was easy. I took a full set of bottles.

Anyway, I was charged with everything. The evidence the DPP [Director of Public Prosecutions] had was the stolen cutters and the brass nuts, which they got when a house was raided and the people there made a statement that 'John Gilligan asked us to mind them for him.'

Every profession in that trade put their own initials on each brass nut and the cutters. These ones had 'LS' on them. But I used to have a very good friend who had the exact same tools who used to lend me his set for a few pounds, and his initials on them were 'LG'.

On the day of my trial I got a friend to come to court with his cutters and screws and brass, with his LG initials on each one.

I said to my solicitor, 'This is my friend and he always lends me his if I need them, so why would I rob other ones? Let's go over to the exhibits and I will show you they are the same. I am entitled to view the exhibits in law. So, ask the Garda to move out of the way there.'

They did – they just kept yapping away. So, as I picked up each exhibit to show the solicitor, they all looked like twins. But, with sleight of hands, I put my friend's ones back on the exhibit shelf and the stolen ones in my friend's carrier bag. He didn't even know what I was doing.

We thanked the Garda and went to our side of the courtroom.

I said to my friend, 'Leave here asap. Don't leave them in your car. Don't leave them at home. Just put it offside.'

'Am I not getting called as a witness?'

'It'll be tomorrow. Please do as I say.'

Anyway, the trial got under way. The Garda was called first, as in all cases. He pointed to the exhibits in court and said I had used these stolen tools when robbing the factory. I told my legal team not to cross-examine him. So, the man got an easy ride in giving his evidence. A few more Garda gave evidence, and the State's case against me was completed ... or so they thought!

The case was adjourned until 10 a.m. the next morning. I got my solicitor to call my friend as a witness. I had told him outside the court about the stroke I had pulled the previous morning with the exhibits.

'Everything on that shelf is your property,' I told him.

'John, you're a bollocks!'

We both laughed.

He got into the witness box and said that he had lent them all to me. 'My initials are on the brass nut and on the cutters,' he said.

It was only then that they saw LG and not LS on each one. The jury was told to find me not guilty.

After that, I never got a jury trial again. My next four cases were all in the Special Criminal Court.

Was that the only occasion?

I was charged one time [for theft] and the exhibits were in the Ballyfermot police station. They were Wrangler shirts and jackets and jeans.

I was after being pulled in for an armed robbery [at the same Garda Station]. They held you for forty-eight hours in them days.

So the cleaner came down to me. 'Do you want fish and chips or anything, John?'

I said to him, 'Don't say you know me. I'll be getting out tomorrow, because I'm innocent. I'll see you tomorrow.'

I seen him the next day at the bookies.

I said, 'Is there a room at the police station with exhibits?'

'There's a room down there and everything has John Gilligan's name on the exhibits.'

'Is there anything with Wrangler down there?'

'There are four boxes with Wrangler.'

I said, 'I'll give you twenty-five for every jacket and jeans and shirts you get out. When the box is empty then get rid of the box.'

Over the course of the next ten days, he got Wrangler shirts and jeans and jackets out in his cleaning bag. He cleaned the windows and mopped everywhere.

So when I went to trial my barrister said he wanted the exhibits in the court. The prosecutor was told to get them and when they came back in the afternoon they said they were mislaid in the station.

So the jury was told to find me not guilty. These were the reasons I ended up in the Special Criminal Court, because I was pulling a few stunts in court to outfox them. But you can only outfox them for so long.

You're chuckling to yourself. Did you just remember something?

I stole a lot of car tyres and I said to this man in Dublin that owned a garage: 'My friend's after getting a load of car tyres from the North. Would you be interested in buying them?'

'Oh, yeah, if they're smuggled from the North I'll take them,' he said.

He took a vanload. And then he wanted another vanload because he got a good bargain. So these stolen car tyres were on *Crimeline*: 'And if anybody knows anything about it ring this confidential number and tell us.'

The man rang me up and he said, 'They weren't smuggled from the North at all ... ya bollix ya!'

I wasn't gonna tell him. 'I don't know about that. I got them off somebody and he said he got them from the North.'

And then about four days later, he couldn't stop laughing on the phone. I couldn't understand him because he was laughing so much.

He said, 'Do you know such and such a detective? He's after being in here and said, "Did that Gilligan fella try to sell you any tyres?" And I said, "No, he didn't." He said, "Well, he's robbed a load of tyres. We're searching everywhere for them."'

And he then said, 'But he's telling me this and I'm putting four tyres on his cars, and one on the spare wheel! Your man's after been up in every tree in Ireland looking and looking, raiding loads of places for theses tyres, because it was a good friend of his they were stolen from. The fecking eejit is driving around in four of them ... and one of them is in his boot!'

The biggest factory heist you've been linked with is probably the infamous case involving those Ferguson VHS machines worth an estimated £1 million in 1984.

They were the best model on the market in them days. They suspected it was me – but it wasn't me because I was wearing gloves! [*laughs*]

Anyway, I knew my house would be raided. I knew I would be a prime suspect. So, I like to have a laugh and joke with the police. I knew [*names Garda*] would be out. He used to hate me. He used to say to me, 'I can't sleep thinking of all the things you've done.' He was obsessed with me, for some reason or other.

But I went into the shop where they sold them [Ferguson VHS machines] on Grafton Street and I bought one. £933 they were. I photocopied the receipt about ten times, and I put the copies in the bedroom drawers, bedside lockers, and I sellotaped the original one on the video recorder in my sitting room.

So when the police raided my house that Guard come in and he went, 'I knew you couldn't resist to bring one home. Ya fecking eejit!'

I said, 'Go easy with that' – they were unplugging it – 'don't break that ... that's mine.'

And he said, 'That's a stolen one. You're going to jail for this, John.'

'I don't know what you're talking about,' I said.

'John, John … I knew you couldn't resist taking the thing home. Jesus Christ, what sort of a fool are you at all? You're a right gobshite, John.'

'Guard, before you go anywhere, look at what's wrote on the back of the video recorder,' I said.

He looked at the receipt – the smile on his face was gone. He sent a guard straight into Grafton Street to see if it was legit. And a radio call came back through, saying: 'Yeah, he bought it there two days ago.'

I'd made such a fuss so that they'd remember me in the shop. I got charged with them. I got [found] not guilty.[*]

---

[*]   Gilligan was accused of threatening a witness in that case, like countless others, but he denied those charges. If I were to continually put to Gilligan every such serious allegation and rumour made against him it would've disrupted the flow of the Q&A and become too jarring for the reader. Because it would suddenly no longer be a book in which Gilligan gets to tell his side of the story, but instead a tiresome one in which he bats away allegation after allegation, ad nauseam. The entire point of this exercise was to bring Gilligan out of his shell, not make him retreat back into it. But make no mistake: Gilligan was never going to get an easy ride. It was a case of prioritising the hard questions for a project of this magnitude. This book would've ended up with several extra chapters of predictable one-liner denials and occasional rants against some journalists and members of the legal profession if I had published all his answers to every allegation made against him that I raised. Here's one such example of one of those rumours. When I put it to him that he had supposedly once soiled his pants when getting arrested, he quickly replied, 'I never done that in a million years! And if I did, I'd say it. So what if your body got a fright and your body has a function? On my mother's grave, I never soiled myself once. Never. I don't panic.'

You were arrested for stealing from the mail train in Limerick in the mid-eighties, alongside two other criminals; one of them being the late Charlie Kirkwood, who ran a notorious betting ring called 'The Toss School' in the seventies, and the other was called Mick.[*]

I didn't realise the elections was on and some of the political parties were staying in the same hotel down in Limerick. I didn't drink at the time. Charlie got drunk and he went up to bed.

So, me and Mick went down to the train station. I was able to open the main train doors. It used to be the green sacks that had the money in it, but they were getting robbed now and again, so for security reasons, they put the green sack in an ordinary sack. So I was feeling if there was the two sacks in it, I took eight sacks out.

We went down the tracks, over the wall and put them into Mick's BMW. We got back to the hotel at about two o'clock in the morning. You had to ring the bell to get the night porter. The sweat was pumping out of Mick. He goes to the night porter, 'Will you get us a Britvic orange.'

So he gets a Britvic.

I said, 'Just go upstairs.'

But he brought a mail sack into the hotel room, to open it. There was something like £40,000 in cheques in it. And then the porter rang the police and said, 'There's somebody acting suspicious.' So next thing is: I was woken up with a machine gun put to me [face] from the police.

I was a week or two weeks in custody in Limerick prison.

---

[*] Coincidentally, Charlie was also a friend of Gilligan's associate John Traynor, who was Veronica Guerin's main source in the underworld. The other criminal involved in the Limerick job was named Mick, but Gilligan was unsure of the spelling of his surname.

When we were down in the cells, Charlie said, 'John, we'll have to plead guilty.'

I was saying, 'Will you shut up, Charlie.'

I used to always have my wedding band ring on my finger and I used to have it real shiny, and when I'd be in a police station I'd put my hand between the rails and I could see if there was a reflection in my wedding ring. There'd always be a policeman standing up against the wall listening to the conversation in the cells. And I used to say, Charlie, 'There's a policeman outside your cell. Stop talking you gobshite ya!'

But he'd keep talking.

I said, 'Charlie, I'm looking at a cop outside your cell.'

The police didn't know how I was doing it, because they'd just see my hand sticking out through the bars.

What about your other accomplice?

Mick pleaded guilty, because the night porter said, 'He carried the bag up to the room.'

When they found the car key in the room, Mick said, 'That's my car,' and he told them where the car was. There were registered mails in the boot of the car. Mick got twelve months – a deal in the District Court. He should've pleaded not guilty because he would've won on a technicality, but I wasn't telling any of them.

Why not?

I kept it to myself, because a few years prior to that I had told the fellas the charge sheet was typed up wrong and they started slagging the policeman. And then the policeman amended it and I got jail time and they didn't because I took responsibility for the stuff. But if they didn't tell the policeman I wouldn't have got time in jail. So, I made it my business: Never tell anybody your business … a need-to-know basis. If they don't need to know, don't tell them.

How did you manage to get away with the mail theft, because you were literally caught red-handed?

I said, 'I'll represent myself.'

I got it adjourned for two weeks. We came back in two weeks' time and I said to the judge, 'I want open depositions. I want to ask questions about the evidence. I want to check all the mail. I'm entitled to examine the exhibits of a crime that I'm accused of.'

And he said, 'Okay, Mr Gilligan, yes, I'll allow you. Where are the exhibits?'

The policeman got up and he said, 'We gave them back. They were all posted.'

They were all posted! There was money in the bags. They weren't leaving it lying around. I heard there was more than £1 million in them. They got delivered to the rightful companies and banks they were going to, like the children's allowance and the social welfare money.

So I said, 'Well, judge, there's no exhibits, I've no case to answer.'

'Yes, Mr Gilligan you're free to go. Not guilty.'

I'd a big smile on my face. But it's the same as when I get sentenced: the police start clapping and slagging me.

I couldn't blame them for celebrating when one of the bad guys gets locked up.

In the early eighties, I was arrested for an armed robbery and they came into the cell with bottles of champagne. Now, they wouldn't give it to me. But they said, 'Would you like a drop of this, John? Because you won't be getting a drop for the next fourteen years. You're fucked!'

So, I said nothing, but I knew I wasn't fucked. I was taken at gunpoint out of a warehouse in which we were storing stuff. My story was: 'I know nothing about this. I'm an innocent person here. I was in the wrong place at the wrong time.'

But the guy who was with me, he pleaded guilty. I waited until his sentencing was finished. I signed on every day in the police station for three-and-a-half years. I went up on trial. This judge hated me. I knew if I kept acting the eejit in the court I'd upset her and she'd make some sort of mistakes.

The jury was twenty minutes out and they came back out and found me not guilty. I won on technicalities and there was no evidence. The jury accepted that I was only after going in to give him a hand as a worker. The baby face I had at the time!

Then I just said to the detectives, 'I think I'll have that champagne now.' But I had to wait three-and-half-years to say those words.

You were also once or twice caught with your hand in the proverbial cookie jar!

I was arrested one day with a vanload of Mars bars. I was after robbing them out of a warehouse. The police stopped us. I was driving a Volkswagen van, a left-hand drive. I was after getting it at an auction.

So, when we were getting taken out of the cells in Crumlin at four in the morning I noticed the tyres down on the van. I said to myself, 'That's still loaded.'

When I got out on bail I went straight from the District Court [back] to Crumlin. I started the van. The police had the keys, but I just hot-wired it. I heard that a policeman spotted us ... no, the window cleaner seen me.

I said, 'Shush! Say nothing.'

And he looked at me and he ran in the door of the police station. And before I could reverse I was surrounded.

The judge said, 'I don't know how a man can be charged twice for robbing the same thing!'

I got twelve months in prison for it.

I was actually only caught once on the premises of a factory that I was robbing sweets out of. I got eighteen months for that. They should've waited 'til I was driving out with the stuff – I would have got more time in prison. But they came in and got me inside.

And another time, there was that incident from earlier in a warehouse – holding all stuff from armed robberies. I got taken out, with forty-two armed detectives, celebrating with bottles of champagne. I was in custody for a few months. I got out of custody and I knew I'd win the case and the jury found me not guilty, and that was the last jury trial I had.

And by the way, I'm sure I was guilty of that crime. But how and ever.

Did you have any other lucky escapes when arrested?

There was one time four of us were after doing a robbery, but the three other fellas was afraid of dogs. There was three Dobermans in this compound yard.

I said, 'I'll get over the fence and I'll get rid of the dogs. I'll just put them away.'

I had no fear of dogs at all. I'd locked them up somewhere. So, I got over the fence and I stepped down onto a lorry, but I put my foot on the back plate – it was all oiled with a load of grease. I'd seen my footprints on the hub of the lorry. I meant to wipe it off before I left, but I hadn't.

So, we'd done the robbery anyway. The cargo was after going away in the big lorry. The lorry got away and we were going off in a small van to Drogheda. The robbery was after being discovered. We got surrounded by a lot of police cars and taken to the station.

I knew the prints off my trainers were all over the wheel arch of the lorry. I said to myself, 'I'm after messing up.'

So that was my only fear, that they'd have [this] evidence on me. I knew they would get forensic oil off my trainers. So when they brought us into Drogheda Garda Station, when we're getting booked – it's a real old Garda station and there was a big open fire in the station – the sergeant was there burning coal and logs. And I said to myself, 'I'll burn me feet!'

So I said, 'Oh Jaysus! I was working on the ship there. I was an old fireman on the old gas boats. I used to have to do up the fire. I'll get that fire going, because that's not great.'

I put one foot at a time in the fire and I was pushing the coal – I was burning all the rubber off the end of my trainers and melting everything off that. I could feel my toes nearly burning.

I said, 'Ah, the fire will be blazing any second, sergeant. It'll be great. I don't mind doing this for you, sergeant.'

We got put down in the cells. I knew they'd be coming looking for my trainers, [to see] which one of us was after leaving these prints. So, they come down and they opened the cell. There were only two cells in the station. They had two of us in one cell and two in the other cell. I could hear them open the door, but they tried to do it real gentle. And they just jumped on top of me and jammed me to the wall and got me to the floor and they took my trainers off.

I could hear them say to the sergeant, 'What happened?'

'Oh,' he said, 'he was fixing the fire for us.'

'You're a fecking gobshite! He's after burning the evidence. The forensic is gone. They're melted. The prints are gone off them. Jaysus! It's a wonder his feet weren't on fire.'

I didn't even get charged. I just got held for two days and then let go.

Can you recall another time you were held for a few days in prison without being charged with a crime?

I was in a van going to Galway to break in somewhere we'd been told there was a lot of cigarettes.

There was a Garda checkpoint in Maynooth. There were four of us in the van. So the driver and myself stayed in the front seats. I said to the two in the back, 'Jump out here. The police will want to know where the four of us are going.' They went into the field and walked all the way up past the checkpoint.

I wasn't known too well at the time to every guard. We just sailed through the checkpoint and then we got around the next bend. The lads got back in and off we went. But the police came after us then. They pulled us because one of the motorists behind us was after reporting that two men got out of the van and went into the field.

The other two lads got away. But me and the other fella got arrested. Anyway, we got charged. I was in custody in Mountjoy for a week and then I got bail. But, as soon as I got bail, I went down and did the robbery and got what we wanted.

You were up on trial for breaking into a pharmaceutical company in Rathfarnham.

I got [found] not guilty.

But did you do it?

Yes, I broke into Glaxo [SmithKline], which was the biggest drug company in Ireland. I was in it all Saturday and Sunday. I got an order for ulcer pills and they were very expensive tablets. I took out ulcer tablets and heart tablets. That's all I took out of it. I took every one they had. I took two pallets of it.

Now, I got good money for them. I was getting £250 a box. I had a man who would buy as much as I could get. He'd buy a lorry load if he could, but I only got a van load. I got £20,000 for them.

They didn't even know they were broken into, because I was after doing the alarm and [then] putting it back [on]. They didn't know that stuff was missing until they went to get an order. They couldn't understand it and then they discovered there was a break in. And so, that's how good I was ...

People said, 'Did you not know there was millions of pounds worth of drugs in there that you could've sold?'

I could have gotten myself ten million. But I wouldn't deal drugs in them days.

And yet you decided to continue to seek unemployment benefits despite illegally earning such a vast sum.

I only signed on the dole because there was a Supreme Court case in Ireland that if you got arrested and you're unemployed you had to get bail within your means. There was no point in putting £50,000 bail on you, because there was a time that they used to.

As soon as I heard that, I went straight down to the dole office and signed on.

They just give out the money on the slip. When I went to get my slip I used to give it to somebody in the queue.

'Here's a few quid for you, go and collect it.'

I actually never took the money and put it in my pocket. But when I used to get arrested for loads of things my barrister used to say, 'My client is unemployed, he's on assistance.'

And then the judges would put £500 bail on me. I'd probably take ten grand out of me pocket and bail [myself] out.

It sounds like you miss it all now?

No, I don't miss robbing, and ducking and diving. It's like some people say, you get born into crime. Maybe you do, maybe you don't. I entered crime from a young age and I just never got off at a bus stop – I just kept going. Some people stopped after five or ten years, some people stopped after their first sentence. But anybody that I knew that done two or three sentences, they never stopped. It was just the way of life. It wasn't a proper way of life, but it appeared at the time to be the way of life open to you. I mean, there were 364,000 people unemployed. And they have no criminal records and you have a criminal record. How are you supposed to get a job? But when a fella does want to go straight, nine [times] of out ten, the cops might be okay, but that bad cop might try to get you sacked.

TAPE THREE

A PORTRAIT OF A GANGSTER
AS A FAMILY MAN

'Let me tell you somethin'. I don't care how close you are, in the end your friends are gonna let you down. Family: they're the only ones you can depend on.'

– TONY SOPRANO, *THE SOPRANOS*

Gilligan liked to come across as sanguine about his criminal life. I've lost count of the number of times he told me, 'I went into the kitchen and I got burnt.' But he always spoke in a contrite tone when it came to his wife and two children. He appeared haunted by his past and full of 'what ifs'.

Gilligan had had much time to dwell on all of it. Living out his last days alone in a suburban nightmare, he rarely ventured outside. He often compared his existence as being akin to an 'open prison' because he was both broke and no longer able to maintain a low profile. He seemed bored, giving the impression that he longed for company.

Torrevieja was either a party town, or somewhere to live out your golden years on your pension. It was not a place for someone on their own, who was still wearing the same worn-out designer suit as almost ten years earlier.

The boredom was slowly killing Gilligan. He occupied himself by watching old movies and sports, mostly horse racing and soccer, while trying to make a few bob on gambling. But I reckoned Gilligan was the type of character who would start to throw caution to the wind with a few drinks on him. Those tenner bets could suddenly turn into three- or four-figure ones if there was enough in the virtual kitty. Winning streaks could suddenly turn into losing streaks if he was not careful. But Gilligan maintained he put the phone away when he had a skinful on him and wouldn't run such a risk.

Gilligan liked to chat with family and friends on WhatsApp, but could often go days without seeing anyone. It would cost him €10 to get into the city centre if he wanted to go out for lunch, but the local taxi rank was often deserted. Besides, there was really nobody on speed dial to meet up with. He obviously didn't want to be seen in public with the co-accused in his drugs and gun charges case, which was pushed back until the same time as the release of this book in autumn 2023.

Sometimes I wondered if Gilligan missed the camaraderie to be found in prison. If not already taken, The Monk would've been an apt moniker for him at this time.

In many ways, Gilligan was living in the past. His partner had shown me mobile phone footage of him once when he was merrily drunk, as he hugged and kissed and even slowly waltzed with a photograph of his late mother. Gilligan would be the last person you'd think of as sentimental.

'I love her,' he said about his late mother. 'I'd die for her this minute, I would. I'd die to get her back for twelve months on earth.'

Family clearly meant a lot to Gilligan. However, such talk will undoubtedly be interpreted as double standards by many, given that Gilligan was once accused of threatening to sodomise Veronica Guerin's child. That allegation was a subject guaranteed to get him riled up.

It was abundantly clear that Gilligan felt terrible guilt over the CAB cases, in which properties belonging to his ex-wife and two children were seized as assets of crime. Did the kids constantly throw it in his face? He wouldn't allow me to broach it. One thing was for certain, such a situation would put a strain on any family.

He often told me that the biggest regret in his life was that his marriage fell apart and that he no longer had much contact with his children. His children were off limits. Perhaps he wanted to protect them or was no longer on speaking terms with them. He would not say.

It was also 'mum's the word' when it came to Geraldine. When I expressed curiosity about her whereabouts, he wouldn't even state if she was residing in Ireland or Spain. But once the tape was switched off, he would occasionally bring her up in conversation, with only good things to say. He seemed to still genuinely care for her.

In 1974, Gilligan married Geraldine and moved into a rented flat on the North Strand. They resided there until they got a council house in Corduff, Dublin West, in 1977. Their daughter, Tracey, was born a few months after the wedding, and their son, Darren, was born the following year.

He once told me, 'I had an agreement with Geraldine – if we were fighting, we'd meet in the middle of the floor at 8 p.m. and we'd hug each other. We'd never let the row go on after 8 p.m. I had that from the day I got married. I don't care who's right or wrong – after 8 p.m., finish it ... it's gone. I've often had a few rows with Geraldine when I was in prison and they'd go on because she was stubborn – but

when we were together it would never go past eight o'clock at night.'
Geraldine later confirmed this story to me.

There's very little known about Gilligan's private life. Certainly,
there has been plenty of conjecture, but we've been mostly left in the
dark. It was time to put his personal life under the spotlight.

Would you have described yourself as a family man?

I was wrong in not being a better father and a husband by going
out every Sunday or going on holidays with the family. We had
no holidays. My wife and children could go on holidays. But I was
too busy in my own world, robbing places and gambling.

But I said, 'What is the problem? You're not short of money.'

I bought them all brand new cars. I got them whatever they
wanted – but they wanted me. I couldn't grasp that. I was wrong
not to see that.

Why couldn't you see it?

Because I never seen that when I was growing up. My brothers
and sisters were starving because my father didn't provide. So,
the only education I had about married life was: make sure your
kids don't go hungry and that they don't wish for anything.

And I used to say, I'm doing my duty, I'm a good guy. But I
was lacking it. I accept that now: lacking. And I regret that in my
life. And it broke my marriage up. I'm raging my marriage broke
up. But no woman is going to put up with that from any man. A
woman would be silly. Geraldine put up with it for long enough.

Even though a lot of women used to say to Geraldine, 'Jaysus!
You don't know how lucky you are having John. He's a great
provider. He doesn't stop you going anywhere.'

But they were only looking at it because they hadn't got money and they couldn't wait for their husbands to go out. But I was the opposite: I gave money and I wasn't under her feet. I was either inside the factory or inside a jail or on a ship or in the bookies.

She always wanted me to go straight. We had millions of arguments about going straight. But going away to sea, gone straight, it was like prison because you weren't with them – you were away for four to seven months.

I'd say, 'Sure, I'd be better off just going robbing and putting money on the table.'

I always thought if the father provided enough money for his wife and kids and all the bills, you're a good guy. But that's all I thought. I was wrong. You have to be with your family, and bring them places. And most of the things I didn't do [was] because: one, I'd be at sea; or two, I'd be in prison; or three, I'd be down the bookies. So, in a sense, I was a bad man, that way – but not intentionally. I thought I was Mr Wonderful by leaving twenty grand in the drawer: 'Spend that if you need it.'

So, it took its toll on her and we were having arguments. I couldn't see that Geraldine couldn't see my picture and I didn't see her picture. But I see her picture now. I regret how wrong I was. I do feel terrible because of the things I done.

You and your young family first lived in a flat in the North Strand, but then moved out of there when you eventually got a council home in 1977.

Geraldine's aunt used to mind the [then] Lord Mayor of Dublin, Jim Mitchell when he was a baby. They lived next door to his mother.

Geraldine's aunt said, 'I'll get you a house, because you're the eldest granddaughter.' They went down to Jim Mitchell's office and he said, 'I'll get you put on the housing list.' And we got a house in three weeks. We got 13 Corduff Avenue in Blanchardstown.

It was unlucky thirteen for you, when CAB seized the property.

They took it back and said it was bought from the proceeds of crime; that the rent wasn't paid. Geraldine and I paid the rent. That rent was paid every week out of Geraldine's wages for the few months in factories, here and there, and anytime I worked on the ship. I worked a good few places. And when I was on the dole, your rent went down and you paid it out of your dole. All the rent was paid for thirty years.

Also, Geraldine bought that house in Jessbrook on her own out of a claim she got in work. And the police know that, because it's in paperwork when the money came out of the bank to pay for it in 1986. They just wouldn't give Geraldine back her house, the Jessbrook house – just the house, not the whole estate. So, yeah, I feel terrible that she lost something that she worked hard for when she wouldn't take stolen money off me. I mean, we lost a family home.

Geraldine had a love of horses from an early age. Her passion presumably led to you purchasing the Jessbrook estate in 1995, and transforming it into the largest equestrian centre in the country. Did you have a fondness for horses too?

It is reported in many newspapers and books that Geraldine used to come down to Lough Conn Road on a piebald to meet me. I never went around Ballyfermot on a horse with Geraldine, or through wheatfields. There is no such place as a wheatfield across from my mother's home.

I am terrified to get up on a horse. I've never rode a horse in my life. I sat on a horse that was £6 an hour for a lesson. I got terrified, because I'm a small man. I've always been a small man; my little legs wouldn't go around a big piebald. And I felt no control whatsoever and I started screaming: 'Get me off ... get me off.'

And they walked the horse over to a 40-gallon drum and I jumped off it. I've never been on a horse since. I am terrified to get up on a horse.

I read that you would steal from hardware companies to fit out the equestrian centre at Jessbrook.

Yeah. Geraldine was after buying five acres and a derelict bungalow. I got stables built for the kids. And I stole in a builder's providers yard whatever I needed for the stables.

Let's say, I robbed £20,000 worth of television sets, and there were three of us. Well, for £20,000 worth of television sets when you'd sell them, you'd only get about £7,000. So share £7,000 after paying £1,000 for storage. So share the £6,000 between three people, you'd get £2,000 each.

And if you went down to buy £2,000 worth of hardware equipment, the builder would come back with the stuff in the boot of a car. You wouldn't get much for £2,000 for building equipment.

And then if you got caught with the televisions, you'd be getting charged for £20,000 – but you're only after getting £2,000. So you're getting charged ten times the amount, in a sense.

So I just thought to myself, 'Why don't I ask the builder what does he need?' And if it's £3,000 worth of material I'll just go in and rob £3,000 worth of material. And if I get caught my charge sheet is not £20,000 or £100,000. So, I did that, just for ponies for the kids. That was in the eighties. Yes, money was paid part in crime for the main building and the stables and the luxury apartment over it and the judges' box, and all the indoor arena and the outdoor arena. But it was also paid from my money exchange deals. I made a couple of millions each year from that, and millions from cigarettes. But Geraldine bought the house.[*]

Geraldine was portrayed as being the godmother of Irish crime, in the 2003 film *Veronica Guerin*.

I wouldn't let nobody know my business. She only ever saw cigarettes, that's what she thought I was only doing. Sure, they said in the court to the judge: 'Mr Gilligan doesn't tell his right hand what his left hand's doing, or his left hand what his right hand is doing.' Why would I want my family involved in anything? It beggars belief.

You're not trying to tell me that your wife didn't have a clue what you were up to?

No, she hadn't. She wasn't dumb, but she never had information about it, like details. She knew I was a criminal. I was an armed robber when I met her. She was giving out to me that I was away, that I was her boyfriend and she can't go out with me because I'm away at sea. I gave up the sea. But I was doing a lot of armed robbery then.

---

[*]   Geraldine was once accused, and subsequently found not guilty, of selling stolen Atari machines at the factory she was working at in Blanchardstown. She received £20,000 compensation over that allegation in the High Court and, according to John Gilligan, used that sum of money to purchase the house in Mucklon, Enfield, aka Jessbrook.

How did you feel when you were incarcerated on the first few occasions, being away from your wife and young family? In July 1977 you received eighteen months for receiving stolen goods, and then the following September you received twelve months for the attempted armed robbery of a bookies, and a further three months for larceny.

It didn't really bother me so much because a jail cell is very similar to a cabin at sea. We used to go to New Zealand and it would take weeks. And we'd go to the Far East, South Africa, Hong Kong, China, Japan, Yokohama. I went everywhere on ships.

And when you come out of your cabin and you go on deck ... all you see is the ocean. The same as when you come out of your prison cell and you go to the exercise yard. It's very similar. So, by the time I got a sentence, I was used to that type of scenario.

What's one of your fondest memories of a day you were released from prison?

It was 1978. I was released from prison in Mountjoy at seven o'clock in the morning. I said, 'Sure, I'll get the bus home.' It was a new housing estate in Corduff. We got out there in 1977 and [soon afterwards] I got eighteen months in prison. But you only served thirteen months, because you get a quarter remission off.

Our house was a corner house and all the newspapers and all the rubbish and bags used to blow into that corner. I was always coming out and having to clean it. But, as I was approaching the gate, I saw this big rat running under the papers. I had him cornered and I danced on him through the papers. I killed him. I kicked him out the gate.

I goes up to bed and I do what you're after not doing with your woman for thirteen months. So I'm in bed with her and then I heard cries outside from one of the neighbour's children, a young boy about nine years of age. And he goes, 'Somebody's after killing me hamster!'

His hamster was after getting out when his sister went to work. It looked to me like a rat from the distance!

I said to Geraldine, 'Oh Jaysus! Don't say it was me.'

I got Geraldine to give him the price of a hamster. But we always laughed about it, even though it was a tragic thing for the poor hamster.

Did you ever attempt to give up your life of crime?

Yes, I tried to go straight. In 1978, I told me wife, 'I will not commit any more crime again.' I had a few pound from crime. I opened a garage down in Grand Canal Street called Economy Car Sales. I still had some charges before the court.

Grand Canal Street is down the road from Pearse Street Garda Station. I would lock up the garage at six o'clock at night and bring the toolboxes home, because the garage was often broken into. I couldn't complain because I broke into a few [such] places myself. But the police would stop me and take the tools out of the car ... and charge me with having housebreaking instruments!

I was in front of a judge one day after the police took a bar and toolbox off me: the type used to take a bumper off a car, or wing off a car when I'd buy a crashed car. I used to buy loads of cars and put new and second-hand wings and bumpers on them. And over that I was charged with having housebreaking instruments! Now, housebreaking instruments in the law is between 2100 hours and 0600 hours in the morning – but they would stop me at ten past six [when] it wasn't even a crime to have them. It's not a crime in law until 2100 hours. It's called having housebreaking instruments without lawful excuse.

But the judge found me not guilty, because he asked me, 'What was the hammer for?'

I said for hammering.

'And what was the lever bar for?'

I said, 'For levering'.

It just became a joke.

And the judge said to me, 'Mr Gilligan, I can't give you a guarantee that you won't be arrested walking away from the Bridewell with them.'

He gave them to me, back in the court.

The police stopped me from going straight. I said to them, 'Listen, I know I've got up yousser nose. But bring me around the side of a building and beat me up and I won't say a word. Let me go straight, will ya?' And they wouldn't. They bullied me, week in and week out.

I gave up the garage and I went back to crime.

During one lengthy phone call when Gilligan was still in Portlaoise Prison, he told me that he gave up alcohol in the mid-seventies while still living in a flat with Geraldine on the North Strand. He didn't touch a drop again until his children were all grown up. Asked why, he said at the time:

I was cranky on drink. I'll tell you why exactly I gave up drink. I'm ashamed of it but I'm not ashamed to say it – when my son was born I got drunk. And I was drunk for three or four days. I came home drunk and Geraldine was doing the ironing. I walked in and hit my foot on a stool and I picked it up and threw it in the corner. And I didn't realise – I was after getting a pram for my son and Geraldine had lifted the top off the pram – you know the way you can lift it off? – and put him in it, on the floor in the corner.

But I threw the stool and it bounced off the wall and it landed in the end in the pram. When I seen it, I just sobered up instantly. If he was turned around the other way I think the stool would have killed him.

I went, 'On his life I'll never drink again.'

She said, 'Just drink shandies from now on.'

I said, 'I have to go. I'm going.'

I went downstairs and she came down.

She said, 'John, don't go.'

I said, 'Fuck, that nearly killed him. If that pram had been turned the other way he'd be dead.'

I didn't drink for twenty years because of that. One night Geraldine, Tracey and Darren said, 'Listen, you are doing every-thing for us. Will you have a drink?'

I said, 'I'm afraid. If I have a drink. Don't give out to me, I won't have a row because I'm afraid to have a row.'

And I had a drink. I can tell you now that I get more happy on drink than anything else.

Was Geraldine a big drinker herself? She's always got a can of beer in her hands in a couple of the pictures of you two taken in pubs during your halcyon days.

Geraldine only drank three bottles of beer every three or four days in the house. One time she used to drink three bottles of Harp a night. She wouldn't even take a fourth bottle, and then she went from Harp to three cans of Tennent's.

The lorry drivers that I knew used to bring in a pallet load of what they used to call little green bottles. They used to get them in Holland or Belgium. I used to buy a pallet load of that. But she'd only drink four or five of them. She wasn't a drinker, and she never drank spirits at all. A lot of people think she drank whiskey and brandy, and she was sitting down in meetings with us. What fucking meetings? She never ever sat down with one of the guys I did things with. She wasn't involved in that shit.

Did you ever lay a finger on your kids?

No, I never hit my kids at all.

Did you ever hit Geraldine?

Yeah. I think I gave her a few boxes over the years. I can't remember what it was [over] exactly. I won't say I've never hit her from the day I met her until the day we got separated. I apologised for hitting her, but whatever it was … my temper, such and such.

But I wouldn't beat her. I've always been a small little man, five foot. Sometimes I say I'm only four foot nine. But I was always strong. It is the only gift that God gave me in a sense. I was always extra stronger than the average guy. I was actually the strongest man in Portlaoise Prison. Now, I didn't do competition, but the [amount of] weights I could lift in Portlaoise Prison; it can be confirmed by a lot of criminals and prison staff.

You're changing the subject. Do you accept it's never right to hit a woman?

Of course it's never right to hit a woman. And if you're going to kick a woman, you should always take the shoes off … only messing.

You shouldn't joke about domestic violence.

I know. Sometimes I forget what I'm talking to you for. I do feel we're only having a yap and banter, joking. Sorry.

Did she ever end up with a black eye?

Yes, I gave her a slap. And you could see my five fingers on her. And I asked her to put ice on it and she wouldn't put ice on it.

I said, 'Geraldine, you'll get a black eye.'

And two or three days later you could see yellow and black.

Was she ever hospitalised?

For a fight? Not at all, not in a million years. No, never.

Have you ever hospitalised any woman?

No. Who? Why would you do that? Are you referring to some-body? If you are, say it, because this is all alien to me. I wouldn't have any dealings with women. I'd only have dealings with fellas that I'd be stroking with, breaking the law with, or selling drugs to. And I never had a problem with anybody. My word was 24-carat gold. People always say that about me. Ask people.

I presume you hospitalised a few men in your time.

No. You'd have a straightener with people and then you'd get up and shake hands, end of story. Why would you put them in hospital? If I had a fight, small enough as I am, mostly the other guy would be losing. And I wouldn't go to town on nobody. If you know you're beating somebody, why would you hit him again?

That's my philosophy. I don't believe in it. But I know a lot of animals that do bash people, hit him, and hit her. They're dirt, the people that does that. Dirt!

So, you're telling me that you never killed anyone or never ordered the execution of anyone?

No. If you think I did, say it to me: ask me who you're referring to. Because I didn't ... why would I?

We'll come to the murder of Veronica Guerin soon enough. Back to the subject at hand: when did your marriage break up?

I think about two days after getting married [*laughs*]. No, my marriage broke up in 1990. We always said we'd stay best friends. She was a fantastic friend to me. And I believe I was a good friend to her. She was [even still] coming down to [visit] me on the four-year sentence for receiving stolen goods.

It broke up from arguments because I was robbing and robbing and robbing. And the house was getting raided by the police. We were nearly putting a plate down for their dinner – we knew they'd be coming.

So, she didn't want me robbing. She used to say, 'You can work at this and that. Go back to sea.'

And I'd say, 'But if I go back to sea I'm away from you. Sure, if I bring in money, what's the matter where I get the thing from?'

I know it was stupid and thick. I couldn't see that she didn't want stolen money. I gave her loads of stolen money. Sometimes I'd be broke and she'd say, 'Are you not going gambling today?'

'I've no money, but I'll get money tonight. Don't worry about that,' I said.

'Take that money,' she said.

'What money?'

'I never touched that money that you gave me, that's in the drawer,' she'd say.

She wanted nothing of it. She used to annoy me. I'd be after getting a good lot of money after breaking the law and coming home and being Mr Big and then saying, 'Here, there's a few quid,' putting a few grand on the table – ten/twenty/thirty grand.

She'd say, 'I don't want that.'

I'd go, 'Will you fucking stop. I'm after getting it for us. We'll get this house. We'll buy this house.'

I had the money to buy a house in 1979. We picked a house but she didn't want it because it was with stolen money. She wouldn't take the house. And them things that they say about her in a movie, that she wanted to be with the horsey set people … what a load of bollocks. Anything but!

Was there any third person involved in the break-up of your marriage?

No, there wasn't. We're legally separated from 1994. I used to be with Carol Rooney from 1995. Then, I think, in 1997 or 1998, Geraldine got a partner. I wish her all the very best in the world. She was a lovely person.

How did you meet your lover, Carol Rooney?

Now, she was a beautiful, beautiful girl. A real good girl. First class. She was a perfect female. She was working in a bookmakers' shop where I used to gamble and I got on very well with her mother, Bernie, who was manageress. And then when I asked that girl out

I said, 'If you don't want to come out with me, don't tell anybody in there because I don't want to be embarrassed.'

And she said, 'You don't tell Bernie.'

I said why?

'She's my ma.'

I didn't know it was her ma; I wouldn't have asked her out. I went out with her a good few times, for weeks and weeks, before it became anything more than steak, egg and chips.

Did she know you were a drug dealer?

She had a clue because her friend was going out with my friend. And he was telling his girl what John does, and she said to me one day, 'Are you doing drugs?'

'How dare you accuse me of doing drugs!'

I stopped the car and I got out and walked away. I didn't want her in trouble. I didn't want her involved. So, I didn't tell her anything. She knew nothing about that, anyway. Once she didn't know she was not breaking the law.

Did your wife ever confront you about your affair?

No, because we were legally separated.

Did you love Carol Rooney?

No, I didn't love her.

Did she love you?

They're not questions to be asking. She's her own life. It's not right that question. I'd rather that be taken off this tape, but it's up to you. But it's not fair on her. I don't know, maybe she's got three or four children, and it would embarrass them.

In a previous taped interview circa 2013 Gilligan told me he conspired to hide their relationship from Carol's mother. He said:

Her mother [would] say to her, 'Are you going out with John Gilligan? He's gambling every day in the shop.'

Carol Rooney had a girlfriend, and she was after telling her friend she was going out with me. That we were going for meals. Carol and her friend had a little falling out and her friend was giving out about Carol to her mother.

The friend told her own mother, 'She's going out with John Gilligan.' So the mother of the friend told Mrs Rooney, 'You'd want to check out your daughter's boyfriend. It's John Gilligan.'

Then the mother asked Carol, 'Are you going out with John Gilligan?'

And she said, 'No, Mam, no, no. It's actually a friend of his that I'm going out with. I do be in his company for a half an hour.'

We'd all go to the Silver Granite pub for coffee and there'd be ten of us, all the gamblers, so she wouldn't be sitting in my company. The mother was not convinced and told your woman, 'Don't be saying that about my daughter going out with John Gilligan.'

I asked Brian Meehan would he get a mate of his to get a photograph with her [to fool Mrs Rooney]. He picked Speedy Fegan. I couldn't believe it but I didn't know. They got the photograph, gives it to Carol to show her mother who put it in a frame and it's on the mantelpiece!

And then, about a year later, two years later, he was murdered.

Next thing he [Fegan] is all over the news headlines that he's after being shot as a drug dealer in Northern Ireland.

I was speaking to Meehan about it.

'Why did you get him to be in the photo?'

Meehan said, 'I know him, he's a mate.'

I said, 'How could you fucking do that? He would have been well known.'

The bubble would have burst for him. This was supposed to have been kept sweet and low profile.

I said, 'What the fucking hell are you doing?'

As it was, he [Meehan] wasn't the brightest. So that's where that came out. The mother believed it 'til she seen it all over the papers. I was in jail at the time when it happened.

How did your relationship with Carol Rooney end?

I didn't see a future with Carol Rooney. Her brother went to Australia with his friend while I was dating Carol, and I told Carol, 'We're finished,' and she didn't want to finish.

So she asked me not to break it off with her, but I broke it off with her. I said, 'Go out to Australia.'

'I don't want to go. Will you come?' she said.

'I'll follow you.' I wasn't following her nowhere.

So, she went out [to Australia]. I was living in Belgium at the time, and she was ringing me. She said, 'You coming out?'

'No, I'm busy. I've things to do. Stay there.'

I was hoping she'd fall for her brother's friend and forget about me. She rang me and she said, 'I'm coming home. I can't live out here without you.' I met her at the airport in Belgium. We were together for another few weeks. And I said, 'Carol, I really don't want this. Would you please go back to Australia.'

She went back to Australia. And I was after getting £8,000 punts and I changed them into Australian dollars and I hid them in her a suitcase, because she wouldn't take money. And off she went with it. She didn't know [about the cash] until she landed there. The customs didn't even stop her with it.

I told her, 'Don't make any contact with me. We're finished. Don't ring me. Don't do nothing.' And she gave me her word. I gave her a big hug and big kiss, and off she went. And that's the last I heard of Carol Rooney.

While in prison in Belmarsh, I seen a photograph in the newspaper of her working as a barmaid in Australia. And then there was another [one in which] she was pushing a trolley with a suitcase in Manchester Airport.

I haven't heard from her from that minute to this minute, and I've no intentions of finding out anything about her, because the girl's an innocent girl. I didn't tell her anything about my business. But I said to her, 'If I ever get arrested, never try and make contact with me. Never ask anything about me or contact my family or friends.'

And that's what happened, when I got arrested at the airport [in London, 1996].

Did you frequent whorehouses back in the nineties?

I was never in a whorehouse in my life! I think I know the book you're referring to. It said that I used to go to a bar in Belgium. Tommy Gore's wife used to work in a bar there. They said she was running a brothel. In court, the CAB barrister said it was before I knew them [the Gores]. I was never in a brothel. And if I wanted to do it, I would have done it.

So you don't believe there's anything wrong with prostitution?

Not as long as the price is right. And I never charged any of them [*laughs*]. We know prostitution is the oldest trade on the planet. But if a woman does it she should be able to do it for herself and keep all the money. It's not acceptable to be a pimp. A man shouldn't make money off a woman – that's just a low life.

TAPE FOUR

THE GENERAL AND
HIS CONSIGLIERE

'Reform school was my primary school, St Patrick's
Institution my secondary school, and Mountjoy my
university – they taught me everything I know.'

– MARTIN CAHILL

You obviously need a brass neck to become a filthy rich criminal. Yet for someone who spent decades throwing his weight around in the underworld, John Gilligan is surprisingly small in the flesh.

Gilligan probably has a Napoleon complex, judging by the way he often jokes about his height. The man never misses the opportunity to tell a gag and probably would've been the class clown if he had bothered his backside to show up for school.

He might at times come across as the pantomime villain, but Gilligan is anything but. He is, in his own words, a 'strong little fucker'. Gilligan has a muscular frame, with a neck built like an ox. In old prison photographs of him lifting weights, he looked akin to a dangerous human pit bull. No doubt it enhanced his fearsome reputation whenever such a picture of him appeared in print.

He repeatedly insisted that his bark was worse than his bite. Gilligan liked to give the impression that he was thick-skinned ... up to a point. However, he can become relatively riled up if you know the right strings to tug at. CAB ... certain reporters ... cops ... barristers ... or judges ... or 'certain cunts', as he referred to Brian Meehan and John 'The Coach' Traynor. The latter two made his blood boil the most. In his mind, Gilligan was not hoisted by his own petard. He blamed all his problems on 'those two backstabbers'.

As Martin 'The General' Cahill's consigliere and later as a close associate of Gilligan, Traynor participated in many of the biggest crimes ever carried out in the Irish state.

'I'd say I'm one of the only people in Dublin who knows who did 90 per cent of the hits in the past year — who do you think killed Paddy Shanahan,' Traynor once boasted.

Gilligan told me, 'I always believed that Traynor had Paddy Shanahan killed.'

John Traynor was always somewhat of an enigma. He grew up as one of eight children on Charlemont Street in south Dublin. The black sheep of the family from an early age, he was arrested for breaking into a house at only age nine. He came from a good family and was always smartly dressed, according to one of his childhood friends who said it always puzzled him as to why Traynor got involved in crime.

In the mid-eighties, Traynor was the prime suspect in a £1 million scam involving the theft of Revenue Commissioner cheques, but was never charged.

With too much heat on him, Traynor – whose other convictions include assault, firearms and fraud – decided a change of scenery might be for the best and moved to England. However, it backfired on him when he received a seven-year sentence for handling stolen bearer bonds in London in 1992.

But then something peculiar occurred: after serving only two-and-a-half years of this sentence, Traynor was temporarily released on compassionate grounds for a weekend to see his family in Dublin. Not only did he fail to return to England in order to finish his sentence, but there wasn't even a warrant issued for him at that time.

'In reality, Traynor had agreed to act as an informant against the then "Mr Big" of Irish crime, Martin Cahill, well known as The General,' according to the Irish Independent *in 2008.*

Incidentally, it wouldn't be until 2010 when the UK authorities decided to extradite Traynor from that same small Dutch town where he had been picked up with Meehan, in order for him to serve out the rest of his sentence. He would be released two years later, in 2012. Why didn't he receive a longer sentence for absconding?

It all seems rather odd, as does Gilligan's decision to partner up with Traynor. Gilligan was at a fork in the road when he teamed up with Traynor to smuggle cannabis into Ireland. There is never a right turn for a criminal, but things would have worked out very differently for both of them if their paths had never crossed.

Was Traynor your right-hand man?

No! John Traynor was a gobshite. A gobshite! He was an alcoholic. He was a fool on drink. He'd drink three bottles of vodka and make all sorts of stupid phone calls.

He was on Antabuse tablets. I fell out with him [over it]. He used to you say, 'I'll come out to you and pick you up and you give me my Antabuse tablet. I'll leave them with you.'

'Stop! Are you serious? Do you hear yourself?' I said.

A couple of times he'd show me it. But I found out he'd be drunk that night. He threw the tablets away and put sweets in it that looked like tablets – and he'd be taking them!

Sure, I wouldn't be caring if he was taking them or not, because you wouldn't be thinking he was gonna mess up again and again. But he couldn't help himself from messing up.

Yet Traynor, a 'gobshite' and a 'fool on drink' you say, remained part of your cannabis smuggling empire. Why?

Partly, in the beginning. I let him in with me for his share of the cheques and traveller's cheques he was getting cashed [to help fund the operation in its infancy]. I gave him an opportunity. But every time he got drunk, he got on the telephone and he would make a hames of what we were doing, because he was a dope after drinking three bottles of vodka. He'd take Antabuse tablets, and then drink two bottles of vodka and he'd be getting sick, but it didn't matter to him.

I got rid of him a few times, over a short period. And he would say to me, 'Look, I'm taking me Antabuse.' But he had peppermint sweets in the tube!

You say Traynor was a 'fool on drink'. Can you give me an example?

In the early stages, I was dealing with the people [drug dealers] on the continent and they only knew me as John. And they used to say to me, 'Go on, we'll get your plane ticket.' And I'd go, 'No'.

And Traynor would go, 'John, they want to get us our plane tickets? We'll save 800 quid.'

'Are you fucking serious? We're making hundreds of thousands. And you're worried about less than a grand?' I said. 'They don't know who we are. They know our first names, Little John and Big John.' By the way, I'm Little John [*laughs*].

And then he let them go to the airport one day and book the ticket ...

I'll give you a funny instance about Traynor. I was in Holland with him and we went into a sex shop in Amsterdam. He was after getting a double-sided dildo. It was a rubber penis. He told me that some of the girls in the shop are lesbians as well.

But Traynor wouldn't get on the plane until he was drunk. So we're at Schiphol Airport. He put it in his briefcase. And the girls was looking at the X-ray and looking at him and looking at this [dildo]. They were scratching their heads looking and then they started laughing. They didn't open the case. They were looking down at him and laughing at him.

And I said it to him when we got home, 'Why didn't you put it in your suitcase?'

He said, 'I wasn't gonna bring it back and then at the last minute when I got a few drinks into me in the hotel I put it into me briefcase, you know.'

How did you first meet John Traynor?

It is said in a book that I was in prison with John Traynor. I was never in prison with Traynor. If Traynor was in Mountjoy when I was there in the seventies, I didn't know him. I don't believe he was in the prison when I was there.

It is said that I was on the B&I with Traynor. I was never on the B&I with John Traynor. I knew nothing about him.

I read I was also in Mountjoy prison with Martin Cahill. Martin Cahill was never in prison with me. I never spoke to Martin Cahill in any prison. I was in Portlaoise Prison with his brother, Eddie.

I found him to be a very nice fella. And John Cahill is a very nice fella. But I was only in prison with them.

I think I met John Traynor for the first time in 1986. I had some cheques and some postal orders for sale and somebody introduced me to him. Traynor was a fraud man and he could do bank fraud, with cheques, traveller's cheques, and printed up drafts.

How did these scams work?

You'd buy a bank draft for £10,000 and then you make three or four copies and you put them in three or four different banks. And then you'd change the original bank draft, because they couldn't refuse that. You would get paid for half of them copies and half of them they'd stop the payment. Some banks you would get away with it because they wouldn't check so much.

There would be a lot of these cheques to be got in the post. And then you lodged them in a bank account and you'd alter the person's name that they'd be payable to. Or else, you'd put them in your solicitor's client account – and that sailed through the system, and then you get your money back off the solicitor.

Were there shady solicitors in cahoots?

The solicitor wouldn't know. Traynor had a few solicitors that he could put into the client accounts and say, 'My friend is buying a property and he wants to lodge this money in the client's account.'

And then Traynor would go back and say to solicitor, 'That deal fell through. He's not going to buy that property anymore. He's after falling out with the guy. So can you give us the money back and just take your fees out of it.'

So the solicitor would give him his cheques, and then Traynor would get somebody to change the cheque in the bank. The bank wouldn't blink an eye once it had gone into a legal solicitor's client account ... big massive cheques for hundreds of thousands.

I came across a lot of really good cheques payable to some companies. They would be stolen. The names would be slightly altered to go into an account.

And then an opportunity came up. There was a good printer outside of Ireland and he was able to print traveller's cheques and bank drafts. You could lodge them into some banks, and they would go under the radar and clear because they wouldn't be checking too much.

So, there was loads of fraud with Traynor that way. I'd get a share of it.

John Traynor also ran brothels. Did you have any?

No, I'd none whatsoever. Traynor had brothels about ten years before I met him. When I met him, he still had one going. He said he hadn't. But I found out that he had, because he said to me one day: 'I had a bit of trouble the other night in my business.'

I said, 'What business?'

He didn't say brothel. He said, 'I have a girls' club,' or an 'exclusive club'. And he said, 'A couple of fellas got messy. Will you help me?'

'No, I won't get involved in any of that. Now, if somebody is picking on your family I'll go with you, no problem whatsoever. But not the likes of that,' I said.

So you didn't approve?

That's low life, getting money out of women. If you're a criminal, just rob the thing. I know that's not the right thing to be saying, but if you're a criminal you're a criminal. I'm not ashamed of being the criminal that I was.

It was often claimed that John Traynor was blackmailing judges and politicians with compromising photographs taken at one of his knocking shops.

Yeah, I heard that too. He had a brothel in Aungier Street and anybody that came into it were recorded. I think a lot of the reasons why he didn't get charged was because he had footage on them.

He was a twisted character in his head. He had young girls in the brothel and he would bully them. I found out after how bad he was. Some people came to me and said, 'You know what he wanted a friend's daughter to do?'

I said, 'Why don't you break him up? He didn't do it on me. Break him up.'

He was a horrible man the way he used women. He would give his [own] girlfriend out to clients for money: 'I'll get you this. Do you want her? Do you want that?'

I believe Traynor would have sold his two daughters and his wife. That's how evil he was. But you don't know it from day one. You only learn that over time.

You said he sold 'young girls' for sex. Were there minors involved?

I don't know. I don't believe he did. He would be capable of it if somebody asked him and he got a few quid. I don't know of any [incidents], but I would believe it. I wouldn't be shocked.

Yet, you were still good friends with Traynor?

At times. When you make money with people you become happy with them and friendly with them. But not when they start messing and telling lies and doing stupid things, and telling you that you didn't get paid on this one when you know you did get paid – that'd be robbing you.

You'd say, 'Listen, I know you got paid for that. So with the next one, stop messing and just split it,' whatever the deal was.

Surely you're not naive enough to believe that there should be honour amongst thieves?

Once I'd done something for a lot of money, just under a million quid. There was an Englishman involved in it and I'd to give him £273,000. I was a very young man and he was older than I am now. But I delivered that money to him.

Two people that were involved with us said, 'You're not going to give him that money, John, are you?'

I said, 'Yes, sure, that's the deal we done. You have to have principles. And just in case you think I'm not going to give it to him, I want you to travel with me.'

And the three of us travelled over to England and I met the man and I gave him his money. They kept saying, 'I couldn't believe you gave him that money. I wouldn't have given him that money. Sure, what could he do about it?'

I said, 'It doesn't matter what he can do about it. You do a deal with somebody, you stick to do the deal. Have principles.' The most important thing is, you must respect people. Because if you don't respect people, you're not respecting yourself.

How many times did you fall out with John Traynor?

I'd say a dozen, or more. If you told me it was twenty, I'd say yeah. He was always sly. I fell out with him a good few times over his stupid lies. He was a sleevan. It used to turn me off him.

Brian Meehan would be saying, 'He's alright. He was just drunk. He's sorry. Just give him another chance.'

And then he [Brian Meehan] was back working with him for five or six months that I didn't know anything about.

I wouldn't see Traynor [frequently]; it'd be every three or four weeks. I went to the continent with him, okay. And then when Jessbrook was getting opened, he came down with his wife and children. He was only there for an hour. But I wouldn't be in Traynor's company. I was never in a pub in Ireland with John Traynor, to my memory. Nobody could ever say I sat down and had a pint with Traynor.

Your ex-wife Geraldine once told me that she didn't like John Traynor. Why not?

Geraldine used to always say to me, 'John, don't be with him.'

I'd say, 'Why?'

'I get a bad feeling off him. He's sly. The hairs stood up on the back of my neck.'

She really didn't like Traynor at all. She said, 'John, don't bring him to the house. He's evil. I can sense the evilness off him.'

And she said the same about Meener [Brian Meehan]. She said, 'The minute he came in the hair stood up on the back of my neck.'

I said, 'No, Brian's a good fella.'

She said, 'John, you just can't see, you're too close to them. They're evil.'

And she was proven right. She had some sort of sense about her because anybody she said it about something always came true. Her feeling turned out to be accurate. She just had some sort of psychic powers.

Did you ever fall out with The General?

Yeah, once. John Traynor was with me over on the continent one time. Simon Rahman, our drug supplier in Holland, was talking about the war zones in Bosnia and Croatia. The soldiers were all throwing down their Kalashnikovs on the street and putting civvy clothes on and running away.

It was just a conversation while we were having pancakes and coffee. I didn't drink when I'd go [to drug deals]. I'd do my business and get out because I didn't want to be seen with anybody. I didn't want to have any notoriety in case the Dutch police were following them and then I'd come into the picture. So, the less time I was with anybody, the better. It was just 'low profile, low profile' with me. I never wanted to be another named crime boss. It's just not good for business to be talked about.

But Simon turned around and said, 'The kids are picking them [Kalashnikovs] up and selling them for eighty quid.'

Traynor was Martin Cahill's right-hand man, in the sense of running around for him. He didn't do any serious criminality with him. He'd do research and paperwork for him.

Traynor said, 'I was telling Martin about what Simon Rahman was telling us: that you can get the AK47s for eighty quid. So, he's after bringing me around 240 quid to get him three.'

'You're an awful gobshite!' I said. 'That's what they get in the war zone. By the time they get them from there down to here, they're probably gone up to two grand. Anyway, I won't be bringing back any guns.'

I went down to Cahill because Traynor said he was going mad. I knocked at Cahill's door and he wouldn't open the door to me.

So, when I was walking away he opened the door and he said, 'You mind your own business.'

'What you mean "mind your own business"?'

'Traynor has all that transport [smuggling operation],' he said.

'What are you on about?'

He closed the door again.

Traynor was lying to him – the transport was mine. I had people to do it. Traynor organised nothing. But Cahill thought I was stopping Traynor doing what he wanted. You couldn't trust John Traynor. John Traynor was a Walter Mitty. Any person he had any dealings with he either let them down or shafted them, sold them out.

Cahill actually came and apologised to me three or four days later in a neutral house.

What was Traynor's response?

Traynor didn't stay home for a week or two. He went missing. He had several people asking, 'Can he come home?'

'Are you gonna beat him up?'

'Are you gonna hurt him?'

And I said, 'What the fuck are you on about? I won't do anything.'

I said to Traynor, 'Why are you telling lies, stupid stories and doing dopey things? Why do you want to bring attention ... and talk about guns?'

He said, 'I just said it to him to keep him happy.'

So Martin comes up and he said, 'I'm sorry, I didn't know.'

I said, 'It doesn't matter, it's no problem.'

I liked Martin and that's when I used to give Martin 300 quid a week wages. Then I upped it to 500 quid a week. And Martin would always go, 'Oh, I can't wait for Friday 'til John gives me £500.'

You gave Martin Cahill a so-called wage! You're claiming he was in financial trouble? The General masterminded the theft of £2 million of jewels, diamonds and gold from O'Connor's jewellery factory in Harold's Cross in 1983. He also carried out the Beit Art Heist from Russborough House in Wicklow in 1986, which was the biggest art theft in the history of the State, worth an estimated £30 million at the time.

He wasn't going too good. Martin had nothing. They got £243,000 out of that robbery – there was £6 million in the safe! The fella that went in and got the money couldn't count. He robbed £2 million worth of diamonds and gold from O'Connor's. Sure, the mark up on gold is 400 to 600 per cent. They got about twenty grand each. It was the only stroke they got for a year.[*]

But even a low five-figure sum was a substantial amount of money in the eighties.

I mean, he robbed paintings – they were no good. They're worth hundreds of millions, but they're only paintings if you can't sell them. He had great bottle, but he wasn't money successful.

---

[*]   In 2014 Gilligan told me, 'As far as I know John Traynor paid for Martin Cahill's funeral. Or helped to pay for it. Traynor did love Martin.'

When Martin Cahill bought Cowper Downs, one of the lads that he was working with lent him what money he was short of to buy it.

Martin done crimes more to annoy the police than to get money. Martin's share of any robberies was nothing. It was a few quid. Apart from the house he bought, Martin had nothing else.

They said Martin went out and robbed small things. I don't know if he did or not. But he certainly had no money to lend anybody. In the end, I used to give Martin a few quid because I liked him. And if he wanted somebody in Blanchardstown sorted out, given a few punches, I went out and done it.

You beat up someone as a favour for him?

Martin had a friend, a lady, I don't know if it was a family friend or something, in Blanchardstown. There was a couple of bullies who used to park their car at the lady's gates. She was about 70 years of age. Now, I'm 70, but she was an *old* 70. And they bullied and screamed and shouted at her.

Martin said, 'Would you sort that?'

I went out and I punched the head off the fellas for Martin. I made them apologise to the lady, and that was the end of it.

Did you ever rob banks with Cahill?

I'm not going to incriminate myself, but when Martin and me got together we weren't saints. He ended up with money and I ended up with money. Is that a fair answer for you?

Do you think the police monitoring Cahill and his gang 24/7 impinged them?

I think they only got followed for one or two years. The police followed maybe eight to ten of them. But they were losing the police. There was a few of that crowd that done armed robberies in the meantime and got arrested in their houses! They'd say, 'If you were watching me 24/7 how could I do that armed robbery?'

The Tango Squad used to follow me places. I noticed them following me. And then they ended up taking the squad off me, because I was getting more of a buzz out of it, losing them. So, there was no point in following me because I would lose them every time I wanted.

The police were picking on me, charging me for stupid things. I won every stupid thing that they charged me with. It was just to keep me down at the court and one detective said to me, 'John, we're told from the top to have you monitored every day and to know where you are. So, the only way we know where you are is if we charge with you something stupid. And we know that you're spending all morning, all afternoon, at the District Court. The factories are safe then.'

What was your reaction when you heard Martin Cahill had been murdered? He had four bullets pumped into him by a professional hitman outside his home in August 1994. He was only 45 and left behind five children.

It wasn't his lucky day. The same as if I was shot dead, it wouldn't be my lucky day. I'm not really squeamish about things like that. If it happens, it happens. I wouldn't be worried about it. As I said to the police one time, 'I don't worry about the next time somebody will come to get me because the next time they'll empty the machine gun into my head.'

Martin Cahill was a lovely fella, in my book. He was up my street, in a sense. I respected Martin Cahill. He was a good, honest criminal. And he was staunch; he would never grass on nobody. The man had tons of bottle. He wasn't afraid to do what he wanted to do.

What ran through your mind when the media had you pegged as a suspect for Cahill's cold-blooded murder?

It was laughable. For what? You know, if that had been the first story about me I'd probably have gone nuts, but at that stage there was so many stories in the paper about me. You just got immune to it.

Do you feel the rumour linking you to Cahill's murder could have had you killed?

I don't believe that could have got me killed because his family and his friends would know that I didn't [do it]. Sure, Paddy Holland was supposed to have killed him. And Martin Cahill's brother, John Cahill said Paddy killed him for me. When Martin Cahill was shot dead there was two people sitting side by side in Portlaoise [Prison] yard on exercise: John Cahill and Paddy Holland! And that muppet believes the newspapers. Then he said Paddy done it because I was supposed to have ordered it. That's how stupid people get.

It was widely rumoured that Martin Cahill lent John Traynor and you the so-called seed capital in order to start up your drug empire. But you didn't want to pay him back and decided to take him out of the equation.

Martin Cahill had no money. A lot of people thought Cahill had tons of money. I heard all sorts of money: a half million, a quarter of a million, £100,000, £160,000. If I wanted somebody whacked in them days, you could get it done for £10,000. If you were that type of a piece of shit, which I ain't, you'd have a murder [arranged] for ten grand.

So, if there was any truth that I owed Martin Cahill any amount of money, whatever money it was supposed to be, why would I not pay him and give Meener the balance? I gave Brian Meehan £1 million as a thank you in 1995 for doing work for me, just normal work.

'Normal work' includes PRSI! Why did you give Brian Meehan, the only person convicted for participating in the murder of Veronica Guerin, seven figures in cash?

Nothing serious – selling hash. I give him a million pounds in one go, as a friend at the time. The police know that Brian Meehan got it because he put it in his account. He got £600,000 out of his account in Austria.

I said, 'Don't let anybody know you have this money.'

But Brian told everybody!

And all the people ringing me up: 'Oh Jaysus! You're great ... you gave him a million! When am I getting a million?'

And Brian said, 'I couldn't believe it. I had to tell everybody I was a millionaire, and you gave it to me.'

One theory is that Brian Meehan was involved in Cahill's murder?

I don't believe he was involved in that. I believe that the police know every single detail of what happened to Martin Cahill and who was involved.

I'm glad nobody got caught. Because you're either a criminal or you're not. And a criminal would not want another criminal to be caught. Because, in a sense, even though it's not personal, the police are on one side, and you're on the other side. They're the good guys and you're the bad guys. But, seeing as you're a bad guy, you might feel in your head you're a good guy. But you don't want the other side to beat you, or to beat anybody that's doing similar things to yourself. You say, 'Good luck to them.'

When I hear somebody gets a big score, I go, 'Wow! Fair play to him. Nice one.'

Martin Cahill was a good guy. It's a shame what happened to him. But if he done wrong, he done wrong. So, he got what was coming to him if he did wrong.

As Martin Cahill's body was lowered into the ground, a dozen of his relatives sang 'Que Sera Sera', accompanied by a family member on a guitar. Why weren't you there to see off your old friend?

I didn't want to be seen. For me to go down and do that it'd be a headline in the paper. I was gone off the radar. I wasn't on the radar. There's a book to be printed there now – how did the police not know I made so much money, that I brought [into Ireland] so much drugs, and I spent millions of pounds on property? The police didn't know because I was under the radar. I didn't want any notoriety. I tiptoed around.

In more recent years, after the IRA took credit for the murder of Martin Cahill,* it was claimed that you used prison football matches between prisoners in Portlaoise Prison to forge links with the IRA and that you were the person who told them The General had helped the UVF and had been involved in the botched Dublin bombing of 1994, in order to have your gangland rival taken out of the picture. Is that true?

It never happened. There was never a football match between criminals and IRA, or even the INLA. There were guys that some time in their lives may have been with some groups, but had long left them or may have left as they served a sentence. The freedom fighter, in a million years, would not play with crims.

My mind keeps thinking of all the bullshit they write about me. People believe so much of things that can't and don't add up and if they took a little moment to ask themselves is that a fact what they just read, they've got to know there is not two Saturdays or Sundays in a week – but if it's in the press they believe in it. It sometimes feels like whoever is feeding such stories to the papers is trying to get me set up.

---

*   A senior IRA member once confirmed to me that the Dublin Brigade was responsible for Martin Cahill's death. The notorious criminal had apparently ended up in their cross hairs because he refused to bow down to the IRA's extortion for a cut of the O'Connor's Jewellers heist and as a result of his ill-judged dealings with Ulster loyalists. It's also been claimed that he supplied them with a safe house for their botched attempt to blow up The Widow Scallan's Pub in Pearse Street, while a Republican fundraiser event for 200 people was taking place there, in May 1994.

TAPE FIVE

GILLIGAN'S DRUG EMPIRE

'If you think we were bad, wait until
you see what's coming after us.'

– LARRY DUNNE, AFTER BEING SENTENCED ON
HEROIN DRUG TRAFFICKING CHARGES IN 1985

During the early nineties, it was somewhat ironic that Moore Street's famous open-air fruit and vegetable market in the heart of old Dublin became a hub for black market cigarettes and tobacco.

Most days of the week, you could witness as many illegal cigarette operators openly peddling their wares as you would find ticket touts on the night of a U2 gig at the old Point Depot venue down the docks.

And, in all likelihood, the cigarettes flooding the Irish market at the time were chiefly sourced from John Gilligan, who had overnight become the main player in this illegal racket. There were plenty of foreign brands and knockoffs, but the shrewd crook also smuggled in genuine iconic labels, too.

Gilligan had become a master of reinventing himself out of necessity. He might have been a self-described criminal with 'plenty of bottle', but this was one hardshaw who was never afraid to retreat when he no longer liked the odds.

Up until now, armed robbery and burglaries had been his modus operandi. 'If there was two banks beside each other, you could rob one and then run in and rob the next one. You'd come out with the money and you could nearly run in next door and lodge,' he told me in 2008. 'You could do stuff like that back in them days in the seventies. Loads of people did two banks – they'd run out of the Allied Irish and run across the street to the Bank of Ireland. I've often pulled 12 strokes – one after the other – with the money still on me!'

Gilligan had given up on bank jobs because he was convinced certain guards had a bullet with his name on it. He feared getting shot dead the next time he burst out of a bank's doors, brandishing a firearm and a sack of money over his shoulder.

After his first experience of Portlaoise Prison, he also had another change of heart about breaks-ins, if they were not going to be on a grand scale. In November 1990, it shook him considerably when he was dragged up in front of the Special Criminal Court for the first time and given a four-year sentence for receiving stolen goods worth a measly £3,063. Such risks, he knew, just didn't add up on a financial level.

He was kicking himself throughout that sentence and vowed not to put himself in a situation where he would be caught red-handed again. Gilligan was running out of options until he stumbled upon the idea of smuggling cigarettes and subsequently cannabis. But it all led to the widely-held perception of him having the dirtiest hands in Irish crime, at least until the Hutch–Kinahan feud kicked off.

After serving the four-year sentence in Portlaoise Prison you next began to smuggle cigarettes.

I was smuggling millions of cigarettes and vast amounts of tobacco into Ireland. I discovered that the law hadn't been changed since 1886; it was still the same in the early nineties. The maximum penalty for smuggling cigarettes into Ireland, no matter the amount, was under a £1,000 fine. No prison. The law was only changed in 1999. I actually educated them on that. They were listening to my telephone calls. They'd bugged all my legal visits in Portlaoise Prison and in England. It's [now] six years for smuggling cigarettes.

I always knew the police were listening to my phones. So sometimes I used get into giddy moods, and I just talked a lot of bullshit on the phones and say this and say that. I said all sorts of weird stuff. And I know they'd be scratching their heads and they wouldn't know what to do. I could visualise them in me mind's eye running around like blue-arsed flies and writing this down and trying to make head or tail of it.

'What the fecking hell is Gilligan saying?'

'Is he talking in code?'

It would be just a load of bull, but I used to get my entertainment out of it. Even when I had mobile phones in prison I used to do the same thing because I knew they were listening. I always believed 100 per cent that the cell was bugged. So it didn't bother me. I used to waffle. Now, that's just banter.

How much did you smuggle into the country on your first attempt?

I would've brought £40,000 worth of tobacco. I probably made £20,000 – 50 per cent profit on it. And then I went up to £100,000 and I'd be making £50,000.

And then I was getting cigarettes from all different places. I ended up getting cigarettes, proper, not counterfeit cigarettes, I got them at a great price. We used to take the cigarettes out of a container that was supposed to be going to Nigeria.

I had them disguised as something else in trucks. I would send them through companies that had a great reputation. I got them to send [shipments] to Ireland as different commodities. I had success every time. I didn't lose any of them. I got every shipment in. I made massive money on them.*

How many shipments did you smuggle into Ireland?

Maybe twenty-eight. It's a lot of shipments when you're bringing in millions. It could be more. I don't know, because I brought a lot of tobacco in. I used to have lorry drivers just to bring tobacco for me. Most lorry drivers would bring fifty or a hundred boxes of tobacco. So, if a fella wanted to make himself two grand he might bring in X amount of boxes.

Where were you sourcing all these cigarettes from?

A man was able to get me containers of cigarettes. The cigarettes where from London and they were in a bonded warehouse in Rotterdam. And when the place closed and the customs went [home] at six o'clock at night, the man used to open his warehouse and I used to send a truck in and unload the first two pallets of cigarettes and leave them down and we'd take all

---

* It was also alleged that Gilligan once hijacked, at gunpoint, a truckload of cigarettes worth an estimated seven-figure sum, but he merely laughed and refused to comment when the subject was broached.

the ones at the back, and then we put the first two ones back [in place].

But we also came with the truck full. I employed people to take the cigarettes out of the cigarette cartons and put them into plain brown boxes that were the same size of the cigarettes. I had foam and a stone-and-a-half of sand to make up the weight put into the box.

The box was weighed and then sealed properly and put back on the pallet and loaded back into the container. We used to put in a bit of furniture into the container to allow for the weight.

And when the container would go to the docks, when the crane man picked the container up, it weighted the exact same weight and it would be loaded onto a ship. The payment for the corrupt customs over there [was inside the containers]. And that went on for a whole year.

How did your first drug deal come about?

John Traynor was after being in prison in England and he knew a Dutch guy that could get hash. Traynor would send the money out [to Holland] for one kilo and I'd send the money for six or seven kilos, but I think only about four kilos came back. I know I was left short of three or four [kilos] from the first time. And then more money went out to get ten kilos, and I think seven or eight come back, and then the money went out for fourteen or seventeen.

You kept paying up front even though you were being left short?

I got Traynor to let me speak to the fella. And I said, 'Listen here, I want what was paid for.'

'Oh, it was. They were all there.' And then he said, 'Let me check my car. Oh, sorry, there's four kilos in the boot of my car.'

So, I trusted him the next time and that never went right.

It all sounds very naive. So what did you do?

I went over to hurt that guy. He was to meet me, but Traynor rang him and said, 'This man is too dangerous. He's gonna do damage to you.'

And your man never turned up. I had a row with Traynor [over it] and I fucked Traynor off. And then I gave him another chance. So Traynor was nothing to me. Nothing! I built it up myself.

According to countless reports, your main source for drugs in Amsterdam was Simon Rahman. Is that true?

He wasn't a big drug dealer in the way some papers say he was. He used to go sourcing for me, or anybody else that asked him, and he'd make himself a few quid. Simon Rahman was a runner.

Every time I was making money from crime I was adding it to the drug money and I was able to buy more and more.

How close were you to Simon Rahman?

Simon Rahman was the only man that would collect stuff and deliver it or get me an introduction to someone that would have a good amount of material. I'd give Simon Rahman a few quid now and again, because he was really just a worker, and he would have no money himself. Simon was living in a small flat. Simon wouldn't be able to put his hands in his pocket and take £10,000 or £20,000 out. Whereas I could put my hand in my pocket and take £200,000 out.

How did you and Traynor part ways for good?

I gave Traynor £1.4 million. I got rid of Traynor in, I'd say, April 1995. I wanted nothing to do with him. I gave him stuff [cannabis] and money, and it came to £1.4 million. Then he bought his garages.

Ballpark figure, how much did you make from smuggling cannabis into Ireland?

I would have been touching £10 million.

And now?

I haven't got ten bob. I have no money. That's the truth.

How did you meet Brian Meehan?

I robbed some factories, and he bought some stuff off me. And I had traveller's cheques for sale and he bought them. And then I had a good bit of jewellery for sale, not out of robbery now. Fellas were selling me jewellery. I was making a stockpile of gold. And some fellas would ask me would I have a good watch, a good chain, and I'd sell it to them for a few quid more than I paid. I'd be getting them at low costs. People would be desperate to sell them. I'd often buy off them in the bookies and at the pitch and toss. And people asked me for something and I'd say, 'Yeah, I have one of them.'

So I met him that way. And then we did a few robberies together.

Did you do any armed jobs together?

Oh, we done a few robberies together. I thought he was a good fella. He had great bottle. Like, bottle means that when a criminal does things and people think you're fearless. You'd say, 'He's got great bottle.'

Why was he nicknamed Tosser?

The Gardaí arrested Brian Meehan and took him to Bridewell Garda Station for a drug search. They got him to take all his clothes off and they took them away to X-ray them. Then they sent a female Garda into the room to ask him something – so he put his hand on his dick and asked her does she want it. True fact.

Was Brian Meehan taking a lot of drugs back then?

I didn't know much about drugs. I didn't know if a fella was after taking a load of drugs and loads of tablets to do a robbery. But people often said that to me – and I thought they're jealous about him – 'What you think of Meener?'

I'd say, 'I think he's a good fella. He's sound. If I'm going in the front door I know he's going to come in the back door. He goes in the back door, I go in the front door.'

He would stick to the plan. I took him as a top guy that way. But people said, 'Do you not know he's stoned every time he's doing something with you?'

'Well, he doesn't look stoned to me,' I said.

'And what does stoned look like, John?'

'Falling over the place.'

They said, 'That's not stoned, John.'

It doesn't matter. We done things together and he was very good. We were close enough, but I had better friends than him.

You were both pulled in once for a major heist of £1 million worth of Adidas in Cork.

Tracksuits ... trainers ... football boots. The safe was also broken open, money taken. Plus, the very special new brand of aluminium/shiny tracksuit that was to be their new masterpiece. This new tracksuit wasn't even on the market.

Well, Paul Ward, Brian Meehan and a guy from Cork and I were arrested in the Harp Bar. We were taken to the Bridewell Garda Station. After we got our allowed phone calls to tell our families, Brian Meehan's dad came to the station to leave him in a few sandwiches ... but wasn't he only wearing the shiny tracksuit!

The Garda said, 'You can give the grub to Brian yourself ... as you're nicked! That's the tracksuit every Garda in Ireland is looking for.'

A million pounds worth of Adidas and he walks in with the one taken out of the safe! A fucking gobshite!

None of us went on trial for that. We all got a Section 30 on it. And we got let off and the file was sent to the DPP. The DPP might be walking around with that tracksuit!

How did Brian Meehan get involved in your drug empire?

What happened was, he asked me one time to get him a 'drop'. He was going to do an armed robbery. And I said, 'No I'm finished with armed robberies. The police told me they'd whack me. My armed robbery days are over.'

So he begged me to get him a 'drop'. So I got it for him. They went after a payroll and they got the whole payroll. So, I didn't want any money off them. I had my own money. And I said to him, 'Forget about armed robberies. I'll give you work and you get more money with me than you will with armed robberies, if you do what I ask ya.'

And that's what he done. 'Nobody else, just you and you alone.'

Was John Traynor still with you at this point?

At that stage, I was doing it myself. I was working on me own. I had left Traynor. I said, 'One day a week is all you have to do, two or three hours' work and you'll get a good few grand. You'll have more money than you ever did with robbery.'

And then he [Meehan] was doing that for a while. Then he asked me could he get Paul Ward involved.

And I said, 'No, no.'

And he said, 'John, Paul is a fantastic driver. The police won't catch him. You'll never lose your stuff.'

I said, 'If you don't tell anybody anything, nobody knows what we're doing. Keep everything low profile. Nobody knows. You won't lose anything.'

But eventually he asked me that many times I said, 'Okay, get Paul. Nobody else but Paul.' And then behind me back he had Peter Mitchell. I said Mitchell was to not be involved as he's an almighty mouth. I only found out six months later. I was proved right. And then Peter Mitchell employed Charlie Bowden. Mitchell and Meehan got Bowden to collect the boxes of hash at the Ambassador Hotel.

How many times did you meet Charlie Bowden, one of the key witnesses in your downfall at your trial?

I'd say I met Charlie less than five times. He wasn't in my company. It was like, we'd have a meeting for five minutes and he was standing there. I just heard that he was a karate expert and he beat up people in the army, because they were gonna give statements against him that he threatened them. He told them all what to say at the court martial. He wrote a statement down for them to say, they practised the statement, what they're going to say, and all that. And then I think, one of the privates broke [rank] and said, 'We were threatened.' So Charlie got demoted and then he left the army.

By this stage Russell Warren had started working for you. How did your paths first cross?

Derek Baker was supposed to be bringing money out to me to the continent. Doing the cigarettes for me. I thought [only] Derek was collecting the cigarettes for me, because that was his job.

But [one night] the sailing was delayed. The cigarettes didn't get in until two o'clock in the morning.

And I said to Derek, 'Does your missus ever give out to you for coming in late?' She didn't know about him going out with a woman.

And he goes, 'No, sure I'm in at ten o'clock every night.'

'What time were you in last night, Derek?'

He said, 'Ten o'clock.'

'Are you sure you were in at ten o'clock last night? Who did the cigarettes?'

'I did it.'

'No, Derek you didn't do the cigarettes, because the cigarettes didn't get in 'til two o'clock in the morning.'

And then I found out Russell Warren was working for him for the last three months. I didn't know anything about Russell Warren.

Do you remember the first time you met him?

Derek was to bring my money out to Belgium. I think it was £480,000 exactly. He'd go over to Holyhead on the ferry, [then] go to London on the train and get the ferry across to Belgium, because it was a big holdall bag of money.

So when I waited there to meet him, I seen this fella come along. He recognised me.

'Who the fuck are you?' I said.

'Russell, Derek sent me,' he said. 'I have your money.'

So when he gave me one bag of money, I said, 'What's in that second bag?'

'Money.'

'Well, give me it.'

'No, that's not yours. It's Brian Meehan's. I've to bring it to your bank and exchange it and get a draft. He wants a draft for £300,000, because he's gonna put it in another bank.'

So I said, 'Give me that money.' I took the £300,000 off him.

I rang Brian Meehan.

'What the fucking hell are you up to?' I said. 'What's this guy doing with three hundred grand?'

And he started choking. He said, 'He's just getting me a draft.'

'A draft from the place where I change my money? My place where I've got authorisation to do it? You're sending him in?'

'What's the difference?' he said.

'The difference is, if you come on top then it'll blow where I'm changing my money. I'm trying to keep everything under the radar. I don't want anybody to know I exist or what I'm doing, or anything. That's how I'm surviving. I'm after taking the money off him. When you get the next money in, take your £300k back.'

I would bring in about six or seven or eight hundred grand a week, so he could take it back.

You were obviously smuggling cannabis into the country by this stage. Why didn't you deal in cocaine and heroin, too?

My mother was still alive and I wouldn't embarrass my mother to the best of my ability. She would've been ashamed. That was the reason. In the nineties there was no demand for cocaine on a large scale as there is today. Cocaine, I think now, is equal to cannabis, or more. But at that time there wasn't too many people on cocaine – other than the judges and the guards and the politicians and the church people!

I've never heard that allegation made before now. But you were missing out when it came to ecstasy because there was a big demand for it in the nineties.

But with the people doing ecstasy [already], I didn't want to be greedy and step on their toes. Let them do ecstasy, I'll do hash.

Did you ever smoke cannabis?

No, I didn't. I was afraid it would stunt me growth. That's why I didn't smoke cigarettes. I was afraid I wouldn't grow, and I didn't [*laughs*].

Did John Traynor ever ask you to get involved in dealing heroin with him?

No, because he knew I wouldn't. I was staunch on that. I used to speak bad about people that done it when it would come up. I'd go, 'Fuck them. Would they like that done to their son and daughter? Other people's sons or daughters are in a heap.'

Do you feel there's a big difference between being someone who deals in cannabis and Class A drugs?

Nobody ever died from smoking cannabis, or became addicted to cannabis. You know, it's like beer: you can only drink so much. And you can only smoke so much hash. But heroin you can inject it 'til you overdose. Nobody has ever died from an overdose of cannabis. And cannabis is legalised in an awful lot of countries. Governments wouldn't be legalising cannabis if it was harmful, or if it was the so-called gateway drug to heroin.

So you believe it's morally wrong to sell cocaine or heroin, but it's acceptable to sell marijuana?

Yeah, that's what I believe, once I know it's not doing any harm. You'd say, 'Well, if it's not doing any harm to the people that's doing it and they're not inflicting any more harm to the people around them, they're not doing any harm at all.'

It's a known fact that the people that smoke marijuana are all happy. In prison people smoked marijuana and they're as happy as Larry. And the prison officers say, 'As long as they're happy, it makes our job better. We were under too much stress, and now there's no problems.'

They could use prisoners as an example if the prison officers are saying, 'There's no trouble in our prison if they're just smoking.

We turn a blind eye for them to get a bit of cannabis in.' It would be the same in society, I would think, and say, 'Well, if they are not doing any harm with it. None whatsoever.'

Yet members of the Gilligan Gang sold Class A drugs?

I wasn't their boss. I was their supplier that was sending it to them.

Is there a difference?

Of course there's a difference. The supermarkets supply your groceries. They're not your boss – and I was like a hash super-market.

But wouldn't you have more than the one item on the shelf if you were a supermarket?

No. But I had tons of hash on the shelf. Brian Meehan imported ten kilos of heroin into the country while he was in prison. Ten kilos of heroin!

What would you have done if you'd found out earlier that Brian Meehan was dealing in heroin?

I would have gone mental. He'd have been gone. I wanted a low profile, and anybody dealing in heroin can't stay under the radar. I never took cocaine. I never took marijuana. I never took any class of drug whatsoever.

The politician Tony Gregory, he went after all the heroin dealers. He said something nice about me. He said more time was spent on John Gilligan, a cannabis dealer, rather than [focusing on] the heroin dealers in the inner city. He said, 'We're trying to stop heroin – John Gilligan is not a priority.'

Why did Brian Meehan attempt to kill Martin 'The Viper' Foley in 1996? Foley must be a proverbial cat with nine lives because there's been four attempts on his life. Foley was also abducted by the IRA but escaped when there was a shoot-out between his kidnappers and the police in 1984.

He was telling people that they were selling smack. John Traynor was going mad over Foley and Veronica [Guerin] because his neighbours across the road, the husband and wife, were senior detectives in Store Street Garda Station. Traynor had two sons and two daughters. The policewoman used to bring Traynor's kids out with them. And they didn't know too much about Traynor. He was going mad because this was going to come back on his son. 'He won't be able to play with his pal.'

Traynor used to go mad, especially when he would have two or three bottles of vodka.

I used to say Traynor, 'You don't cause no fucking problems for me.'

But the scum that he was, he didn't give a shit.

But didn't you say Brian Meehan was working for you?

But I found out years later that he was doing heroin with Traynor and Bowden. I had no control over them. I always said, you give the drugs to clients on the southside and you get paid on the northside, or you give the drugs on the northside and you get paid on the southside. You'd never have both together, because if the police get lucky or get information, they're gonna stop your transport: you're gonna lose the money and the drugs. You'd have a double whammy. This way will give you a chance to lose one thing: money or drugs.

I was very trustworthy in regards to people with buying [drugs] and a lot of time they would pay me £300,000 before they even got the merchandise to make sure that they were getting served. That's the way it was in the nineties. People trusted me.

But when I was in Portlaoise Prison a couple of people that bought off me said, 'Jaysus! John, you know what? That van was often going around and it would have 300 kilos still left in it and there'd be more money belonging to you than there would be in some of the security vans getting held up.'

It was ridiculous. 'Cause that's the fool he [Meehan] was. His da's famous saying in prison is: 'Don't insult me intelligence.' You know what I mean? Intelligence!

And then I pressed him and he said, 'So what? We didn't lose anything. What's the problem?'

I have no respect for that man. He couldn't do anything he was paid to do. He'd lie. He was driving around with a van load of money and a van load of drugs.

You mentioned earlier that you made £10 million from smuggling cannabis but sounded unsure.

£10 million or more. I wasn't counting because I was getting it and spending it. When you'd be dealing with people on the continent, the drugs, they'd always ask you for a favour. I'd say, 'What's that favour?' 'Will you sell some for us.' So, I sold a lot of cannabis in Ireland for them. It's the norm in the drug business if you buy drugs off somebody, you're buying hundreds of kilos they'd say,

'Can we put a half a ton on for us and return us back X amount of money? We'll make sure you get top quality stuff.'

Everybody says you laundered a lot of your drug money through gambling.

No, I didn't launder any money through gambling. It's laughable. There's a certain guy in the newspapers said John Gilligan used to put £10,000 on each horse in the race. And when the winner would win, he would put all the losing tickets into a bin and look for a cheque for the winner.

This is how ludicrous that is: in the average horse race there's ten runners; but there's some horse races with fifteen or sixteen horses. And if you put £10,000 on ten horses, that's £100,000. And the winner might be a one-to-two favourite. You'd get £15,000. So you'd just have thrown away £85,000 to get £15,000.

There's no such thing as laundering money. It's a myth, laundering money in any country in the world, because once the authorities come down on you they have your money. They'd go, 'Where do you get that money from?'

If you're stupid enough to say, 'I won it on the horses,' they'll say, 'Where did you get the money to put the bet on? You never paid tax.' So, you can't win.

I was gambling heavy, but I was winning most of the time. I wasn't doing a heavy bet and winning to say where I got the money from, because I already was covered it: I had a £4 million pound loan from Joseph Sammona and I'll show you that documentation very soon.

I often put £40,000 or £50,000 on a horse. I had my own horse that was in my wife's name. I had £100,000 on it. One of the winning bets was very close to £300,000. CAB had records of that bet.

But when I'd have other bets, if I put 20k on a horse in a bookies, which I done hundreds of times, that meant the bookie had £20,000 in the till, plus my 10 per cent tax: that'd be £22,000. If the horse won I would ask for cash. If it won at 6/4 my return would be £50,000. So I'd get my £22,000 back plus £4,000 or £5,000 off the bookies and then they'd give me a cheque for the rest.

So how many millions did you blow away on gambling?

Ah, millions. I'd say from 1970 to 1996, I would have – and this just sounds far-fetched but the truth – gambled and lost very close to £20 million.

I would have gambled between £400 and £600 million [in total]. And the way I say that is, if you go into the bookies with say £20,000 and you put ten grand on and it loses you've only ten grand in your pocket. But if you put six or seven grand on a two to one, you've £18,000, plus the two or three that you have in your pocket, so you're nearly back to twenty. And then if you put ten grand on an even money shot and you win ten grand, now you've thirty grand. Now you put twenty grand on a horse and it loses you've ten grand in your pocket. And then if you won with the ten grand on the two to one you'd have thirty grand back again.

So, in the course of the day, you'd probably put £200,000 across the counter, but you didn't *gamble* £200,000 of the money you came in with. It would be after a win, a losing bet, a win bet. It's like somebody in the casino, putting ten chips down, losing them, putting the next ten chips down and winning it, and then putting five or eight down and winning or losing. So if you were to count how many chips you put on the table in a couple of hours gambling, that you changed £200 at the counter, you go, 'Jaysus, you're after gambling £3,000 there.'

But you know you only lost 200 quid, it's the same money going back and forward.

But in real money, I would have lost close to £20 million. I'm not proud of it now. I'm stupid. I am a dope. But I paid tax on all my bets. So, I paid millions in tax and that tax went into the Exchequer. I gave millions over the years and the court told me I only paid £7 in tax.

You were quite successful yesterday with your gambling on your phone – showing five figure bets – in front of me while we had a coffee break in between filming.

I was. I don't want to go into that, how much I have. So do not say it. I know you seen in it black and white. But I don't want to. Why would you want to say that? I don't want that – that's my life today. I'm talking about my past life. And the reason why I'm doing this is my past life.

Do you know the way people say, 'Do you believe in the hereafter?' You know, the only time I believed in the hereafter is when I used to go into a factory and I'd say, 'I'm after this. I'm here after these televisions.' So when I'm dead, that's the only hereafter I believe in.

Did you have any other money-making schemes over in Amsterdam?

I was a registered money-changer in the banks there. I had a card. There was two fashion houses, nearly the size of the towers in New York that were bombed, in Amsterdam. On every floor there was money departments and they would have hundreds of thousands of guilders but they would need Irish money and sterling. That was how they could buy their materials for their factories.

I used to get my money changed there as well. I changed millions. I changed people's money for them in maybe two goes, three goes. People come along and buy the guilders off me and the monies they would pay me for that, I'd go back and change them again. So that's the reason why I changed sixty to ninety million in the Bureau de Change.

I was changing hundreds of thousands for people from all over England, Scotland, Wales, and Ireland, and anywhere else. And it was said in court: 'Why would they not do it themselves?'

I said, 'Because they were afraid to walk into a Bureau de Change or the bank and put £200,000 up on the counter. Because they would think the people behind the counter would ring the police and the police come and take the money.'

But the word got around that the Irish guy, John Gilligan, can change any amount of money for you. Because I would have the money already changed. I always had a million Irish pounds changed and I'd always have two or three million guilders.

And once I counted their money and they agreed the rate I wanted to give them – what they got across the road in the Bureau de Change after they changed fifty quid and got whatever rate after commission – I'd go, 'I'll match that rate.'

I used to do that and I used to make 6 or 7 per cent. I done that day in day out, for over two years. And I made a fortune. And if you do the maths, you'll find out you'll get £80,000 or a hundred grand a week. I stopped doing a certain amount of drugs, because I was making plenty of money.

The people that sold the drugs to Irish, English and Scots people would have lots of different notes and I'd change it for them out of my stockpile of guilders. Most times I'd have 2.5 million. I gave them the rate that holidaymakers got.

Were there any other illegal practices going on in Ireland?

The managers [at the Bureau de Changes] there knew me. They said, 'We won't record this transaction.' They didn't want to declare so much money getting changed.

When they found out I was doing it all the time, they accepted me as a respectable money-changer, a businessman. I actually got that done in Dublin Airport. I had the Bank of Ireland Dublin Airport change the money for me because they thought I was an antique car dealer. They changed millions for me into guilders at Dublin Airport.

Now during my Section 3, Peter Charlton, who is now a Supreme Court judge, put the case to me that I changed £16 million, between pounds and punts, in the Bureau de Change at the Central Station in Amsterdam.

I said, '£16 million? That's not true at all. No, the figures [would] be more like £60 or £70 million.'

Were you reading the daily currency exchange rates just as much as the racing papers?

The rate of exchange went up or down every day. I would find out what the rate was and if the rate suited me Tuesday, I'd probably change a half a million to three-quarters of a million.

And if I found out the rate was any better Wednesday and Thursday I'd changed more. And if the rate went down lower, I wouldn't change any more. But I found out that on Thursday afternoon and Friday the rate always went down, and it'll always start creeping back up Monday morning to dinnertime. So the good days for me to change money were always Tuesday and Wednesday when the rates got higher. And I still think it works that way. Even if people Google rates now every different site offers them higher rates, but there was no such thing as Google then.

Overnight you'd become the biggest criminal in Ireland at the time ...

Well, not in height [*laughs*]. I'll accept I'm the smallest, in stature in Irish crime. I think I've midget blood in me. But I would accept when they would say I'm the biggest criminal in the sense that I stole more than another criminal. I would agree with that. I would also agree that the bookmakers were the biggest receivers because they got all the money. So why don't they go after the bookmakers? Because I got the proceeds of crime and I gave it to them by losing bets. I'm only messing.

They [the authorities] didn't know I was up to loads of skulduggery. When they come down and seen how much money I had, and the buildings and what I was after buying my family, they were in shock.

People were saying, 'Why didn't you keep an eye on this fella?' 'Why weren't you watching this fella if he got so rich in two years?' 'Why weren't they on top of him, watching every movement?'

The reason why they weren't was because I was keeping a low profile. And they admitted they didn't know. They said it many times in evidence in court: 'We were totally shocked.'

It's known in history now, they say, as the biggest drug business – cannabis and only cannabis – to ever hit the history of the State. But they didn't realise the volumes that was coming in. They [only ever] found a few old kilos, and the truth was they were Peter Mitchell's.

And those four years in prison had taught me, 'Keep your head down and you'll be successful.' I was successful and then people brought the whole heavens down on top of me.

Was Paddy 'Dutchy' Holland really involved in your drug empire?[*]

I don't want to answer that question. Why would I? He was a decent guy and never done any damage on anybody. I know the man's not with us, but I'm not going to say a bad word about a good man. As far as I know, he was a good man. I've no evidence he ever done anything wrong on anybody[†] ... other than going to chapel! He was the most religious man I ever came across. When I was in prison with him, he done the altar in the chapel. He was recommended by all the governors and all the Welfare Board and all the priests that he should go to Shelton Abbey for the last three or four years of his sentence. The Minister for Justice said 'that gang will not be getting a day off'. And that's why I even believe I done six- or seven-weeks overtime, with a smile always on my face. They did not break me.

---

[*] Documents found in the Gilligan gang's warehouse recorded that someone named 'The Wig' had been supplied with cannabis. Holland denied in court that he was known as 'The Wig', but later confessed to me that this was indeed his moniker.

[†] Gilligan would later change his tune and affirm Holland was a hitman.

TAPE SIX

VERONICA GUERIN

'To me the story is a dance of death between Veronica and John Gilligan. Because even though they are totally 180 degree the opposite, they are very similar in some respects. They are both extraordinarily successful in what they do, they both have very big egos and they don't stand down for anyone ...'

– DIRECTOR JOEL SCHUMACHER ON HIS FILM *VERONICA GUERIN*

The summer of 1995 was the greatest period of tranquillity and happiness in John Gilligan's entire life. He was making money hand over fist from smuggling cannabis and was enjoying a jet-setting lifestyle with his much younger lover, Carol Rooney.

Yet, it was amazing how such an astute criminal mastermind appeared oblivious to the heavy storm clouds swirling around him at a rapid pace, which would presage difficult times of biblical proportions.

Gilligan might have been desperate to remain 'low profile', and he obviously felt untouchable but he was too clever for his own good. It was difficult for him to remain anonymous when he and Geraldine built the country's largest indoor equestrian centre, with a 3,000-person capacity in Jessbrook, near the Kildare–Meath border. Sooner or later somebody was going to come snooping around and ask Gilligan some awkward questions.

How could he go from residing in a small council home in a tough neighbourhood to, almost overnight, living such a lavish lifestyle?

He didn't have a plausible tale to spin. Even more peculiarly, when the media pried, the Gilligans claimed they had legally separated circa 1994, despite still working together on the estimated €1.5 million venture during 1995–96. It also included thirty-eight stables and an apartment on the forty-acre site.

It's rare enough for separated couples to remain on speaking terms. But theirs was certainly one of the most amicable splits I've ever observed. I was even half-convinced that they were still a couple from the way they were play-acting with each other when I was invited to interview John Gilligan at Jessbrook in late 2013. As it turned out, they weren't still together, and, from what I understand now, they haven't seen each other in several years.

The equestrian centre was a fine-looking venue, but the house itself was slightly run down by the time I got to see inside it, as they had unsuccessfully fought a sixteen-year legal battle to stop it from being seized by CAB. Yes, it was a spacious bungalow with a nice kitchen, and its centrepiece was an impressive games room with an old-school wooden drinks bar, one with plenty of light from large windows overlooking pleasant views of the nearby woodlands. But it was certainly nothing like the Camelot it has been portrayed as in the media. As an aside, Gilligan somehow managed to ship that bar to Spain.

Gilligan's house of cards first began to unravel when the then 37-year-old journalist Veronica Guerin decided to visit Jessbrook on

14 September 1995. By then Guerin was one of the biggest names in the Irish print media, thanks to her exclusive interview with Bishop Eamonn Casey, whom she had tracked down in Ecuador in 1993. But even though she had branched out into crime writing, Gilligan claimed he was still unaware of her.

'I wouldn't know who Veronica Guerin was to save my life in them days.' He only seemed to read the racing pages at that time. Even now, Gilligan is not motivated to check the news online, often waiting a few days before learning about the latest major scandal or crime story in Ireland.

It's strange that Gilligan wouldn't have been able to pick Veronica Guerin out of a police line-up, because her face had been plastered all over television screens and newspapers when she was shot in the leg at her own home, with a .45 revolver.

He had to be either truly self-obsessed or living under a rock if she wasn't on his radar. Gilligan's old partner in crime, John Traynor, whom he claimed to have cut all ties with by 1995, after giving him the underworld's equivalent of a golden handshake, had been arrested and questioned over the first shooting at Coolock Garda Station. 'No, I did not know that about Traynor,' Gilligan said.*

But Gilligan was not going to forget about Veronica Guerin in a hurry after she doorstepped him and later pressed assault charges against him.

After conducting many hours of interviews with Gilligan, I was never surprised and always expected the unexpected from him. But, much to my utter astonishment, Gilligan even wanted to dispute the

---

*   It's a subject we would discuss later on during these taped interviews, in which Gilligan made a controversial claim that Veronica Guerin had asked John Traynor to shoot her in the leg to help increase her profile! It should be noted that that was not the first time such an allegation had been aired.

long-established narrative that Veronica Guerin had called out to Jessbrook because she wanted to expose him as Ireland's new Mr Big in the drug trade. He will undoubtedly be accused of attempting to rewrite history here.

How did you believe Veronica Guerin first heard about you?

I was after giving John Traynor £1.4 million. I got rid of him. He was a thorn in my side. He was a disaster when he got drunk. And with that money, he rented garages in Church Motors, Dun Laoghaire, and Naas. His daughter was in the one in Dun Laoghaire, he was in the one in Church Motors, and his brother was in the one in Naas.

Nobody knew at the time that he was feeding a journalist from the *Sunday World* [with information] all about Martin Cahill, like his love affair. John Traynor was reading the *Sunday World* one Monday morning and his landlord came in and said, 'What do you think of that guy Martin Cahill?' The landlord said his niece was Veronica Guerin. Traynor was impressed because she was after writing a negative story that the police didn't like.

Traynor said, 'Would she speak to me?'

And the landlord said, 'Yeah, I'll get her to talk to you.'

So, she came up and seen Traynor. She was asking Traynor:

'What do the police do when they arrest you?

'How bad are the police?

'Do they set you up?

'Do they stitch you up?

'Do they plant evidence?

'Do they type up statements and add your name?'

Yes ... yes ... yes ... and yes again. Sometimes people got their penises burnt by the police. There was a policeman called the

Pig Man and often he burnt people on the penis, bullied them to make statements.

I knew the police plant evidence. I knew the police got into the dock and told lies during my trials. Equally, I got into the dock and I didn't tell the truth.

She found out that Traynor was Martin Cahill's right-hand man.

'Would you get me an interview with Cahill?' she said.

Traynor said he would try. Cahill met her a good few times in her house. Also, The Monk was in her house, having tea and scones. These guys [had] done absolutely nothing wrong. They're top criminals. I've always looked up to them.

They were led to believe that they would spill the beans on the horrible corrupt police and that she was going to print it. So, they told her everything they could to print about dirty Gardaí.

But she was lying to them for her own gains! She was doing research for a movie, but nobody knew that. It could happen to anyone that wanted to print about bad cops. Michael Sheridan was doing a movie script with Veronica. They used to meet in a café in Stephen's Green to work on this. It was called *Double Cross* and the two characters in it were based on Martin Cahill and Gerry 'The Monk' Hutch.

Martin Cahill said, 'Really, the man that would tell you an awful lot of what the police do, chapter and verse, is John Gilligan, because he is meticulous in a lot of things.'

And that's not blowing me trumpet. I'm telling you what he said.

You're actually claiming Veronica Guerin wanted to approach you for information about corrupt members of the Garda Síochána and

that it had nothing to do with her seeking to do a story on your drug empire? Up until now the widely accepted narrative has been that she was there to investigate your unusual wealth, which she understood to be from the proceeds of crime. How were you approached?

They knew Brian Meehan was working for me. They approached Brian and said, 'Will you ask John would he give her an interview? She's going to print it all. We could blow the lid off the crooked cops.'

Meehan came down to me on a motorbike.

'Martin and The Monk fella sent me down to ask would you give her an interview?'

'No, Brian. Get the fuck out of here. I want nothing to do with it. I haven't even got a car. Brian, I'm trying to stay under the radar.'

I wouldn't even go to parties. I was never in a pub. I never clubbed with them.

I said to Brian, 'I don't want to associate with you [publicly], or anybody else. Let people think I'm dead or something. I don't want any limelight. None whatsoever.'

Why didn't you drive anymore?

When I was in Portlaoise Prison doing my four years sentence, I vowed never to drive again because when I had a car I had a scanner and I could hear the police talking on the police radio. They would say, 'We're gonna stop John Gilligan here. He's gone down Thomas Street.' Every policeman in Ireland is hearing your name coming over the radio!

Out of sight, out of mind. And I was doing very well. It would've brought heat on me if I had given any interviews. I didn't trust anybody in that way. Why would I do it? There was no gain in it for me to give people stories. I'm giving these interviews now because I'm sick for the last twenty-five–thirty years hearing stories about me. There's only been one side of the story out. My side of the story has never been told, to give the public a chance to say, 'He's a nut,' or, 'He's actually telling the truth,' or, 'I don't believe him,' or, 'I do believe him.'

You speak about keeping a low profile, yet you did go on a lavish trip to St Lucia with your ex-wife and Brian Meehan and gangster Peter Mitchell to attend the wedding of Brian's sister Leslie in April 1996. [*]

I told Brian Meehan to take what money was needed to pay for his family and sister's trip to St Lucia, and he got me a ticket for St Lucia. It was a stupid thing on Brian Meehan's behalf. It was the last place I wanted to go. And the last place I wanted to be was on video. But that dope Peter Mitchell was cam recording

---

[*]   Gilligan claimed to me in 2008: 'The only one in Ireland who didn't have a flash lifestyle was me. I never went on holidays. When I came out of prison the last time, I promised Geraldine that I would go on holidays. I was out about a year-and-a-half and she kept saying, "You promised to go on a holiday." So she booked one with a friend of ours who works in a travel agent. I've only had three holidays in my life. I went to the French Alps and it was not enjoyable because Geraldine was after falling and breaking her wrist before we went. I couldn't really ski. I was in kindergarten over there trying to learn how to ski. Then we came home and decided to go to the Caribbean but it was actually a disaster because our marriage was finished – and neither one of us wanted to be there. It was just a stupid thing to do, but we'd been talked into going. Then, three or four months later, I was invited to a wedding and I didn't really want to go – but they had the tickets, so I went. That's the three holidays I had in my whole life, and I'm 56 years of age. It's nothing. It was all in the space of a few months.

everything. He wanted to go over and hit Prince Nassim to try knock him out! Prince Nassim was smaller than me. But he was a fantastic boxer.

And I said, 'What are you doing, Peter?'

'I'm videoing it.'

'Get away from that. Don't make a fool out of us here, you moron.'

Prince Nassim came over and he said to a good few people, 'Take photographs of me no problem. I'll get in photographs, but please leave my girlfriend alone.'

But Mitchell was taking photographs of her. And I think Prince Nassim would've knocked him out. Just stupid. You have to have respect for people.

And Mitchell had them [the video recording] all at home and the police raided his house. They got the receipts that he had where he left them all in to Pete's Video Shop to get them videos done. And that's where the police got them and they gave them out to the press.

A video of the trip later emerged in which Brian Meehan leaned into the camera and said, ominously, 'This one's for you Veronica.' Laughing, he then added, 'Crime doesn't pay.' This was two months before her death.

This is a true fact: all the papers had printed many, many times that John Gilligan, while in the swimming pool with Peter Mitchell, Paul Ward and Brian Meehan, drinking champagne, Gilligan raised his glass and he said, 'This one's for Veronica!' And Gilligan was laughing with the other three guys.

It was to be used as corroboration against me. The president of the court one day ordered the prosecution senior counsel to set up a video machine in court the next morning so the court could see the evidence of John Gilligan saying that and also saying crime doesn't pay. The next morning the court said to the senior counsel, Peter Charleston, 'We don't see any video machine set up.' He replied to the president [that] he watched the video three times and it was Brian Meehan, and Peter Mitchell [who] said it twice. He told the court the reason there was no video machine set up in the court was because there was no evidence of value in it, as Mr Gilligan was not present. He was not party to them in the pool.

I did not know what went on. The court indicated [that] the case of a murder charge was thinning out fast. My legal team told me if the press would not have tried to help the Garda with the set up, I would not even have been charged. The dirty thick Garda went along with Traynor to put me up for it, and after that they could not stop – they were chasing their tails.

Veronica Guerin doorstepped you in Jessbrook on the morning of 14 September 1995. There had been a party at the estate the previous night for your son's 20th birthday and some of your family and guests were sleeping off their hangovers when Veronica knocked. What happened next?

When she came in the car I actually said to Geraldine, 'There's a woman in a red car. Will you go out and see her.'

And she said, 'Oh, that's the woman from an equestrian centre. She's supposed to be here today. Will you tell her we have a hangover?'

'Will you not do it?' I said.

'No, you do it.'

I didn't buzzer her onto the property. And it was going through me mind, 'How the fecking hell did she get in the gate?'

The gates were locked, remote control locked. The penny only dropped after. We looked on the cameras: she came to the gate and the gates opened. They can only open when you press the remote control button on the zapper you have in your car. The only ones who had zappers to the gate were my son and daughter and Geraldine and myself. The police were stopping my son and daughter in their cars all the time. They were taking the zappers off my son and daughter, and seven days later Veronica Guerin came down to me.

They used to ring me up and say, 'Da, the police stopped me in Kilcock.' Or, 'Da, the police stopped me in Dublin and took the zapper out of the car.'

I said, 'It doesn't matter. They're only twenty-five quid, get another one.'

So, she zapped herself in. She opened the gate herself and drove up to the house.[*]

It's very easy to sully the name of someone who is unfortunately no longer around to defend themselves. Veronica had a valid reason, as an investigative reporter, to doorstep you: she wanted to know how someone who was supposedly living a hand-to-mouth existence could afford such trappings of wealth.

She was coming down looking for help from me about the police. Why would I want to help her, a journalist? I wanted to be low profile. I didn't want to be even remembered.

---

[*]   I next asked Gilligan why the Garda would give a zapper to Veronica. On reflection, I decided against typing up his tendentious explanation.

It was suggested that Geraldine didn't answer the door that morning because you had given her a black eye on the previous night when she confronted you over Carol Rooney. It wouldn't have been the first time you assaulted your wife, as you've already admitted.

That's a total lie, because if Geraldine wanted to, or anybody else in the family wanted, they could show all the photographs and the video of the party that night, because it was my son's birthday.

Did Geraldine confront you that night?

No, she didn't. That is a mirror image story of what was supposed to have happened [later on] at Geraldine's 40th birthday party.

It was also claimed you assaulted Geraldine on the night of her birthday party too, which occurred shortly after the murder of Veronica Guerin.

I went away on 25 June; I was in Holland. But I came back on 18 September 1996 to make sure everything was in place for Geraldine's 40th birthday party. They hired out the Spa or Springfield Hotel. At that 40th birthday party, there were no less than ten reporters. There were no less than a dozen policemen. They were standing there looking like vultures.

There must have been fifty to sixty people [in attendance]. But I wasn't there, because I was after leaving the country before the party. It [the alleged assault] was reported in the newspapers. Geraldine went on the Marian Finucane radio show. She was asked that question: 'You were waltzing up and down the floor with John, but when you confronted him about his young lover he punched the head off you and gave you two black eyes?'

This is what Geraldine said to Marian Finucane, 'The only person that wasn't at my 40th birthday was John Gilligan. I would've loved him to be there because we parted as great friends, and we will be friends forever.'

It never happened. And after the party, she went to a nightclub. That was the first time for her to go to a nightclub in her whole life. But the papers said I punched her black and blue. I wasn't even there! If I did go they would have taken lots of photos. There's no photos of me because I was not there.

Which door did Veronica knock at on that fateful morning in September 1995?

I went to the patio door to open it because that was mostly the door used [to enter and exit]. They didn't really use the hall door. The patio door was where you parked your car and you could get straight into the house. So, I looked and she wasn't there. I went back into the sitting room. I looked at the cameras. She wasn't at the hall door. She was at the back utility door. She said in a statement she was using a knocker on the door. There's no knocker on the door to this day.

I opened the door. The newspaper said I had a designer silk coat on. I had a cheap one out of Dunnes Stores.

'Hello?' I said.

'John Gilligan?' she said.

I said, 'Yeah'.

'I'm Veronica Guerin.'

I knew who she was as soon as she said the name, because I was after telling Brian Meehan no to the interview. I said, 'Get outta here,' and closed the door. She was after putting her foot to the door. She came in after me into the utility room.

'John, I want to talk to you. Will you have a talk with me about bad Garda?'

I didn't let her speak anymore. I just turned around and I said, 'Get the fuck out of this house,' and I grabbed a hold of her and I pushed her outside and slammed the back door. And the car went up the driveway a hundred miles an hour.

Veronica later went to the Garda and made an official complaint about you allegedly assaulting her. She stated that you, in a fit of paranoia, ripped open her blouse because you were convinced she was wearing a wire. You've always denied the assault charges, but how do you explain the photographic evidence of the bruises on her face?

The newspapers took photographs of her. She had photographs done in make-up, that she had bruises on her, like what they do for a film, or *Coronation Street*. But she wouldn't be able to use them in court because they weren't official.

But when she went to the police station, if she had black and blue marks, the police would have had to do their duty. The first thing: take police photographs. It's got to be only Garda photos for a court case.

The next thing to do would've been to hop into a police car and go down to Jessbrook asap to arrest me. I was never arrested.

I was never going to be convicted of that charge, because in the Garda forensic report it's stated there was no pull, no tear, nothing [to her jacket]. The stitching on the pocket was taken out by hand. There was five buttons supposed to be missing on her blouse. Five buttons couldn't have came out of no blouse, but that's the evidence. The Garda forensic report stated that the stitching from the five buttons was taken out by hand. There was no blood on the shirt. Nothing.

Surely the authorities wouldn't have pursued an assault case against you if they weren't satisfied with the evidence?*

Six months later, I came home from Holland to get a summons. I wasn't running anywhere. I didn't have to come home: it was only a summons, like, really, a civil thing. If she was assaulted the way the papers report it, sure, you wouldn't get a summons – you'd get charged with GBH – grievous bodily harm. For sure, a sex case assault charge. You can't rip a woman's blouse open and not get a serious sex charge, a ten-year sentence – not a civil summons.

The police interviewed me and they let me go in three or four hours. I didn't even have to apply for bail. It would have been a golden opportunity to have me in custody for about two years until the trial come up in the Special Criminal Court. The police would not have missed this opportunity. The guards wanted me to be locked up at every opportunity.

I've been in custody several times in prisons and got found not guilty in the court case, but they were laughing at me. They would say, 'At least we kept you off the street, you little bollocks.'

They wouldn't have missed this opportunity to come down and arrest me and bring me to court and charge me. Instead, five months later, a different police inspector rang me and asked me to come home to be interviewed.

Nobody in their right mind would give a summons if you're after beating up a woman and making her black and blue. Were they having a laugh? And they want people to believe that. You beat up a woman, you leave her black and blue and they don't even come to arrest you? They didn't even call to the house.

---

* The court date was set for Kilcock District Court on 25 June 1996 but was adjourned until 9 July. Veronica Guerin was murdered the next day, on 26 June.

No person on the planet, especially in Ireland, can go into a police station battered and bruised, and say, 'Somebody's done this to me.' And the police go, 'Ah, well, we'll think about it, we might interview them in six months' time.' It's a joke. And anybody who believes that is a fool. Well, that's my opinion.

And there were loads of people in the household during the night of my son's birthday. The next morning, there were still eight guests in the house. They seen and heard what was going on and they were coming to court to give evidence [about] what actually happened. That was one of the reasons why I was so anxious to get the case heard. Every time I was in court I demanded my case to be heard. I demanded three times to get my case on. Three times.

But things soon went pear-shaped with the court case.

The day it was going to be heard the judge was handed up my file and [accidentally] seen my convictions. So he said he would have to debar himself from the case. My solicitor told him, 'Mr Gilligan waives his right to object to you hearing his case. He wants it heard today.' That was also proved at my Special Criminal Court trial and accepted as true.

The judge said he'd hear the case at eleven o'clock. Veronica Guerin was there. Graham Tully was there. The police was there. All my witnesses were there if I needed to call them. But no doctor had been called, no staff were called to say she 'came to work in bits'. Nothing! Why? Because it did not happen.

The police and Veronica Guerin, they went into the café on the corner over the bridge in Kilcock, and we went into the nearest pub. We had cups of coffee. We went back at eleven o'clock to hear the case. And the judge then decided to get a judge from

Dublin. And we demanded yet again to get the case on and he refused it. I was screaming to get my case heard, three times. So this nonsense about [how] I [supposedly] offered £100,000 to Veronica Guerin to drop the case when I was screaming to get it on … if I am not telling the truth now, I would be in Portlaoise Prison. The Special Criminal Court and the prosecution accepted that I tried to get the case on three times.

Why would you pay £1,000? Never mind £100,000. Why would you want to give a fiver when you knew 100 per cent you didn't do anything and you wanted to win your case? Because to do that, you're admitting you're guilty.

I don't even know if Traynor offered her that money. Maybe he did, maybe [he] didn't. Because he was a Walter Mitty; he'd make things up. Why would you want to give money to somebody to drop something? You know, let's say there was truth in that and Veronica Guerin was to double cross me, or set me up and say, 'There, look, there's the money he gave me, his fingerprints is on that.' You'd be shooting yourself in the foot. I couldn't wait to get their case on because I had the videotapes [on the home CCTV]. I don't believe she went to the hospital.

It was then alleged that you started to stalk Veronica.

She said I followed her places, including [one incidence] on a motorbike on the Naas Road. The police went down to Geraldine while I was living on the continent and they said, 'Where's John?'

'I don't know. I've no number for him. I only speak to him when he rings me,' she said.

Plus, if I threatened Veronica Guerin on the telephone – I don't know if I got accused of it at that time – they would have my phone number.

But when Geraldine told me that the police was looking for me, I rang the police and they said, 'Where are you?'

I told them where I was, in the Hilton Hotel, Amsterdam.

'Can you prove that?' he said.

I said, 'Hang on.' I went over [to the hotel reception] and got the number. I said, 'I'm gonna hang up, ring back and ask for me.'

And that's what I done.

The policeman said, 'Yeah, I'm satisfied you're over there.'

'What's this about?' I said.

'Veronica Guerin says you're chasing her around Dublin on a motorbike. You're behind her and pointing the gun in the window, having a laugh and joke at her.'

Laughing at her!

And I said, 'Well I'm here.'

'I know that you're there.'

And that happened a second time. And I had it verified where I was, again, in Amsterdam.

You then allegedly phoned Veronica Guerin when she was in the presence of a barrister on 15 September 1995 and told her, 'If you do one thing on me, or if you write about me, I will kidnap your son and ride him. I will shoot you. Do you understand what I'm saying? I will kidnap your fucking son and ride him. I will fucking shoot you. I will kill you.' Is that true?

I never spoke to Veronica Guerin once on the telephone in my life, or in her life. If I did threaten her there'd be phone records. I was asked, 'Did Mr Gilligan ever speak on the phone to Veronica Guerin on his phone?' The answer was no, in my trial.

'Did she ever ring him?' The answer was no.

There were no records because there was no throwaway

At 14, John Gilligan dropped out of school and got a job on the B&I Ferries. He would remain at sea, on and off, for a total of eleven years, until 1982.

Gilligan pictured at the family's council home in Corduff, Blanchardstown, Dublin West, which they moved into in 1977.

A rare photo of Gilligan's parents, Sally and John Snr, in happier times. Gilligan was in Belmarsh Prison when both his parents died.

It was a proverbial shotgun wedding when Gilligan married Geraldine Dunne at Our Lady of the Assumption Church in Ballyfermot in 1977. Their daughter, Tracey, was born a few months after the wedding, and their son, Darren, was born the following year.

'I was with Geraldine since she was 14. She told me she was 16! But she was tall for her age ... she was a well-developed female,' he recalled. They married when she was 17.

At a family gathering, with Gilligan's late mother, Sally, sitting directly behind him. 'I love her,' he said with great pathos. 'I'd die for her this minute, I would. I'd die to get her back for twelve months on earth.'

Gilligan said that the biggest regret in his life was that his marriage failed. 'I was wrong in not being a better father and a husband ... but I was too busy in my own world, robbing places and gambling,' he reflected.

In an effort to stay under the radar, John Gilligan often booked two or three hotel rooms when conducting drug deals in Amsterdam, because he feared 'getting followed' or undercover cops 'taking photographs of me'.

The Gilligans had legally separated long before John ended up in Portlaoise Prison in 2001. Nevertheless, Geraldine regularly visited her ex-husband during his time locked up. And as is evident from this photograph, they still genuinely seemed to care for each other.

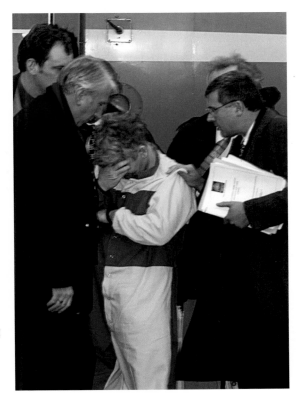

The iconic picture of Gilligan stepping off a flight at the military airport in Baldonnel, having been extradited back to Ireland from England.
© Collins Photo Agency

Gilligan had originally been handed down twenty-eight years for illegally smuggling huge amounts of cannabis resin into Ireland, widely perceived as a murder sentence by default. The sentence was reduced to twenty years on appeal. He would clock up more convictions while incarcerated. But he still somehow walked free after serving only seventeen years.

© Collins Photo Agency (top); Alamy (bottom)

The mafia boss showing off his prowess at the gym in Portlaoise Prison.

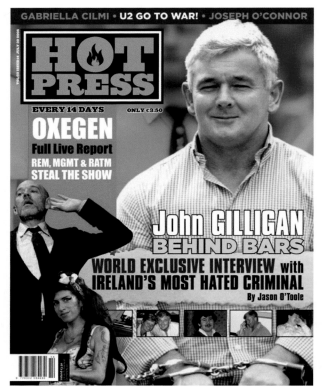

The author conducted a controversial interview with John Gilligan, which ran over two parts in *Hot Press* in 2008. There was praise and hysteria in equal measure. It resulted in the Minister for Justice, Dermot Ahern, ordering an investigation into how O'Toole managed to obtain a prison visit with the country's most infamous inmate. The magazine itself was subsequently banned from Irish prisons.

There was a big media circus at the gate of Portlaoise Prison when Gilligan was released on 15 October 2013. © Collins Photo Agency

Gilligan posing for the camera at the harbour in Torrevieja on the Costa Blanca coast, June 2022.

Gilligan pulling a pint in the original bar from the Jessbrook estate, which he somehow managed to get transported over to his bolthole in Spain before CAB eventually seized the property after a lengthy legal battle.

Gilligan pictured soaking up the sun as he strolls along the seafront promenade at Torrevieja in late summer 2022.

As the author hit the record button, Gilligan leaned back in his chair and waited for the Spanish Inquisition to begin ...

In total, the author recorded approximately thirty-five hours of interviews with Gilligan on camera, plus many more hours of phone conversations.

phones [in] them days. I had to prove that there was no phone calls made whatsoever, because a lot of people won't realise in 1994–96 there was no such thing as having a telephone that you could text on, or take photographs on. There was no such thing as 'Ready To Go' phones, or throwaway phones; they came out in 1998, I think. In 1996 to have a mobile phone you also had to have a landline, that's when you were granted a mobile phone. These are all facts and they can be all checked. If that was the truth what they spoke about, I'd still be in prison.

But could the call not have been made from a different number?

During my [murder] trial the court ordered that they trace every phone call that Veronica Guerin received, not only on that day, but for the whole week, just in case you got a day wrong. Every one of the phone calls received and made for that week has been traced to her family and friends and her job, or her colleagues and politicians, and the policeman she was working with. They were all traced to them people. So there was no phone call [from me].

If there was a phone call, that was the motive. I would've been convicted of murder. That was the evidence they needed to convict me of murder. The judge said on transcript 'this is detrimental to this case'. But that lack of evidence destroyed the prosecution's case. The State now accepts there was no such phone call.

I feel very lucky that they said I said it 'on the telephone', because if they would've said that I said it to her face I couldn't have proved that I didn't.

What did you make of Veronica Guerin?

I never gave her a thought. When I was down in the courts, I'd look at her and I used to just laugh. I couldn't help laughing at the waffle that was coming out. Because I had the tapes of the CCTV cameras and I had the eight people as witnesses. That's why we were so anxious to get the case heard. It was a walk in the park. Everything she said was all lies. I wasn't worried about going to prison: I was going to walk out of the court.

You claim the guards seized these tapes during the murder investigation and you have no idea what happened to them. You would've imagined any such CCTV footage of Veronica Guerin at Jessbrook, if it did exist, would surely have been used as a key piece of evidence during the murder trial?

Yes, tapes taken from Jessbrook, and that wedding trip to St Lucia. None was used in court. My tapes helped me regarding the Kilcock case, the other one, they confirmed to the court, I was not in it with them for their sick jokes.

We had CCTV from Jessbrook. I had five cameras around the house, outside the house, and also inside the halls of the house. And I had them at the entrance and those cameras down the drive. So I had all that ready for the court case, because that's how we knew we were going to win the case, hands down.

I had the tapes and when CAB came down to Jessbrook they took all these tapes and what I find extraordinary is, if I would have done anything wrong, I have no doubt in my mind the police would have given this tape to the newspapers and it would have been shown on RTÉ. But they looked at the tapes and there was no assault taken place.

TAPE SEVEN

THE KILLING OF A BRAVE JOURNALIST

'Only three weeks before her murder, we had asked
Veronica to change to political writing. Her usual
reply was, "I'm interested, but not just yet." I know if I
had stopped Veronica writing on that stuff she would
have quit and another paper would have signed her
up straight away. In hindsight, I should have let that
happen. I didn't want her to leave us, but I should have.'

– AENGUS FANNING, EDITOR OF THE *SUNDAY
INDEPENDENT*, SPEAKING TO THE AUTHOR IN 2008

*26 June 1996. It was the first time the veteran newspaper editor Paul
Drury ever had to say those immortal words: 'Stop the presses!' In
fact, it might have been the only time he said it during his stellar
career, which also included stints in senior editorial roles in* The Star,
the Irish Independent, Ireland on Sunday, *and the Irish edition of
the* Mail *newspapers.*

Word had filtered through to him at the Evening Herald's *offices
on Middle Abbey Street that their sister paper's crime correspondent,*

Veronica Guerin, had been shot dead at traffic lights at Newlands Cross, Naas Road.

Those traffic lights may no longer be there, but nobody from Ireland will ever forget where they were on the day Veronica Guerin was murdered. It was our very own JFK moment.

The Sunday Independent *editor, Aengus Fanning, had just arrived in London when word reached him of the murder. 'I can recall feeling shock, first of all, which leaves you kind of without emotion. You're just numb and dazed. I'd just arrived in London and got the call and I turned straight back. The next day or two were just a blur. The enormity of what happened takes time,' he told me in 2008, shedding a few tears in the process.*

I, myself, as a cub reporter, was boarding the ferry from France back to Ireland when I heard the news. I'd been away on my first foreign assignment for the Evening Herald. *Little did I know that over a quarter of a century later, not only would I interview the prime suspect, but I would also give John Gilligan the first opportunity to publicly name the person he claimed was the gunman.*

At the time of the murder, Gilligan was holed up in one of two rooms he had booked into at a hotel in Amsterdam. When the news was broken to him, Gilligan claimed his initial reaction was, 'Fuck off! She's not fucking dead, is she?'

But she was ... and all hell was about to break loose.

Did Geraldine ever ask you straight if you ordered the murder of Veronica Guerin?

Yes. She cried and cried. 'Look what you're after doing.'

And I said, 'I didn't do anything.' And I didn't.

'We're going to get an awful lot of problems with this,' she said.

'But so am I. I didn't do anything. You seen the way I was, Geraldine. I didn't even have a car. You had a car. Tracey had a car. Darren had a car. Youse had everything. You had a jeep. You had horseboxes. You had a horse in your name. I'd nothing in me name. I had nothing. I kept a low profile. I got a taxi or a lift off a friend of mine. I wanted to be forgotten ... low profile, low profile, low profile. Why would I do that? This is after fucking me up. Big time.'

The optics don't look good here. You knew Brian Meehan, you knew John Traynor. You knew Paul Ward, who was dating Meehan's sister. These people were all in your close circle. You have admitted that you met Charlie Bowden, who confessed to loading the gun. And you're claiming they coincidentally conspired without your knowledge! Even your close friend Paddy Holland was accused of pulling the trigger.

I've no education, but I'm certainly not a nut. I'm clever enough. I know that would cause mayhem. It's mental, I was trying to get my [assault] trial on. I was screaming and shouting to get my trial on. If the judge would have put the case back for two days I'd have been back in the court; I wouldn't have left the country. He gave me permission to leave the country. Why would I be ordering anything? It would be ludicrous.

I didn't get anybody whacked. Why would I get anybody whacked? Why ...? To get somebody whacked they have to do something on you. Sure, the police would know all about it.

I shouldn't be saying this on camera, but I don't know if I'm capable of killing somebody. I think I could, right? But I do know if I would have to do it, I'd trust nobody – I'd do it myself. And I know I wouldn't tell on myself. But to ask somebody else to do a killing, that he could turn on you in five minutes, you'd want to be mad. You're signing your own prison warrant, because some day it will come back and bite you. I wouldn't ask anybody.

In your view is Brian Meehan as guilty as the actual killer? The man has blood on his hands. Is that right?

It's the same difference. They are [both] guilty. You don't have to pull the trigger to be the murderer ... once you're there.

I remember one time there was a murder down in the Strawberry Beds in a pub. They went in to rob that pub and the driver outside was sitting in the car to drive them away. There was a 21st birthday party going on. And when somebody produced a shotgun, the son jumped up and grabbed it, and I think either the father or son was shot. The people inside pleaded not guilty and got off. But the driver outside? They done him for manslaughter! So, I know that you don't have to pull the trigger. I know loads of cases. You could even be at home and if you've played a part in it, you're as guilty as the gunman.

It's been suggested that the only reason Brian Meehan didn't pull the trigger himself was because of his two botched attempts to take out Martin Foley. He shot him on two occasions at close range, even hitting his target five times with a full sub-machine gun in The Liberties in January 1996.

That was put to Bowden in court: Brian Meehan was a 'miss man' but Bowden was a winning army marksman – won all shooting competitions.

Was Brian Meehan 'proud' of the fact that he was the architect behind this gruesome murder?

No, I wouldn't say he was proud of it; I don't think anybody could be proud of that. I suppose he thought it was the right thing to do at the time, because it was going to interfere with him. [He knew] I was going to be finished in six months, because I was making massive money. I was gone, new life. But they were going to continue on. But he'd already started [acting] behind my back, because I didn't know what was coming in. His man Charlie Bowden was collecting the boxes coming in, but I didn't know. If I thought there was six boxes coming in, sure there'd be twelve to fifteen boxes coming in – and they'd have guns and everything in it. I didn't see, because I didn't go near any lock up.

On certain days, he'd see the funny side of things. He was sniggering like when he was fucking [somebody's partner] behind his back! And then he was telling everybody [that same person] was his best friend ever, he was like a brother to him. He was like a spare prick to him.

It's an awful shame that the actual murderer was never charged and put behind bars. Isn't it?

Exactly. I feel the same way. Well, I don't and I do. I'm a criminal to my backbone. When somebody does something, I don't like them to get caught. But that is a horrible crime. And I always said there's three crimes if I ever saw somebody get convicted of, I'd be happy. [One], if they interfered with a woman – rape; [two], or a child; or [three] a murder of an innocent person.

Like, if somebody shot me over this tape, I wouldn't want him or them to be caught. Yes, I'd hope they'd get away if somebody shoots me over this for telling the truth, but I'm not grassing.

I'm telling you what's out there. What the people have said themselves. Brian Meehan never shut up in the prison [about being guilty]. He told everybody in the prison; he told everybody in the life support group and everybody on the parole board and welfare people.

I know plenty of people in them places and they go, 'Jesus, you want to hear what he's saying about you.' Because he's happy that's what they want to hear. He's dancing to their tune. It's ridiculous. People pulled him and said, 'What the fuck? We know Gilligan didn't have anything to do with it – so it was you?' And he admitted that he done it.

If it wasn't you that ordered the cold-blooded murder of the journalist, then who was it?

I was in prison when Brian Meehan told me. He told me he was on the bike. And he told me the reason why they done it: Traynor wanted it to be done because she was going to print a story that he was dealing in heroin. He got an injunction against her. It would destroy all their families. He was playing the trump card of his children's safety. So most courts would give the injunction.

It seems like Veronica Guerin was bullying and blackmailing John Traynor when you read Emily O'Reilly's book. It goes into detail about all of the pressure Veronica Guerin was putting on John Traynor – when it comes to John Traynor's affidavit and all the accusations he made. John Traynor was a liar, but you can't say too many lies in an affidavit. She was threatening and bullying to get down to this meeting:

'I'm going to print this about you ...

'... I'm going to print that about you.

'... I'm going to say you deal in heroin.

'... I know it's not true but we're printing it tomorrow.'

Read Emily O'Reilly's book, it's all in it – backed up by other people in the media. Now, she still didn't deserve to get shot – but the bullying that was going on was unbelievable: demanding him to turn up at this meeting, that meeting, every other day. And demanding he get information off other criminals on who committed this crime and who committed that crime.

Veronica was just bullying him and demanded things, day in and day out, for the last two or three months. Now, that's not John Gilligan saying that – that's in Emily O'Reilly's book. We used to think Saint Veronica – after reading that you wouldn't say Saint Veronica. It was still wrong what happened.

It does sound plausible that Veronica Guerin was offered £100,000 to drop the assault charges.

I didn't offer her £100,000 – I was screaming to get my case on. But maybe they [John Traynor and Brian Meehan] offered her £100,000 to say, 'Drop the story, drop the story.' And maybe she just refused. That was the reason why Traynor wanted her killed.

He was doing heroin with people from the UK. The police knew he was doing heroin. She was going to appeal that injunction and get it sorted that she could print the story about him. So, he had to kill her.

You have repeatedly denied ordering the murder of Veronica Guerin. So who do you believe actually killed Veronica Guerin?

Charlie Bowden did it. Even on the day they killed Veronica, they, Meehan and Bowden, were drinking in The Hole in the Wall

[pub], bragging as they watched England play against Germany in the football. He told a few people what he and Charlie had done but none of them would give evidence.

Meener could never keep his gob shut. He only wanted to brag, brag, brag. He said he was like a king. He could do in life whatever he wanted until the bitch was driving Traynor mad, saying he was going to be all over the papers as a big supplier of heroin to kids. They only saw themselves as victims, not what heroin was doing to Irish children.

They loved themselves, partied and every holiday weekend they went on mini holidays. Brian Meehan bought a big house out of the £1 million I gave him. The house was already converted into eight flats and there were people renting each flat out. But some flats just had women in them. He would bring coke down to them, trying to get the girls to party with him.

The girls would say, 'Our landlord is so cool. He gives us free coke and he ain't worried if we're behind with the rent.'

He only wanted to fuck them.

You're saying Charlie Bowden, the State witness who admitted to loading the gun, was the one that pulled the trigger on the Naas Road?

According to Brian Meehan, Bowden certainly knew how to handle a gun. He had learnt how to become an excellent marksman during his time in the Irish Army. He won all the competitions for marksman [there]. Brian Meehan told me that Bowden was going to take her out for Traynor for £50,000 – a rifle shot.

I said, 'I can't listen to this shite.' And I fucked off out of the cell. Some of it used to make me mad and I had to walk away.

So did Charlie Bowden and Brian Meehan receive £50,000 each from John Traynor for murdering Veronica Guerin?

Charlie Bowden was to get £100,000. He got £50,000 up front and £50,000 after the job. I don't know if he got the rest of the money after the job. But I'd imagine he did, because he did it. Brian Meehan would tell different versions. I don't know, to tell you the truth, if Meehan got anything, because he was more involved with Traynor in the Class A drugs they were doing.

Was that considered a lot of money for killing somebody back in the nineties?

No, it wasn't, because there wasn't that many killings in them days. There was a £250,000 hit put on my head when I got out of prison. And there's other people, I'm not going to name them, who were supposed to have a half million or a million on them. It depends on who wants you dead and it depends on who you are.

Did you ever ask Brian Meehan why they murdered Veronica Guerin on the Naas Road?

I did. It was ridiculous. I don't know why somebody would follow somebody from a court down the country in Naas, all the way back to Dublin, to shoot them. Did they know that the traffic light was going to turn red? If there's somebody from Dublin and you want to murder them, sure, you'd murder them going in or out their hall door, many people have been killed getting out of their car. The people that done that were just stupid.

Killing is killing. But I think the way they went about it made it really newsworthy: coming down the Naas Road, shooting people at a traffic light. I believe there wouldn't have been as big an uproar if they would have shot Veronica Guerin at her house.

Okay, a murder is murder, it is a bad thing. But I think the fact that they were so stupid to do it on the Naas Road – they were very stupid to do it in the first place. You could see they were brain-dead for what they did. And to do it in that way, it was just ludicrous.

Why did they have to go to court to find her? Traynor was meeting her, so he could have told them to follow her to her house, you know. I'm sure if you'd done a bit of research, you'd have found out where she lived. I think there might have been reports out that she was shot at home before that. So you would know where the house was.

During your conversations in prison with Brian Meehan, did you ask him about the gun they used?

I said, 'Why would you use a Magnum? Why would you not use a silencer? Why use it on the Naas Road? You could have been rammed off the bike.'

And that nearly happened: a man followed them and then [that witness] bottled it.

He said, 'Bowden was just so excited about the Magnum. He had a hard on for the Magnum. He couldn't stop talking about the Magnum. From the time the Magnum came in – the people in Holland sent it over – Bowden couldn't stop talking about it morning, noon and night. He wanted to go out doing practice shots with it.'

The hard man Bowden and the expert Bowden with firearms, he wanted to use the Magnum. He was just a gun lover. I suppose it's like a golfer who likes to play golf. Guns were his thing; the same as the bookies was my thing. He was a loose cannon.

Do you think Veronica Guerin was the first person he murdered?

You talking about Bowden? I'd imagine so, because I don't think he was involved in serious crime up to that point in his life. [Before that] Bowden was selling E's for Peter Mitchell when he was a bouncer in a pub somewhere near Croke Park.

Why do you believe Bowden even confessed to loading the gun?

He wasn't too sure if he left his fingerprints on it. I think the police said they found a gun.

But they never found it. What do you think happened to the gun?

Well, whatever Charlie Bowden and Brian Meehan done with it, they done with it. I don't know. I asked Meener many times, 'Where's the gun?'

He said, 'It's gone. It'll never be found.' They wouldn't answer you. I always thought they had it hid somewhere and they were afraid I'd say it to somebody and somebody else would say to somebody else and somebody else would tell the police.

Well, how long ago is that now, 1996? And it hasn't been found. So it makes me think it must have gone into the sea. If it has been buried in the ground, I think with buildings going up and down, there's a good chance it would've been found. So I think that went in to the water somewhere, deep water. That's an educated guess.

Do you think the police reckoned Bowden was the killer?

Yes, 100 per cent. I don't know if they knew straight away he done it. They had already got him to make statements against Paul

Ward, Brian Meehan, Paddy Holland, and me. And they weren't going to start backtracking. They were scum.

With all them [guards] listening to phone calls, they knew Bowden did the shooting, as most witnesses said it was a big guy. From the bike he put his foot down on the ground and bent over to shoot Veronica Guerin. A small guy could not put his foot on the ground.

John Traynor ordered the murder of Veronica Guerin and it was carried out by Charlie Bowden. And the man on the bike was Brian Meehan, 100,000,000 per cent. Without a shadow of a doubt. They're dogs, they're dogs. They're low lifes. They're the lowest form of life going. There was no need to do any of that.

Why did the guards point the finger at Dutchy Holland as being the killer?[*]

Most witnesses said it was a taller man, a big bulky man on the back seat. From the bike he put his foot on the ground and bent over and shot Veronica Guerin. A small guy could not put his foot on the ground. He put his foot on the ground and leaned over and broke the window. Some say he broke the window, and some said he shot through the window, but it's the same thing. But the gunman was able to put his foot on the ground and lean over. Paddy Holland wouldn't be able to do that. Paddy Holland wasn't much bigger than me and my short legs certainly wouldn't hit the ground off any motorbike, even a Honda 50 –

---

[*]   It should be noted that Holland was a middle-aged man with a badly broken nose but no eyewitnesses described such a distinctive feature on the killer. In 2008, Paddy Holland told me, 'An eyewitness at the scene saw the gunman through the visor of his helmet. He said that the gunman was in his thirties. I was a lot older than that at the time.'

it was supposed to be a big bike. So definitely his feet wouldn't reach the ground.*

It has also been reported that the killer stepped off the motorbike when he pulled the trigger.

Somebody said he jumped off the bike and ran across, but I think that's somebody listening to stories from the twenty-second car back behind. But the first eight or nine cars seen everything and the lorry driver seen everything. I mean, a lot of witness said that's what they seen. They might get mixed up with 'he was wearing dark blue clothes' or 'black clothes' but you wouldn't mistake that the guy was able to put his feet on the ground from the bike and lean over without getting off the bike.

Why did they blame Paddy? Because Traynor couldn't tell the truth if he was paid. Traynor was speaking to the cops and reporters and putting the finger on somebody else, like Paddy, because that's what Traynor done all the time. He'd always blame somebody else. That's just an educated guess.

Was Dutchy a hitman?

He might have been a hitman. He might've done six or eight hits. But the rumour was, he was a hitman for the Chicago Mafia and he done a lot of hits there. I know he done a lot of bank robberies and he was a good bank robber. Whoever he was doing the bank

---

* But Holland told the *Sunday Tribune* in 2005: 'Witnesses say Veronica was killed by a big man, which is why it was linked to me. But Bowden's a big man too. If you check who was in Gilligan's gang, he was the biggest man physically. And Bowden can't account for his movements on that day. He doesn't have an alibi.'

robberies with, he always made sure everybody got away first and then he would walk away from the bank. He's always had a disguise of a wig on him and this and that. He was a good armed robber. But I suspect he was a hitman. If I was to believe half the things I was told, he was a serious hitman. I heard he was paid to kill Christy Delaney, who was a ticket tout seller [in 1995]. It wasn't Paddy Holland [who murdered Veronica Guerin], because I know 1,000,000 per cent it was Charlie Bowden because I was told in prison.*

What would you say to Charlie Bowden if he was reading this?

Charlie, come clean. Tell what you done. If you have any remorse, or even if you haven't got remorse, say it. Say it, for the sake of

---

*   Holland was never even put on trial for murder. He had been accused of pulling the trigger in a number of the most high-profile murder cases that have occurred during the last two decades in Ireland. He was the prime suspect in the execution of the major underworld figure Paddy Shanahan, who was gunned down in 1994. It has also been alleged that Holland assassinated one of Ireland's most notorious criminals, Martin Cahill. But the IRA claimed that particular hit and it's highly unlikely that they would've needed to outsource their dirty deed to a professional contract killer. Dutchy was also accused of being the hitman hired by Catherine Nevin, nicknamed 'The Black Widow', to execute her husband Tom. 'Look, even if I had [murdered somebody] I wouldn't admit to it,' Holland once told me. Unlike other notorious Irish criminals of his generation, Patrick Holland came from a respectable, middle-class background. Born in March 1939, he grew up in Chapelizod and unlike his gangland contemporaries, he did not participate in any criminal activities during his youth. But his life went in a very different direction when he emigrated to Chicago, Illinois. According to rumours it was there that Holland learned his future trade as a so-called gun for hire. It's been claimed that Holland

all the hurt that my family [are] after getting out of this. You've got that immunity for anything you say. You won't be charged. Admit it, Charlie, say it. Go on a radio station somewhere ... make a phone call to Jason O'Toole ... tell the truth. I'm only telling the truth because all the cases are over and I'll more than likely die soon, and for my family and friends, as I said. There's no money in this for me. I'm not getting any money. So the truth is the truth.

How do you think Charlie Bowden is able to live with himself?

But he's a low life, and low lifes don't feel nothing, as far as I know. I know a man up where my mother lived and he knocked down a child and the child died. He couldn't live with himself. He killed himself. So, that's what good people do.

Is Brian Meehan able to live with himself?

Yeah, he is. I believe he's not remorseful. He thinks he's hard done by. They all think they were hard done by.

Do you think you were hard done by?

No, I don't. There's two answers to that. I have feelings about what happened to my family. They shouldn't have gone after my family.

---

joined the elite United States Marine Corps and served in Vietnam. 'Again, that's not true. I wasn't in the American Army. The myth is that I was a top hitman in Ireland because it's been reported in the media that I learned how to become a killer in the American Army. It's just nonsense. I was involved for a while with the Republican movement, and it was bandied about that I was a hitman for them. Again, utter nonsense,' he claimed.

The police know what my family genuinely owned themselves. So, they should've left them with that, but they didn't care. They just took everything and said, 'We're taking everything.'

They didn't care about hurting innocent people, taking innocent people's things. So I feel a bit hard done by, but not for myself, because I was a criminal all my life. I done it all my life, with respect. I know that sounds crazy robbing 'with respect'. I've principles; there's certain things I won't do.

Why was John Traynor never even questioned by the Irish police?

John Traynor has told loads of people he done it, but John Traynor couldn't be arrested. Traynor was arrested in Holland with Brian Meehan, but they couldn't bring him back because he had a file on the judges – sexual. With judges and priests, all having bondage sex and somebody died, they were strangled.*

He was a suspect. One hundred per cent he was a suspect, but

---

*   Gilligan is referring to the murder of Fr Niall Molloy who was killed in mysterious circumstances at the home of businessman Richard Flynn in Clara, County Offaly in 1985. Veronica Guerin had written in the *Sunday Independent* that The General had stolen sensitive files on the case from the Office of the DPP and, rumour had it, that he would only return them on condition that John Traynor was released from prison over in London in the early nineties. When Traynor returned he told the Irish government, 'Here's the files back but I've made twenty photocopies of everything. And if I'm ever arrested again they'll be leaked.' If the files had been made public it would have been very embarrassing for the government. 'They had files on stuff like that priest – what do you call him? – who died in strange circumstances? Fr Niall Molloy,' Gilligan told me in 2008. 'The only reason he wasn't charged is because he got the files and he gave them back when he got out of prison. He and Martin Cahill were working together. That's a fact. He told me that himself.'

because he had the file robbed from the Department of Justice, they were terrified to come near him. But they still should have ... the file would have been the truth. Why were they afraid of the truth coming out? So what if a few judges and clergy were involved in it? And politicians. If they done something wrong, they done something wrong. They're no better than me.

You maintain that John Traynor was not arrested for the murder of Veronica Guerin because he still had copies of these files. It all sounds far-fetched, but it's hard to think of any plausible explanation for why Traynor was never extradited back to Ireland after the journalist's death.

Traynor had them over a barrel because he had the files out of the DPP's office up in Stephen's Green – that's why they didn't come after Traynor. As I said before, he was arrested with Brian Meehan in Holland and they held Brian and let Traynor go.

So, Traynor had that file. Martin Cahill got that file and he said, 'If you try ever to take us in and stitch us up we'll produce this.'

And to protect all that, Traynor got the freedom to do what he liked. And maybe that's the reason why he knew nothing could happen [to him]. Why was he not even taken in and charged? Why was he not charged when they knew all this thing about Traynor? Why was he not brought back when the police had him? They could have extradited him on the backs of the warrants. They just let Traynor do what he wanted. So they had to have a fall guy – so that was me.

After Veronica Guerin's murder, you knew it was John Traynor and, at the same time, the media was pointing the finger at you, but you didn't really do much about it.

I was on the continent. I didn't want to make contact with nobody at that stage of the game. I must've [been] after bringing maybe £2 million out of the country. I was travelling with money all the time. I was doing loads of trips. Each time I carried £300,000–£500,000 out of the country. My concern was getting me money out of Ireland. And I got it out. I was more interested in finishing up what I was doing and getting things sorted. And tomorrow was another day. 'I'll get around to that another day.' And then I got arrested.

You told me in 2008 that Traynor tried to frame you for the murder.[*]

Yes, I told you that he used me as the [fall] guy in his murder

---

[*]   Gilligan stated to me at the time, 'He [John Traynor] was after ringing me – bad, bad drunk. He rambled on and rambled on and he goes, "You're down for it, John! It's all over the paper!" I said, "What's going on? How did you conveniently have a crash, down in Mondello? And you go to Naas General Hospital? What was that about John? Was it an alibi?" And he went, "She was going to ruin me and I told her – and I begged to her. I gave her loads of stories. I gave her everything that has ever occurred." I went, "Jaysus, what sort of a fuckin' eejit are you?" We had an argument, but he was mad drunk. Then he tells me, "I was going to try and set you up for it." I said, "You were going to try and set me fuckin' up?" And he said, "Yeah. I was trying to get your telephone off you for Warren [Russell]. And you didn't go for it." He was trying to get me telephone, to have her shot at the house – and drop my phone in the garden. That's what he told me when he was drunk. Traynor only done all these things with drink taken. That's what I found out in the end. It was always drink … drink, drink, drink. Vodka … vodka … vodka. The cops used to fill him full of drink and he'd then spill the beans.'

plot. He put the blame on me. Traynor knew I would come into line for it because of the assault charge of Veronica Guerin. So people were able to put two and two together and get five. You would have to, as a normal policeman [might] think, 'Who would do this? What would be the motive for this? Who had trouble with her?'

I see it now in Emily O'Reilly's book, what Veronica Guerin was doing to Traynor. She pushed him to kill her. She was bullying him. Read the facts in that book.

I believe he was setting me up all the time. He was saying I was doing this and doing that, and winding Veronica Guerin up. John Traynor once showed Veronica a briefcase with £80,000. But he lied and said there was a half million in it and her eyes nearly popped. He also then claimed, 'Gilligan owes me another half million.'

So, he was showing Veronica Guerin that he was dealing in drugs. Partly in Guerin's defence, he was making her come after him, because he was putting it in her face: 'Look at that money, I got that out of criminality.'

So she obviously said, 'I must be on the right road here.' He was a fool to brag. A lot of criminals brag.

But Veronica Guerin never wrote a story about me.* She was

---

* Veronica Guerin might not have mentioned Gilligan by name in any of her articles, but she clearly referred to him as 'Criminal C' in a piece titled 'Top 20 Crime Bosses' published in the *Sunday Independent* on 27 February 1994. In it, she wrote: 'Criminal C comes from the Blanchardstown area of Dublin. He has done a number of armed robberies but his speciality is warehouse robberies. He is considered an expert at disconnecting complex electronic alarm systems. He has served time previously for armed robberies but like a number of his peers has escaped conviction in recent years.'

making chapters for this movie. And then she thought it was a good idea when other newspapers said, 'Oh, she doorstepped me.' So, I think that gave her an idea. Because she didn't doorstep me to ask me about any taxes, or anything. Because the police didn't even know. So how would she know? Other than what Traynor was telling her.

So, if you hadn't been arrested do you think you might have had John Traynor killed?

No.

But were you not worried?

I said, 'It is not down to me. I've no worries, I didn't do anything.' There will be no evidence that I had anything to do with it – other than them blaming me. All of them used my back for grip. Every one of them used my back for grip, because they were going along with the story in the paper, 'Oh yeah, it was John Gilligan.' I would not do that to no man. I'm not trying to get anybody here in trouble. This is thirty years on. Nobody can get me into trouble, it's the truth.

Why didn't you tip off the police?

But what difference would that make to me? Even if I actually knew who'd done it I wasn't going to go to court and say, 'Excuse me, it was him.' You don't do that to [other] criminals. The only reason why I'm doing this now is, I'm over 70 years of age, everybody's been through the system, and Brian Meehan has admitted to the parole board, admitted to everybody in the prison, what he's done. The whole world knows he was there. Charlie Bowden the same, but he's saying he wasn't the hitman, but he got the gun he wanted to use.

Yet you stood in the High Court and pointed the finger at John Traynor.

Meehan asked me to say it to get him a Section Two. What a Section Two is, when you go for your appeal, you cannot go back into court with your case until you apply to the court for a Section Two. And a Section Two has to be new-found evidence that wasn't known before or used in court before. So to help Brian Meehan I spoke up.

All of the good guys on the E1 Landing said, 'John, don't do it for him. You'll make a show of yourself.'

'No, I'm going to say it. I'm going to help if I can help him. There was good days and bad days with him,' I said.

A good criminal wants to beat the police at every hands turn, if you can. So, I stood up and said it. And, every one of them got asked, 'What is Gilligan trying to do ... get a deal to get his property back?'

And they said, 'No, to get Brian Meehan a Section Two for a new appeal.'

And one of the reasons why I'm bitter now is because Meener told me he asked the solicitor if he had that type of evidence he would get a Section Two in ten seconds. I expected after I said that he'd apply for the transcripts off the court and get an affidavit off me. From that day to this day, no solicitors came to me on Brian Meehan's behalf to do an affidavit because he was just a lying fucker. He's no respect for nobody.

He didn't even appeal the severity of his sentence for the drugs. Like, Paddy Holland got twenty years and he got it cut down to twelve. Brian Meehan got twenty years. He probably would have got that down to fifteen and then I would have got my sentence to maybe twenty.

And the next guy in court for a lot of drugs, his legal team could say Meehan only got fifteen years and he was convicted of tons: 'My client had nothing like that,' so he could only get six or seven years. Meehan did not care, only for himself. See the point?

If you met Brian Meehan today walking down the street, what would you say to him?

I won't meet Brian Meehan today walking down on the street. So I don't need to go into that scenario, ifs and buts, and me granny. Brian Meehan will be out on licence for life. Meehan won't be able to leave the country unless he gets permission off the court. And I'm not worried if Brian Meehan tries to get somebody to give me a dig in the head or something. I've no worries, no fears. I wouldn't be afraid of them. Not for half a second I wouldn't be.

Do you think it's fair that Brian Meehan will be free in the near future?

I'm not going there. The system is the system. I'm not going to knock the system. I don't believe a man killing a guard or ten guards should be released when he serves thirty years. It's ludicrous.

What about killing a journalist?

This is the law today: if a Garda gets killed, or six of them, the guy gets forty years. He has the right to get out in thirty years. But if a person kills an ordinary person he gets life and could be held for seventy years in jail. He has no right to be released, but the Garda killer has. The good Garda's life is worth less by that system.

I wouldn't see a journalist anywhere near the highest value of a policeman. Because the policeman is going out to protect the public. Journalists just make up a load of lies, but they still shouldn't be killed. I think the legislator got that wrong. If anything happened to a good policeman the persons convicted of that should die by hanging or lethal injection, or die in prison. If somebody shoots somebody else, you could give them forty years to make sure they do thirty. It's the wrong way around. In my book they have cheapened the life of the Garda Síochána.

Do you agree with the death penalty?

I don't know. Yeah and no. Monday yeah. Tuesday no. Some murders, if it's a woman or a child, you'd say they should be hung. But then you look at it another way: life in prison. It's obvious when people get life in prison and the government let them out, they don't feel like that they should have been hung and then they don't feel like they should be left in prison.

In Emily O'Reilly's book, one theory put forward is that Veronica Guerin could've shot herself in the leg. She wrote, 'Senior Gardaí, even those deeply loyal to Veronica's memory, admit that the theory was given some consideration. One such source told me that he had ruled it out, because anyone who did such a thing would have had to be insane.'

She asked Traynor could he get somebody to shoot her in Coolock Shopping Centre outside RTV Rentals, because there were cameras there, Traynor told me. He went to Niall Mulvihill and Niall got the gun, sold her the gun for 250 quid, an old gun. He made a statement to the police about that and the police told him 'get out of the station', because her senior guard friend told them: 'Release him, don't take him in.' And he got out.

So then she shot herself in the leg. The police knew it couldn't be true. But then when the forensic tests came: at the angle, the [trajectory] of the bullet, no man could stand over her and shoot her because she had scorch marks on the leg where the bullet went into her leg, into the flesh or into a bone or anything, it was shot at an angle that would come out. It was only a flesh wound. They knew that didn't make sense. The scorch mark on her leg could have only come for her putting the gun up to her leg and shooting her[self]. She probably wanted to make sure it didn't go through a bone. It was a flesh wound, you know.

Why would she possibly want to carry out such a strange act?

The police are satisfied 100 per cent that she shot herself and every journalist in the country knows that Veronica Guerin shot herself in the leg to get notoriety. She wanted to be a high-profile journalist. She needed it for her movie. She was putting that part into the script of her movie. It only came out after her death that she was doing all those mad things, because she was making a movie and she was going to put all that into it, [in order to portray herself as a] high profile reporter.

And I only found that out years and years later, and in hindsight, when I come back from England in February 2000. It was probably back about two months before I got any disclosure served on me and I got 3,600 statements, and an awful lot of statements are stamped on it 'Private and Confidential: Do not give to the defence.' Well, I got all that. I got boxes and boxes and boxes of it. And I found all that material. And I gave it to my legal team and they said, 'It's great material to use in court but we don't want to embarrass Graham Tully or the Guerin family any more, They've been hurt enough.'

I said, 'What about my family? I'll sack youse if youse don't use them.' The next one said they'd do it, but never did. I was promised they would. They didn't use them. They were always going to, in the morning, in the afternoon, tomorrow, the next day. And, before I knew it, the trial was over. It took forty-three days.

What about the gun shot that went through Veronica Guerin's window the time before that?

I don't know if she got that done herself or if John Traynor done it. I haven't got a clue. But I do know that she asked John Traynor could she get shot at in Coolock Shopping Centre. She shot herself. The police said the only one that could've shot her is herself.

For someone wanting to stay 'under the radar', as you continually state, you must've felt completely desperate when you gave not one but two sit-down interviews in 1996. It would be the last time you spoke on the record again to anyone in the Irish media until 2008 when I visited you in Portlaoise Prison.

I did not feel desperate. It was in all the news [that] it was me, the prime suspect. My family said, 'Say something to prove it was not you. To say nothing looks like you're guilty.' That's what I was hearing, so I gave two interviews.

There was a journalist called Liz Allen. I didn't know her from Adam. But maybe a couple of days after the murder, she went down to Jessbrook and climbed over the fence and went into Geraldine.

Geraldine was very upset with all the things they were saying in the paper. So she spoke to her and she said, 'Will you ask John to give an interview and tell him I won't exaggerate, I won't fabricate it, I'll tell the truth.'

She convinced Geraldine. So Geraldine asked me.

'No, Geraldine, I won't give anybody an interview,' I said.

'Please give her an interview. You need to speak. You don't know what's going on here. They're blaming you on everything – and when you're getting blamed we're getting the backlash of it. People are giving us dirty looks as we're going around to the shops. So, you have to speak. You have to explain that you weren't in the country, that it wasn't you,' she said.

'I really don't [want to] … they're not going to stop. They're vultures.'

The lies coming out in the newspapers and the radio stations and the television: it was like trying to pull back water with a rake. It's an impossibility. So I said, 'I won't bother.'

But she begged me. She said, 'Will you do that for me?'

'Give me her number.'

I rang her and I said, 'I won't be going home unless the police wants me, but if you want to come out I'll give you a story, if you give me your word you won't mix it up and leave things out. Exactly what I say.'

She said, 'I give you my word.'

'Okay, ring me up. That's me number there I'm after ringing ya on. So come out when you're coming out.'* I said, 'I don't want

---

*   Gilligan said the crime reporter rang him back several times and asked him not to let her down by being a no-show when she travelled over to to talk to you, but I'm after telling Geraldine I'll talk to you. I won't go back on me word. I'll talk to you. Okay.'

It was later claimed that you had her followed over on the flight.

She said she was coming out – I don't know what day, say a Thursday – and I had a grin on my face because I knew Brian Meehan was coming out to me Thursday morning. So I was going to the airport to meet Brian Meehan. I didn't know she was on the same flight.

So, the next thing is, she rang me and said, 'Will you be there when I land?'

'I'm actually here at the airport. Don't say another word. I'll show you how honest I am. I will call out the flight number you are on.'

So I went over to the arrivals. I looked at the screen and I could see the Aer Lingus flight. I read it out the number to her.

'So, I'm here. So don't be worried about that I won't be here. I won't be making a fool of you. See you when you're here,' I said.

I hung up and I rang Brian Meehan and I said, 'Is there a blonde girl there, Geraldine says she's a blonde girl. There's a reporter coming out to me called Liz Allen.'

'Well, there's a reporter here. I thought it might've been for me. She's with a guy with a camera. He's got all his camera equipment,' he said.

'Okay, that's sound. Don't come near me. I'm going to go to the Hilton Hotel with her.'

Amsterdam. Gilligan claimed she said, 'I'm paying for it out of my own pocket. And if I go out there and you make a fool out of me, I'll be a laughing stock.'

Why were you still speaking to Brian Meehan at that stage, when he just participated in the murder of Veronica Guerin?

We were in businesses, doing cannabis. There was still shipments paid for and they were on their way. I did not speak to him on the phone [again after that call in the Dutch airport] as the Garda would have heard about the next shipment of hash. I did not know his part [in the murder] at that stage, until I got back into Ireland on 3 February 2000. I got to know bit by bit. I never met him until I went back to Portlaoise Prison. I think he was coming over [on that occasion] to his girlfriend, not his partner.

And I came back to Ireland on 18 September 1996 to sort it out and Geraldine's 40th birthday and [to] sign an affidavit to state I knew nothing about Veronica Guerin's murder. I was scared shitless that the cops might try to stitch me up and say I made a statement if arrested. I was gone out of Ireland on the ferry on 20 September 1996.

You're saying you didn't even have an inkling at this stage that Brian Meehan was involved in the murder?

No, I didn't. I didn't want to be talking on the telephone. I'd want to have been the biggest eejit on the planet to think that the police weren't listening to our calls. I wouldn't talk to him again until back in Portlaoise Prison and then I discovered an awful lot of the truth.

And why would you tell Liz Allen what flight she was on? It was actually viewed at the time as a form of intimidation, as it was felt you were having her followed.

I said to her, 'I'm here. I'm telling you what flight you're on to stop you worrying while you're coming through customs if you think I'm not going to meet you.'

And why meet her at the arrivals hall with flowers?!

I rang Geraldine and I said, 'What do I do with this woman? How do I treat this woman? I've no experience meeting guests and that type of thing. So, do I get her flowers or something?'

'You can get her a bunch of flowers.'

So I went to the stand. Amsterdam is a flower country, like, not only tulips. So, I got her a bunch of flowers for ten or fifteen guilders. So when she came through the doors, I said, 'I don't know if you want to take these or throw them in the bin?'

She said thanks very much and she took them.

I said, 'We'll go to the Hilton Hotel across the road there.'

She said, 'We'll go to your hotel ... wherever you're staying.'

'I've no hotel. What hotel are you on about? I'm not staying anywhere in a hotel. We'll go up to the Hilton.'

It's three or four minutes from Schiphol. So we walked across the road.

'You've a cameraman there,' I said. 'I don't want him listening to me when I'm talking. I want to talk to you first. I want to talk to you about ground rules, so to speak.'

And what were they?

'Are you gonna tell the truth? Are you gonna edit this? Are you gonna twist it? Are you gonna be fair?'

So we went into the Hilton Hotel bar/restaurant. The photographer sat across from us. She agreed that she'd tell the truth, the whole truth.

A criminal's side of the story is not necessarily going to be the truth, is it?

I mean, the answers wouldn't be twisted, or it wouldn't be added to through an actor's voice, or anything. So she agreed to that. So, we're talking for a bit and then we went and had a meal in the restaurant.

And then she said, 'Can we go up your room? I want to get a photograph of you in the room.'

I said, 'I've no room. You staying here tonight, or what?'

She said yes.

'I'll go to the counter with ya,' I said.

At that stage we're after letting the cameraman sit in the company with us. I think he did sit with us at the end. So the three of us went to the counter. She booked a room for her and a room for the cameraman.

And I said, 'Can I have another room, too.'

'Sir, can I have your passport,' the receptionist said.

I gave her my passport. I was showing Liz Allen the honesty of myself, that if I had a room the girl behind the counter would've said, 'You have a room already.' They could see that people behind the counter didn't know me.

I can't remember if we went to my room or her room with the photographer. And we got a photograph. So that was it, we said goodnight.

'I'll see you in the morning,' I said.

As soon as I went to my room I opened my door and put the Do Not Disturb sign on the handle. I waited about five or six minutes and I came out of the door. I didn't use the lift, I walked down the corridor and I came down the steps and within an hour-and-a-half I was in Belgium. I got a taxi all the way down to Belgium; three quarters of the way I stopped at a train station. I got out of the taxi and got another taxi to another train station, and there from that train station down to somewhere I could walk the last half a mile to where I was staying.

You were obviously very pleased with the printed article because you sent Liz Allen a thank you note and signed-off with the word 'love'!

She said everything in the paper. It was a very honest story. She didn't backstab me, so I was delighted with that. So I talked to Geraldine and I said, 'How do I thank this girl? What will I do? Will I send her a present or whatever?'

'No, I think you've done enough. You know, you did the interview. But do what you want John. But I'm just telling you as a friend,' she said.

'I'm going to write to her and thank her,' I said.

'Yeah, do that if you want to.'

So I wrote, 'Thank you very much for the interview. You stuck to your word, you were very honest. You said it the way it was ...' And when I got to the end of the letter I just went 'love ya'.

It was suggested during your murder trial that you were infatuated with her.

I think I put L.U.V. Y.A., like slang. It made the whole court laugh.

I tell you the reason why she [Liz Allen] was a witness in the Special Criminal Court. She said to me, 'Could I say that you're sorry for hitting Veronica and what you said about her son?'

I said, 'You won't be saying that at all. Because that's not true. That wouldn't be nice.'

But she said, 'John, it will give you credibility.'

I said, 'Credibility or no credibility, I ain't admitting to something I didn't say.'

What you're alleged to have said about threatening to sodomise Veronica's son was nothing short of repulsive.

Yes, Jason, you're right – it's filth. Filth. I did not say it. There's no phone call for that horrible statement ... a vulgar statement. A man should be put to death for saying such a thing like that. And I believe that.[*]

And if a man kicked my head and left me in hospital, because he believed that I said that, sure, I wouldn't fall out with the man, because it's a horrible, horrible thing to say. Only a dirt of a person would say that.

---

[*]   At this point Gilligan appears agitated.

TAPE EIGHT

BELMARSH PRISON

'You are now essentially in the closest thing
that you could be to a grave, to a coffin.'

– MOAZZAM BEGG*

Four months after Veronica Guerin's murder, John Gilligan was finally detained in London on 6 October 1996.

He was arrested by British Customs at Heathrow Airport with a bulging suitcase filled with £330,000, while attempting to board a flight to Amsterdam. The UK government later charged him with possession of Class-C drugs, too.

It would be a lengthy extradition process; Gilligan did not return to Ireland until 3 February 2000. In the period in between, he was incarcerated at HM Prison Belmarsh in south-east London. The maximum security prison is an 'A' category jail for high profile

---

*   Moazzam Begg, a British-Pakistani citizen who was accused of terrorism, speaking about the prison in the Channel 5 documentary *HMP Belmarsh: Maximum Security* in 2022.

prisoners. *Charlie Kray, the eldest brother of the notorious Kray twins, was locked up there at the time of Gilligan's arrest. In total, Gilligan was there for three-and-a-half years. On a personal level, it was also a traumatic period for Gilligan, as both of his parents died while he was at Belmarsh.*

His father went first. But Gilligan didn't give a monkey's when he heard about his death. 'I would not have gone to his funeral if I was out – that's how much I hated the cunt. He's dead. I don't get sentimental over bad people. He was a bad da,' he admitted to me in 2008.

And more recently, he revealed: 'I'm not proud of it: I beat my father up twice for hitting my mother. And when I say beat him up, I beat him up with my fists and a six pack of Harp – I smashed it on his head for hitting my mother.'

One of Gilligan's younger brothers eventually threw their old man out of the family home. It wasn't until Gilligan was extradited back to Ireland that he heard the full story about how his father died.

A detective said to him, 'John, I was the one who found your father dead in the bath in Ballymun.'

John Gilligan Sr had been reported missing by the family.

'I think my sister said, "We haven't seen my father for three or four days," and they rang Ballymun Garda Station. They said, "Will you check on my father?"' Gilligan recalled.

'People said they hadn't seen him around for a few days. So they kicked in the door. And he was dead in the bath. So my family didn't even tell me that. The policeman told me.'

It hit him hard when his beloved mother died. Gilligan retreated into himself, as he processed it. Speaking of his late mother he said with great pathos, 'I won't explain, because I couldn't put it into words how much I miss my mother. She was one of the nicest, best women on the planet.'

Where did it all go wrong for you at Heathrow Airport in 1996?

I wasn't travelling with [Michael Cunningham], we were separate, but going on the same plane.* Just before I was going through the scanners with the money – packed so it wouldn't show up on the scanner – I was after leaving my telephone down.

I said from a distance, 'Michael, pick the telephone up. I don't want that telephone just in case I'm stopped and my telephone starts ringing. So you hold onto me telephone.'

I got through with the money, no problem whatsoever. And then he went through the scanner and when we sat together in the lounge, waiting to board, I said, 'Have you got me telephone?'

'Oh, Jaysus! John, I never picked it up. I have to go get it.'

So, he went [back] through the X-ray machine and, with that, they held him. He was wanted for something else in England. And then they came down to me and asked had I got anything?

I didn't want to tell lies, so I said, 'Yeah, I have £300,000.'

'In cash?'

'Yeah, in that suitcase.'

They were shocked at how I knew how to beat the X-ray. There was a technique of getting money out of the country, that it wouldn't show up when it goes through the scanner [at the airport]. I never told anybody how to do it, because I was using it myself. I brought every time £400,000 or £600,000 out with me. I made £10 million or more [from smuggling cannabis into Ireland]. I wasn't counting because I was getting it and spending it.

The scanner was only overhead and underneath – it would scan down and that picture of the money would come up. But

---

*   Michael Cunningham died at the age of 65 in 2015. Cunningham had, with his brother John, masterminded the kidnapping of Jennifer Guinness in 1986.

I discovered if you put it that way [sideways], the only thing the X-ray machine would [pick up would] be paper. There would be no picture. And a customs man wouldn't suspect it. It would sail through.

I had the largest handheld briefcase I could buy. But it wasn't huge. It probably looked out of place me carrying it, being so small and the briefcase being so large!

They said, 'Come with us.'

So they took me off [the flight], and the rest is history. I went to court and they remanded me in Wormwoods Scrubs. I was put in a stinking cell with another prisoner. Stinking! They were on twenty-three hours lockup.

And then the cell opened about two hours later and a prison officer said me, 'Come out here. You're going somewhere else. You shouldn't be with any other prisoners.'

He brought me to another part of the prison, which was very clean. I was happy there. And he said, 'You could be getting transferred tomorrow to another prison.'

What happened was: the English police were after speaking to the Irish police and they said, 'He'll know too many people in there and he'll be able to get messages out. We want to isolate this fucker.'

So, they went back to the judge and they got another warrant, to move the goalposts, to ship me off elsewhere. But, really, that was illegal, because when a judge gives a warrant to remand you to a certain prison your body is supposed to be in the court, but they didn't care that my body wasn't in the court. I was already on the way to Belmarsh.

While in Belmarsh, I was on remand for money charges firsts. And then after a few months, maybe a year, the prosecution went to the High Court and got a voluntary bill of an indictment that meant they could add extra charges. I was charged with importing twenty-two-and-a-half tons of cannabis into England from Holland, by using territorial waters in the English Channel. People were saying, I'll never get of out jail in England.

The reporter Liz Allen famously visited you in Belmarsh Prison in 1996.

People told me, 'You probably won't get a visit for [the first] six or seven weeks because you're top security and we have your category as a Treble A, the highest [security]-rated prisoner in the United Kingdom.'

It was alien to me. You had to apply for it. You've got to fill in forms. They've got to send them to the Garda Síochána. I said to myself, 'I won't get a visit when they get a hold of the forms.' So they kept just throwing them in the bins. I didn't get a visit [from family and friends] for months and months.

But I was in prison a couple of days and a prison officer comes out and says, 'A visit for John Gilligan.'

Everybody's looking at me in the yard, wondering how am I getting a visit because they [prisoners] didn't get visits for weeks. I wouldn't take a police visit in prison, because you don't have to. I said, 'Is that a police visit?'

And the lady officer said, 'No.'

'Well, who is it?'

She said, 'Come out on the visit.'

'No, I'm not going out until I know who it is. Is it police? Because I'm not going out if it's police. I'm not doing an interview with anybody,' thinking it was the police. If it was a solicitor they would've said it was a legal visit.

The lads were saying, 'Ask if it's private visit?'

I said, 'Is this a private visit?'

They said, 'Yeah.'

'Who was it?'

They said, 'Come out on the visit.'

They opened the gate of the exercise yard and I goes in. When you go on a visit in Belmarsh, you have to be stripped naked and leave your clothes on one side of the room and walk across to the other side of the room and put your sterilised civvy clothing on, which have already been checked in an X-ray machine and metal detectors. Dogs sniffing them out. Everything.

So, I put my clothes on. Now, the lady wasn't in the room – it was [male] prison officers in the visiting stripped room. Afterwards I said to her, 'Where am I going for this? I really don't know who this is.'

'I'll tell you now that you're in your civvy clothes. It's your girlfriend,' she said.

You obviously presumed it was Carol Rooney.

Of course, I thought it was Carol Rooney. Sure, she couldn't get in here, I thought.

'Girlfriend? What colour hair has she got?'

And she said blonde. Carol Rooney was blonde. I don't think so, I thought. I felt I was getting set up.

'Can I have a look in the room? Tell me where it is. I want to walk behind you,' I said.

I walked behind the lady prison officer. I said, 'Stop when you come to the visiting door.'

I was after asking what the visits were like and there were five or six doors and each one had a visit room. Some were behind the glass for legal visits or when you haven't yet been passed by security. And then when you're passed by security, there's no glass there. But this visit was behind glass.

So I just looked in the door and I pulled my head straight back.

'That's Liz Allen ... that's a reporter!' I said.

The lady officer said, 'Is she not your girlfriend? She told us ... we gave her a special visit because she was very upset.'

'Get the governor down here.'

So, in that prison there was five governors; one to five, in their seniority. The number five governor came down. It was a lady governor. I'd never seen her in my life.

'You say this is not your girlfriend?' she says.

'That's a reporter out of the newspapers. I gave her an interview in Amsterdam. I don't want to go in there. I want her arrested.'

'Stay there,' she said.

She went out and she said to her, 'You're not his girlfriend – you're a reporter? Give me identification. We will be referring this to the police and you'll never get into another prison in England again. We will send a file to the Home Office.'

But I knew it wouldn't get done.

The governor said, 'Bring him back to his cell.'

'I was on the exercise yard,' I said.

'Bring him back to his cell,' she said.

Is it true that you lost all your hidden cash reserves while in Belmarsh?

Where did my money go? How did I have no money when I came out of prison? When I got arrested, I had it in three different houses on the continent and all them people grabbed it and left the country.

Paddy Holland went off and collected some money in Dublin that I was owed. He collected £660,000 and he thought the best thing to do was to bring it down to Geraldine. He arrived down to Jessbrook with the £660,000 and he said, 'Here Geraldine, this is John's money.'

'Paddy,' she said, 'I've nothing to do with John's business, or wherever he does. I don't want that. I won't take John's money, or any criminal money whatsoever.'

'Take it because somebody's going to try and get him out on bail.'

She went, 'You give it to whoever is going to get bail for him.'

'Tommy Coyle* is after being onto us and he has a man in England that will get him bail.'

So Paddy spoke to Tommy. Paddy went over to London and met Terry Wingrove and gave him the £660,000 and he said, 'That's for John's legal fees and to get him bail.'

No one could speak to me because I was locked up in the top security prison. I couldn't make contact with nobody. I didn't even get a chance to speak to Geraldine for a good while until her number got cleared in the prison, and to clear them it has to go through the Garda Síochána, and they didn't [want to] clear anything for me. Nothing. They wouldn't lift a finger to help. And rightly so. I'll say, fair play for that, that's part of the game. So nice one, lads!

Wingrove gave the money to the solicitor for bail and [he] came up to the prison, and he said, 'I'll represent you.'

'I don't need representation. I'll be going back to Ireland to face trial for murder,' I said, because there was enough about it everywhere. Other inmates were telling me that their families said that they'd seen it on the television that I'm in jail here.

---

*   Gilligan was referring to the same Tommy Coyle, who at the time was described as the biggest fence to ever operate in Ireland. He then mentioned Terry Wingrove, who was well-known for money laundering.

'No, we'll try for bail for you.'

I said, 'You won't be getting me bail. I've charges here, but it will be no time at all before they'll be coming to get me back to Ireland. I know that for a fact.'

He turned up each time I was in court. I'd say to him, 'I don't need you to represent me. You're talking a lot of waffle anyway. You don't know much about what you're talking about.'

He was told not to turn up [again]. But the day before the hearing date, he came up to me and he says, 'I won't be appearing for you tomorrow.'

'That's great, because I told you not to appear.'

'No, I want to do it,' he said.

'I don't want you to. What part don't you understand?' I said.

He said, 'No, it's because Terry won't authorise me to take it out of the bank. I have the money in my client account. It was the only way to keep it safe. And he won't authorise me to take another £30,000.'

'Another £30,000! How much did you go up to now?'

'I only got £89,000,' he said.

I went for him. The prison staff had to pull me off him.

'I didn't want to spend £10 on legal fees because I wasn't going to win anything. It's a waste of time,' I said.

I didn't know at this stage that money had been originally offered to Geraldine, because I was hoping to get it to her and my two children, to help them survive. Because I knew what was coming down the line. You could see it: it was like rocks rolling down a mountain. It wasn't gonna stop.

The judge awarded me costs, seeing how the crown prosecutors hadn't gone ahead with my case for Class-C drugs.

TAPE NINE

A SHOCK JUDGMENT

'Never in the history of the state has one person been responsible for so much wretchedness to so many.'

– JUDGE DIARMUID O'DONOVAN ON
JOHN GILLIGAN, MARCH 2001

It would've been the murder trial of the twentieth century if the Irish State had managed to get John Gilligan in the dock before his court case began in 2000.

Four years on, we were still struggling as a nation to come to terms with the first assassination of a journalist in the history of the state. Gilligan had already been found guilty in the court of public opinion, but still managed to be found not guilty in the juryless court case.

'The only court capable of finding an innocent man guilty of a crime is the Special Criminal Court, but they couldn't even do it with the most hated man in Ireland at the time – according to the press – because there was absolutely no evidence,' Gilligan insisted to me during a phone call from his prison cell in 2008.

The Irish public has always had an almost insatiable thirst for true crime, but even so, it is surprising how many members of the public are convinced John Gilligan was found guilty of the murder. Instead he was handed down a twenty-eight-year sentence for cannabis smuggling, widely perceived as a murder sentence by default. It clearly irked Gilligan.

'If I was to go around threatening everybody who was calling me a cunt, I'd be dead before I'd find the last fella or woman. So, I'm not going to go down that road. It goes over my head,' he told me during that same phone call.

It probably doesn't help his case that the redtops still constantly refer to him to this day as the culprit accused of the murder rather than his innocent verdict. 'I understand why people back up their own – journalists write negative stuff about me because Veronica was one of their own. But, at the same time, they fail to remember that I was acquitted of the murder.'

His guilt by association would never help his case in the court of public opinion. He was good friends with Paddy Holland, who was accused by a female Garda in court of being the triggerman, but was never formally charged. And Gilligan was closely linked with Brian Meehan, the only person ever brought to justice for the murder. Last but not least, he was on a first name basis with all the other members of the drug gang: Russell Warren, Paul Ward and Charlie Bowden. The optics weren't good. [Gilligan said he was 'disappointed' by my assessment.] But you could say the exact same thing about John Traynor, who also had a clear motive. Undeniably, there are compelling reasons to point the finger of blame at him too and it's a mystery how he also didn't end up being charged.

The guards believed the hitman was Paddy Holland. 'Holland was only just out of Portlaoise Prison and he became the number one suspect. I arrested him and he was held for 48 hours but never charged,' *retired Garda detective Gerry O'Carroll wrote in the* Evening Herald *in 2009.*

I'm not the only one who questions Holland's involvement in the killing of Veronica Guerin. Vincent Browne wrote in Magill *magazine in 1997, 'We understand that there is only a vague piece of hearsay evidence to suggest Paddy Holland had any involvement in the murder. This is certainly not enough to convict him of the murder. Neither is it enough to charge him of the murder, nor is it enough to justify the spate of media reports that he was the culprit. Of course our sources could also be mistaken, but are they any less reliable than the sources that have grounded the spate of sensational media articles "naming" Patrick Holland as the murderer?'*

Brian Meehan was also heard to claim that Paddy Holland had no involvement in the murder when he rang up Charlie Bowden's partner and threatened her in a conversation recorded by the Garda Síochána. It's often hard to detect any sarcasm when you don't hear the actual recording of the audio transcript itself, but Meehan told her, 'Paddy Holland came home to clear his name. He's innocent ...' He next said, 'Holland had nothing to do with what Charlie got done for.' Then shortly later he added, 'He's clear of the murder, Holland is, because they didn't do him with it, 'cause they've no evidence, right?'

Traynor, who was almost double the age of Veronica Guerin when he shuffled off this mortal coil at the grand old age of 73 for a criminal in 2021, was the classic example of a gangster who went to his grave knowing where all the bodies were buried.

In the house of mirrors that is the criminal underworld, one thing is certain: John Traynor had a clear motive to want Veronica Guerin murdered. He had once been one of the crime reporter's most valuable and trusted sources, but he took out a high court injunction against her on 13 June 1996, because she threatened to expose him as a heroin dealer. This was just thirteen days before her death.

'The story would destroy my family and my business and perhaps lead directly to my death,' Traynor said in his affidavit.

Traynor knew Veronica Guerin was going to be in the Naas court on that fateful day, because she had mentioned the speeding charge in passing to him. Traynor, who gave this information to the others involved in the murder, made sure he had the perfect alibi on the day: at around the same time as the unidentified gunman pumped six bullets into Veronica Guerin, Traynor was only a few kilometres away doing laps in a racing car at the Mondello racetrack. The car dramatically flipped over when he took a corner too fast, according to eyewitnesses. Many believe he did it on purpose. I'd agree.

Ironically, he was rushed to the very same hospital where Veronica Guerin's lifeless body was shortly brought to, too. Coincidence? According to some rumours, Traynor had let slip to one hospital staff member that he knew the identity of the victim before it was even announced on air. You'd imagine, if true, it would have helped to nail him. Yet, Traynor was never questioned and charged.

He fled the country soon afterwards, but why was he never apprehended and extradited back to Ireland? It's not as if the authorities couldn't find him. There was the perfect opportunity to bring him back in September 1997, when he was pulled in alongside Brian Meehan by Dutch police while the two thugs were on the lam over there in the small town of Amstelveen.

It's puzzling how Meehan himself was extradited, but Traynor was let go. The Gardaí felt he had a 'watertight alibi', according to newspapers. The mind boggles at how Traynor, a prime suspect in the first two shooting incidents involving Veronica Guerin – the shots through the window and the one in her leg – and a man who had just taken out a court injunction against the journalist, was never brought back and questioned.

To make matters worse, according to one of her closest garda sources, 'Traynor too had assaulted her very shortly before she died,' Emily O'Reilly wrote in her controversial book, Veronica Guerin: The Life and Death of a Crime Reporter. Yet he somehow slipped off into obscurity? You don't need a calculator to know that something doesn't add up.

Gilligan hoped to change the narrative with his many controversial claims about his former associates in these pages, but there was always the danger that he could just end up digging a bigger hole for himself. He was convinced the media would twist his words, but hoped enough people would read or hear the tapes in order to make up their own minds. I suppose he saw it as a calculated punt. Besides, as he kept telling me he was an old man now, running out of time. It was the gambling addict's one last throw of the dice.

On 3 June 2000, after three-and-a-half years in Belmarsh Prison, Gilligan was finally brought back to Ireland, soon after his extradition application had been rejected by the High Court in London. The then 47-year-old was taken from Highdown Prison in Surrey to the Royal Air Force station, RAF Northolt, where he was handed over to two Garda detectives and flown back to Casement Aerodrome (Baldonnel) on an Air Corps CASA jet.

Gilligan was dressed in a bright green and yellow jumpsuit. He looked like one of the children's characters from the BBC's Teletubbies, according to the popular press, who were happy to poke fun at it.

Gilligan was not shy about posing for a photographer in Amsterdam and for a crime reporter in London when trying to clear his name in the court of public opinion.

However, in shackles, as he stepped off the flight at the military airport in Baldonnel, Gilligan bowed his head and shielded his face with his right hand when he was frogmarched by five plain-clothes detectives. That aroused suspicion that he must have been guilty as sin. What's more, it was a futile exercise: Gilligan was fast on his way to becoming one of the most instantly recognisable faces in Ireland.

He was bundled into the back of a white Garda van and whisked off to the Special Criminal Court at Green Street Courthouse, and later that night he was charged with Veronica Guerin's murder. It was just three weeks short of the fourth anniversary of Guerin's brutal death and one month shy of what should have been her 42nd birthday.

Gilligan, who by this stage was still hoping he'd be acquitted and would then reclaim his money stashed away in secret locations in Belgium and Holland, stated his address in court as his old council home in Corduff Avenue, Blanchardstown, Dublin 15. But his obscene wealth from drugs, which would've been enough to buy that entire housing estate, was now long gone. He learned the hard way that there was no honour among thieves.

After the first hearing, Gilligan was remanded in custody and brought to Portlaoise Prison. Brian Meehan, Gilligan's henchman, had already been sentenced to life in prison for murder as the driver of the motorcycle that transported the unknown assassin to the Naas Road.

While Meehan would be the only member of the gang convicted of the actual murder, Paul 'Hippo' Ward was then sentenced to life in prison as an accomplice for disposing of the gun and motorbike, only for that conviction to be eventually overturned on appeal.

Paddy 'Dutchy' Holland, who was the man Bowden claimed he had handed the loaded gun to, had also been sent to Portlaoise. He was convicted of possession of ten kilos of cannabis and sentenced to twenty years, which was reduced to twelve years on appeal. Soon after his release, Holland was arrested in London for his naive involvement in a honey trap plot to kidnap a businessman. In 2009, he was discovered dead in his cell on the Isle of Wight.

Gilligan was probably the only person in the country who was convinced that he would be found not guilty of murder when his trial finished on 15 March 2001. A ripple of shock ran through the packed courtroom when the verdict was read out.

Judge Diarmuid O'Donovan might have had 'grave suspicions', but the three judges felt they had no option but to acquit Gilligan because the evidence from one of the prosecutor's main so-called supergrasses, Russell Warren, was found to be unreliable and uncorroborated.

One of the other two criminals who turned state's witness against Gilligan included the so-called Greenmount Gang's quartermaster, Charlie Bowden. Gilligan believed he only did so because Bowden feared the Gardaí had already discovered the weapon and would find his fingerprints all over it. The Colt Python .357 Magnum used in the hit was never found. Nor was the motorbike.

Bowden, who was originally from Finglas in North Dublin, also dealt in ecstasy before he became involved in Gilligan's cannabis operation and later confessed to selling cocaine on Brian Meehan's behalf.

'Garda didn't want the defence to know what deals and money they [the three supergrasses] got and to disclose if other family members also got other crime charges dropped to get them to make up lies.

'As soon as the supergrasses gave evidence against me they were let out of jail as part of the deal, as Bowden said to the Garda he may not give any evidence against Gilligan if they don't do a deal fast. He got his deal asap. Bowden was well ahead of them, he outsmarted them, month in, month out.'

Bowden became the first person to ever enter the Irish witness protection programme. He served six years in prison and later relocated overseas with his second wife, and his mortgage was paid by the Irish State. It is an offence under Irish law to make contact with Bowden or publish his whereabouts. His new identity and whereabouts are unknown.

The third protected witness was John Dunne, who was at the time serving three years for importing cannabis resin into the country. He was the operating manager at Seabridge, an international freight company in Cork, and confessed to receiving £1,000 every time he arranged shipments of drugs for Gilligan between early 1994 and 1996. He said they occurred at regular intervals of three to four weeks.

Dunne said that he once travelled to a pub in Palmerstown, Dublin, to get paid and was met by a man named John. He described him as 'small, a low-size, stocky man with black hair', in his mid-40s. Dunne said the two men met on several other occasions between 1994 and 1995. It certainly sounds like Gilligan, apart from the hair colour.

Gilligan was also found not guilty of four charges of possessing weapons and ammunition. But Gilligan knew his goose was cooked when the judge said the court would reconvene after lunch.

As far as those judges were concerned, Gilligan was public enemy number one. He was found guilty of smuggling cannabis on the evidence of the supergrasses who had been given immunity by the State. He was handed what most people would consider a ridiculously lengthy prison sentence of twenty-eight years for importing 20,000 kilos of cannabis resin worth £32 million sterling. It was – and probably still is – the longest-ever prison term handed down to a mere hash dealer anywhere in Europe. On appeal, the term was reduced to twenty years, but even that was extreme.

What ran through your mind when you received twenty-eight years in prison for importing cannabis into the country?

I laughed at the sentence. All the reporters were looking at me going down the spiral staircase, and I [dramatically] stopped. There were officers in front of me and officers behind me. And I did this [counting] with my fingers. I was just having a buzz.

I went, 'I'm out on a Tuesday. Yep, I'm out on a Tuesday.'

And that was the day I got out. How funny was that?[*]

Somebody else said they took the smile off me face. I never lost a smile in court. Never! I went into the kitchen and I got burnt. But this time I got furnaced! I took it on the chin. And I'm still taking it on the chin to this day. They shafted me. I'd have been released if they had stuck to their own rules. But I spent a long time in prison because they had to break their own rules. But I won't cry about it, because I wasn't so innocent.

I'll say that if I got convicted of [being found in possession of] twenty tons of cannabis I would've said, 'You know what? That sentence is about right. I'd agree with that sentence.' But I was charged with importing cannabis resin into the State on a date unknown, between July and December 1994. No amount of cannabis on a date unknown. So they didn't know in that six-month period what date. Nobody could defend that.

My second charge was: between the first day in January 1995 and 30th day in June 1995, on a date unknown, I imported cannabis resin into the State. Nowhere in the twenty-six counties was named. Where in Ireland are they talking about? I mean, their own rules is: if no evidence, don't convict. There was no evidence of drugs.

My third charge was: between the first day of July 1994 and the 31st day of December 1994, on a date unknown, I imported cannabis resin into the State.

My next charge was: between the first day of January 1996 and 30th the day of June 1996, on a date unknown, I imported cannabis resin into the State.

---

[*]   Gilligan next said he wasn't going to give the press the opportunity to write, 'Oh, he started crying,' as he was led away in handcuffs.

My next charge was: between the fourth day of July 1996 and the 30th day of October 1996, on a date unknown, I imported cannabis resin into the State.

Now, how on God's Earth could you defend them charges? I don't even know if them are proper charges under the constitution. If they gave you a date, you could say where you were on a date. But unknown! It's totally ridiculous.

The police actually stopped me and said, 'We fucked you good, didn't we?' Many of them said it to me and had a good laugh.

Not a tiny bit of hash was found on or near me; all the State had was Bowden saying he collected hash for me, but I did not ask him – he was Meehan's guy. So it was hearsay. Plus, the court ruled his evidence all out, like in The Monk's case he [Bowden] was found to be a liar and accepts he lied in all trials. He [Bowden] did it: he was the killer.

What ran through your mind when you were found not guilty of the murder of Veronica Guerin?[*]

I never thought I was ever going to be convicted, because I didn't do it. The way the case went, the police drip-fed the media evidence and they exaggerated the thing. It was all about phone records [of threatening to kidnap and sodomise Veronica Guerin's young son]. There were only mobile phones attached to the landline, there was no texts in them days; it was a bill phone. Every phone call could be traced.

---

[*] It should be noted that for various legal reasons much of what John Gilligan claimed about the alleged threatening phone call was omitted here.

Theoretically, you could now confess to having organised the murder if you wanted to.

Yes, there's no double jeopardy. I didn't, but if I did do it, I could say: 'Yes, I ordered the murder of Veronica Guerin.' I could even go further; I could say: 'I was actually on the motorbike. I actually shot her off the motorbike.' And there's nothing the State could do. But I wasn't there. I didn't know anything about it. Nothing. Traynor had Veronica Guerin murdered.

Why did you represent yourself during the first few weeks of your murder trial?

I done it on purpose because I knew the other legal teams hadn't got any undisclosed material. When they applied for undisclosed material for Paul Ward off the DPP and the Gardaí in Lucan investigation team, they refused to give it.

They didn't want the defence to have certain documentation to stop the truth coming out. They came to an agreement that, at the end of every day of the trial, they would go up to Lucan police station and get a look at the files, and any documents that the defence required, that the police would photocopy it and give them a copy – if they were happy enough to give them a copy, because they were claiming privilege on a lot of documentation.

The police would automatically tell the prosecution, 'This is the line of questions they are going to go down.' They were forewarned.

So, I'd heard all about that when I come back, because it was over a year before I went on trial. I represented myself and I demanded to get all of the disclosure. I said, 'I'm entitled to have everything under the constitution. I want everything.'

The judge eventually made the order, that I got everything. I got Brian Meehan's, Paul Ward's, Paddy Holland's transcripts. I have all them and that's when I quote anything [here], on camera, the transcripts are there for proof. And don't forget, it's nearly thirty years [ago now, which means] every citizen in Ireland will soon have a constitutional right to go and look for the papers on that case, in totality, under the Freedom of Information Act.

What did you glean from these documents and your own snooping?

Brian Meehan forced Paul Ward to get into the witness box to give evidence that he was a drug dealer. Paul Ward was never charged with drugs. He was charged for one charge: murder. Brian Meehan was charged with murder, firearms and the sale and supply of cannabis resin. Paul Ward's a very good fella. I like Paul. But they never charged him with drugs, or firearms. They just charged him with murder. I don't know why.

And was he involved in that murder?

No, he wasn't. I think Paul Ward wasn't even in the country. I read Paul Ward came back that night, twelve hours after it. I know they said he got rid of a motorbike and the gun. But I don't think he was in the country. I don't know; I was in Belmarsh when his trial was going on.

All the problems were caused by Brian Meehan. I wouldn't give him any credit for anything. I call a spade a spade. So Paul Ward's trial came before Brian Meehan's, I think.

Paul Ward was dating, or living, with Brian Meehan's sister, Vanessa. And Brian Meehan told Paul Ward to get into the box and say, 'John Gilligan is a drug dealer.'

And he said, 'I'm not getting into the box.' Because Paul Ward wouldn't tell on nobody. Paul Ward is a stand-up guy, as far as I'm concerned. I respect him. But Meener told him, 'Vanessa, will never speak to you again if you don't do it.' And, it's going to help him and help Paul. And Paul loved her.

Brian Meehan says, 'So you have to go into the box and say this. You're only charged with murder.' No, not 'only' murder, but that's just saying his one charge was murder.

Brian Meehan said to him, 'The reason why you should do this: it's a very clever move, Paul. When you tell the court that you done drugs for John Gilligan, and he was a drug dealer, the court will see that you're telling the truth and the prosecution will be happy with you saying it and the police will be happy. And then they'll say, "We must believe him", that you weren't involved in the murder whatsoever.'

Paul said he wasn't involved in the murder. Meener kept forcing him to do it. So, there's a few people in the prison that knew a bit about law, good criminals. I'm gonna name two of them: Frank Ward was one good fella and Larry Cummins was another good fella. And they were saying, 'Paul, don't say that. Don't do anything he's telling you to do. He's trying to sell you down the river and he's trying to sell John down the river. The court will say, "Paul, if you agreeing with 80 per cent of what Charlie Bowden is saying, why would we not believe the other 20 per cent that he was saying? So we'll convict you, Paul."'

And that's what a lot of other fellas who knew a little bit about law told him that, too. But Meener says, 'Don't mind them. They don't know what they're talking about.' So, Paul gave evidence in the dock about that.

Meehan must have felt his goose was truly cooked when he heard Charlie Bowden was going to sell everybody down the river.

Paul Ward got word to Meener that Charlie was going to sell him out after being moved to Arbour Hill Prison.

He got a fella to go out to Bowden's house in Castleknock and knock on the door to say to Bowden's partner, Julia Bacon: 'Brian Meehan wants you to ring him. You better ring him.'

If he had a brain in his head, he should have sent the fella down and got your man to ring Brian when he was at the hall door and then put her on his phone, say what he had to say and off he goes – there's no evidence. But no, the 'brains anonymous' I call him, told her to ring him! So, as soon as the guy was gone, she reported it to the Garda Síochána.

They brought her down to the Hole in the Wall pub. They blocked it off, one end of it. They got the technology people down who could do recordings – the judge authorised it – and they got her to ring Brian Meehan.

Brian Meehan started threatening her: 'Charlie better not turn on me. If he starts going belly up on me I'll have him whacked.' The threats he made!

So, it was all recorded and it was used against him in his trial.

I heard it was Brian Meehan who secretly bailed out Charlie Bowden so he could have a word in his ear. Is that true?

Meener asked Paul Ward to put up the 'joke' bail money for Bowden. Meener said to Paul, 'All my money is out of Ireland. If there's bail involved will you put the money up? I'll give it back to you when my drugs get in and sold. I need to talk to him.'

Paul said, 'I'll give you the money.'

It got delivered to Bowden's family, or someone. Brian Meehan started telling everybody he put up the bail money!

Didn't Bowden skip bail?

Brian Meehan got him out of the country, to go over to England. Bowden got nervous and he went back to Ireland.

Nobody knows if Bowden got arrested in England, or gave himself up in England. There's about six or seven different stories. I think he was away for four to seven weeks.

He broke his bail. He should have lost all his bail money because if anybody else ran away you'd lose your bail money. But Bowden came back and he started making statements about everybody and [that] he was innocent of everything.

Paul never got paid back. Bowden was handed back over £29,000, but he kept it. Bowden sold his house and he was able to keep the money for his house – and that was all the deals Bowden got with the police to make statements against Paul Ward, Brian Meehan, Paddy Holland and myself.

Bowden must've felt like he was between a rock and a hard place?

I suppose I would've felt he was left out to dry. Meener should've been fair with him and helped his co-defendant, instead of running away and going partying on the continent and going to brothels, and all this sort of thing. Meener wouldn't give a fuck if they had charged Charlie with the murder as long as he wasn't charged.

When you're in things together you help people. It's kind of a criminal code. Sometimes you do things you don't want to do to help – if I don't help them I'm rowing for the other side, which is the police, the prosecution.

Do you think Charlie Bowden is living in fear of his life?

At the moment? No. I'd say he's in Australia, New Zealand or Canada.

What about Russell Warren's statement that you fought tooth and nail to pull apart?

Russell Warren said anything that the police wanted him to say, because when they raided Warren's house they found a big lump of cocaine. So, he said he was ordered by Brian Meehan on behalf of John Gilligan to follow Veronica Guerin to Naas, to go down and look for her in Naas and go to the courthouse and see her car and follow her up. And he said he drove all the way down there.

He said he parked outside the town hall or the social welfare office and the post office. And he met a policeman down there. And the policeman directed them to the court. Every policeman in Naas was asked, 'Did you ever meet this man?' Every one of them said no, because I got that in the disclosure.

But here's proof that he wasn't on the Naas Road and he wasn't in Naas town and he wasn't parked behind Veronica at the traffic lights, for this: I got served on me hundreds of security tapes [as part of the court case], and they had to buy a machine that cost £14,000 for me to view these tapes, because security tapes have a special machine that it goes slow over 24 hours. You wouldn't see them on an ordinary video [machine].

I went through these tapes which were from every shop that had a camera in town, outside every bank and post office, every jeweller shop. I had tapes from both sides of the road. Also, [I had] copies of the tapes from every petrol station on the way down from Dublin to Naas and you could see the traffic on the left- and right-hand sides of the road. There was an awful lot of factories all the way down the Naas Road and they also had security cameras out onto the road.

And nowhere did his van pass, and nowhere was he seen walking up and down the town. He was never there. He also said he was the second and sometimes the third car behind Veronica Guerin at traffic lights.

He was asked in court, 'When you were the second car behind Veronica's car and you decided to get out of there had you any problem manoeuvring from that outside lane to the fast lane to the slow lane, and then go down Boot Road?'

'No,' he said, 'it was clear.'

It was clear! The judges said they didn't believe a word he was saying because the cars were backed up maybe two to three hundred yards. And everybody in the traffic, nobody drove away.

Only one man went after the bike and he said in evidence that he stopped because he was afraid that they'd shoot him when he thought about it.

Every witness in my trial was asked: did you see this blue HiAce van? Nobody seen him. And everybody was accounted for, inch by inch. But he still insisted he was there. The police made him say it, because they were building a case against me. They were fabricating things and putting things in to try and stitch me up.[*]

---

[*]   In a text message to me in early 2023 Gilligan wrote the following: 'I meant to say this to you [a] few times, Russell Warren's van was seen in Castleknock at 11.30 a.m. on the 26th June '96. Higgins's SC put it to him how could he be in Terenure giving BM a bike at 10 a.m. as his statement said, and it said BM told him go straight to Naas, to look for VG's car. He was asked why was he spotted in Castleknock at 11.30? He said that's the way he would go to Naas. The true reason, it came out in court: he

It was claimed that you had a propensity for threatening witnesses, which is one of the main reasons why you ended up being sent to the Special Criminal Court on several occasions. Yet, despite all that, the authorities still believed you intimidated certain witnesses during your murder trial.

I didn't threaten any witness. But let's say that happened for a moment: if I did threaten the witness how would anybody know about it? This is just a makey-up story from the journalists. There seems to have been an awful lot of witnesses that were afraid to speak about me. Sure, what's the police doing? Why don't they come and arrest me? You'd get arrested [for that].

Carol Rooney was terrified to testify against you. Is that true?[*]

The baloney that the police say, and they keep saying it, 'Only for she was afraid,' and I bullied her and I terrorised her, 'she would have made a statement against me.'

Now, I got stopped at Heathrow Airport and I got locked up. So how could I bully her not to give evidence against me? I got arrested at the airport in England. She's on the continent. I'm put into custody. How could I bully her? I was supposed to bully

---

was fucking his best friend's girlfriend or partner. The Garda never put that in the book of evidence. There was [a] statement [that] his van was in Castleknock, but nowhere on the Naas Road, or Naas town ... all the premises in that town had cameras. Cameras showed up and down that town and around the court. He or his van were not anywhere ... he said what Garda asked him to say to get a small sentence.'

[*] Gilligan was also accused of threatening the Dutch-based drug dealer Martin Baltus if he testified against him. It was reported that the man's eldest daughter had been held against her will overnight until her father had a change of heart. Again, Gilligan denied the allegation.

her, according to their Garda and press statements. That's how stupid they are. They didn't say people went on John Gilligan's behalf and bullied her. I'm in custody. That's how sick they are. That's how stupid they are. My trial accepted there was no phone calls to Veronica Guerin, and no phone calls to Russell Warren. So how could Carol Rooney hear me on a phone when there was no phone calls made? The Special Criminal Court and DPP confirmed that.

It was claimed you threatened Carol Rooney when she overheard you speaking with others on the day of the murder. It was also alleged that Dutchy Holland intimidated Rooney over in London on your behalf, saying to her: 'Get yourself a new boyfriend, forget about John and everything you've seen and heard and everyone will be alright.'

No, that never happened. There is no such thing as a person that can give evidence that the police don't bring them to court as a witness, and especially in a high-profile case like this. She would have been used as a hostile witness and remanded in custody on contempt of court for not answering questions. When you're ruled as a hostile witness your statement is read to the court as evidence.

Now, that's what they would've done. But she'd nothing to tell them, because she's told the Garda the truth. 'Where was he?'

'He wasn't with me.'

Now, I never spoke to her, but I know she couldn't have said, 'I was with John, I listened to him.' Because I wasn't there. And the proof of the pudding is, they didn't bring her to court. There's no such thing on this planet, especially in Ireland: 'Oh, she said she didn't want to make a statement.'

That will go down in a case to do with a summons or

something – but a murder? You have to give evidence. You witness something and you decide not to help the police as a citizen? Get real! There's no chance of that happening. If you just examine what happened, the logic of it, the waffle that they're giving jumps out at ya.

Did Carol Rooney make a statement against you?

I got 3,600 statements – and that's on record – and there was no such statement from Carol Rooney. And I've asked many times for Carol Rooney's statement to be produced as the Garda were saying on radio she had made one. She had never ever given a statement about me [being] in a hotel with her as I was not, and she could not have made a statement that she heard me on the phone because there was no call on the 26th of June 1996, to Russell Warren. The Special Criminal Court and the DPP confirmed that. The Garda gave a lying account out to the press.

So where are these quotes coming from? For example, there's a quote from Rooney saying that she overheard you speak to Dutchy after the murder and you said to him, 'I heard you put a smile on her face.'

If there would be just maybe even 5 or 10 per cent of truth what was written about me in the newspapers and books, we wouldn't be doing this interview – I'd still be in prison for murder.

You're claiming Carol Rooney never heard any of your conversations on the day Veronica Guerin was murdered, including you threatening Russell Warren to keep his mouth shut ... or else?

Yeah, that's right. She just realised how much of a bad man I was supposed to be! It's very strange Carol Rooney was always standing beside me, or a couple of feet away when I was making these threats on the telephone, when the police listened to me telephone? I'm no moron by any stretch of the imagination. And I wouldn't be so stupid. It wouldn't interest me to make threats, but I wouldn't make threats on the telephone.

I often had three hotel rooms in case I was ever getting followed or [they were] taking photographs of me. But that particular time I had two hotel rooms. Carol Rooney was in one and I was in another one because a couple of people wanted money exchanged. I had two and a half million guilders; it was a million quid. And one of them wanted £400,000 and the other fella wanted close to £300,000 changed. I used to make money on the exchange rate. They were afraid to change money. They'd be afraid the bank would ring the police and it'd be taken off them. So they'd come to me, because I would have a good reputation of being a straight, honest guy. I would change it and I'd make good money. And sometimes I used to say to the bank, because it was a bank I went to and not a bureau de change, I'd say, 'No, I'm not happy with that rate. I'm going.' And then they'd up it another three or four cents. And changing £600,000–£700,000, it'd be a good few thousand for me.

So, let's get this straight: you're claiming that you were effectively money laundering for over £1 million for some shady characters at the time of Veronica Guerin's callous murder?

I was changing money – that's how I know I wasn't talking to Carol Rooney until very late that night.

Why not?

Because I didn't bring the money back to my hotel. I had the money somewhere else. I won't tell ya where. I had a place where I could keep me money. I had two meetings: one first, and one a couple of hours later. I went down and got a cup of coffee – I made sure I wasn't gonna be drinking with business – and waited for the other guy to come, and I gave him that thing [cash] when I felt safe. I went to put the money away, and then I headed up to Carol Rooney. So, she was nowhere next to near me at that time.

Yet the narrative is that Carol Rooney fled to Australia and refused to come back to Ireland and give evidence against you because she feared for her safety.

There's loads of cases where people are doing prison sentences for contempt of court because they wouldn't answer questions. But they have to get into the witness box. So what was done with Carol Rooney if she had something to say? They didn't say, 'Jesus, go ahead there. We really want John Gilligan for this, but if you don't want to say it it'd be okay. You have evidence that will convict him but, go on and enjoy yourself.'

How pathetic is that? When you analyse it, any man and any woman listening to what I'm just after saying will say, 'Well, why didn't they?' Because she had nothing to say! That's why. Her statement would have been read out to the court if she did not answer in the witness box.

The only reason I got found not guilty of the murder was that the evidence in the newspapers they were saying about me never existed in real life. It was fictitious. I challenged every bit of it. And I won, and that's why I'm here now talking to you, Jason.

But you supposedly had a propensity for making threats even outside of the courtroom, even in your day-to-day dealings.* **What about the times you allegedly threatened members of the Garda Síochána?**

That did not happen. You'd get a charge sheet and be in custody for a long, long time. You cannot be arrested for something and during the interrogation threaten a member of the Garda Síochána and not get charged. Apart from that, you'll be battered in the station. They'll kick the fuck out of ya and they'll say they're only restraining ya and they had to use as much force as possible, because that happened a thousand times. But it didn't happen to me.

You hit or threaten a guard in a station he'd want to be an awful gobshite not to charge you and bring you to court. I mean, I have two convictions for threatening prison officers. It's all baloney that, 'Oh, it was your word against his.'

Like, another time I was charged with an armed robbery [in 1981]. I was in custody for a few months and when I went before the jury, the jury took twenty minutes to find me not guilty of everything. And then the police said, 'Gilligan, the next time we charge you you'll go on to the Special Criminal Court.' You don't get justice in the Special Criminal Court. It's a corrupt court. It's an unconstitutional court. And the Special Criminal Court is only supposed to be opened under the constitution if the country is in a state of emergency; they can have a Special Criminal Court in Dublin only or Cork or Limerick, if they class that part of the country in a state of emergency only – that's the legislation.

---

*   For instance, it was claimed Gilligan made threats against local farmers and landowners in and around Jessbrook during the expansion of the equestrian centre, which he also vehemently denies.

I think either Amnesty International or United Nations, or perhaps even both, have condemned the Special Criminal Court.* Peter Pringle, the last innocent man in Ireland to have a death sentence overturned, who was incarcerated in Portlaoise Prison at the same time as you, once told me that the Special Criminal Court was a de facto sentencing tribunal.

But they haven't closed it down. It's ridiculous. It's either a good court or a bad court. But Europe said there is nothing wrong with a Special Criminal Court if all the citizens have a trial without juries. But you can't have a jury trial for some and no jury trial for the others. It's not right. So until they sort that out Ireland is paying millions of taxpayers' money [in fines] to the European Court because they won't close that court. Do you know that Ireland pays a fine every year about it?

---

*   Even the Irish Human Rights and Equality Commission has also stated that the Special Criminal Court and repeal of the Offences Against the State Acts should be abolished. Speaking in 2021, their Chief Commissioner Sinéad Gibney stated: 'The extension of the Special Criminal Court to tackle organised crime has seen it evolve into an institution that is far removed from the circumstances it was established to address in 1972. Ireland's criminal justice system is capable of effectively confronting the problem of organised crime without resorting to a parallel criminal justice system that deprives the accused of their right to trial by jury. The fundamental rights of individuals need to be carefully balanced against the rights of victims, national security concerns and the public interest in having an effective criminal justice system. Any restrictions or limitations of the rights of an individual must comply with the principles of legality, necessity and proportionality. The use of the Special Criminal Court has led to two criminal justice systems in Ireland, and subsequently has compromised the fundamental right of equality before the law.'

Yes, I did indeed know that.

Okay, thank you. They have never produced a certificate to Europe, that Ireland's in a state of emergency. So that's the reason why every single year Ireland have to pay the European Court the money for having a Special Criminal Court, because every citizen should have equal rights. Sometimes citizens get a jury trial and the others get the Special Criminal Court. And that court came about when the Troubles happened; it was supposed to be only used in a state of emergency. And they locked up loads of innocent good men on no evidence, all on the word of a lying superintendent.

But, John, is it fair for you to be able to profit off crime full stop?

No, but they have to prove you committed a crime; if they don't within their own legislation and rules prove you did then they can't say you profited off crime.

How did you feel the day you had to hand over the keys or have to sign off and give the State Jessbrook, your pride and joy, after such a long drawn-out legal battle?

I accepted that we were robbed in a corrupt way. Okay, I done drugs. If they done the case proper and right, I would have said, 'Well, fair play. They can prove I was a criminal and done this.' I understand that. But I didn't make the rules – the government made the rules. They set the rules down that they will, under the constitution of Ireland, [conduct] business with the right procedures. But they kept moving the goalposts.

It sounds like I'm more bitter than I am. I'm not. They didn't give you your rights. I know a lot of people say, 'If you're a criminal, why give you rights?' Well then, with that attitude they shouldn't even give you a fair trial – just bring you to prison. Just come into your house, kick your door down and take you to prison and say, 'Ah, stay there for ten years or twenty years.'

Nobody in Ireland would like that, so there's laws brought in and there's rules in that legislation. And they should abide by it, because that's what they're supposed to do. The judges swear four times a year that they'll be impartial and independent – but they weren't impartial and they weren't independent. In my book, they're lying scumbags. They're corrupt.

[An example was] when it came to the major point in the CAB, that was to explain better to the court that the Section 3, in 1996, had to be a legal right in the Gilligan case. CAB used the one granted on 16 July 1997 to apply for a Section 4 disposable order. The Supreme Court had stated during the appeal hearing they were not with CAB on that one, as they said it was plain to them that none of the Gilligans had got any legal representation at that hearing as the Supreme Court had, in May 1997, squashed their legal fees order the Section 6 for it to be filed and heard fresh to see if Gilligan would be granted one, and they stated that the hearing did not take place in the High Court until 31 July 1997. So, it is crystal clear we were not legally represented on 16 July 1997, so we should have won, as the Garda and CAB were telling people they will get a winning judgment from the Supreme Court, but they did not give us our constitutional rights.[*]

---

[*] Throughout the course of these in-depth interviews Gilligan constantly vented his anger at his legal representatives and made several libellous allegations, none of which can be printed under Ireland's stringent defamation laws. He is convinced one of his legal team felt he was guilty of the murder. Gilligan said, 'Meener was after telling him, "It was all John Gilligan."' Regardless, this certainly didn't prevent Gilligan's legal team from successfully defending the murder case.

And when I got found not guilty of the murder, because [of] what was in the newspapers, everyone thought: 'Mr [Michael] O'Higgins must be Houdini. He must be great.'

I said, 'I'm going to get twenty-five years. Brian Meehan got twenty years. So I'm put down as the ringleader. So I'm going to get five more.'

When they found me guilty, the judges asked if we wanted [it] to be dealt today or next week. 'Do we need time?' I said, 'Leave it a week, let the dust settle.* It's better if we wait a week and let them do all their speculation. And we'll get the case done right.' Because I know I'm gonna get twenty-five years ago, but Meener has twenty years – he might appeal that. So that might help me.'†

So I said, 'Well, when they sentence me make the application only when they sentence me, to get the sentence backdated.'

So he made the application beforehand. And there was an argument going on for forty minutes. And then the judge goes, 'Oh, yeah, we'll allow him the time.' And when they went in to work out the sentence, I said, 'They'll add the three years on top of twenty-five now.'

And that's what they done!

I have observed you on several occasions becoming irate when it is claimed your case against CAB cost the taxpayer up to £20 million.

No £20 million of taxpayers' money was used on the Gilligans'

---

*   Gilligan claims his legal team advised him, 'No, you're better off doing it now.'

†   Gilligan again claims that his legal team urged him to go ahead with the sentencing on that day.

case! Yes, it may sound not so exciting about the Sections two, three, four, but the courts did not give the Gilligans their legal rights under law and procedures and protection under Irish constitution ... that is wrong.

Yes, I know the murder is more exciting to read about ... Traynor ... methamphetamine ... Bowden ... the shooter. But one of the main reasons I am doing these interviews is for my family – they lost their homes.

Tracey's, Darren's and Geraldine's homes [were seized by CAB], plus our Blanchardstown family home ... 123 acres ... cars ... land, horses and horses boxes ... machinery ... tack room ... saddles ... and Geraldine's bank accounts – all that was used to pay legal people. In total what they got paid was £800k. Our properties came to almost £2m!

The government of Ireland make the laws and the rules. The courts and judges' hands are tied – they can't go outside the rules. The rules are protected by the Irish constitution, giving citizens protection in all courts in the land. Everyone has heard the saying, it is better to let go nine guilty out of ten if you don't know the innocent one out of the ten.

When the proceeds of crime came into law on 4 August 1996, there was no legal aid in it; that came in after 2003 in the new 2005 Act, I think. The P.O.C.A [Proceeds of Crime Act] 1996 is the act CAB used to bring the first one hundred and more cases to court. The Gilligans were number ninety-four.

The P.O.C. Act 1996 is governed by the constitution of Ireland, [and] also by its owns rules of its legislation that became part of Irish law.

Read the P.O.C. Act – you will see the first steps. One is called Section 2 Interim Order. CAB don't have to tell you they're going to the High Court for it, but once they get it, they must do two things: one is, they serve it on each person named in it; the other is, they must apply before twenty-one days is up for the next order, as the Section 2 order dies on its twenty-first day.

The next order is a Section 3 Interlocutory Order. They have [a] little longer for a hearing on that once it's filed in court before [the] twenty-one days is up. Now, here is what I want to make crystal clear: once CAB serves you with the Section 2 Order there was no legal aid P.O.C.A. until years later.

You've got to go to some solicitor office with the Section 2 Order just served on you. In that Section 2 Order from the High Court it will state [that] all your bank accounts and all your properties are frozen. You can't sell or put your properties up to get a lend off them.

So no solicitor will take your case. He can't get you barristers, as no funds. But in the P.O.C.A. 1996 there is a section that the 'solicitors only' can apply for funds to be paid. That is called a Section 6 Order. If he is granted that Section 6 Order, then he can take your case and look to see what barrister will also take your case.

How a Section 6 Order works is, if you lose your case then any money and properties [frozen] is sold and the first person to be paid is your legal team, as there is no legal aid. So, you pay your own costs – not like the media claims I cost the taxpayers £20m.

We did not get our rights – [as] guaranteed to the Irish citizens under the rules of the P.O.C.A. 1996. Legislation and the courts did not protect our citizens' rights and the rights of the law.

On 5 December 1996, CAB went to the High Court looking for a Section 3 Order off the President. He gave them it. On 24 January 1997, they went back to him [and] asked him to change it, said they did not call evidence. He said no. But before that in January 1997, CAB went back to the High Court to file more papers. The judge gave them a second Section 3 Order, also without them calling any evidence – they went to the High Court on 24 January to try and fix it.

By this time my family solicitor and barristers went to ask for a Section 6 Legal Fees Order. In February 1997, at the application, the President granted one with one condition, which was this: if another judge hearing the trial thought that [the President] should not have given the Section 6 Order it could be taken back. The barrister said, does that mean we've been working up to seven years to trial and our fees may not be then paid? The President said yes. The barrister said he couldn't take a case on that [basis]. He appealed the order.

The appeal came up before the Supreme Court in May 1997. They quashed the Section 6 Order with the clawbacks in it and sent for a new Section 6 hearing to rule if the Gilligans [can] get it or not. That hearing did not take place until 31 July 1997. But on 16 July 1997, a new judge granted CAB another Section 3 Order – that's the [same] Section order CAB used to apply for the last order, the Section 4 Order.

The Supreme Court said on our appeal, the Section 3 Order of 16 July 1997 is of no use, as this court had sent the case back to the High Court in May 1997 to see if that court would grant a Section 6 to the Gilligans – and that hearing did not take place until 31 July 1997. So the dogs on the street know the Gilligans had no legal people to defend them in court for the Section 3 Order on 16 July 1997. So it's not legal, but they still took our properties.

It really irks Gilligan that he is pigeonholed as the main culprit who propelled the Irish government of the day to bring forth emergency legislation to establish CAB in 1996. He told me, 'They [the media] stirred it up. They blamed me on the CAB. People thought the CAB came in because of John Gilligan. CAB didn't come in because of John

Gilligan. Well, in that [TV] programme, State of Fear, *there's a man from the Department of Justice that done the legislation for CAB and [he] says CAB didn't come in because of John Gilligan. He said this didn't come in because of the murder of Veronica Guerin or the murder of Jerry McCabe. This fire was already lit. And the proof of the pudding is that that woman got murdered, brutally, on 26 June 1996 [and] CAB legislation was signed into law on 4 August 1996. A lot of people say it was October/November. I'm telling you because I know, because I fought my CAB case for twenty years. CAB came into law on 4 August 1996. No legislation can pass through the Oireachtas in that amount of time. It's an impossibility. It has to be up and running on 'white paper', 'green paper', and all sorts of papers. And it has to be agreed with all the different parties: Fianna Fáil, Fine Gael, Sinn Féin, and whatever. They have to agree to this and it has to go back and has to be drafted and redrafted and redrafted. They didn't just run down on 27 [June] and start writing up legislation and bring it forth on 4 August, because it has to be legally checked and then it has to go to the Attorney General for him to give his approval. That's how legislation comes into it. So it is an impossibility to go down that fast and the man said [that] on the television. I don't know the man's name. But anyway, you should check that and put into this [book] because that happened.'*

TAPE TEN

THE JAILBIRD YEARS

'I don't cry over it because I did get away with
plenty ... but I just take it as part of life. I also
done crime that I got away with. So it's swings
and roundabouts, that type of thing.'

– JOHN GILLIGAN SPEAKING TO THE AUTHOR IN 2008

Old habits die hard, it seems. On the final day of my third trip to
Torrevieja in August 2022, I was feeling ebullient after recording
several hours that morning at the hotel I'd picked this time, which had
splendid views of the marina. We were both tired from talking all week.

As I was taking apart the cameras and folding up the tripods,
Gilligan suggested we take the short ramble down the promenade to
one of the popular restaurants with an outdoor terrace for a spot of
lunch, before we parted ways. By this stage, I had over twenty hours
of tape, and I didn't know at that point if Gilligan would be available
to conduct any further interviews, because of his impending trial for
membership of an illegal gang, possession of a handgun and drugs:
both sleeping pills and cannabis.

Despite Gilligan's belief that he would get a suspended sentence, I reckoned that there was a good chance that they would lock him up. Gilligan didn't want to speak about it too much, but I got the impression that it was not, by any stretch of the imagination, a big operation. He was sending it out in small amounts to Ireland. It was a far cry from the days of smuggling massive amounts in containers on ships. He had gone from the top back to a dealer on the virtual street corner.

It was fascinating to watch Gilligan eat. I had half expected him to put his arm around the plate to shield the food, like many ex-cons and children from large families will instinctively do. He didn't and he didn't eat very quickly either. He took his time sipping his cola, and then when his massive steak arrived, he meticulously cut the fat off all around it and then sliced the meat in half. But what he did next certainly took me by surprise: he picked up a large piece of the meat with his bare hands, took a big bite out of it and happily chewed away, unselfconsciously.

I figured it must have been an effect of all those years locked up behind bars where nobody bothered with table manners, nor watched their Ps and Qs. Still ... I looked around at the other diners, but nobody batted an eyelid. I said nothing and ate my meal, using the traditional knife and fork etiquette. I wondered if he was testing me in some unorthodox way, or if he really didn't bother much with cutlery.

When Gilligan said he couldn't remember how many times he had been in jail, he wasn't playing mind games. As far as he was concerned, it was part and parcel of the life of a so-called career criminal: 'It's very hard to answer that, as an accurate record, because there was many times I was charged with crimes and I'd be locked in prison for three or three months on remand and then I'd eventually get bail. So, I'd done two months here, a month there, six weeks there, seven months here, and this,' he explained.

Gilligan could count all his bona fide prison sentences on one hand prior to becoming a household name in 1996. There had only been four of them, which was a relatively small number for a career criminal.

'I got six months for taking scrap off an old building site in 1975 or '76 – but it was suspended. Then in 1977, I got eighteen months for receiving about sixty cigarette lighters.* I did that time and then, in

---

* During my first ever interview with Gilligan he told me about his first sentence: 'I had to be the unluckiest man in Ireland to get jailed in 1977. Do you know why? In 1977 there was an amnesty going. There was a huge number of cases backlogged. Cases were taking five years. It was told un-officially to every barrister that if your client pleads guilty he'll more than likely get a suspended sentence – even if it was for armed robbery, banks, post offices – everything. I know loads of fellas that were up for three or four post office robberies who would've normally pleaded not guilty and tried to win them – but they all pleaded guilty. The whole town pleaded guilty.

'But I wouldn't plead guilty. The fella downstairs on the North Strand was after having these cigarette lighters. When they raided the flat, they took them from downstairs and they brought them up and threw them on my floor. When they'd charged me, the copper realised that I wasn't a bad fella – that I was at sea and all my family was at sea, because I was after being at sea for about seven years at that stage. He asked me to plead guilty. He said, "I don't want you to go to jail." But because I pleaded not guilty, I was sent across to Judge Martin's court. With that judge, if the law was in your favour you got it, but if you got found guilty he'd give you the worst sentence you'd ever get.'

The way he tells it, halfway through the trial, Gilligan changed his mind and pleaded guilty. 'They should have sent me back to the other court to get sentenced. I gave up my seaman's book and the judge said he'd never seen a reference as good as it. He said, "I'm going to give you half the sentence I had in mind." I was told I was only going to get nine months, but the judge gave me half the sentence he had in mind which was eighteen months! I went up to the Joy and I got a visit the next day

1982, I got twelve months for stealing forty large cartons of Mars bars. The biggest one was in the Special Criminal Court in 1990, where I got four years for receiving £3,062 worth of hardware goods – trowels and shovels and that. And in between, I got six months here and there for driving with no insurance,' he told me. 'But I didn't really worry about it because I would always delay the tax insurance case until I was convicted of one of the [more serious] crimes and then I would plead guilty to no tax and no insurance and that sentence automatically ran into my criminal charge.'

According to one court report, Gilligan had at least twenty-seven previous convictions by the time he received his twenty-eight-year sentence for smuggling cannabis into the country in 2002.

He had essentially only set foot inside Portlaoise Prison when, ten days later, he was found guilty of assaulting one prison officer and then threatening to kill two of them in 2002. Even more convictions would be clocked up during his time there, such as when he smuggled mobile phones into the prison. After his release in 2008, he would be arrested two more times, in Belfast and then in Spain.

Gilligan was surprisingly sanguine about these long stretches behind bars. 'It's swings and roundabouts. I just laugh. Loads of things I done I got away with. There's very few things I got caught with. I did a lot more than what I got convicted of. I was lucky, clever, or whatever,' he told me in 2008.

I got the sense that Gilligan would probably agree with some of the profound thoughts Albert Camus had on prison in The Stranger, in particular this rumination: 'And the more I thought about it, the more I dug out of my memory things I had overlooked or forgotten. I

---

from Geraldine. I got five-and-a-half months off for remission. But it done me good. It smartened me up. That's the truth. But it smartened me up as a criminal.'

realised then that a man who had lived only one day could easily live for a hundred years in prison. He would have enough memories to keep him from being bored. In a way, it was an advantage.'

I felt it would read better if all of Gilligan's thoughts on prison were included in one chapter, rather than bits and pieces, here and there, in a chronological format.

Were you always regarded as a violent man?

I read that the police were saying I was known as a very violent man. I don't know how they could say that because the only assault case I was convicted of, in fact, was [for] my brother. He's dead – Lord have Mercy on him – but when I was doing that eighteen months in 1977, he gave someone a dig. It was common assault – and that conviction got put down to me. The first violent incident I ever had was when I hit a chief officer – which I did. I gave him a box and I got six months for it. I was never known as a hard man. The papers made me out to be a hard man.

It's an obvious question to ask, but what did you miss the most when you were locked up?

You miss all your family: your wife, your children, your mother, your father, brothers and sisters. You'd miss your freedom.

You sound sanguine about it all, but do you have any major regrets?

I regret two times I was in prison for something I didn't do. And the first thing I didn't do was, I didn't wear gloves and they got my fingerprints! And the second time I didn't wear my balaclava and I got identified. They're the only two things I'm sorry I didn't do.

I'm not going to cry and feel sorry for myself.

Do you really want everybody to believe it was like water off a duck's back for you?

It didn't bother me when I got locked up, because it was like when I'd go away to sea in the merchant navy. I think prison, for me, was fairly simple, because my trade was to go away to sea. And the reports saying I didn't want to go to jail for six months [for assaulting Veronica Guerin] ... I would do six months in the shed. It wouldn't bother me.

There were reports of you becoming very depressed when you were once locked up in Cork.

No, that's not true. Every prison officer in Portlaoise Prison, if they were asked, they'd say, 'Gilligan laughed through his sentence, and he holds the record of being locked up into seg [segregation unit] in Portlaoise Prison. Nobody would match him, the amount of time he was locked up.'

Now, I'm not proud of that.

Yet you assaulted a prison offer at Portlaoise Prison during your first stint there, doing the four-year sentence in 1992.

I had a run in with him many years ago when I was in Mountjoy in '77 or '78. He used to pick on me an awful lot and I was fed up with it. I had no tolerance for him.

In them days in Portlaoise Prison, you could ask the prison officer on the spur of the moment: 'Could I have a copy of me warrant?' and he'd go and get a copy. Now, in other prisons, you'd have to put your name down to see the governor and make an application to ask him for permission to get your warrant.

I had about four or five copies of the warrant in my cell. I got called for a visit with my wife and I'd planned to give her one of the warrants to pass onto my solicitor. While I was nearly all the way out to the visitors room I remembered I was after forgetting the warrant.

I said to the officer who was bringing me out: 'Excuse me, could you get a copy of me warrant please? I'd have to go back on the landing to get it.'

He said, 'Yeah, that's no problem, John.'

So, he went off to get a copy for me. Then he came back and he said the chief officer was after saying, 'You'll have to get your solicitor to apply for it.'

He was doing Dublin rules. He was being awkward.

I said, 'Just tell him I'm entitled to it down here. This is not Dublin, this is Portlaoise. Or else, I'll go back to me cell again.'

To cut a long story short, I didn't get the warrant. But I said to Geraldine, 'Will you wait outside the prison gate. I'll get one out of the cell and the officer will leave it out to you. Wait there twenty minutes. Don't stay any longer, because they won't tell you they're not coming, because the chief, he's not a nice fella to me.'

I went back to my cell to get a copy of the warrant and I gave it to the prison officer to give it to my wife. But he came back to me and he says, 'John, the chief won't let me do that.'

'Tell the chief I want to see him,' I said.

I was going out to the prison yard and the prison officer called me over.

'The chief wants to see you.'

I said to him, 'Chief, can you give the copy of the warrant out here? My wife is waiting in order to get it. Please don't have her hanging around there.'

And he goes, 'No.'

I got angry. They were letting him out of the security gate. I said to the officer in the bubble that pulls open the security gate: 'Please don't open that gate.'

I closed it back.

'Chief,' I said, 'if I go out there I'll punch the head off you.'

'You'll punch the head of me?'

Now, this was a big fella. I said, 'I'll punch the head off ya. So I don't want to go …'

He said to the officer, 'Open the gate.'

The officer said, 'He doesn't want to go out.'

The chief said, 'That's an order, open the gate.'

I walked straight out and I punched the head off him – one good hard box. Everybody just turned and looked. Next, I went out to the yard.

They were saying, 'Come in.'

I said, 'I'll come in at five o'clock when I'm ready.'

That was at four o'clock. 'If you want to take me, try and take me.'

I came in an hour later and I was put in the seg for a few months. I got charged for it. I was lucky that I wasn't brought to the Special Criminal Court over it. I got brought to the District Court in Portlaoise. So when I got brought to court, I got sent down to a Cork prison in isolation for punishment.

I had a couple of court appearances about the assault. I got brought back up the Portlaoise Prison for the court case. My solicitor says to me, 'Will you apologise to the chief?'

'I won't apologise to him at all. Are you serious?'

'John,' he said, 'if you don't apologise to him, you're going to end up in the Special Criminal Court. Be clever. Say you're sorry to the man.'

'I just can't do it.'

'Do you want six months? Or, do want you four years?'

'I'll take the six months?'

'Apologise,' he said. 'I'll go over and have a word with him first. I'll tell them you're getting a hard time down in Cork, down in the seg, that you're sorry. It was just spur of the moment and you'll never do anything like that again. And you're remorseful. We'll see what he says.'

My solicitor went over to talk to him. Then, the prison officer brought me across to see the chief and I said, 'Chief, I'm very sorry. I shouldn't have hit you.'

You don't strike me as being the remorseful type.

I never meant a word of what I said to him. I hated him. I was trying to be a smart arse.

He said, 'Are you getting a hard time in Cork?'

'Ah, I'll manage with that, chief, thanks very much.'

I sat back down. The case gets called. The policeman gives his evidence, that he charged me, and all that. And then the lady judge was looking down at me and I could see she was thinking, 'He's only a midget!' The chief was a big man.

Looking at the height of me, she said: 'How did this come about?'

My solicitor said, 'Mr Gilligan has apologised wholeheartedly to him in the court this morning and the chief accepts his apology. The man had anxiety in prison. He's pleading guilty.'

'Put it to him.'

I said guilty. She gave me six months. She didn't even give it consecutive, she just gave it concurrent. I was over the moon. So, I was walking by the chief and he says, 'John, now good luck to you.'

'Go fuck yourself,' I said, which I shouldn't have done. But I'm telling you the truth. I'm not going to butter it up.

The *Veronica Guerin* movie directed by the late Joel Schumacher and starring Cate Blanchett was released in 2003 while you were behind bars. Did you ever see the film?

I never watched the full movie. But every time I went to the seg in the later years there was a television there; before that there'd be nothing in the seg. But when I used to get put into the seg they used to play the *Veronica Guerin* movie on Monday, Tuesday, Wednesday, Thursday, Friday. They used to kick the door and they'd say, 'Your telly is not even on, John!'

I'd just knock my telly off if I seen that film coming on. The prison officers would want to know if I was watching it.

I've seen bits and pieces of it maybe twenty or thirty times, but I did not see that movie once from start to finish. I'd be doing legal work [on my appeal] and then I seen it was on and I'd be looking at it and then it just got knocked off.

You're portrayed as a nasty piece of work in it.

That was the idea of the movie. If it wasn't me, it was somebody else. You weren't gonna see this nice guy, no matter who was in it. Everything that they put in that movie was shown to be bullshit in a court of law.

The tabloids claimed you were viciously attacked by a dangerous prisoner as a result of our interview in *Hot Press* in 2008.*

No, it never happened. Like, one guy came at me and he just got put up against the wall. The prison officer down there she used to laugh at him all the time.

'You'll never try that again. The little fella was well able for you,' she said.

But that's water under the bridge. Like, when you're so many years in prison and you're getting bad news from your family – something's happened, somebody's sick in your family – you'd be a bit down. So people would snap. But the fights in prison don't last long, it's over and done within a half an hour and you shake hands. It's like a straightener on the street. It's not like in the movies, with the fights and stabbings.

It might be now. There's an awful lot of stabbing down in Mountjoy. There's fellas going to the hospital every ten minutes – forty stitches, sixty stitches, eighty stitches. I think that's disgraceful. It shouldn't happen. People should realise that everybody in prison is going through some sort of pain or anxiety. And they should just let it go.

I could do prison in a dustbin. It wouldn't bother me. I don't

---

* Inmates were apparently angered that the authorities had clamped down on the number of visitors allowed as a result of said article. The Minister for Justice ordered an investigation into my visit and the prison authorities then said that new X-ray-style airport scanners would be introduced in Irish prisons as a result of my controversial visit, but such devices were already in place when I visited Gilligan in Portlaoise Prison. I even wrote about them in the piece itself. I felt it was irresponsible journalism when one redtop wrote a front-page piece in which I was essentially blamed for the reduction of visitors being allowed to make visits. It made me a target for some irate family member or ex-con to take a swing at me, or worse.

care where they put me in a prison. Even if I got arrested today for something, and they gave me life in prison and they put me in the dustbin to live, I'd live in it. I'd put up with it after three million cases in the High Court, without a doubt.

When I interviewed you for *Hot Press*, the go-between you used to get documents and photographs to me was a young woman working in a bookies. She said she was your girlfriend.

I had a few very good-looking young girls visit me. I'd be talking to them on the mobile phone in the prison and they'd say, 'Can I come down and visit you?'

There was this regular girl who came down to me every second week, and she always dressed really sexy. She'd be holding me man thing and I'd be feeling her boobs and feeling between her legs and we'd be kissing.

But there was a prison officer present at all times in the visiting room when I met you in Portlaoise Prison.

The prison officers just turned a blind eye to it and they put the head behind a newspaper. But this particular newish fella in the prison – I think he was after coming from the Midlands – was there on this particular day [when] she'd a real loose dress on her.

I said to her, 'Jesus, you're gorgeous. I'll tell you what, I'd love to go down on you.'

'I'd love you to go down on me,' she said.

'Do you want me to go for it?'

'Please, John, go for it,' she said.

I got down on my hands and knees and I was kissing her pussy. I couldn't stop kissing it. It was lovely.

And the prison officer said, 'John, what are you doing?'

I just picked my head up and turned around and said, 'Twenty-two years,' and I continued on sucking and licking. It was a laugh.

When I was going back to the prison wing, he said, 'You shouldn't be doing that in front of me.'

'Don't look then,' I said.

It wasn't allowed, but in that particular prison they turned a blind eye to it, in order to keep the peace. But I had plenty of visits from females. I must've had more females visit me for my notoriety than the whole prison put together. So, use your imagination there.

You're making it sound like you had groupies.

No, they only came in one at a time [*laughs*].

Apparently Elaine O'Hara's murderer Graham Dwyer has received so-called fan mail, which is bizarre. Did you?

Ah, buckets of it. Loads. People my age, or maybe even older. And they'd say, 'John, never lose that grin off your face. You're beating them. We know what they done to you. We know you didn't do it.'

Now, I'm blowing my own trumpet, and I don't want to. 'You do things for people and you wouldn't stoop so low. We know and we take up for ya.'

There were many people who got into trouble taking up for me. Got into fights. Men and women, but an awful lot of women got into fights. Neighbours. When I was home one time a neighbour told me she got into loads of fights taking up for me. She said, 'I class him as me second da. He's a gentleman. He would never do that. He took up for us when we were kids. He doesn't let anybody touch families.'

Anyway, I'll say no more about that.

There was video footage in the news of you doing commentary on football matches between inmates in prison.

The lads used to play football in the yard. I couldn't play football because my legs are too short!

They'd only give us so many footballs, probably a half a dozen. There was a fence with the yard and then there'd be a barbed-wire fence and chain-link fence and then, say, six feet over, there'd be more chain-link fences to block you. But when the footballs used to go over the fence and they'd land in the middle, they wouldn't give the lads another football.

Now, Portlaoise Prison is one of the most secure prisons in the whole of Europe. The army is on the roof with machine guns and there's big M60 machines on the roof and no planes or helicopters can fly over the airspace. It's a no-fly zone. The army is patrolling inside and the outside of the grounds.

I was well used to going through fences from my robbing factory days. I could open a fence in seconds. So I said to the lads, 'Just stand in front of me and I'll get the ball.'

I'd be undoing the chain link wire and the army would be shouting down: 'Move out of the way!'

'Gilligan get away from that fence.'

'Get out of the line of fire.'

Like, they were gonna shoot me. They would shoot you. They'd often shot at people in that prison when they got near the fence. They'd let shots off. But once the people were blocking me – because I was small and they were tall – I got the balls back for them. We were happy to get one over them. Once you walked away from the fence they weren't going to shoot you.

The crowd from the local football team outside used to come and play the lads. Some of the prisoners were very fit; they'd be doing the gym a lot and they'd be exercising and playing football.

I was always doing the video recordings. I'd be standing up on the seat doing the commentary. We used to get the tapes and send them out to our families, to let them know that we were okay.

But we never played football against the IRA. They didn't mix with us. They kept to themselves. They didn't walk with us. When we were in one yard, they were in the other yard. We never associated with each other, but we'd acknowledge each other by just giving a nod passing by, respect for each other. But they were freedom fighters and they were fighting for their rights, to get England out of Ireland. But that's got nothing to do with me. That's not my business. I'll keep my nose out of that.

You also assaulted a second prison officer shortly after first entering Portlaoise Prison in 2002.[*]

I was going to the tuck shop one day before a legal visit in Portlaoise. We had the shop six days a week, but you get the tuck shop seven days a week if you got a legal visit on a Sunday. Brian Meehan and I were going out to see our solicitor and barrister. There were facilities there for you to make your own tea and coffee, and get Kit Kats for them, to show respect for your legal team.

---

[*]   Gilligan was found guilty of said assault and death threats made to two prison officers on that occasion in the Special Criminal Court. There were other incidents when Gilligan was reported for using abusive and threatening language on prison officers, including two incidences in Belmarsh.

I asked the ACO [Acting Chief Officer] to let us go to the tuck shop and he said, 'You're not getting nothing, Gilligan.'

I said, 'We're entitled to get them for the legal people.'

Anyway, he wouldn't do it. So, I said I was going back in to see the acting chief governor up in his office. I knocked on the chief officer's door and I said, 'Excuse me, chief, me and Brian Meehan is going out on a legal visit to our solicitor and our senior counsels. So can we get something from the tuck shop?'

'Yeah, no problem,' he says, 'whichever officer is with you, tell him to come here and I'll authorise it.'

I said, 'Thank you very much, you're a gentlemen.'

So when I come out, there was a second officer out there. I said, 'Would you come with me and go into the chief?' And he says yeah.

We had to go through two security gates now. As I was walking up to the ACO, I said, 'The chief said you've to open the tuck shop.'

The other officer had given him the nod. But he still said, 'You're getting nothing.'

I said, 'Listen, open the tuck shop.'

He said, 'I'll do nothing for you.'

And I gave him such a smack. I just lost it.

So he said, 'Get back in ...'

I said, 'We're on a legal visit. You can't stop us going out on a legal visit.'

We went out on the legal visit and I told the solicitor what happened. And, of course, I actually denied I'd hit him.

'He pushed me and I hit him,' I said, like defending myself. 'He was just getting rough with me.' But he hadn't. I didn't need to hit him, you know. He tried to push me through the door. I said, 'Don't put your hands on me.' And I saw him move again, so I just give him a box.

So during the visit Brian Meehan kept going out to try and quieten it down. And I said, 'Leave it. It doesn't matter what he does.' I really didn't care. I wasn't going to cry after doing it.

We never got tea and biscuits for them. So when the visit was over, there was about ten or fifteen officers there, waiting. One of them said, 'John, you have to go to the seg. Is there any problem?'

I said, 'No, there's no problem with me at all. But put your hands on me and we'll take it from there. But I'll walk, no problem.'

So, I went down the seg for a few months. I got charged that time. And because the Dublin police got involved they brought me to the Special Criminal Court and they gave me five years on top of the twenty-eight – that made it thirty-three years.

They topped up your sentence, so to speak, on other occasions, too.

Also, after being convicted of the drugs, based on how much I profited from drugs, they gave me an [additional] ten-year sentence if I didn't pay £14 million. I wasn't able to pay. So when I'd finished the thirty-three years, I would have had to start a fresh ten years, a civil ten years and you don't get any remission [there]. And then I got into trouble again after that when I got caught with a telephone in my cell and I got eight months consecutive off that [in 2011].

You appeared a staggering forty-eight times in court to deal with that mobile phone charge. You were also caught red-handed smuggling phones into prison.

When I was in the court, I was representing myself over four or five days in the court and every day in the court somebody was after coming in before [the trial] and strapping two phones under the table. I used to bring the two phones back to the prison every night. I had six phones over three days.

And then on the fourth day, as soon as I took them from under the table – they were stuck with double-sided tape – I was jumped on.

'Do you have something you shouldn't have?'

I said, 'Yeah, a big sentence.'

I got another six months consecutive for that.

Yet you didn't do anything like thirty-three years in prison.

I would've needed to pay €14 million, or do ten years of a sentence. But the High Court said the Special Criminal Court hadn't got jurisdiction to deal with civil matters. So the State wasn't happy. They appealed to the Supreme Court and they lost. So the ten years went out the window.

Then, when I went up on the five years for the assault to the chief officer, the court took my age into consideration, and they put it down to two years consecutive to the sentence. The twenty-eight-year sentence was knocked down because I wasn't convicted of any amounts of hash. It was just on six days on dates unknown over a two-and-a-half year period. So, they said twenty years in prison is enough for cannabis resin.

How else did you smuggle phones into the prison?

I put my earlier trick with the magnets into action in Portlaoise Prison. The prison van used to go to the shop seven days a week. The tuck shop was next to the gym. You'd get somebody to put cling film around a couple of telephones and a magnet, and when the van was in the car park of the shops a guy just went over and stuck it under it. So, it was drove back into a top-security prison, with the army there.

And as it was getting unloaded, you'd say to one of the trustees that worked in the shop, 'Get that for me.'

You would have a shop order and the trustee just put your two phones and your magnets in the bag. And then you'd give it to him the next day when you'd be going to the gym: 'Stick that back under the van.'

And then the fellas started getting drugs in that way to the prison. All that's after been stopped, because somebody talked about it. So the van gets checked every time – they put mirrors [underneath the van] and put the [sniffer] dogs on it.

It's probably nothing short of a miracle that they finally let you out after seventeen years in 2013.

They wouldn't tell me my release date until very late on. And then when the date came out, all the lads were going to have a party for me the night before my release. But the governor and the chiefs came down and said, 'There'll be no party.' They all got locked up an hour early.

The prisoners said, 'We'll come down and see you in the morning.' But they wouldn't even let them out for breakfast until they took me out of the cell. They didn't take me out of the cell until about quarter-past nine. Normally, you're down to the reception at seven in the morning. I was waiting an hour or two in the holding cell. They didn't want me to talk to nobody or see nothing until I got out the gate.

Did you speak with Brian Meehan prior to your release?

I remember about three weeks before the end of my sentence, I was in my cell and the prison officer opened my door and Brian Meehan was there holding his food tray in his arms.

I said, 'What do you want?'

'Would you do a bit of work for me?'

I said, 'I would never be in your company again. Me and you are finished. You're dirt to me, Brian.'

And he goes, 'Oh, no, no … we could get back as good friends, as we were.'

'No, Brian, you killed everything we had. I know about you now. I'll do nothing with you. If you could make me twenty million, I'd have nothing to do with ya,' I said.

'Can we not do things when you go out, with me brother?'

'If you could make me 100 million, I'd have nothing to do with ya. 100 million! I'll get out and if I want to get money I'll get it myself,' I said.

'Are you going to give an interview when you get out?' he said.

'What the fuck's it got to do with you if I give a fucking interview or not? Who do you fucking think you are? You done this … you fucking done this, not me. Now get you. Do you want a fucking problem? I'll give you a problem. Do you want to have a go?'

And he goes, 'No, no, I'm not fighting.'

'I doesn't give a fuck if you're fighting. You done fucking all this. You and that piece of shit Traynor, all youse. Now, fuck off out of me cell.'

And he said, 'I'll come down and shake your hand before you go.'

'Get the fuck out of it,' I said. 'I'll have nothing to do with you.'

He went out of the cell. There were six prison officers outside of the cell listening. And then one of the prison officers came to me and said, 'You alright?'

I said, 'Yeah.'

Brian Meehan was on the fourth landing and I was on the one landing. The further away from my cell the better. Even when we were on the same landing, we didn't speak.

The fourth and third landing used to come down for their meals first and when they went back up and got locked up, then they used to allow the second landing and the first landing out to get food.

'John, go down and get your grub now while the cell doors are open,' the prison officer said to me.

So, I walked down and a couple of my friends down there said, 'What's wrong with you, John? Your fucking neck ... your face is standing out. You're as red as a berry.'

I said, 'That fucking piece of shit ... do you know what he's fucking done? He's asked me am I planning on giving an interview to the press when I get out. The fucking tramp ... him and fucking Traynor and that fucking Charlie. Fuck them!'

What was his game coming down to me? You know, what did he want me to do? Give him a clap on the back or something for what he was after doing. I'm surprised that wasn't leaked to the newspaper. I never spoke to him since.

It sounds like you felt like killing Brian Meehan.

No, not killing him. I've got hatred for him. Sure, during his trial he was putting it all down to me. Some of the barristers, the same ones that were on his [case], were looking at me like I was telling lies, because Brian Meehan was after giving his version. So, it looked like I was the bad guy.

It was affecting my family – my ex-wife and my children and my grandchildren and my brothers and sisters. And he didn't give a shit. So it's time for me to say the truth, the way it was and to take up for my family, and just give my side of the story. I could say much more, I could probably talk from now to Christmas, but it's not going to do any good.

Brian Meehan is coming up for parole.

He actually said to me, 'John, don't you know, when I go to the parole board, they won't give me parole unless I fully confess?'

This is the way it works in the prison system: if you don't admit to your crimes you won't get parole because it sounds like you're not rehabilitated. But the funny thing about all that is, there's no parole board in Ireland whatsoever. There's a 'letting on' parole board called an ad hoc parole board. A parole board has never been put on a statutory footing in Ireland; all around Europe it has, but Ireland won't do it. The Department of Justice keeps putting it off because the police didn't want it on a statutory footing. So the Gardaí are winning all the time on that argument.

But Brian Meehan said to me, 'When it comes to it, John, I'm going to have to say you done it.'

'No, Brian, you won't be saying I done it. It had nothing to do with me – this was you and others. It had nothing to do with me.'

'I know that, John, but they won't believe it. They just want to hear it's you,' he said. 'If I say you didn't do it, they'll believe I'm taking up for you and they'll never let me out of prison.'

I said, 'No, don't say that about me – I'm warning ya!'

But my belief is, he would have said all that. He would have gone into great detail blaming me – agreeing with anything that was wrote in the press about me, everything the prosecutor said about me. I don't only believe it, I know it, because others in prison said it to me. He told them that he had to say this and say that when he went to be interviewed by the 'letting on' parole board.

And they said to him, 'That will send Gilligan mad.'

He said, 'What can I do about it? I won't get out of prison if I don't blame him because they won't believe it was anybody else but him.'

I got told he admitted to the parole board: 'Yes, I drove the bike. Yes, I done this. I was ordered by John Gilligan.'

So why should I have any respect for that piece of shit?

Would you take legal action against Brian Meehan if he ever gave an interview on his release from prison and publicly claimed you masterminded the murder?

I would, yeah. I think it is possible, and I would do that.

From the way you talk about him, I'm surprised you even had any conversations with him in prison.

Brian Meehan and I had some arguments that came to near blows in prison. We fell out four or five times. He spent five years down in the basement, so I wouldn't be able to see him for five years. But he never stopped talking about me to other people up on the E1 Landing in Portlaoise Prison. He got the furthest away from me.

He only came to me to help him when he'd a court case coming up. And I gave him the best help I could. Because when you're a criminal you're on one side of the fence. We class the bad guys as good guys. The cops, they're on the right side of the fence.

We used to look at them as bad guys. Obviously we were more bad. And they'd look at us as the bad guys – and rightly so. One of the reasons why I waited 'til now to tell my side of the story was because Brian Meehan was waiting to get out of prison.

Why would you do that for someone you don't even like or respect?

He was convicted for life in prison and I had to be fair to him because one time he was a good friend. I'd be fair to him, because I knew he'd have to go to the parole board and say this and say that.

You're claiming Brian Meehan only told you the full details about the murder while you were locked up?

Brian Meehan was doing drugs in prison. He was on heroin. And when he'd be stoned, somebody would say to me, 'He's stoned over there.' I used to go over and bring up the subject and he'd tell me a bit more. But he wouldn't tell me anything when he was sober.

There was a big media circus at the gate of Portlaoise Prison on your release on 15 October 2013. Your own solicitor Joanne Kangley, who is now no longer practising law in Ireland, after she was arrested for smuggling contraband into a client in prison, showed her greenness when she unnecessarily hyped up your release by claiming that you wouldn't conduct any interviews even if offered €1 million. You were really playing to the gallery as you got into your brother's waiting car and sped off.

I had some plans to get out of that gate. When we were doing the sentence, we'd be having a laugh [about it]. The yellow jumpsuit

I got dragged in with [during his extradition to Baldonnel Aerodrome], a couple of good men in the prison were going to get their wives to make one of them suits and send it into me. I was going to come out in the suit. But I was going to get a blade and cut it all in ribbons. And when the gate opened I was going to dive on the ground, [looking] like Robinson Crusoe.

And then another plan was: a fella on a big motorbike and a fella in a HiAce van were going to come down. But the police weren't going to let them up to the prison door. My brother had to prove who he was when he came down to get me. But they were going to get the fella to get off the motorbike and hand me a helmet. And I'd put the helmet on my head and then the fella in the HiAce van was going to take out a little three-wheeled scooter – one about this size [*he points to his knees*] – and I was going to get on it and peddle down the road. Just for the crack.

We knew there would be people to make fun and jokes at my expense. So I said, 'I'll join in the fun and jokes.' But we never got around to doing it. I just came out as I did. I was on television coming out the gate and there must have been fifty photographers outside the prison walls. Then they followed me from there up to my brother's house. I could've lost them if I wanted to, but I said I wasn't going to run from anybody.

You went from there straight to a knees-up at your younger brother Thomas's home in Lucan, County Dublin.

People were kissing and hugging me, but I was numb. I knew the prison part of it was all over, but I [also] knew all the shit was gonna start over and over again, and all the waffle. I knew I was going to get followed here and there, with the journalists looking, and if you said a word they were going to twist it.

Like, the journalists were all parked outside my brother's neighbours' houses and they came out and said:

'Get away from him.'

'He only got convicted of cannabis.'

'He's a good guy.'

And, 'Get away from my gate. I can't get my car out of my gate.'

So, a reporter came to me brother and said, 'Will he give us an interview?'

I didn't want to talk to them. Thomas said, 'John, the neighbours want them all to go. And they said they'll go if you say something, and then the neighbours could get out. Because this is going to kick off. There's a few fellas out there and they said, "Does John want us to ram these fuckers?"'

There were ten stolen cars ready to ram all them reporters, if I wanted it done.

I said, 'No, please don't cause any scenes. Do nothing. Just leave it. Tell the reporter [I'll do it] if he gives me his word that as soon I talk they'll go. Because this is going to get sloppy. There's a lot of people not happy with the hassle they're giving me. And they are ready. They have balaclavas, they have gloves on them and they've stolen cars.'

They were just going to ram them and ram them and ram them. I was afraid some kid or woman would get hurt. People in their houses would be terrified.

Anyway, I came out and they were gone in five minutes, bar a few of them. A couple of people came and they said to my brother:

'There's still one at that corner.'

'There's still one there.'

'There's still one across the road over there.'

You know, hanging on to try to get the last photograph, thinking I was going to walk up to the local. But you have to accept all that. I don't mind; it's other people that I worry for. That shouldn't happen to them. Their lives shouldn't be interfered with. If somebody hasn't done anything wrong why should they get hassled?

Were Geraldine and your kids at the house that night?

No, but there was a friend of mine from England there and he said, 'They should be here.'

I said, 'I'd like them here,' because I was a great friend with Geraldine. She was a lovely woman.

I presume there was a lady friend waiting to see you later that same night?

No. I wasn't interested. That wasn't on my mind. I actually don't even know when the first time I did 'that' again. Was it one or two weeks or ...? I don't know.

TAPE ELEVEN

THE CAT BURGLAR WITH NINE LIVES

'I lay on the floor – I just played dead. I thought
I was a goner for sure. If I hadn't done that,
I wouldn't be here to tell the tale now.'

– JOHN GILLIGAN IN CONVERSATION
WITH THE AUTHOR IN 2014

It wasn't yet even nine when my mobile rang early one chilly morning in December 2013. I didn't recognise the number flashing up on the screen. But the voice on the other end of the line was impossible to forget: 'Hello, Jason,' he rasped in his Dublin vernacular. 'It's your old friend ... John Gilligan.'

A slight chill ran down my spine. While it was obviously professionally useful to be on speaking terms with one of the most notorious gangsters in Irish history, knowing that such a man had my phone number was unsettling, to say the least. Still, as a journalist, it was my job to talk to all sorts of people – including those who might be regarded with horror and revulsion by many.

I had reason to be extra vigilant when we made arrangements to meet up and do an interview – there had been an attempt on his life just a couple of days prior to this call.

On 4 December 2013, a Dublin criminal gang decided to take Gilligan out of the equation. They knew he was going to be in the Halfway House on the Navan Road in Dublin at a certain time that day. Shortly before 4 p.m. the hitman, believed to be a well-known armed robber, barged into the pub wearing a motorcycle helmet and brandishing a 9mm pistol. He started walking around, looking for his target, but quickly became frustrated and yelled out, 'Where's Gilligan?' to the stunned audience, before running around the venue like a headless chicken. When it became clear that the 'pint-sized' criminal – a description often used in the redtops – wasn't there, the hitman fled the scene.

He raced off on his motorcycle towards Finglas. A Garda patrol car spotted the suspect on the Ratoath Road and attempted to intercept him. Panicking, the motorcyclist tossed away the gun and then somehow managed to give them the slip. He might not have had his 9mm pistol anymore, but Gilligan must have known in his heart that the killer would try again. After all, he wasn't going to get his big bounty until he had wiped Gilligan off the face of the earth.

'I hope you don't want to meet in the Halfway House!' Gilligan cackled when we agreed to meet up and do an interview, which was subsequently published in the Irish Daily Mail. It would be his first and last major interview since his release from prison in 2013 ... until now.

During that phone call on the week of the botched hit on him, I ventured to ask whether he was not in fear of his life after the terrifying incident in the Halfway House?

'No, I'm not worried at all,' he boomed. 'I'm not worried a bit. In fact, I'll be in the Harp, seven o'clock Sunday ... singing!'

It was all bravado. He knew he was a marked man: but being John

Gilligan, his answer, as always, was to make a joke out of his own predicament. However, speaking to me all these years later, he readily admitted, 'I didn't know what was happening, and that was kind of a shock to me in a sense.'

But at the time, for a man who was supposedly not afraid for his life, Gilligan took some pretty serious precautions when we met. I was instructed to take a Dublin commuter train and then told to get off at a certain station, where he had someone waiting to pick me up and ferry me to a secret location.

As we took off at breakneck speed, my driver regularly looked in the rear-view mirror to ensure that we weren't being followed. We eventually pulled up outside a bungalow that Gilligan was using as a safehouse. With the engine still running, the driver made a phone call. Suddenly another man appeared out of nowhere and escorted me to the front door. He knocked several times in code before the door swung open and John Gilligan ushered me inside.

He was wearing an old Aran sweater and tracksuit bottoms: it was certainly a far cry from his once ostentatious lifestyle.

Closing the curtains 'for security', Gilligan agreed to talk to me about the previous attempt on his life. He was meant to be in the pub at the appointed time to meet someone. Acting on a gut feeling, though, Gilligan said he pulled out of the planned meeting shortly before the gunman arrived: 'I was halfway there and I just didn't feel right ... I changed my mind,' he said. 'I went for a pint elsewhere. I'm lucky to be alive.'

With those prescient words, Gilligan then went on to say, rather less accurately, that he was no longer under threat.

'It's gone,' he said simply.

Walking into court for his CAB case in December 2013, Gilligan told an RTÉ camera crew that the episode was a 'Halloween prank too late' ... in December! The gunman shouting, 'Where's Gilligan?'

before fleeing the scene had led many to wonder whether the entire episode was a joke, or some kind of bizarre set-up. Another theory at the time was that Gilligan orchestrated a fake murder attempt because he wanted the Gardaí to offer him protection. But it was a genuine attempt to murder him.

'No, I wouldn't take Garda protection,' he said. 'If they were giving me wages for Garda protection I wouldn't take it.'

There was a double irony, of course, in these contemptuous words. Gilligan was shot six times and ended up in the care of armed guards at Connolly Hospital in Blanchardstown on 1 March 2014.

And, it seemed, wages – or money of any kind – was exactly what he was sorely lacking. It was his attempt to squeeze money out of former associates that led to him being shot, according to word on the street.

'I'm skint. I haven't got any money whatsoever,' he told me that day in the cottage. 'A few friends of mine threw me a few pounds.' He paused and looked at me, then added: 'I know you don't believe me!'

A few weeks before he was shot, I met Gilligan at The Reform Club in London to kick the tyres on the possibility of a book. As we sat there at one of those tables with a buzzer to summon a waiter on the first balcony floor, we were surrounded by judges and barristers, who undoubtedly would've been horrified if they discovered someone of his ilk was in their midst.

I had read the seminal non-fiction crime classic Wise Guys *about the Irish-Italian criminal Henry Hill, which was written by the journalist Nicholas Pileggi in 1985. It was, of course, later brilliantly adapted for the screen by Martin Scorsese as* Goodfellas *and deservedly won several Oscars.*

I wanted to chronicle Gilligan's life story in a similar fashion to Pileggi's book. I was a big fan of John Boorman's film The General *but, like many others, felt it went overboard with the humour.*

Gilligan's story, in the right director's hands, had the potential to be an Irish version of The Sopranos.

Phileas Fog might have famously been able to make a wager in that very same club to travel around the world in eighty days, but I wasn't able to come to an agreement to get Gilligan for such a book. The idea was a non-starter because Gilligan at that time was still in a legal battle with CAB and, as a result, he didn't want to talk on the record about being a drug baron. It would have been akin to interviewing Lance Armstrong without bringing up the proverbial elephant in the room.

We parted ways. As I watched Gilligan pull a woolly hat down over his head as he sauntered off down Pall Mall, I was convinced that our paths wouldn't cross again.

Incidentally, Gilligan was wearing the same grey suit in London that he turned up in when we met eight years later in Spain and I asked him to relive the attempt to murder him.

It's nothing short of a miracle that you're alive to tell your tale, considering you were left for dead in a pool of your own blood on your brother's kitchen floor. It happened on the day your family were holding not one, but two christening parties in the same pub in Palmerstown, Dublin, on 1 March 2014.

I knew certain people would be looking for me. It had already happened when my niece had a birthday party in The 79 Inn on the Ballyfermot Road. Plus, I knew the journalists would be there. At every one of my family's functions there were [always] no less than ten journalists trying to get photographs, and no less than twenty detectives there!

I didn't go to any family functions because I didn't want anything to happen to them by accident. Because when a hitman runs into pubs, people get pushed and bullets go off, here and there – and innocent people get shot.

So, there was a christening [party] from my sister's home and a christening [party] from my brother's home on the same day. They were both held in The Silver Granite [public house in Palmerstown] in two different function rooms, but they were altogether. They were all happy.

I had presents for them. I flew up to my brother Thomas for ten seconds to bring presents. My nephew wanted to see me, so I waited three or four minutes.

They were watching my brother's house. I was looking out the window and I seen the jeep pull up outside. Two black African men* got out of the jeep, one with a machine gun and one with a handgun.

There was nothing I could do. The front window is down to the ground. There's a window in the [front] door and a window in the parlour door. I double checked the window. I lost valuable seconds, but I don't think I would've got through the house and out the back door.

What were you thinking at that very moment?

I said to myself, 'This is me out of this life. God, I'm sorry for all me sins, please forgive me.'

---

*   I let Gilligan know that his description of the hitmen sounded ridiculous. Hitmen don't turn up without hiding their identity, which would make it hard to even recognise their skin colour. But he maintained it was true, with one of those self-described 'smirks' on his face.

Why didn't you carry a gun?

Why would you carry a gun? When I knew my life was in danger I was offered many guns. Many people came to me to say, 'John, I have this.'

I said, 'Mate, I can't carry anything. Because if I have a gun in me pocket and I'm walking down the road and the police jump out of anywhere and search me they'll say, "Ten years, John."'

So, I had to walk around with no gun. I couldn't walk 100 yards without a policeman seeing me, a detective, an undercover detective, or an ordinary police car driving by. And them guys are professionals; they'd smell you have something on you. They'd know you'd have something on you – whatever it's the body language or you'd be hyper, or this or that. So, I couldn't carry a gun.

So, what happened next?

I tried to get down the hall, which was stupid. They came bursting in. They kicked in the door as I was running down the hall. He shot me in the leg. When I was hopping down the hall, I tried to throw a dig. I said to myself, 'I'm gone! Fuck! I'll go out with a bang' – not like a bang of a gun, but that was going to happen, too.

I turned around to throw a dig and the bone came out of my leg and I fell down. I didn't even know there was a bullet in me! I just knew I couldn't use my leg. I didn't even say, 'I'm after been shot in the leg.'

He shot me again in the kitchen. And then they started shooting into my back. They shot me in the head.

You must've been in considerable pain?

I didn't feel any hurt with the bullets. A lot of people think when somebody shoots you, you go 'Uhhh!' When a bullet goes into you it's so warm that you don't feel anything. You only feel it when the bullet cools down. Then you feel the pain if it's stuck in a bone, or in your side, or in your head.

They really wanted to make sure you were dead if they shot you six times.

They thought I had a bulletproof vest on, because I'd my overcoat on. I never had a bulletproof jacket. I wouldn't wear one to this day. I couldn't live my life that way.

And when he put his hand down my Crombie overcoat, I pulled his hand and the bullet went across my chest – it [just] missed my heart. That bullet is still in me.

Then he put his hand up the bottom of my coat to shoot up into my chest. I pulled the gun [away] and the bullet went across me. And that bullet was still in me when I was discharged from hospital on 17 March 2014.

And when he took the last shot, he stood over me and missed and hit my face. But when I heard it go [off], I smacked my face against the floor like I was dead.

It's amazing that you were quick-witted enough to play dead.

When I looked at movies and you see soldiers [in similar situations] moving. I know it's only a movie but I'd say, 'Why the fucking hell would you move? Pretend to be dead and when they're gone, get up.'

I always said that in my head: 'That's what I'll do.' It just came to me. I knew when he shot again to just bang my head like I was dead.

'He's gone.'

I was expecting to hear the machine gun going off, but it didn't. Like, good criminals, if you can do something without firing a gun, the gun can be used again for something else. But once you use it [because of] the ballistic report, you have to get rid of it. Some people don't dump it, but it's clever to dump it. It doesn't matter what it cost you – dump it.

I could see in me mind's eye that the one with the machine gun was waving his arms. 'He's gone.'

I could [en]vision them in the back of my head. Then they ran out the door.

What exactly do you mean by this?

I was going to tell you off the record, but I'm going to tell you [on the record]. I was face down, because I went forward. I seen myself opening the back door and going out the back door – but I never got fifteen feet near the back door!

I always laughed when I used hear stories about people when they're in a hospital bed and they were able to say what was on top of the wardrobe. 'There was pennies on top of the wardrobe,' or something. You'd hear stories like that over the years and you'll say, 'What a load of baloney.' But that actually happened to me. I could see myself crystal clear opening the lock with the key in the back door and going. I never got near there.

Would you consider that an out-of-body experience?

Well, it must be. After I left Ireland, I was talking to my sister-in-law on the phone. She was there in the kitchen when it all happened.

I said, 'You have to answer me the truth. I need to know this just for my head, out of curiosity. Did the fella standing over me do that?' [*Gilligan waves his arms across his chest to signal that he was dead.*]

She said, 'Yeah, how did you know?'

'I knew because I visualised it in my head.'

But I will tell you one thing: I believe people when they die come back to life.

You mentioned that you didn't feel any pain when the hitman fired six rounds into you at close range.

I didn't feel pain until I went to have a heart attack, because there was that much blood pumping out of me ... everywhere. And then I felt it.

My daughter was standing there.

I went to say, 'Oh Tracey ...' But then I said to myself, 'Shut up, John.' I bit down on my lip. I didn't want to be crying in front of my daughter.

'You alright, Da?'

I said, 'Yeah, I'm alright. I'm alright.'

All my family is on their knees saying, 'Please don't die ... don't die ... don't die.'

My bet was on the mantelpiece in my brother's house. Tottenham and Liverpool were after winning that day.

I said, 'Fuck! I'm not going to die. Are you serious? I'm after getting a winning double bet. I'll be going and collecting that bet.'

And they were all laughing. They still talk about that to this day.

It would've been an unusual sight: family members breaking the tension by laughing while a loved one is next to death's door on the floor.

I said, 'And by the way, did anybody ring an ambulance?'

Nobody had rang an ambulance!

I'm surprised the police weren't tailing you at the time of the botched hit.

The police would have known, and I don't blame the police. The same as with Martin Cahill. I have no badness for the police on that topic. They were around but they just went offside. They knew there was somebody coming for me. But they didn't do anything. But I wouldn't want anybody caught anyway.

That's a very serious allegation to make without any proof to back it up.

I don't believe they rushed to the house, right. And by the time they came, I said, 'I think you drove around the block three or four times to give me time to die.' I probably deserved that, you know that way. They don't feel sorry for me. I went into the kitchen and I got burnt.

Or rather, on this occasion you went into the kitchen and you got shot. It was touch and go whether you'd survive. You even received the last rites at Blanchardstown Hospital.

I must've lost two stone in hospital because, while they were cutting me open and sewing me up, I was only getting fed water. They were just wetting my lips with water.

After I was there so many days they then said, 'We're giving you jelly and ice cream tomorrow.' And a couple of days later they were giving me potatoes. The nurses were lovely. There were six different doctors over me, and physiotherapists.

But the police were pushing to get me out of the hospital asap.

How can you make such a claim?

The nurses told me. On the second day I was in there, the physiotherapist crowd came around for me to do physio on my leg. But the lady doctor said, 'On no condition are you to do anything for six weeks with that leg. Don't move it. Don't put it on the ground. Don't do anything.'

I said, 'Well, I can't move it.'

The physio team came in for me the next day. Two beautiful looking girls.

They said, 'Right, we'll just bring you around the ward.'

'How do you mean?'

'We'll put you on a frame.'

'I'm not going anywhere,' I said.

'You have to.'

'No. Sure, I can't walk. The doctor told me not to,' I said.

They went off. The head fella came in.

'Are you refusing?' he said.

'No, I'm not refusing. I'm not being disrespectful to nobody. The nurses will tell you my manners is very good. But I can't walk. I can't even go to the toilet. I'm using the bedpan in the bed. I can't move me leg.'

And he goes, 'Well, we'll try in the morning.'

'The lady doctor said I couldn't ...' I couldn't think of her name. I said to the nurse, 'What's the lady doctor there?'

She said, 'She will be around at ten o'clock in the morning.'

I said, 'Would you please come back around ten o'clock.'

And he said, 'Yeah, we'll be here because you need to do physio. Sooner the better.'

The nurses told me, 'If you do that physio, if you even try to move from here to there, if it takes you an hour, they'll sign you off and you're out of here. Because they want you out of here, John. You're not a problem to us at all.'

They were saying other patients in the ward were complaining about me but there was nobody complaining. They were all people saying, 'Guess who's in there?' You know that way?

So, the doctor came around the next morning.

I said, 'Excuse me, can I speak to you?'

She said yeah. I said to the nurses, 'Tell them physio people to come in.' I said to the doctor, 'These physio people want me to walk on me leg. Will you tell them?'

'This man is not to put that leg down on the ground for six weeks,' she said.

So I said, 'I'm very, very sorry about this just, I won't be doing physio.'

There's a famous photograph of you looking frail in your Crombie coat and a flat cap pulled down to mask your war-like wounds, as you were wheeled out of the hospital and whisked off to the ferry over to the UK.

I didn't know how bad I was. When I left the hospital I was black and blue. I had black eyes. I didn't know because I never seen a mirror because I was only in the hospital bed.

Were you then given a police escort, as reported in the media?

I didn't get a police escort! The police wouldn't protect me. They drove behind to make sure I left the country. There was an Irish and a Welsh rugby match that weekend. So it was hard to get a boat ticket.

What did your first taste of new-found freedom feel like over in the UK?

It must have been about four in the morning when we went into McDonald's. I was so happy because not one person turned around to look at me. But if I went into any shop or pub in Dublin, the whole pub would turn around and look at me. So the freedom of being left alone was great.

Did you make peace with the person who ordered the hit on you?

They had a talk with me on a phone and it was all sorted out. It was a mistake. The police had told them that I was going to kill them. The Garda set me up after I got out of prison.

How could they possibly set you up?

The police were pulling in a lot of drugs runners and they were saying, 'When Gilligan is out he's going to kill youse all.' And journalists were trying to get interviews off criminals and they were saying, 'What are you gonna do when Gilligan gets out? He'll be coming to get his patch back and if anybody stands in his way he's going to kill them.' So they wound people up.

Again, that's another serious allegation to be making. You've made known your dislike of the Gardaí and crime reporters loud and clear now. But do you not have any hard feelings towards the person, or persons, that ordered the hit on you?

No, none at all. I made my peace with the two black African men over shooting me. It's water under the bridge.

Some reckon it was the Kinahans who ordered the hit on you.[*]

No, 100 per cent it was not them – they're white people! I've no enemies. They said I've an enemy in Daniel Kinahan. I've no problem with him or anybody else in Ireland whatsoever. I've nothing to do with any feuds. I don't take sides in any feuds. It's none of my fecking business. So why would I try and stick my nose in where my nose is not accepted?[†]

---

[*]   According to media reports, the cartel had sanctioned the hit after Gilligan had a bitter falling out with their associates Michael and John Cunningham, convicted kidnappers. Gilligan denied the Cunninghams were behind the attempt on his life. The now deceased Michael Cunningham had been arrested with Gilligan at Heathrow Airport in 1996. In 2014 Gilligan told me about the botched kidnapping plot: 'When the police came on top of them, Mick and John Cunningham, and Anthony Kelly were in the house. They were on the telephone from Waterloo Road, surrounded in the house, to Corduff Avenue [Gilligan's home]. And I said, "Can I come down and get yous out?" And they were just laughing and at one stage they were going to kill themselves. And I talked them out of killing their fucking selves.'

[†]   Gilligan said, during one of our in-depth interviews in early 2014: 'On my mother's grave, I have no bad blood on the planet with Christy Kinahan and there's no hidden agenda anywhere. There's no bad blood between us. We hugged when he left jail. I was in Mountjoy in the seventies when Christy was doing twelve months. The next time I met Christy was in

I really don't know how you're able to keep a straight face while claiming it was two black hitmen. Were you offered any compensation?

I don't really want to go into it. When I give my word it's over, it's over. Don't speak about it. It's a code I have. The mistake was made. And thank God I'm alive to talk about it, but I don't want to talk about it. And I'm thankful to them for acknowledging that it was a mistake. They're not afraid of me, by no means. They could well kill me next week if they wanted to. Not a problem.

But I couldn't live my life in fear. I don't duck and dive. I walk where I want to walk. I don't drive, I walk. So, if anybody wants to come after me, they only have to walk behind me. OBE: one behind the ear.

I've never killed anybody, but if I was confident that somebody was going to come and kill me I'd have no hesitation in trying to get to him first. I'd eliminate my problem and thank God I've never had to.

How do you feel about it now, looking back on it all?

It's just an embarrassment to me ... because other people think different. But then I go, 'Well, if people think different about this, well God love them. They don't know John Gilligan.'

Portlaoise Prison. He was back from England and he was doing a sentence. He done another two or three years while I was there. We used to buy a birthday cake and we'd all cut it and put it in our sweet bowls. And he goes, "John, give us yer bowl." There'd be thirty-two of us on the landing and the fellas we didn't like, we wouldn't give them a bit. When he was going he got steaks for everyone, he didn't get steaks for three people he didn't like. He gave me a steak and we all shook hands and hugged each other. And he left the prison and I couldn't say a bad word about the man. I don't believe the man could say a bad word about me.'

I'm a good age now, 70. And I survived six bullets going into me. So the next time I won't survive, you know, if there is a next time. I hope there's not a next time, but if there is, there is.

The gangster described as your driver and minder was murdered around the same time you were released from hospital. Stephen Douglas 'Dougie' Moran was shot outside his Lucan home by a lone gunman and later died at Tallaght Hospital on 15 March 2014. Moran was a cousin of the infamous Dundon-McCarthy brothers in Limerick and was a key member of the Limerick Murder Inc. gang.

I didn't know that man from Adam. When I was in prison, Tommy Coyle was a very good friend of mine and he was a very good friend of Tommy Coyle.*

But that man [Moran] used to visit Spain a lot and go to the Judge's Chambers – the pub my daughter used to own. He used to say to Geraldine, 'I heard some great stories about your man.' Now, I don't want to be blowing me own trumpet. So I'll water it down: 'I heard some good stories about your man. I'd love to have a pint with him.'

One day I was down in the Supreme Court and I said to Geraldine, 'Ring that fella and I'll have a pint or a cup of coffee with him, whatever he wants.' He said he had a bar in his house.

---

*   Coyle was once described as the biggest fence in the country, who handled stolen goods for both the paramilitaries and criminals such as The Monk and George 'Penguin' Mitchell. He also attempted to dispose of the pilfered British Treasury bonds worth £77.3m sterling, which had been brought to Ireland. Coyle died from cancer at the relatively young age of 51 in 2001.

You obviously got on like a house on fire, because he was reportedly driving you around.

The man wasn't my driver or bodyguard. I [once] said to him, 'I'm down in the court in the morning.'

'I'll bring you out,' he said.

I got into his four-wheel drive and I said to him, 'Jesus Christ! Them fucking doors weigh a ton.'

'They're all bulletproof,' he said.

'Why would they be bulletproof?'

'My life's in danger. My brother got shot.'

I think it happened in Laois, or somewhere down that part of the country. A knock came to the hall door, and they shot his brother in the face. He survived. So all his family is in England. I never met them.

But that was the extent [of my friendship] with that man. He treated me very respectful. He was a lovely gentleman to me. I would have met Dougie max five times in a short space of time.

I went up and had a look at his gravestone, which is half the size of this hotel room.

TAPE TWELVE

GILLIGAN'S BELFAST BLUES

'I don't talk about outside prison [when
incarcerated] because I think that would do
a man's head in. I don't think about it. That's
the gospel truth. On my mother's grave.'

– JOHN GILLIGAN SPEAKING TO THE AUTHOR IN 2008

John Gilligan may have wanted to keep a low profile, but he appeared doomed to be stuck perpetually in the spotlight if he remained in Ireland after his release from prison in 2013.

It was time to get out, but Gilligan was either too stubborn or too reckless. However, he had a change of heart on his release from hospital after his close shave with death. The killers were still on the loose, and he needed to keep his head down until he could clear up what he liked to describe as a mere 'misunderstanding'.

Gilligan started to go off the boil once he was out of the country. Out of sight, out of mind. But there was still an appetite there for him. In 2017, one newspaper's circulation jumped by a phenomenal 11 per cent when they ran a series on him.

No doubt Gilligan would've continued to feature regularly in the Irish press if he hadn't prudently decided to slip away to the UK, following his release from Blanchardstown Hospital, in March 2014. No longer the main villain in town, Gilligan soon found himself recast in a supporting role following the rise of the Kinahans and their cruel tit-for-tat feud with Gerry 'The Monk' Hutch's family, which started in 2015 and has so far claimed eighteen lives.

Gilligan miraculously managed to maintain a relatively low profile between 2014 and 2018 – no mean feat for a criminal once considered public enemy number one. He escaped lightly, with only the occasional screaming tabloid headline about him being down on his luck and hiding on halting sites in England. The only other time Gilligan's name popped up during this five-year time frame was when it was alleged that he had threatened an English solicitor during a heated discussion over money.

But, apart from these two episodes, things were quiet for him in the south-eastern Spanish province of the Costa Blanca, to where Gilligan had relocated.

Away from the eagle eyes of the Gardai and the Irish media, Gilligan had grand notions about getting back into his old business: smuggling hash. It was clearly one of the reasons why he picked the drug-infested city of Torrevieja, but Gilligan also went over there because his daughter Tracey had resided in that city for many years. She offered to put him up while he got back on his feet.

At the time, Tracey still owned a bar called The Judge's Chambers.*

---

*   It was claimed Tracey's former partner, Liam Judge, who died from a massive heart attack in 2004, was John Gilligan's bagman in Spain, laundering money for him. As Gilligan told me in 2008: 'That's a load of bollocks. They can have anything that's connected to me in another country. I don't have anything – but if they find it they won't even have to fight for it. They can have it. I didn't know the man from Adam. It's

Most bar receipts would simply thank you for your business, but the one at her bar couldn't resist a quip with 'The Jury's still out' printed on the bill. Unintentionally, Tracey introduced Gilligan to his then new partner, a 50-something English woman named Sharon Oliver, who worked as an embalmer. There was, perhaps, a twisted paradox here, with Gilligan's alleged reputation for threatening to put people in the morgue.

According to Gilligan, it all went south for him when he put together enough money for the deposit to rent a villa for himself and Sharon. The then 66-year-old was suddenly catapulted back into the limelight when arrested with a suitcase full of money at Belfast International Airport in October 2019.

Where did it all go wrong this time?

I was coming back to Spain. I had €8,000 to bring back with me. But a man owed me money for over three years. I spoke to him the day before I went back.

'Would you have the money what you owe me?' I said.

'I will have. I'm borrowing money off a sister of mine. She's coming into a good few quid,' he said.

'Can you bring it over to me?'

I asked for the money because I was going to rent a place for twelve months [in Spain]. I was staying in my daughter's and I promised her I'd only stay a few weeks.

---

hard to believe, isn't it? Nobody seems to believe that. From what I'm told, he was a lovely, lovely fella to my daughter and my granddaughter. But then I didn't know him. When I was in prison, my daughter was going out with him. I never set eyes on him. Nobody can ever say that we met or had a phone call or were seen together – in any country in the world. I challenge anybody to say otherwise.'

I'd been talking to an estate agent over in Spain and he said, 'You can't get a place because of who you are. You're high profile and you have no bank account in Spain and you have no NIE [Foreign Identity Number] in Spain. You will need twelve months up in advance.'

I said okay. He showed me three properties. I picked one. I said to myself, 'When I go back with the €8,000 I'll give it to him. Then when I get some more money I'll give it to him and see if I can talk him into letting me have the property.'

I got up the morning I was leaving. I got some breakfast and showered and cleaned up. My niece came and said, 'Uncle John, a man's after knocking at the door. And he said, there's your €14,000.'

So, I now had €22,000. I went to the North because there was no flight in Dublin. The flights in Northern Ireland were really cheap.

I had the money in my suitcase. I didn't get stopped by the customs, but when I was boarding the flight the woman [at the desk] said to me, 'You're not on this flight.'

'There's me boarding pass,' I said.

'Oh,' she said, 'I think you'll be taken off it.'

And then she called the customs man and said, 'Is this the man that you want to see?'

And he said, 'John Gilligan?'

I said yeah.

'You any money?'

I could've taken a chance, but I didn't want to tell any lies.

'I have about €1,000 in me pocket, but I have €21,000 in the suitcase.'

'Where's your suitcase?' he said.

'It's on board. It's for rent. I've the papers with it in me suitcase for the rental.'

'Come with us,' he said.

He was after saying to one customs officer, 'Go down and get his case, right.'

I only walked three minutes across the floor. So, by the time we got across the room the case was coming through the door – so they already had it. So, I was delighted I told the truth.

'Am I getting on the plane?'

And he said no. A couple of customs officers said, 'We think you'll be getting your money back. Our boss has just gone to make another phone call to the Criminal Assets Bureau. It's them guys that's picking on you. It's them guys who want you locked up and the money taken off you. But you didn't hear that from us.'

What happened next?[*]

They brought me to a police station and then brought me to court and got me held in custody. The maximum sentence for that was six months in prison. You got 50 per cent remission off. It should be only three months inside. But I was in prison for five-and-a-half months. I applied for bail ten or fifteen times.

You mentioned off camera that you later had a bullet removed while you were in a Belfast prison.

I had two bullets inside me. One of them moved. It came through my ribs and got jammed in them. It swelled up my whole side. I

---

[*]   You must declare cash of £10,000 or more to UK customs. Gilligan was charged with money laundering offences, which included the claim that he was attempting to remove criminal property from Northern Ireland.

went to see the prison doctor and he said he'd give me tablets. And then I put down my name five or seven times to see the governor and he wouldn't see me.

I couldn't lay on the bed because it hurt any time I moved. I couldn't even take my shoes off. I was in a cell with another man, and in the morning he used to have to open my shoes for me and let me put me feet in them. And then he'd tie my laces, because I couldn't bend down. It was swelling like a tennis ball.

So I went down to the doctor for an X-ray. They brought me to the nearest hospital. I was told, 'You'll have to defer the appointment to another day.' But he couldn't tell me the day in case I was trying to escape.

As I didn't know when I was going back to hospital, it was hurting so much that I got a razor blade and I broke it and I ripped the swelling open. I was pumping blood. I put my finger inside and I got my hand on the bullet. I pulled it, but I couldn't get it totally out. My hand was covered in blood.

I kicked the door. The prison officer opened the door.

'Bring me down to the surgery. I need a tweezers to take this out,' I said.

They brought me down and a nurse said, 'Oh my God! You'll be brought to the hospital in an ambulance or in a prison van. Go back up to your cell. You'll be getting brought in twenty minutes.'

I went back up to my cell and about an hour-and-a-half later the doors opened and there was a senior nurse and a load of prison officers.

You could see the bullet sticking out, but it wouldn't come out.

And a prison officer goes, 'What's that?'

'Can you give me a tweezers to get it out?' I said.

And the nurse says, 'Ah, that's been like that for the last two months.'

'That has not been like that for the last two months! I'm after cutting that out,' I said.

She said, 'No, no, we'll monitor you every couple of hours.'

They were after saying, 'Don't send him to the hospital – he's trying to escape.'

So nothing happened. I was in pain. They didn't come back in an hour. So the next thing was, I broke a disposable razor blade and I cut it some more and I pulled it out. It came out on a string.

I hid the bullet. I knew they'd come looking for it. But I know how to hide things in prison, where they won't find it – and I don't mean in my body! I put it inside metal. When they'd be doing the metal detector, they'd say, 'Well, that's steel.'

I said to one of the cleaners, 'I'm after getting the bullet out. So that's great. I've no pain now whatsoever.'

So then the governor sent for me.

He says, 'I heard you got the bullet out. Have you got it?'

'No, I threw it in the bin,' I said.

'Why didn't you hold onto it?' he said.

'Why would I want to hold it?'

'Did you never hear of forensics?' he said.

'I know more about forensics than you ever would,' I said.

And he says, 'But if you gave the police the bullet they'd be able to find out who shot you.'

'Sure, I know who shot me and I won't be telling anybody on the planet. So why would I need a bullet to know that? Listen here, governor, you go fuck off! I'm after being six weeks up there in agony and I put my name down five times to see you. And you wouldn't see me. You were asking officers, "What's it about?" So now you know, you want to talk to me as a friend?'

Did your English partner Sharon Oliver visit you in prison?

I didn't want the media to know who my partner was. So I got my family to make a phone call for me and tell a friend to get false identification for her to get a pass into the prison.

So when she came to visit me in the rec hall I gave her a big hug and kiss. I noticed the staff were looking at me kind of funny. Later a prison warden said, 'Youse are very friendly.'

'I love her,' I said.

She'd go to Belfast from England. She'd stay three days, so she could come in to visit me the next day. You could save up your visits.

The next day I was kissing her. Everybody was watching. I said to myself, 'There's something going on here.'

So, I said, 'What name did you give?'

'Mary.'

'Mary what? Just in case they ask me.'

'Mary Gilligan.'

'Me sister! I'm standing in the middle of the floor kissing ya when you come in, and I'm kissing you when you go out, and a big fucking hug and tell you I love you – and you're me sister! No wonder that they're looking at me. Ya gobshite, ya!'

She said, 'I wasn't thinking. I just thought I'd get in to see you if I was your sister instead of coming in as somebody else. Because people told me the only way to get in to visit you is as your family.'

Did you have a few words with the guy that made that fake ID?

When I met him in Spain I said, 'You're an awful gobshite! What name did you do it in? Mary Gilligan! And I'm kissing her ... me sister!'

And then we just got drunk that night, laughing and talking about it.

But it was no laughing matter when you ended up spending five-and-a-half months behind bars on that occasion.

So, the judge said, 'What's the maximum sentence?'

'Six months,' I said to the judge, representing myself at a time because I was on a video link. 'I'm over time. I'm after having served five-and-a-half months in prison. I should've only served three months in prison.'

'Mr Gilligan, will you hang on,' he said.

'No, Judge,' I said. 'I want to be released. I'm after doing the full sentence. And I'm innocent.'

And the judge says, 'I will be releasing you, Mr Gilligan.'

All the Criminal Assets Bureau was there in the court. I could see them on the camera. They objected. They told the court: this is only the tip of the iceberg.

'He has done the sentence,' the judge said. 'He has done double the sentence that I can give him in law. I could not sentence him to another day in prison if he was found guilty.'

I got out on bail. I had to sign at a police station. They asked me what address I was going to say, but there was already an agreement not to give the address I was going to be bailed to. But this was a different judge.

Why would there be such an agreement?

Because the journalists would be knocking at the door. I was using the trump card that my life was in danger, even though it wasn't.

So, the solicitor representing me gave the address. And while I was still in the court, the address got a phone call: 'Do not let that John Gilligan fella stay in your house. He's a drug dealer, or we'll kill you. Not John Gilligan – we'll kill you!'

The woman was crying on the phone. Two minutes later, there's a knock at the door. Two policemen.

'Did you get a threatening phone call?' they said.

She said yes. She was balling crying.

They made a phone call and they came up to the house.

You really believe the Northern Ireland police would actually break the law in order to impede your release?

I know that it was the police, because the woman got a knock within two minutes, not ten minutes or half an hour – two minutes! She'd just put the phone down and there was a knock at the door. The only one who made that phone call was the police, on behalf of the Criminal Assets Bureau.

The police had to check out the address so I was held for another week until I got another address. And then they let me go back to my sister's house in the South.

Were you still obliged to then attend court after all that?

I told my barrister, 'I won't be going into evidence. We don't need it.'

He said to the judge, 'Mr Gilligan has given instructions. We're not going into evidence. There's no case, you can rule on what the prosecution said.'

And the judge said, 'I'll raise now and make my decision.'

He came out ten minutes later. 'Mr Gilligan, you're free to go. You're not guilty.'

The judge said to the prosecution, 'There's no evidence. I would have expected to see even a text message on a telephone about something to do with money or crime or drugs.'

I had to go then and sort out the cash. This took a few trips back and forth. I was after flying back to Belfast twice and it was costing me. The prosecution knew this, and they would get an adjustment. And it would be twenty policemen coming up from Dublin. All the CAB officers, all suited and booted. And what was it to do with them? They couldn't give evidence ... nothing to do with them. They weren't even called in the case.

So, the border force police went to my solicitor and asked him would I take half of the money back and not fight the case.

I did the mathematics. I said, 'Well, I've gotta go back over there, and if I lose the case I've got to appeal it and I've got to get more flights.' So I took it. I must've spent close to £10,000 [fighting it]. Because I went over there with me partner and we had to stay in a hotel, and that.

They transferred the money into the solicitor's account. He couldn't give it to me in cash. He had to serve it. It had to be transferred into a bank account; that was part of the deal, which is ridiculous. So, I nominated me son's bank. I gave that money to my family.

I could sue them, but there's no point because it would take years and years and years.

TAPE THIRTEEN

AN EX-CON IN EXILE

'I think to be in exile is a curse, and you need to turn it into a blessing. You've been thrown into exile to die, really, to silence you so that your voice cannot come home. And so my whole life has been dedicated to saying, "I will not be silenced."'

– ARIAL DORFMAN, SOUTH AMERICAN NOVELIST AND HUMAN RIGHTS ACTIVIST

The online transcription services are a godsend for journalists. They will typically have up to 80 per cent accuracy for most neutral accents, saving you hours slaving over the computer. But it didn't work very well with John Gilligan's Dublin vernacular – maybe a 30 per cent success rate at best. I immediately threw in the towel when a mundane comment was freakishly translated into Gilligan boasting that one part of his anatomy [insert vulgar word here] was 'lovely'.

I decided against farming it out to a dictation service out of fear that excerpts of it could be leaked and opted to transcribe it all myself. It took me approximately five weeks of a nine-to-five schedule to

plough through most of the tapes. After personally transcribing close to twenty-five hours of tapes, I felt it would be a worthwhile exercise to visit Gilligan again – armed with a few pages of follow-up questions.

I made the long trek back out to Torrevieja only a week before Christmas 2022. It was my fourth trip in seven months, each one taking up a full working week.*

Waiting to meet with him, I stood at the very same spot along the promenade where we had first met in May of that same year when I embarked on this project. The rain in Ireland had reached almost biblical proportions that December, but there the sun still shone brightly in a cloudless sky, and many passers-by were dressed casually, some even in T-shirts. At that time of year the weather in Torrevieja was unpredictable and it would turn cold enough to need a jacket after lunch.

As I sat at a restaurant's outdoor terrace, swarming with patrons in nothing more than jumpers and obligatory sunglasses as they tucked into their poor man's version of traditional Spanish dishes, I spotted Gilligan almost a mile away as he strolled towards me in his Crombie, which looked like it was the very same one he had on him when leaving the hospital in Blanchardstown. Amongst the tourists we both stood out like sore thumbs dressed in heavy jackets. I too had acclimatised to Spain and shivered if the weather dropped below 25 degrees.

It struck me that Gilligan had turned up on time for every one of our meetings, which was close to twenty-five times at this stage – only failing to do so once, which went to show his determination to get his side of the story out there. But at least he had the good manners on that occasion to text first thing in the morning and ask

---

* I would go back again in February 2023 with a film crew to work on the documentary.

if we could postpone that day's interview until after lunch because he was down in the dumps. He had lost his shirt the previous evening after gambling heavily on football matches and had gone to bed with a skinful after the final whistle. But he had bounced back to himself by the time we met up. We ended up recording more hours on that day than we did on any other.

On the surface Gilligan appeared to be his cheerful and chatty self when we got together in December, but you could tell that there was something else on his mind.

I presumed I would have got through all my follow-up questions in one simple sitting, but I was still there listening to him talk some three days later.

For his part, Gilligan had some questions too, asking if I would be writing about X, Y and Z in the book – mostly relating to his murder trial and legal battle with CAB. He seemed relieved when I assured him that I'd be covering all the broad brushstrokes, and, in the process, examining the ever-increasing graduation of hue between black and white, more commonly known as the grey.

During it all, I got the impression that he was either lonely, or preoccupied with the upcoming court case. I soon learned that it was loneliness when he mentioned that his partner was back in England. Later I knew Gilligan was also preoccupied with the latter. While we walked back down the promenade to the taxi rank, he asked me, 'Will you please send a copy of your book to me in prison if I'm in jail when it comes out.'

In 2021, Gilligan had been arrested at his Spanish villa and charged with drug trafficking, illegal possession of a gun, and membership of a criminal gang. He was charged alongside his partner Sharon Oliver, his son Darren, and an associate named 'Fat' Tony Armstrong, who was a prime suspect in the 2006 murders of Westies' gang leaders Stephen Sluggs and Shane Coates. Those two young men were found

buried six feet under cement in an industrial estate in southern Spain.
Despite the fact that Fat Tony had been linked to the warehouse in
question, there apparently wasn't enough substantial evidence to
prosecute him. Coincidentally, the deceased men lived only a stone's
throw away from the Gilligans in the Corduff housing estate.

The trial was one of the very few topics Gilligan didn't want
brought up. 'I don't want to go into that, because that case is still
pending. I haven't got me passport. I have to sign on every month and
I've done time in prison for it. You can say that it's the smallest case in
Spain. The judge acknowledged it,' he said.

Gilligan was perhaps the most unpredictable character I have ever
met, but at least he will now be much less of an enigma as a result of
this book and corresponding documentary. While I'm always hesitant
to give credit to a criminal, at least he came forward and told his
story, unlike John Traynor and others, who hid in the shadows like
cowards.

As I bid farewell to Gilligan on my last trip to see him in early 2023,
I couldn't help but feel our paths might never cross again, because he
could die in prison. At his age even a twelve-month prison sentence is
akin to dog years.

But it wouldn't affect the book, because at this stage, I had asked
him practically every question under the Spanish sun.

I reminded myself that I was convinced we'd never meet again
when Gilligan had been shot six times, some eight years earlier, but
the man has always been full of surprises. Something tells me we have
not heard the last of him.

Are you retired now when it comes to crime?

No, Jason. I robbed two banks yesterday! [*laughs*]

Do you have any future plans?

Rob another bank tomorrow!

Joking aside, it must be difficult being in your seventies, based in a foreign country and not speaking the local tongue?

No. My life is, for the want of a better word, over. And I'm not going to cry up that. I lost about thirty years of my life through my own stupidity. I wasted my life, but I can't cry over that now. It's not gonna make a difference to me. And believe me, if I thought crying or spending two hours on television would change my whole past I'd cry for hours.

You've been in Spain now eight years. How are you finding it?

Hot and cold, and we'll leave it at that.

Do you miss Ireland?

No. Ireland's the last place I'd want to go back to. I just don't like the way Ireland is. Ireland's a police state.

Your daughter no longer has her pub, The Judge's Chamber, in Torrevieja.

The pub didn't go that well in the end. My daughter hadn't paid a mortgage – probably too much shit about me. The bank was taking it back. So instead of fighting it, she decided to give it back. I tidied it up.

She was renting it to a couple of friends before I came out of prison and they never paid her, because she was in Ireland and they were here [in Spain]. They were just drinking what was in the pub.

And then when I came over I got a Swedish crowd to rent it off her. So instead of getting the money off the Swedish crowd and paying it off what she owed, Tracey – who wasn't getting any money off social welfare – had no choice but to live on the rent from the Swedish people.

It's a gold mine that pub ... it's just a pity. The police didn't help. See, the police was coming over and sitting in the pub. The presence and the smell off them in the pub was putting people off coming into it. So the police bullied her in Spain. Things didn't go right after that.

I know you don't want to talk about your present life, but I suppose you must regret the fact that you don't have much contact with your family.

I don't have much contact with family and I don't really want to go into it, because, with all the shit about me, they always get a backlash. Like, you asked me the other day for a list of people to [help] tell my side of story. And I said I could give you 100 names, but I won't be giving you any, because I don't need them people to be bullied, with journalists calling to their doors, or the police harassing them when they would tell the truth about me or take up for me. So I don't need other people to get into trouble over me. And then the police would be stopping them and saying, 'No, you haven't got enough rubber on your tyres.' They would get done – and that would be all because of John Gilligan. It's like going to my family funerals: I didn't go to any of their funerals. And I wouldn't go to any of their weddings. I was asked to go back, but I said, 'Please forgive me, I don't want to – it would be a circus.'

You have been widely described by the press as the most notorious and reviled gang boss in the history of Irish crime – is that a fair comment?

No, I don't believe that. That's fiction. I've been hearing that for the last twenty years. Well, I might have a reputation of being notorious. I'd probably half agree with that. But vile! I wouldn't agree with that. That's just journalists adding things to make a spicy story, exaggerating the truth. Sometimes the journalists are economical with the truth. And sometimes they just exaggerate it by tenfold.

When we first met in 2008, you claimed that you were 'the most hated man in Ireland'. Do you still believe that to be the case?

I remember saying that to you, but I didn't explain myself properly. I was referring to the police, politicians, journalists, judges, and, more than likely, a lot of legal people – that they would hate me second to none. And I believe nothing has changed there.

But I think some normal people could hate me because they're under the [wrong] assumption. I pity them in a sense for it: they think whatever is written in a newspaper is the truth, and nothing but the truth. When I was younger I always thought the newspaper could only print the truth. I always believed that any story in a newspaper was after being properly researched – not something that happened last night and then [they're] given all the facts the next day. I mean, there's people that write in the newspapers that have more evidence than the police can gather! And if it was true, everybody would be convicted. They just make it up as they go along. But that 'evidence' they print never reaches a court of law, because it's pure fiction.

Do you revel in your notoriety?

No, I don't. It's been a thorn in my side. The real fact is, as I look at myself, I'm a fool! I've served close to thirty years. How could I say, 'I'm great' when I got caught and was in jail? It's a myth. It's crazy for people to think that I feel great over being, for the want of a better word, a gobshite, doing time in prison.

You accept that selling drugs was wrong?

It wouldn't be fair in the man-made laws, but there's nowhere it says in the Commandments that you can't sell drugs. It's not a crime in the Ten Commandments!

But there weren't any drugs at the time Moses wrote those Ten Commandments.

How does anybody know that? I think they were all stoned! It's not there – thou shall not sell drugs. We're talking about what law is.

Thou shall not steal is in the Ten Commandments.

If you take somebody else's property, that's a crime. Yeah, that's not right. It's not right for you to abuse anybody, or hit anybody. I'm not a religious fella now, but I don't see anything wrong in selling hash.

Thou shall not kill is in the Ten Commandments.

Yeah, that's right, it's 100 per cent. Nobody should kill nobody.

Another thing that was a big no-no in the Ten Commandments was infidelity.

If you go with another woman, or whatever, I don't see it as a big deal. Like, I wouldn't be up for obeying the Commandments. But I'm not really talking about the Commandments. I'm talking about legislation.

Do you believe in heaven and hell?

I think I'm going to hell. But, no, I don't believe in it. Some days I do and some days I don't. You know, I suppose a lot of people are of the same mind as myself. Normal people. But I'm not saying I'm normal. Some days, they will believe it, and some weeks they wouldn't. Sometimes, when a member of my family is sick or anything, I pray to God to please help them. And then when there'll be no crisis, so to speak, I probably say, 'Ah, fuck that!' That's me being totally honest.

I don't know if there's a purgatory or not. I know when you sin, rumour has it that you're going to hell. I don't know anybody who's come back and told us. But rumour has it you're gone to hell. I still say you have to do something wrong to sin against our Lord Jesus Christ – but selling drugs is not against Lord Jesus Christ, in my book.

If there is a hell, John Traynor surely must be there right now.

I would say he is. And I'd say a lot of judges in my trial and an awful lot of the prosecution legal team and hundreds and hundreds, if not thousands of guards, are all down there.

I want to ask you about your favourite crime film. Is there anything that you watched and thought, that's realistic?

I always liked *Heat*. I love that film. I used to read books when I was at sea, but I'd be reading cowboy books, you know. But then when I got into trouble, I'd be reading books of evidence all the time, because I'd be studying. People used to think I studied the law all the time. I didn't study the law – I'd study the section I was charged under. I'd look for rulings in the High Courts and the Supreme Court or [what] a European Court gave on that particular section. And if I found something in it that would favour me then I would use that judgment. People think I know an awful lot about the law – I don't. I know a bit of what concerns me. Whatever crimes I done, and if I was guilty I'd always look for a way out if I could use the system against them. They have set rules and if I could use them rules to beat them, I used to enjoy that.

Did Robert De Niro come across as a real gangster for you in *Heat*?

Yeah, he came across like a genuine fella with principles – that there's certain things they do and certain things they wouldn't do. They came across as very loyal people to the people around them. You know, like, I was very loyal to Brian Meehan and John Traynor.

Who would you like to play you in a movie?

Maybe Danny DeVito. Some short arse, anyway, would have to play me.

I thought you were going to say Robert De Niro and not Danny DeVito.

I think he's bigger than me, isn't he? Everybody's bigger than me. I wouldn't know, Jason. It wouldn't concern me. I mean, I'm an old man now. I have one foot in the grave.

Do you have any type of complex about your height?

No, I don't think I do. I think at five foot one I'm fairly tall. I could wear platforms now but they're out of fashion. The problem was, when platforms were in [fashion] I put platforms on and when I looked in the mirror I was a bit taller, but every other six-foot fucker was wearing platforms! No, I've no complex. I'm what? Four foot, thirteen inches. Ha ha!

What about this kind of Napoleonic complex that commentators claim you suffer from?

No. There was a time I was big-headed. Now I'm just perfect. I'm only messing.

It was often suggested in print that you could be more aggressive, more domineering to make up for your lack of height?

No. Sure, most would people say, 'What's that little fucker saying?' What they were talking about them days, there was no fights then. There'd be straighteners and you'd shake hands with the man afterwards. And I could fight because I was small and strong. That was lucky sometimes because if I was fighting a big fella, his arm would have to stretch down to give me a dig.

You'd shake hands after and you'd become friends forever. I don't know anybody that had a straightener and then shook hands after it and they were still enemies. You just respect each other. It doesn't matter who won. It doesn't matter if he got a broken tooth or black eye.

And that's all you get. And if you put the man down you didn't kick him. They're animals now: when you're down they want to stab you. Why would you want to be so aggressive?

I would always back away, because I knew what I could do. I used to laugh inside. Every time I tell this fellow, 'I'm sorry, I didn't do anything wrong. I apologise. I'll shake your hand. I'm sorry,' I knew he got stronger and stronger and was getting tougher and tougher. But it was only mouth. And I'd go, 'Well then, come on, hit me.' And it would be all over in minutes. But there was none of us professional fighters; we were just street fighters.

You're making yourself out to be like Charles Bronson.

I came across a thousand guys that would be capable of knocking the head off me, but they didn't because I didn't give them a problem and they didn't give me a problem. Both of us would fight if that was the case, but I don't think there'd be a clear-cut winner. Both would be hurt. I'd be hurt and the other guy would be hurt.

Do you think much about dying?

I'm not squeamish about death. I wouldn't like to die in prison, but when you die ... what happens when you die? Nothing happens to you. You don't wake up in the morning and say, 'I'm after dying last night.' You're dead. So, it doesn't matter. People say, 'I wouldn't like this. I wouldn't like that. I wouldn't like to be buried there.' But that's only what the living feels. But if I had a heart attack in ten minutes, sure, what difference does it make? You're gone.

It doesn't sound like you shed a tear when you heard Traynor died from terminal cancer aged 73 in October 2021.

I got drunk. I was delighted. When I was in England recovering [after being shot in 2014], I had heard he was down in Margate and I spent the whole day [looking] to see if I could find him. I would have hurt him. He was a scumbag.

Hurt him or kill?

Hurt him ... for all the lies he told about me, and all the trouble he caused. I wanted to have words with him. We'll leave it at that. Use your own imagination, Jason. The man was a clown.

A friend of mine, when I was down in the Supreme Court, told me he and his son was meeting Traynor in London in a café to do a big drug deal. My friend walked over to him and handed him the phone and said, 'A guy wants to talk with you.'

Traynor said, 'Who is this?'

And I said, 'The guy you fucking set up.'

He dropped the phone and ran screaming out of café, saying: 'We're going to be killed!' He ran down the street with his son.

The son you mentioned was Ronnie who, aged only 40, was found dead 'in tragic circumstances' in March 2022. He died less than five months after his father. But 'foul play' was not suspected, according to newspaper reports. It's believed Ronnie lived abroad with his father at one stage.

I did not know that he was dead. I only knew him when he and his brother were boys. But his father was supplying him drugs: coke and brown heroin.

What do you think the newspapers will write in your obituary?

'He's dead. No loss to nobody. We're happy he's dead. Goodbye John, ya bollocks!'

But I wouldn't care about it: I'd be dead. People only worry about the dead when they're living people, but I don't worry about it. Because I have it in my head – when you're dead you're dead. When you're gone, you're gone.

I'm not really worried what they say, because I wasn't really worried what they said about me when I was alive. I felt obliged to speak for my family and friends. I read very little papers. I haven't read papers in the last twelve to fifteen years. I didn't read newspapers in prison. It wouldn't worry me what they write when I'm dead, because I won't be reading them then either.

What would you say to the readers who believe you were involved in the murder of Veronica Guerin?

Well, this is the way I can explain myself: a lot of readers will believe and do believe and kind of have to believe I was involved. Because the majority of the general public, the good people, the working-class people, they actually believe. They're naive in a sense, but I don't say that in a bad way: they just think that if it's in the newspaper it should be true. But those things in the newspapers that they're talking about, what I said on the telephone – it was accepted in a court of law that there was no telephone call threatening Veronica Guerin.

And, if youse know I done something – charge me. If youse want me to come back to Ireland I'll come back to Ireland as soon as I'm able. I wouldn't run.

Would your biggest fear be to die in prison?*

Yeah, I wouldn't like to die in prison. But whatever happens me I don't run, I've never had a warrant out in my life. I don't believe in running. I don't believe in looking over my shoulders. Maybe that's the reason why I don't wear a bulletproof jacket.

I've no doubt in me mind if I was dying in prison that they would make sure I would die. The prison officers wouldn't want that. I don't even think the governors, or the nurse and the doctors would want that. But they get ruled by the Garda Síochána. And then again, I'd say, 'Fair play to them', because they would say, 'Fuck him'. In their book I don't deserve any respect because I was a robber. They worked hard for their wages, according to them.

If you had your whole life to live over, would you get involved in crime again?

No, I wouldn't. It doesn't pay. I got involved in crime at a very early stage, so I don't know what it would be like [without it]. But I'd imagine life is better without crime. And with crime, there's too many ups and downs. There's more downs than ups.

I was successful in many robberies, but when they caught me I paid for all them. So, I've never won. People think I outsmarted

---

* There's a strong possibility that Gilligan will be behind bars in Spain when this book comes out – if the court case in Spain finally goes ahead, after several delays already, in September 2023.

the police. No, I didn't. I can admit that. I'm a gobshite. I was wrong. I'm a fool.

And if I had my life to live over again, next time I'd wear gloves! No, it's the wrong path to go down. But saying that, I'm not crying about that at all. So, that's just the way it is, Jason.

But crime doesn't pay. If anybody is listening to this tape – if I'm alive or dead – don't get involved in crime. It's wrong. But I understand if you do [so] because there doesn't look like there's any light at the end of the tunnel, to get a job. It's not by choice that you'd want to become a robber.

But nobody is going to take the smile off my face. I'm going to die with a smile on my face. And, if for some reason, I don't die with a smile on my face, I am going to pay the undertaker to put a smile back on my face.

ACKNOWLEDGEMENTS

I'm tremendously grateful to Niall Stokes of *Hot Press* and film producer David Harvey, literary agent Linda Langton, as well as Merrion Press publisher Conor Graham, commissioning editor Patrick O'Donoghue, their copy-editor Dermott Barrett and publicist Peter O'Connell for all championing this project.

ANY DAUGHTER

M000229645

Charles Abood

Anybody's Daughter is a work of fiction. Names, characters, places, and incidents are the products of the author's imagination or are used fictitiously. Any resemblance to actual events, locales, or persons, living or dead, is entirely coincidental.

All rights reserved. No part of this book may be reproduced or transmitted in any form or by any electronic or mechanical means, including photocopying, recording or by any information storage and retrieval system, without the written permission of the author, except where permitted by law.

Please do not participate in or encourage piracy of copyrighted materials in violation of the author's rights. Purchase only authorized editions. Sale of this book without a front cover may be unauthorized. If this book is coverless, it may have been reported to the publisher as "unsold or destroyed," and neither the author nor the publisher may have received payment for it.

2022 White Bird Publications, LLC

Copyright © 2022 by Charles Abood
Cover by E. Kusch

Published in the United States
by White Bird Publications, LLC, Texas
www.whitebirdpublications.com

ISBN 978-1-63363-576-0
eBook ISBN 978-1-63363-577-7
Library of Congress Control Number: 2022933288

PRINTED IN THE UNITED STATES OF AMERICA

Acknowledgements

As with anyone who has published a book, I have many people to thank for their help and support. For starters, I am indebted to the extremely talented members of my writing critique group, The First Draft Writers. Pam Kelso, Margaret Berkhousen, Elizabeth Holland, Joette Rosanski, and Judith Scharren all read for me repeatedly while this project was in the works.

I also want to thank readers of past efforts, including my sister, Patricia Branam, and friends Susan Denny, Art Meyers, Jane Meyers and Linda Mates.

A special thanks as well to my cousin, Bonnie Ammer, for her encouragement beginning decades ago.

Of course, none of this would be possible without Evelyn Byrne-Kusch of White Bird Publications, and her amazing editors. I also would like to thank private editor, Anna Bierhaus.

Most important, however, is my incalculable gratitude to my extremely patient wife, Gail. No one could have a better partner in life. For years she has read the good, the bad, and the even worse, never failing to reward me with the often-painful honesty I needed to become a better writer. Thank you for everything you do, including putting up with me and my idiosyncrasies for much longer than I deserve.

ANYBODY'S DAUGHTER

White Bird
Publications

ANYBODY'S
DAUGHTER

Whiteford
Publications

Chapter One

Footsteps on the stairs.

Eyes now wide open, Traci sat straight up and swung her legs over the side of the bed. The heavier steps were Jason's, for sure. She hoped the others were Belle's. She had been gone a long time, longer than she should have been.

The door slammed open, and Jason shoved Belle into the room. "We leave in two hours. Scrub up, get some food. Tonight, you're a couple of cute little high-school girls. Do the uniform thing."

Belle fell onto the bed. "Fuck you, asshole," she mumbled.

Before Traci could blink, Jason was across the room with his right hand clamped on the back of Belle's neck pushing her face into the mattress.

"What did you say?" he screamed at her ear.

Belle fought to lift her head.

"I asked you a question."

Gasping for air, she squeezed out a choked, "That

hurts…please stop."

Jason tightened his grip on Belle's neck, and she started gagging. Traci wanted to reach out to help her but, instead, sat frozen, cowering in the opposite corner of the bed. She had seen Jason's explosive rages and knew better than to interfere.

"Don't you ever talk back to me."

"I won't… I won't, please stop… I can't breathe."

"You're only alive as long as I say you are, you got that?"

"Yes… I got it."

"And don't you forget it." He let go, gave Belle a slap across the back of her head, then banged the door shut behind him.

Traci reached out but hesitated a moment before gently placing her shaking hand on Belle's shoulder. She knew that sometimes the last thing Belle wanted after being out with clients was to be touched—by anyone.

"You, okay?" Traci asked.

Belle sat up and rubbed her hand across the back of her neck. "Oh, yeah, I'm real fucking okay."

Traci had been noticing Belle growing more and more fragile over the past few weeks. No surprise. When she arrived at the house, Belle had already been there for over six months.

So, what am I going to be like after another six months of living like this? Probably dead…like for real…dead.

When Belle turned to lie back down, Traci scooted closer to her. Belle flopped her arm around Traci's waist and snuggled up next to her. "I wish I could just fucking go to sleep and never wake up."

Traci closed her eyes and stroked Belle's hand. "I told you…you have to stop saying that."

"I don't know how much longer I can do this."

"No…we have to…this can't be how we—"

"Get fucking real, Sweet Pea. We're going to die doing this shit."

Traci tried to think of a response but had nothing to offer.

At least this time we're going out together. Even though she knew it wasn't true, Traci always felt safer when she wasn't alone with the clients.

In search of a few minutes of escape, Traci closed her eyes and allowed herself to drift off to sleep.

Chapter Two

"I can't believe how beautiful it is," Ellen whispered, "and how peaceful."

It was twenty minutes after sunset and the western sky was a stunning dark pink, turning to purple. There was a decent breeze from out of the south, and the forecast was for it to stay that way for the next two days. Perfect conditions for being at anchor in the north bay at Kelleys Island.

"That's the best part of September sailing, still warm but not many people," Adam said. He wrapped his arm around Ellen's waist, and she snuggled back into him. "With the sun gone, it's going to cool down pretty fast."

"No problem, I'm counting on my freshly minted husband to keep me warm."

Adam smiled. "That'll work." He pulled her closer.

Gazing out over the water, Adam thought back to the night almost three years ago to the day when his lifelong friend, Jon Evans, and his wife, Samantha, first suggested he meet Ellen. They were having their usual Sunday evening pizza at the Stardust Inn, a corner bar downtown, when Sam took a swig of beer and said, "She's great, I think you two would get along."

Jon gave a thumb up. "I agree, you should meet her."

At the time, Jon had just started dating Sam, a former big firm lawyer from Columbus who moved to Shawnee Falls to take a job as an Assistant Wendell County Prosecutor. Adam knew that Ellen had been Sam's college roommate and recently relocated to Shawnee Falls to teach at the high school.

"How about here for a drink Wednesday after work?" Sam asked.

As a thirty-seven-year-old pretty set-in-his-way bachelor lawyer, Adam was used to people offering to fix him up. Usually, he declined, but this time it was Jon and Sam vouching for her, and he didn't feel like arguing.

He shrugged, "Ah, yeah…okay, what's her last name?"

"Lane. Ellen Lane."

The following Wednesday evening Adam left his office, made a quick stop at home to change clothes, then drove to the Stardust. Inside, it took a while for his eyes to adjust to the dark interior. He walked past a couple of regulars engrossed in the Cleveland Indians baseball game on the large flat screen TV and waved to owner Bobby Lewis who was stacking freshly washed glasses. Bobby smiled, winked at Adam, and pointed to the high-top table in the corner where Jon and Sam were seated.

Adam had just joined them when they both looked past him and smiled. Adam turned and saw Ellen walking toward them. Dressed in a pink V-neck, short-sleeved shirt, faded jeans, and white tennis shoes, her blonde hair pulled back into a ponytail, she looked like she just stepped off the pages of an L.L. Bean catalogue.

She hugged Sam and Jon then turned to Adam with her hand out. "Hi, I'm Ellen."

He stood and stared at her sparkling blue eyes and high cheek-boned, suntanned face.

Jon said, "This is Adam. It appears your radiance has caused him to forget his name."

She grinned, and Adam took her hand. "Hi, I'm Adam Kennedy." He pulled out a stool, and she sat down. "I hear you're a high-school teacher.

Ellen smiled. "Yep."

After taking a second to untwist his tongue, Adam asked, "What do you teach?"

"Phys Ed, and I coach the girls' tennis team."

The conversation flowed easily from there, and, by the time they all parted company hours later, Adam was thoroughly smitten. The next evening, he called Ellen and invited her to go sailing the following Saturday on the old Catalina 30 he had purchased the year before. She accepted, and he gave her directions to the Shawnee Falls Yacht Club.

The day was sunny and warm. Ellen arrived at the dock dressed in a gray University of New Hampshire T-shirt, dark-blue athletic shorts, and white tennis shoes with a backpack slung over her shoulder. To Adam, she looked more like a school kid on her way to a soccer game than a high-school teacher and coach.

"I think I'm supposed to ask for permission to come aboard," Ellen said.

Adam smiled. "Permission granted." He pulled the boat closer to the dock, and she climbed into the cockpit.

"I've spent a lot of time on water but never on a sailboat. So, you'll have to show me what to do."

He gave her the thirty-second tour, then they headed out. The wind was perfect and, after they put *Rose Marie* through her paces for a few hours, Ellen asked, "Is there some way we can jump in the lake and cool off?"

Adam smiled, "I think that can be arranged." He brought down the sails, maneuvered the boat into a protected cove near the shore, and put Ellen behind the wheel while he went forward to drop the anchor. As he came back to the cockpit, Ellen was peeling off her shirt and shorts, under which she was wearing a one-piece Speedo swimsuit. She looked very fit and toned, with a small waist, muscular but shapely legs, and a perfectly rounded butt. She dove off the back of the boat and swam away. Although he had spent his entire life in and around water, Adam knew instantly never to challenge her to a race. It was obvious that, at some point in her life, she had been a competitive swimmer as well as a tennis player.

Once they had cooled off, Adam climbed back aboard and went below to grab a couple of towels. Ellen followed and, when he pulled a plate of cheese slices out of the refrigerator, asked, "Do you have any beer to go with that?"

"Sure do." He smiled, the attraction growing by the second.

Two hours later, in the glowing yellow light of the setting sun, Adam sailed back to the yacht club where they grabbed a table overlooking the water and ate, drank, talked, and laughed until they were politely ushered out at closing time. Deliriously happy, Adam walked Ellen to her car under the shimmery stars, as hopes of seeing her again danced in his head. As it turned out, the attraction was mutual, and they had been together ever since.

Adam recalled how, for a long time, he felt intimidated by their ten-year age difference. After stewing about it for another two and a half years, he finally convinced himself that Ellen might agree to marry him and forged the courage to pop the question. Even then, he was surprised when she responded with an enthusiastic "Yes."

Adam leaned down and kissed the top of Ellen's head, thinking perhaps he should pinch himself just to make sure he wasn't imagining this, that life really could be this good after such a disastrous beginning to the sailing season. His prior boat, the Catalina, had been destroyed in an arson fire soon after launch in early May. After spending the entire summer looking at boats, he and Ellen decided to use the insurance money, a chunk of Adam's savings and a low interest rate, to treat themselves to a major step-up. The ten-year-old, 42-foot Beneteau they finally found was everything Adam ever dreamed he might someday own. It had two staterooms, one forward and one aft, two heads, a large galley, and a spacious salon with a table big enough to seat six for dinner comfortably. They had done a few day sails in the three weeks since they purchased her, but this was their first full weekend outing on their new boat.

"Are you sure you aren't going to regret not having a real wedding?" Adam asked.

"Absolutely not. Spending the last three months trying to plan the wedding of my wacky mother's dreams has been a real pain. When we get back from our honeymoon cruise, we'll call my family, break the news that it's a done deal, and let them throw us whatever kind of party they want." Ellen twisted around and planted a kiss on Adam's cheek. "For now, I just want to wallow in spending my wedding night on our beautiful new boat."

"I wouldn't exactly call a weekend on a sailboat on Lake Erie a *honeymoon cruise*."

"Sure, it is. The best kind, just us."

Adam lifted his head and surveyed the 360-water view. "It is pretty nice out here."

"How'd the boat feel on the way over? That's the heaviest weather she's seen since we've had her."

"Amazing. Over eight knots on a broad reach in twenty-three-mile-per-hour winds."

"It felt pretty wild to me. I wasn't sure how much you were enjoying it."

"I've been out in a lot worse. It gave me a chance to get a feel for the boat in that kind of air." Adam had grown up sailing with his childhood buddies, Jon Evans and Nick Cromwell. As adults, they were still best friends and continued to sail and race together.

Adam and Ellen sat in silence as the last of the color faded from the sky, replaced by a million pinpricks of light wherever there was a break in the clouds.

"I don't think I've ever seen so many stars," Ellen said.

"It helps that the moon isn't up yet and there's almost no light from the island."

Ellen gave a little shiver as she turned and snuggled her face into Adam's neck. "I'm glad you closed up when you did to keep it warmer down below."

"It shouldn't be too bad. The water temperature is still close to seventy. It'll keep it from getting too cold inside."

After about ten more minutes, Adam said, "I'm starting to get a little chilly. Are you ready to pack it in?"

Ellen hesitated, then said, "It's a little early to go to sleep, but I bet we can find a way to occupy ourselves for a while."

Chapter Three

When Belle rolled onto her other side, Traci curled up behind her. Staring at the peeling yellowed wallpaper with faded tiny pink flowers and green vines, her mind went to how she had gotten into this horrifying mess.

After a couple months of online chatting, she finally agreed to meet Jason in person. When he walked into Starbucks wearing gray slacks, a blue button-down collar shirt, navy blazer, and striped tie, he looked just like the bank accountant he claimed to be. Her first impression: totally geek.

Traci had never been one to push boundaries and, from the beginning, the idea of spending time with this older guy, even just meeting him for coffee or having lunch, was exciting in a way that was different from anything she had ever experienced. Jason listened to her when it seemed like no one else would. He talked to her about her hopes and dreams, encouraged her, and made her feel like she mattered.

For a while, she wasn't sure if he saw her as a little sister or something more than that. But then he started saying things that made her feel wanted and warmed all over. No one had ever said she was beautiful the way he did, and no one had ever reached across a table and touched her hand as tenderly.

It was hard for Traci to recall just exactly how she ended up in that hotel room with him a few months later. She did remember, though, how nervous she was, but how her fears were calmed by his soothing voice and gentle touch. When they made love, it was like nothing she had ever experienced before. The way he touched her, the ways and places he kissed her, what he did with his hands and his fingers took her to places she never knew existed. She had no idea anything could feel so good. Everything about it was the exact opposite of the bumbling, thirty seconds of grunting and panting she allowed her boyfriend, Zack, on the few occasions she snuck him into her room when her parents weren't home.

Traci recalled thinking that Jason was the most amazing person she had ever known. By the third time they made love, she was thoroughly under his spell. Nothing mattered but being with him. She thought about him night and day and was convinced he was telling the truth when he said he loved her—the real her—in a way that no one else ever had or ever would. In her sixteen-year-old mind, Traci believed to her core that she was in love with Jason and couldn't live without him. She trusted him completely and believed him when he told her he would take care of her better than anyone. By the time he asked her to run away with him, she was powerless to say anything but, "Yes."

Traci's thoughts were interrupted when Belle let out a long, low moan, rolled over onto her back and asked, "How much more time do we have?"

"Probably about a half hour. Don't worry, it's not like he's going to let us oversleep."

"No shit." Belle threw her arm across her eyes and said,

"You know…I've been thinking…how about we just kill that fucking asshole? Like maybe when he's not looking, we sneak one of those big knives out of the kitchen. When he turns his back on us, we stab him, cut out his heart, and feed it to a pack of rabid dogs. I mean, after all the fucked-up shit he's done to us…"

After all the fucked-up shit he's done to us. Belle's words echoed in Traci's head. She felt her entire body shudder when she recalled how everything changed the minute Jason pulled his car up beside the farmhouse. With no warning, he snatched her phone out of her hand then dragged her inside and up the stairs where he dumped her into the bedroom she now shared with Belle and locked the door.

The house itself, which Jason had assured her would be her wonderful new home with him, was a disgusting dump. There was a small bathroom and another bedroom that was shared by two other girls on the second floor. Jason's bedroom, a bathroom, a living room, and kitchen were on the first floor.

His *associates*, as he called them, were coming and going at all hours of the day and night. They slept on recliners in the living room, with a huge flat screen TV and a collection of laptop computers lined up on a long table on the opposite wall. One of the associates was a big, burly guy named Ramone. He had a round face and a shaved brown head that reminded Traci of a giant Q-ball. Another, a tall, lean woman with short-cropped black hair, called herself Spade. Sometimes she cooked for the girls, regularly reminding them how important it was for them to eat well so they look good for the clients.

There was one other guy who hung out at the house. His real name was Daveed, but he called himself Denzell and claimed he was only working with Jason temporarily, until he headed off to his real career in Hollywood. He, along with Ramone, took care of some of the nastier parts of Jason's business. Daveed was short and stocky, with coal-colored skin and sparkling white teeth. Traci knew about the teeth because he always had a stupid fucking smile on his face whenever he was doing those things that caused so much pain to the girls at the house. Jason or one of the other three was always there and awake, making sure the doors to the outside were kept locked with keyed deadbolts.

Traci felt her heart rate increasing when she recalled how devastating it was to come to the realization that Jason, this person in whom she had placed so much faith and trust, was really a monster who took pleasure in forcing her to do gross, demoralizing sex acts, first with him and then with Ramone, Spade, and Denzel joining in. When she screamed, cried, and tried to fight them off, they told her it was part of her training and to get over it. Anytime she refused to do something they directed her to do, they hurt her.

Day after day she begged Jason to take her home, but he just laughed at her. When he started sending her out to the clients, her feelings of despair bottomed out and her hopes of ever being rescued from this terrifying nightmare became harder and harder to imagine. When she was with the disgusting men she was sent to by Jason, her very survival depended upon her ability to separate her mind from her body and envelop herself in a brain numbing fog until it was over.

Traci turned her head and stared at the dust particles dancing in the shards of light sneaking around the edges of the blackout blind that hung on the only window in the room. She recalled her conversations with Belle about trying to escape when Jason left them with one of his clients. Belle's response was always the same. "I've tried it, and you can fucking forget it. He'll find us and, trust me, the price you'll pay isn't worth it."

After a few minutes, Traci tired of watching the random movement of dust floating in the air and rolled over onto her other side. The old mattress was hard and lumpy. She winced at the pain in her ribs where Jason stomped on her the day before. The pill he gave her helped, but not much.

She had no idea what it was but didn't really give a shit.

One of the other girls told her that Jason was different from the rest of the asshole pimps out there because he didn't give his "bitches" many drugs. He claimed it was because the clients wanted them alert and looking good, but more importantly he didn't want to finance drug habits for a bunch of dumb fucking whores. It didn't take long for Traci to figure out that Jason actually took pride in keeping them in line with pain instead of drugs.

Is Belle right, is this really what the rest of our lives is going to be? Am I going to die doing this? If I do, will my mother and father even know that I'm...gone? But they probably think I'm already dead. I should have left them a note. I should have told them I love them. I never should have left home.

Chapter Four

For over an hour, Adam had been lying awake, curled up behind Ellen, soaking up the warmth their bodies shared. His heart swelled as he replayed the day in his mind. Ellen had been able to get someone to handle her afternoon practice so she could cut out right after school. He finished a trial that morning and arranged for his friend, Judge Nick Cromwell, to perform their wedding ceremony in his chambers on the second floor of the one-hundred-ten-year-old Wendell County Courthouse. Jon Evans was there as best man. Samantha and Nick's wife, Alison, shared the maid of honor responsibilities. As per Adam and Ellen's request, the judge made it quick and to the point. After an extended round of hugs and more than a few tears, Adam and Ellen took their leave. They made a quick stop at Adam's house to change clothes and load the car and by five o'clock were at the Yacht Club carrying weekend provisions onto the boat.

From the summer resort town of Shawnee Falls, Ohio, on the south shore of Lake Erie, mid-way between

Cleveland and Toledo, it was a two-hour sail to a cluster of islands ten miles off shore. By a little after seven o'clock they were anchored in a quiet cove on the north side of Kelleys Island, and Adam was firing up the grill on the stern rail to cook the salmon he had marinated in a mixture of olive oil, lemon juice, and maple syrup.

When Ellen twitched, Adam kept perfectly still so he wouldn't wake her. He leaned closer and gently kissed the back of her head, feeling Ellen's back expand against his chest with each breath she took. He closed his eyes and conjured a vision from earlier of climbing into the bunk and looking down at Ellen, her blonde hair spread on the pillow under her head and her sparkling blue eyes gazing up at him.

"God, you're beautiful," he said.

Smiling, she roughed-up his full head of dark brown hair. "You're pretty good looking yourself."

For Adam, making love to Ellen was all about giving her pleasure and it wasn't any different that night. Desiring to make it last, he kept it slow and gentle, allowing it to build on its own accord. When it finally did, they were clutching each other so intensely that it was impossible for either to tell where one body began and the other ended.

"I love you more than you can possibly imagine," he whispered, as his breathing began to return to normal.

"I love you more," Ellen responded rolling onto her side and pulling him into a spoon behind her.

For his entire life, Adam had been searching for something, but never understood what it was. Now he finally had found it, and it was better than he ever dreamed it could be.

For the first time in his life, Adam Kennedy felt utterly at peace.

Chapter Five

Traci popped awake at the sound of Belle coughing. She pushed up onto her elbow and leaned over. "Are you alright? Do you want some water or something?"

"No… I'm okay…just tired. I need to fucking sleep for a while."

Traci flopped back down onto her back. "Yeah, I know what you mean." Staring at the brown water stain on the ceiling, Traci reluctantly allowed her mind to slip to the past, her pre-Jason past. Since coming to the house, she had grown to dislike doing that. The shame accompanying those thoughts usually caused her to feel like her intestines were being gripped and twisted by a giant fist with long sharp nails. But sometimes she just had to do it to remind herself that she was alive and still the person occupying her skin.

Traci wondered if her mother and father would even acknowledge that she was their daughter if she ever escaped and showed up on their front porch. They were doctors, her mother a pediatrician and her father a neurologist, and they never made much effort to hide the fact that they expected their only child to follow the same path. She had always done her best to please them - she got straight A's, never missed a swim team practice even though she hated it, sang in the school choir, joined the debate club, volunteered at a local nursing home, and did her best to do whatever was expected of her. But no matter how hard she tried, nothing ever felt good enough.

All Traci wanted was to be an artist, or maybe even an art teacher, but the only thing her parents ever talked about when it came to plans for her future was which college would give her the best chance of getting into med school. She recalled her big moment of rebellion, the day she came home with the small butterfly tattoo on her lower back, and how her mother had flipped out. She shook her head at the thought of how her mom had ranted and raged over it and how shocked she was that her mother had ever even heard the term "Tramp Stamp."

Traci wondered if the police still looked for her. She guessed by now they had filed her away and moved on to some other missing kid. She pictured her mother and father going on the local news and begging for anyone who might know something about her to please come forward. She wondered if tattered flyers with her picture on them were still hanging on the light posts that lined the streets where they lived—where she used to live—in the white Cape Cod house with black shutters and a red front door.

Traci sighed. But all that was gone. Jason had told her over and over again that her past no longer existed. Sarah was dead. Dead to her parents, dead to her family, dead to the world of her past. She was Traci now, and he would be the one to take care of her.

For a long time, hearing him say those words felt like a knife piercing her heart. She was past that now; shame had dried up most of the tears. At some point, she began to believe that perhaps Jason was right when he said her parents had moved on with their lives and had forgotten about her, so she may as well forget about them.

Traci's thoughts were interrupted by the sound of footsteps on the stairs. The door swung open, and Jason stuck his head in. "Spade's fixing eats. Get your asses moving. We leave in an hour. Don't forget, you're doing the sister act." Jason's phone went off. He pulled it out of his pocket and looked at it. "Yeah. They're still—" He slammed the door shut.

Traci sat up and listened to Jason's side of the conversation as long as she could.

"No. They come as a pair." The top two steps squeaked under Jason's feet. "Don't fuck with me. You saw the pics." His voice was fading. "No fucking way, asshole. Fifty each or you can stick it up your—"

Yeah, right…the fucking sister act.

She and Belle were both slim but a little busty with blonde hair and blue eyes and looked like they could be related. At five-foot two, Belle was four inches shorter and appeared younger, even though she was a year older than Traci. According to Jason, they were the sister combo the disgusting old men he sent them to had spent their entire adult lives fantasizing about.

Belle sat up. "What's going on?"

"Same shit. Time to get fed."

"I gotta shower. I feel like I still have that jerk's stink all over me."

"Yeah, I know what you mean. I'll go with you."

Chapter Six

Adam was somewhere between sleep and awake when he heard what sounded like something knocking against the boat. He sat up. Ellen heard it too; she was already pulling on a T- shirt and boxers. Adam grabbed a pair of sweat pants and jumped down from the bunk.

"What is it?" Ellen asked.

Another bump.

"It's coming from the transom. Either we've broken loose or someone else has," Adam said as he hustled through the salon to the companionway. Standing on the second of the three steps to the top, he slid the overhead hatch back and pushed open the doors to the cockpit. As he took the final step, a flashlight beam hit him in the face.

"What the fuck," he exclaimed.

"Stay where you are." A deep voice growled.

He felt Ellen at his back. "Who is that?"

"Don't come up here," he said in a loud whisper.

The light dropped slightly. As Adam's eyes adjusted,

he saw a large figure standing behind the wheel on the port side of the boat. The hand that wasn't holding the flashlight was pointing a handgun at his forehead.

Adam froze, his eyes on the barrel of the gun. *What the fuck is happening? Is this real or a bad dream?* His mind swirled in a blend of confusion and disbelief.

Ellen nudged him from behind. "What's going on?"

"Go back down," he said sharply.

"Come up here slowly, both of you," ordered the voice behind the light. "Keep your hands where I can see them."

Definitely real.

Adam wondered if Ellen could hear his heart pounding as he forced himself to keep calm. He took the final step into the cockpit, holding his hands out, palms up.

Ellen followed. "Who are you?" she demanded. "What are you—"

"Shut the fuck up," the guy with the gun ordered.

Behind the light, Adam could make out a big shouldered, stocky body in a thick dark jacket and a worn Cleveland Indians baseball cap. A second guy stood on the swim platform. In the penumbral light from the flashlight, Adam could see he was tall and lean, with long scraggly hair. He was helping another smaller guy up into the cockpit. This one was wearing a bulky, quilted black ski jacket with a stocking cap pulled down low on his head. Once he was up, the tall guy passed him a duffle bag that appeared to be stuffed full and fairly heavy.

"Put it there," the guy with the gun directed, pointing to the seat next to Ellen.

As he dropped it on the bench seat a fourth guy climbed up from the swim platform carrying another duffle bag. He was a little taller than Ellen, probably about five-six, and looked at lot bigger around, but it could have been because he was wearing a heavy, gray fleece pullover that was too big for him. He also had a stocking cap pulled low, almost covering his eyes.

"Put it there." Gun Guy pointed to the space next to the

other bag. When the fourth hijacker passed in front of him, Gun Guy gave him a push, and he stumbled. Ellen reached out to grab him but pulled back when the guy with the gun screamed: "Keep your hands up." He motioned with the flashlight beam to the seat on the other side of the cockpit. "Sit down there, both of you."

Adam and Ellen sat on the seat on the other side of the fold-down cockpit table.

"That's it," the tall guy said from the swim platform.

"Okay, let the boat loose," the guy with the gun said.

"Fuck no, that's my boat. We can tow it."

"If it'd been big enough, we wouldn't fucking be where we are. Untie it, let it go."

"No fucking way. It's staying."

"It'll slow us down too much. Get rid of it…now."

"Fuck you. I'm not going to—"

Gun Guy swung the gun around.

"What the fuck…are you—"

There was a loud bang and a flash of light, then a splash when the tall guy's body hit the water.

Ellen screamed, "Oh, my God! You shot him!" and started to jump up.

Adam grabbed her and pulled her back down as the gun came back around to her.

"Shut up, or you're next."

Adam's heart pounded, his breath came in short gasps. His instinct was to grab the guy, but he fought against it as Ellen leaned into him, shaking almost to the point of convulsing.

Adam's mind raced through alternatives. His first thought was they must be drug runners and were hijacking his boat, his beautiful new boat on which he and Ellen hadn't even spent one full night. His next thought was, if that was true, they likely intended to kill them both when they were no longer needed.

But they aren't there yet. If they were, we'd already be dead. Have to keep it that way as long as I can.

The guy with the gun pointed the light at the taller of the two remaining guys, the one closest to him. "You, get rid of the boat."

Without a word, he stepped past Gun Guy and climbed down onto the swim platform. Adam could see his dark outline as he untied the line that was holding what looked like a well-worn seventeen-foot Boston Whaler with a couple of decades old 50 hp Evinrude motor.

The light was back in Adam's face, blinding him. "Now, you're going to take us to Michigan."

Adam was stunned. He again considered jumping the guy, but the thought dissipated quickly. The space was too tight. The pedestal and wheel were between them, with less than a foot of clearance on each side. Adam watched the other guy climb back up from the swim platform and guessed that he probably had a gun too.

No, can't do that. Not a good idea to jump anybody…yet. Have to wait for the right time.

Adam felt Ellen's trembling hands grab his arm. He couldn't imagine what she was thinking, how frightened she must be.

"I said keep your hands where I can see them," Gun Guy yelled.

Ellen moved her hands to her lap.

The light was back in Adam's face. "As I said, you're going to take us to Michigan…now."

"That's crazy," Adam blurted out. He knew the closest harbor in Michigan was almost thirty miles away across open water, and that would be after winding his way through the Bass Islands. "It's pitch-black out there. As soon as we get out from the lee of the island the winds could be over twenty with gusts to thirty."

"This is a sailboat. It's made for wind." He pointed the gun at Ellen's head. "You'll take us…or she dies."

Ellen let out a loud gasp.

"No!" Adam screamed and lunged forward, his arms outstretched, putting himself between Ellen and the barrel of the gun. "There's no reason to kill anyone. I'll do whatever you want. You want to go to Michigan? Fine. I'll take you…I just wanted you to know it's going to be a rough ride."

"I can handle it.

The light was back in Adam's eyes.

"You got any weapons, any guns on this boat?"

Adam shook his head. "No."

"If I find out you're lying, she dies."

"We don't own any guns. And even if we did, we were going to Pelee Island tomorrow, and you can't take guns into Canada."

"Huh," Gun Guy grunted. He shined the light on the smaller guy, the one sitting across from Ellen. "Kid, take the flashlight and go down there. Check it out, look everywhere, open everything. If there is a gun and you don't find it, I'll fucking shoot you along with the girl."

He stood up and took the flashlight but didn't say anything. As the beam of light bounced its way down the companionway steps, Gun Guy yelled, "They have phones, don't come back up until you have both of them." He leaned over Adam, his bulk seeming much larger than it actually was, and pushed the barrel of the gun against the side of Adam's head. "Hopefully, for you, there aren't any guns, and I won't have to kill your girlfriend." He backed off and waved the gun at the other guy, the taller one. "You, toss those bags down the steps."

Without a word, he stood and threw the two duffle bags through the companionway and down the steps. Adam cringed when they hit the floor with a loud thud. When he felt Ellen shudder, an almost overwhelming combination of rage, frustration, and helplessness washed over him. Once again, he had put Ellen's life at risk, something he promised her and himself, he would never do. He closed his eyes and clenched his fists. *I have to stay calm. And, somehow, I have to get control of this shitstorm.*

Keeping his voice as steady as he could, Adam said,

"You can't kill her. If I'm going to take you to Michigan, I'll need her to help sail the boat." Not true, but Adam figured this asshole didn't know that.

"Is that right? Well, hopefully, you won't fuck it up and no one gets hurt."

A few minutes later, the flashlight beam preceded the kid back up the steps.

"Any guns?"

The kid shook his head and passed over two cell phones. Gun Guy stashed them in his jacket pocket, took back the flashlight, and turned it on Adam. "Let's get going."

Adam turned to Ellen and whispered, "We have to do this."

"No whispering! I want to hear every fucking word you say…got it?"

Adam felt the barrel of the gun jammed into his ribs. He threw his hands up in front of him. "Okay, I get it, no problem. Just cool down." He stood and glanced at Ellen. She was shaking, maybe out of fear and maybe because all she was wearing was the T-shirt and boxer shorts she had pulled on when they jumped out of bed. He then noticed that all he had on was sweat pants. "There are some things we need to do first."

"What's that?"

"For starters, we have to get some clothes on. It's going to be cold as hell once we get out in that wind."

"Okay, but she goes. You stay here."

When Ellen stood, Adam said, "Make sure all the batteries are on, and bring the warmest clothes we have." Turning to Gun Guy, he said, "I hope you know it's going to be a long, cold trip."

"How long?"

"It's over twenty-five miles. Sailboats don't go very fast, and the wind will be almost in our face. It could take up to eight hours."

"That's too fucking long. It'll be daylight before we get

there."

"Sorry, that's the best I can do." Adam instantly regretted saying that. This asshole might just go ahead and kill them if they don't give him what he needs. He backed it up. "But the wind seems to be changing. If it does, I can cut that down to…maybe five hours."

"You better hope it does. Now get this thing going."

Adam gave Ellen a nod.

Gun Guy said, "Kid, go back down ahead of her with the flashlight and keep an eye on her. If she does anything funny, holler and I'll shoot this one."

Ellen sighed and started down the companionway steps. With the smaller of the two other guys shining the light in her face, she couldn't see anything. Once she was down, she turned on the overhead lights in the salon. "Now you can get that light out of my eyes."

The kid turned off the flashlight. When she saw his face, Ellen was startled by how young he looked, no older than the high school kids she taught and coached, maybe not even old enough to shave. His gaze fell when he saw her staring at him. Since they were in the way, Ellen picked the two duffle bags off the floor and carried them into the aft cabin.

"Don't forget to turn on the instrument switches," Adam called down to her.

Ellen stepped passed the guy, who stood motionless with his head down, and into the forward cabin. She pulled open the top drawer under the bunk to gather clothing but, as she reached in, she began to feel light headed. Afraid she was going to pass out, she sat on the bench seat in front of the bed, bent over and covered her face with her hands.

Oh my God. What the fuck is going on? He just killed someone right in front of us. He's going to kill us, too. We're going to die out here. Gasping for air, Ellen scrunched her eyes closed and concentrated on getting the pounding in her chest to slow down. *Have to get control, this isn't helping. Adam will want me to stay calm.* Taking deep, slow breaths, she felt her heart rate begin to normalize.

"What's going on down there?" It was the big guy with the gun.

Ellen took another deep breath and yelled, "I'm getting what we need."

She noticed the kid watching as she pulled on a pair of blue jeans and a sweatshirt. When she stared back at him, he turned his head away. Ellen grabbed a T-shirt and a fleece for Adam and boat shoes for both of them, then went back to the nav station and flipped the switches for the chart plotter and the rest of the instruments.

When she turned on the navigation lights, Gun Guy hollered, "Turn the Goddamn lights off."

Ellen switched off all the lights and climbed back up into the cockpit.

Chapter Seven

Adam had just begun to feel chilled when Ellen passed him the clothing she had gathered. He was putting on his boat shoes when Gun Guy barked, "Hurry up. We gotta get this thing going."

Adam started the 55hp diesel engine, and then nodded at Ellen. "Take the wheel, I'll get the anchor." As she slid past him, Adam said in a low voice, "Keep cool, we have to do this."

As the grinding sound of chain moving through the windless pierced the cool night air, Ellen gave the throttle a brief shot of forward. Once the anchor was up, Adam gave Ellen the usual signal to move out even though he suspected she wouldn't see it in the dark. He knew he had taught her well when he felt the boat moving forward, toward the west end of the island.

Adam returned to the cockpit and took back the helm. To the guy who was pointing a gun at him, he said. "You do know that as soon as we get around the end of the island, we could have four to six footers?"

"Of course, I know that. Why do you think we dumped the small boat? This thing can handle it."

"So, are you going to tell me where in Michigan we're going?"

"Grant Harbor. You know where it is?"

"Yep, been there. It's at the west end of the lake, just south of Monroe." Adam forced himself to stay cool, partly because he needed Ellen to stay calm, but mostly because this guy had just murdered someone right in front of them, and he knew nothing good could come from pissing off a psychopathic killer...with a gun...on a boat...in the middle of Lake Erie.

Adam glanced over his shoulder and saw Gun Guy perched on the rail seat in the corner behind him. Ellen sat to his right. The two smaller hijackers were sitting across from her on the other side of the cockpit with their heads down. So far, neither of them had spoken a word. They both had their stocking caps pulled down over their eyebrows, but, like Gun Guy, their faces weren't covered. It seemed pretty obvious that their plan was to kill him and Ellen when they got to their destination.

Adam's hands began to cramp from the death grip he had on the wheel. *The only way not to end up dead is going to be to, somehow, outsmart these assholes. But how the hell am I going to do that?*

They were approaching the end of the island when Gun Guy said, "Why aren't you putting up the sails? We need to get there...fast."

From the way the trees on shore were blowing, Adam could tell the wind had picked up and it was going to be rough as hell once they were in open water.

Adam turned and looked at the guy behind him. "Have you ever sailed before?"

"Ah, no...but I've—"

"I'm waiting until we get around the point to see how much sail we can use. My guess is, it's blowing around twenty, or even more. If that's the case, we won't want it all out." Adam hesitated then asked, "So, why'd you pick me?"

"It doesn't take a fucking brain surgeon to know that a sailboat this size can take these kinds of seas a hell of a lot better than what we had. And it's not like I had a lot to pick from. I guess it was just your lucky day."

Adam looked at Ellen. It was too dark to see her face, but he guessed she was looking at him like she thought he was crazy for talking to this murderer as if he was a real human being. Adam knew her well enough to be confident that what she really wanted was a chance to get her hands on him and rip his eyes out. Adam made an up and down motion with his right hand, out of view of Gun Guy, indicating that he wanted her to stay calm. She responded with a clenched jaw and a slight nod.

A few minutes later, they rounded the west point of the island and were met with a huge blast of wind and five-foot waves. When the bow of the boat rose up and smashed back down, a wall of water washed across the cockpit.

"Shit, it feels like more than twenty-five," Adam screamed. The boat continued to rise up and crash down on the other side of each of the close together, hard-hitting waves. "We should go back and wait until it calms down. Maybe by morning it will be—"

Adam felt the barrel of the gun up against the back of his head. "We're going now. I have a delivery to make."

The boat continued to climb each wave and then take water across the bow when it crashed on the other side. When Adam turned off the wind to stop the crashing, the boat began to roll violently from side to side.

"It's not going to be a fun ride. We're going to get wet and pretty much beat to shit."

"Do I look like I give a fuck? Just keep this thing going," Gun Guy shouted.

Adam shook his head. "Ellen, take the wheel, I'll get the sails up."

They were rocking so much that Ellen fell into Adam

as she stood to take his place at the wheel. He caught her and held on until she regained her balance. As they exchanged places, Ellen whispered, "The smaller one is just a kid."

Adam tried to get a look at his face as he moved forward to wrap the outhaul for the furled mainsail around the winch. Although it was dark, he could see that Ellen was right. He looked like he was barely out of his teens, if that.

When Adam got up to the winch, he yelled over his shoulder, "Let off on the throttle and head into the wind."

As Ellen turned the boat into the waves, lake water flew across the cockpit soaking them all. Instinctively, Adam turned to make sure everyone was still onboard. Then, as the boat crashed up and down on the waves, he pulled the mainsail halfway out and secured it. He pointed in the direction he wanted Ellen to go, about ninety degrees off the wind, and set the sail. The forward pounding stopped, replaced by rolling but not as much as earlier with the sail keeping them heeled to starboard.

Adam turned and looked at the guy with the gun. "You're going to have to move over, I need to get where you are to bring out the other sail."

He grunted and stood up.

Adam released the furling line, then slid past Ellen to the other side of the boat and pulled the genoa halfway out and secured it. When he trimmed it in, the boat seemed to leap forward. Once the sail was set, he turned off the engine.

"Why the fuck did you do that? We got to get there as fast as we can."

The sky had cleared and when Adam looked over his shoulder there was enough moonlight for him to see the barrel of the gun pointed at his chest.

"In this wind, the motor wouldn't do anything for us. We're sailing as fast as we would with it running."

Adam was making that up. It was not in his plan to get there as fast as they could and get shot upon arrival. He needed time to figure things out and to get help if that was possible. As miserable as the conditions were, Adam figured the last thing he wanted was for the wind to calm down. All in all, to Adam, it seemed like they were pretty well screwed.

"Damn, this water is fucking cold," Spider whispered to himself. After diving off the back of the sailboat when Ozzie turned the gun on him, Spider surfaced on the other side of the Whaler and hung on, out of sight, watching while the kid untied it. He had no idea why Ozzie would have taken a shot at him but there was no way in hell he was going to give him another go at it. He kept his head down and waited as the Whaler drifted away. The only sound was Ozzie yelling at the people on the boat and threatening to kill them if they didn't take them the rest of the way to Grant Harbor.

After a few minutes, he turned and looked in the direction of the sailboat. All he could see was Ozzie's flashlight beam bouncing around. *I'm far enough away. Have to get into the boat.*

Spider pulled himself up as hard as he could but was barely able to get his head above the gunwale. *Fuck...this isn't as easy as it used to be.* He tried again, this time kicking his feet as hard as he could but not getting any higher. *Shit, I can barely feel my legs. I have to get out of this water or I'm going to fucking die out here.* Spider inched his way to the back of the boat. He reached down and lifted his right foot up onto the plate over the prop on the motor then reached over and grabbed the stern seat inside the boat. Using his leg and arm together, he pushed and pulled with everything he had and flipped himself over the transom into the boat.

He lay there for a full minute before peeking over the side. No longer in the shelter of the island, he was shocked at how far he had blown from the sailboat and the shore. He thought about starting the motor but decided against it. Instead, he pulled out the old canoe paddle he kept stashed under the seats and set to work. *Fuck...in this wind I'm drifting faster than I can paddle.*

Spider had a flash of being found washed up on a beach somewhere in Canada in the morning. Ignoring the pain in his arms and shoulders, he paddled harder. He finally started to make progress when he heard what he thought might be the engine starting up on the sailboat. Still hesitant to start his old outboard motor, he kept paddling. It wasn't until he heard the anchor chain grinding through the windless and then saw the outline of the sailboat moving toward the west end of the island that he finally felt comfortable starting his motor.

Freezing and sore all over, and generally feeling like he had been run over by a train, Spider decided to go to the shelter of the island rather than head out into the big winds on the lake. Keeping his motor at a low idle to keep the noise down, he slowly worked his way to the shore at Kelleys Island State Park.

As he pulled the Whaler up onto the beach, Spider shivered uncontrollably. He climbed back into the boat and from under the seat in front of the pedestal pulled out a duffle bag containing a change of clothes he always carried in case of running into rain when he was out fishing. Hands shaking, he peeled off his clothes. After trading the wet clothing and shoes for dry, he was still cold but not nearly as much as before. He stuffed the wet things into the bag and looked around. Everything on the island would be shut down at this time of night, so there was no reason to go looking for help, at least for several more hours. He grabbed his phone but wasn't surprised that being underwater had rendered it useless. A light went off in his head. "The VHF, I could call the Coast Guard." He grabbed the handheld receiver from a pocket on the pedestal. "Haven't used this in months...hope it still has charge," he mumbled to himself. He pressed the ON button. "Shit, it's dead too."

Spider put the handheld down and bent forward resting his elbows on his knees so exhausted he could hardly hold his head up. When, after several minutes, he didn't feel any better, he curled up in the bottom of the boat and closed his eyes. *This is all so fucked up.*

Chapter Eight

The farmhouse was quiet. The remaining two girls were locked in their room upstairs. Jason and Spade were on the couch in the living room, the only light coming from a computer screen open and running a Star Wars screensaver. Naked from the waist down, Spade straddled Jason, moving her hips slowly in a circular motion while he sipped from a glass containing one small ice cube and a couple fingers of Macallan 18-Year-Old Scotch. When it came to his favorite beverages, Jason didn't believe in skimping.

"How long before we hear something?" Spade whispered while swirling her tongue around Jason's right ear.

"A few hours…at least…maybe more. Ramone's going to call when he has the cash in hand."

Jason never, ever exchanged money for product in person. That was one of Ramone's jobs. It had been five years since Jason picked a drugged-up, bruised and battered Ramone out of the gutter and brought him back to life. To

Jason, Ramone had been utterly pathetic, which was precisely why he put so much effort into saving him. Jason patched him up then sat with him while he went through the disgusting withdrawal process. The seemingly endless days of tremors, retching and seizing, were followed by almost a month of restlessness and depression.

It served Jason's purpose well that Ramone had been a teenage thug before graduating into a self-proclaimed *enforcement specialist* who was more than happy to hurt people for just enough cash to keep his drug habit going. It had worked for him until he ran into someone who was bigger, meaner, and better at causing pain than he was.

When he finally got Ramone to take nourishment and begin to exercise again, it was easy for Jason to convince him that he owed him his life, and to do whatever was asked of him. Ramone was back in the business of doing what he loved most and, having been trained by Jason, was now much better at it.

"If I don't hear from him by then, you're going to pay a visit to Ozzie's family," Jason said.

Jason also never transported product himself, especially when it would be across state lines. The last thing he wanted was to give the Feds an additional reason to be after him, so he outsourced that to handpicked couriers who were made well aware of the consequences of their failure to perform as expected.

"Mm, sounds like fun, almost as much fun as this." Spade quickened her hip movements and began breathing more heavily.

Jason downed the remaining scotch and set the glass on the end table next to the couch. Spade sat back and raised her arms, and Jason pulled her T-shirt over her head. He took one smallish breast in each hand and brought the left one to his mouth. Spade began to hum when Jason circled his tongue lightly around her nipple and then sucked it into his mouth. When he moved to her other breast, she pulled his head hard to her and began to moan. Thrusting her hips back and forth faster and faster, she let out a gasping sound before slowing down and falling into him.

After a few minutes, Jason lifted her and eased her down onto the couch next to him where she curled up and closed her eyes. He grabbed his jeans off the floor and pulled them on. He looked at his watch. It was a little after midnight.

CHAPTER NINE

With the wind holding steady at around twenty-two knots, the boat still bounced and rolled, but not nearly as much as it would without the sails up. Adam knew the autopilot would never hold in these conditions and, if the wind didn't let up, he would have to hand-steer the rest of the night. He looked down at the chart plotter. They were still twenty-three miles out if he kept his current course.

When Adam glanced over his shoulder, the guy was staring back at him. Adam noticed that the gun was in his left hand, on his lap, which meant he was probably left-handed and would only have to point the gun a little higher and pull the trigger if he wanted to shoot him through the heart.

The next time Adam looked the guy's head was down slightly. As far as Adam could tell, he could have been asleep. Adam mused briefly that it might be a good time to jump him. He was still processing that thought when, without looking up, the guy said, "Don't even think about it."

How the fuck did he do that?

Adam looked at his watch. It was 12:30 a.m. Sunrise this time of year would be around 7:20, which meant it would start getting light in a little over six hours. At their current speed, they would be arriving at about 5:30 a.m., but Adam knew he could control that and slow down or speed it up if he wanted to. The question was whether or not it would be better if they got there in daylight.

Adam's mind ran through the scenarios, the different ways this nightmare might end, one at a time. The outcome of each was worse than the one before. He looked at Ellen, her profile in relief against the dark-blue, night sky. She sat up straight, with her arms folded across her chest. While most women finding themselves in this situation would be scared shitless, he knew Ellen and guessed that, along with being frightened, she was pissed off, like really pissed off, at the people who had hijacked their new boat and her wedding night.

No one spoke for the next twenty minutes. Adam pictured the guy behind him falling asleep and thought about how he could grab the gun. Then he recalled that the only times he had ever held a gun was when a firearm happened to be among the evidence he showed to a jury during a trial. He wondered if he would know what to do with it if he got his hands on it. He decided he could deal with the aiming and pulling the trigger part, but it was stuff like a safety being on or off that he knew nothing about. And then, there was the tight space. What if he was wrestling the guy for the gun and it went off and hit Ellen? And what about the other two guys. He had no idea if either of them had a gun but decided he had to assume that at least one of them did.

A deep voice behind him startled Adam. "I know what you're thinking, and you can forget it. I'm not going to fall asleep."

Adam wanted to scream, *fuck you, asshole,* but bit his tongue instead. Gripping the wheel so tightly that his fingers were beginning to cramp again, he concluded that grabbing the gun was not going to work. *Need another plan. But, what the fuck would that look like?*

As the boat lunged forward through the wind and waves, Adam thought about the duffle bags the taller of the two other guys had thrown down below. They weren't very big. Each was only about eighteen inches long and less than a foot high. Whatever they were delivering was small but valuable. He decided his first impression was probably correct, the contents were drugs, probably opiates. He figured there could be a hell of a lot of pills in those bags.

Adam wondered where these guys had come from and where they were going. He guessed they were traveling either to or from Canada by water to avoid customs at the border in Detroit. It was common knowledge that, even with the increased presence of the Coast Guard and Customs and Border Protection since 9/11, the US/Canadian border that ran almost the entire 240-mile length of Lake Erie was still relatively porous and, because of the amount of recreational boating that went on, could provide an easy way to smuggle contraband into or out of the country. For lack of a better theory, Adam decided that must be it.

After a few minutes, Adam asked, "So, what's in the bags?"

"None of your fucking business."

"Actually, it is my business. My guess is, I'm participating in the commission of a serious felony, and I think I have a right to know what it's about."

Gun Guy gave a grunt. "What are you, some kind of fucking lawyer?"

"As a matter of fact, I am a fucking lawyer."

"Is that so? You one of those rich, corporate assholes?"

"Nope, criminal law only. Not the kind you get very rich on." Adam hesitated and glanced at Ellen. He knew she was biting her lip. He couldn't remember her sitting so quietly for this long. Even in the dark, he could see the questioning look on her face.

"So, who the fuck are you? Anyone I've ever heard of?"

"I doubt it. I'm Adam, Adam Kennedy. I have an office in downtown Shawnee Falls." Instinctively, he almost reached out to shake the guy's hand. Instead, he asked, "So, what are we delivering?" When there was no response, he said, "This obviously isn't going as planned. Maybe I can help." In his peripheral vision, he saw Ellen's head swing in his direction.

"No more questions, counselor. Just shut the fuck up, and get us there as fast as you can."

Chapter Ten

Shivering, Ellen wrapped her arms across her chest and buried her hands in her armpits. She tried to focus, but her head spun and her body shook. Maybe it was a lingering effect from seeing someone murdered right in front of them and knowing that, unless something changed, she and Adam likely would be killed upon their arrival at Grant Harbor.

Or maybe it was because she was cold and wet, and it had only been four months since the last time she and Adam were staring down the barrel of a gun, believing they were about to die. Ellen hadn't exactly forgotten that the previous May, Adam was representing a client whom he believed was wrongfully charged with the aggravated murder of a nun in the sanctuary of St. John's Church. When Adam's investigation into the killing brought him too close to the truth, the real murderer came after them. It was only due to some last-minute assistance from Jon Evans—and a healthy dose of luck—that they both weren't killed.

Or perhaps it was because she had just heard Adam

offer to help a drug smuggler and murderer. Either way, she couldn't just sit there. She knew Adam wouldn't like it, but she had to move. If the asshole shot her, so be it. She gritted her teeth and stood up.

"Sit down," Gun Guy yelled.

Ellen stayed standing. She opened her mouth, but no sound came out. She swallowed hard and tried again. "I'm cold, and I'm wet. I need to change clothes, and I have to use the head. If you don't like it, I'm sorry, but I really have to—"

She felt Adam grab at her arm but pulled it out of his reach and held her shaking hands out in front of her. "Adam, don't... I have to go, and I'm—"

"Kid," Gun Guy barked. "Go with her, watch her."

The shorter one's head flew up as if he had been awakened from a deep sleep.

"Holler if she does anything funny."

The kid said nothing but stood and followed Ellen down the steps. When she turned on the lights, Ellen saw that he was staring at her. She scanned his face, taking note of his fair skin, perfect eyebrows, and not even a hint of stubble on his chin. *Can't be much more than sixteen.*

Ellen went into the forward cabin and turned to go into the head. When the kid started to follow her, she snapped, "Are you planning to watch me go to the toilet?"

The kid blushed like an embarrassed teenager and turned away. Ellen felt like she may have screwed up. Perhaps Adam was right. It seemed like he was trying to cultivate communication with these assholes, and maybe she should do the same. She stayed sitting while she worked on gathering her wits. When she felt she was ready, Ellen stood, pumped out the toilet, and came out of the head into the salon—the main cabin of the boat. The kid looked the other way.

"What's your name?" Ellen asked.

The kid slowly turned around. "Belle."

Holy shit, it's a girl!

Ellen was momentarily speechless. A million questions flooded her brain. Finally, she frowned and asked, "That's not your real name, is it?"

The girl shook her head slowly.

"Is the guy up there with the gun your father?"

The girl, again, shook her head.

"How old are you?" When Belle hesitated, Ellen suspected she was trying to decide whether to tell the truth. Their eyes met. "Eighteen,"

Ellen doubted it but didn't say anything. Then, looking closer, she realized the girl's face was a pasty white, and sweat ran down her forehead into her eyes.

"You don't look very good. You better go back up into the fresh air. If you stay down here, you're going to get seasick."

Belle nodded and turned to the steps.

"What the fuck is taking so long?" Gun Guy yelled from the cockpit.

"I was using the head. I still need to change clothes," Ellen said.

"Make it quick. Kid, keep an eye on her."

Belle turned around but kept her head down while Ellen changed into a pair of dry sweatpants, a sweatshirt with SFHS Tennis printed across the front, and a yellow, foul-weather jacket.

"Let's go," Ellen said, motioning for Belle to go up first.

Belle had her foot on the first step when the boat took a hard roll, and she started to fall. When Ellen reached out and caught her, Belle held on for a moment then pulled away, looked Ellen in the eye, and mouthed the words, "Please help us."

Ellen was stunned. She grabbed the edge of the desk at the nav station and hung on. *What the fuck is going on? Oh no...shit, could it be?* When the havoc in her head died down, she leaned in and whispered, "Is the other one a girl too?"

"Yes."

Ellen pointed at the duffles on the floor of the aft cabin. "What's in the bags?"

"Our clothes and stuff."

"Oh, my God, you two are what's being delivered to Michigan?"

"We've been sold."

"Get your asses up here, now," Gun Guy screamed.

Ellen was so incensed she could hardly see. *This asshole is trafficking these young girls, probably as sex slaves.* What she wanted most was to run up the steps and strangle the guy. But then there was the gun, and he had already made it pretty obvious that he didn't mind killing people.

What the fuck are we going to do? There is no way in hell I'm going to help this asshole do this. And what about Adam? Did he just offer to...no, he would never do that. He was just trying to get him talking, doing a—let me help you thing—as a ploy to get him to let down his guard. If he does, maybe we can surprise him, get the gun, and take him down. I should work on that too. Okay...okay, I will. I'll try it. Adam must have a plan. I sure hope he knows what he's doing.

Ellen took a minute to think through her next move, then called up the companionway steps, "Does anybody up there need anything? Can I bring some water or something else to drink?"

"Just get your ass back up here where I can see you."

Ellen reached into the refrigerator and pulled out three bottles of water. She handed one to Belle. "Stay hydrated. It will keep you from getting seasick."

Belle looked up and whispered, "Thank you," then turned and climbed up the steps to the cockpit.

Adam watched as first the kid then Ellen came back up the

companionway steps. Ellen was carrying two bottles of water. The kid had one in his hand. He sat down and screwed off the top. Ellen handed a bottle to the other kid. "Drink a lot of water, it'll keep you from getting seasick."

Adam was surprised when Ellen offered her remaining bottle to the guy behind him. "Would you like some water?"

All she got in response was a grunt, which Adam interpreted as a "No."

Ellen sat down, unscrewed the top and took a drink, then passed the bottle to Adam. From the way their eyes met, Adam sensed there was something she wanted to tell him but knew it would have to wait. He took the bottle from her, relieved that Ellen appeared to have caught on to what he was trying to do to keep them from being shot and thrown into the lake as soon as they docked at Grant Harbor.

Chapter Eleven

When they cleared the channel between the Bass Islands, Adam stood and checked the chart plotter.

Twenty-two miles to go. Another four to five hours, depending on the wind direction and speed, to figure out how the fuck I'm going to get us out of this.

Adam glanced to his left and saw lights on the mainland but nothing that would be of any use to them. The wind was bouncing between seventeen and twenty-two knots. They had a good heel, and the rolling had eased up, but the bow was bouncing like crazy as they plowed through four to five-foot waves. Every now and then Adam tried the autopilot, but it still wasn't holding, so he hand-steered, which he knew was going to get old if he had to keep it up over the next few hours.

As he fought the wind and the wheel, Adam tried to focus on how he was going to keep the two of them alive. Then another thought crossed his mind. He knew there were several militia groups in southeast Michigan and wondered if he had been wrong about the duffle bags containing drugs.

They looked heavy. What if they contain guns or explosives of some kind?

Adam looked over his shoulder and, in the moonlight, saw Gun Guy staring at him. "I know you don't want to talk about what we're carrying but, those duffle bags … could you at least tell me if there's something in them that could blow up?" When he got no response Adam added, "I mean, with all this bouncing around, if we're carrying explosives—"

"Don't worry about it. Nothing's going to blow up."

Adam felt encouraged. He had actually answered a question. But then Adam had a flash of him shooting the tall guy at point blank range and hearing him fall off the back of the boat into the water.

So much for the feel-good moment.

Adam looked at Ellen. She was staring at him, and, even in the dark, he could see the grim countenance on her face.

"Are you okay?" he asked.

She nodded slowly.

Adam wished he could talk to her or hold her and comfort her. He wondered what she was thinking. He wondered if they were going to get out of this alive. *It would be much better if we can somehow get control of this mess out here. We'll be even more outnumbered once we get to Grant Harbor. But how the fuck do we do that?*

Adam looked out over the water, surprised at how calm he felt. Not what he would have expected. He decided to try to get Gun Guy talking. "Will someone be there to meet us when we dock?"

"You better hope they're still there. If not, we're all fucked."

"So, switching to this boat is going to make you late with your delivery?" Adam asked. When he again got no response, Adam said, "I take it that's going to be a problem."

"You could say that."

As Adam pondered what to say next, he noticed that the taller kid was shaking. Pointing at him, Adam said, "He's soaking wet and shivering. He needs some dry clothes."

Ellen started to stand up. "I'll get a jacket and a blanket."

"No, you take the wheel," Adam said. "I need to use the head. I'll get more jackets when I'm down there." He then looked at Gun Guy and said, "Unless you'd like to take the wheel."

He broke into a sinister smile, then lifted the gun and waved it in the air. "Nope. I'm trusting you two to get us where we need to go…and if you don't… I'll blow your fucking brains out."

Ellen stood and moved to the wheel. As Adam slipped behind her to trade places, he said in her ear, "Hang in there. You're doing great."

Ellen squeezed his hand and whispered, "They're both girls."

It took a second for what Ellen said to register in Adam's brain. As he started down the steps, Gun Guy pointed at the taller of the two and said, "Heh, kid, go down and keep an eye on him. If he tries anything, holler, and I'll shoot the girl."

When Adam reached the bottom, he switched on the lights then turned and took a close look at the kid who had followed him down. He was looking at the floor, but Adam could still tell that, yes, it was a girl. A very young girl.

"How old are you?" Adam asked quietly.

Without looking up she answered, "Eighteen."

"You aren't really eighteen, are you?"

She slowly shook her head from side to side.

"What's your name?"

She raised her eyes and said, "Traci."

"So, how did you get involved with this guy?" Adam asked pointing up the steps.

She looked back down at the floor.

"Wait a minute," Adam whispered, "are there drugs in

those duffle bags?"

"No, just our clothes."

"Oh…shit…you're not here to help this guy, are you?" Traci shook her head.

"You two are what we're delivering."

"Yes."

Adam's face grew hot with anger. *I can't fucking believe this. I'm participating in the trafficking of these young girls—kids actually—probably as sex slaves.* Adam fought the urge to run up the steps and grab the guy by the throat. *Can't do that. Ellen and the other girl are up there; he'll start shooting. Too big a risk, have to be patient and pick the right time.*

Adam looked at the girl standing silently in front of him. As he took a second to calm himself, the pain in his bladder reminded him of why he came below. "If you need to use the head, I mean toilet, there is one in there." He pointed to a door on the right.

"Okay," she said, then turned and went into the head while Adam went to the forward cabin to use the other toilet. When he finished, he changed into a dry sweatshirt and fleece then grabbed a foul-weather jacket and a set of Ellen's sweats for the girl. She was waiting for him when he came back into the salon. He handed the clothes to her. "Your name isn't really Traci, is it?"

"No."

"What is it?"

"Sarah." She looked him in the eye and asked, "Can you help us?"

A shiver went up Adam's spine. "We're going to try."

Seeing that Sarah was starting to turn a light green from all the bouncing of the boat, Adam pointed at the companionway steps. "You better go back up and get some air before you get sick. You can change clothes up there.

Adam followed Sarah back up to the cockpit and stepped around the console to retake the wheel. As Ellen slipped past him, he said, "She's very cold and wet. Help her into the dry clothes."

"She needs to warm up. She can't do that up here in this wind. I'll take her back down."

"You can't, she was about to get seasick."

"She'll be okay for a few minutes. I'll give her some water and crackers."

"Nobody is going anywhere. He can…"

When Gun Guy hesitated, Adam guessed it was because he realized they had figured out that the other two passengers were girls.

"…can change right here!"

Before Adam could say anything, Ellen spun around. "She's cold and wet, and I'm taking her down to warm up."

Adam saw the gun move in Ellen's direction. "No!" he screamed as he jumped to his left putting himself between Gun Guy and Ellen. He half expected to hear a gunshot as he felt a hand on the back of his neck pushing him out of the way. Struggling to keep his balance, Adam twisted out of Gun Guy's grasp in time to see Ellen and Sarah disappear down the steps into the cabin.

"You dumb fucks. You both got some kind of death wish?" Gun Guy shoved the gun into Adam's ribs and pushed him behind the wheel. "Just keep this fucking boat going."

When Ellen turned on the cabin lights, Sarah stood in front of her, shivering. Without a word, Ellen put her arms around her. Sarah stiffened at first, then melted into Ellen.

"It's going to be okay, we're going to help you," Ellen whispered.

Sarah pulled back and looked into Ellen's eyes. "You can't, nobody can. Jason will find us and kill us all."

"Well, he doesn't have to look very far to find us, we're all right here. Don't worry, we'll figure something out. There's one of him and two of us, and we're not going to let

Jason do this to you."

Sarah shook her head. "No, that's not Jason."

"It isn't, then who is he?"

"Jason called him Ozzie. I don't know his real name. He's just delivering us. Compared to Jason, he's one of the good guys."

"Ah, what does that mean? He doesn't seem very—"

"Believe me, if that was Jason you two would be dead by now."

Ellen frowned and put her hand on Sarah's shoulder. "What's your name?"

"Traci." When Ellen stared at her, she looked away then looked back. "I mean… Sarah."

"How old are you?"

"Eighteen."

Ellen thought about the high school girls she taught and coached. "No way. You're not really eighteen, are you?"

Sarah looked at the floor and shook her head.

"How old are you, really?"

"Sixteen."

"How old is the other girl… Belle?"

"She's seventeen."

"Oh, my God. You're both just—"

"What the fuck's going on down there? Get back up here," Gun Guy shouted.

Ellen wanted to respond, *fuck you*, but instead yelled, "She's changing, we'll be right there."

When Ellen helped Sarah out of her wet jeans, she saw several bruises up and down her legs. Ellen became angrier by the second as she watched Sarah pull on the sweats Adam had given her. She had no idea how all this was going to end, but she did know that there was no way she was going to help this asshole deliver these two kids into a life of slavery.

Before heading back up to the cockpit, Ellen grabbed a zip-lock bag of Club Crackers out of a cupboard and handed it to Sarah. "When you get up there, eat these and drink a lot of water."

Sarah whispered, "Thank you," and climbed up the steps.

Ellen followed, her rage continuing to build. By the time she reached the top, Sarah was already sitting next to Belle. Ellen stood in front of the companionway steps and glared at Gun Guy.

Chapter Twelve

Jason sat alone on the couch in the darkened living room, the only light coming from one of the computer screens. Spade was asleep under a pile of blankets on a recliner in the corner across from him. Jason was restless and becoming more agitated by the minute ever since Ozzie called and told him he was going to have to dump his friend's boat. He had said it was too small for the weather and he found someone else to take them to Michigan, but it was on a sailboat and would take a lot longer to get there.

Jason had always been very careful about the way he handled his business. To him maintaining strict control over every aspect of all of it was crucial to avoiding risk. The key was keeping his distance in all transactions and limiting the number of people with whom he had personal contact. The only part he actually did face-to-face was recruit the girls and anyone else who worked for him, and he was always very careful about how he did that.

When it came to acquiring girls, Jason preferred sixteen

to seventeen-year-olds. With the age of consent in Ohio being sixteen, it helped keep things simple when he was making his initial contacts with a prospect. To him it was also best if the girls he recruited had limited life experiences as well as problems at home. They were easier to train than girls off the street who, even though they tended to be low hanging fruit, usually had drug habits and could be a pain in the ass to deal with and control.

In his search for girls, Jason believed research was critical. Before ever approaching a prospect, he spent months watching her from afar and communicating with her online. When he actually set up a personal contact, it was always in a public place with safe, trust-building conversation. Even then, he might have one or two meetings and decide to just walk away. Patience was the key.

Jason was equally careful about how and where he found anyone else to work for him. As with Ramone, he hand-picked Ozzie to be one of his couriers. Jason first spotted him sitting at the bar in a downtown Shawnee Falls hangout, with his hands wrapped around a glass of caramel colored liquid and little to no ice. He looked pretty disheveled, with several days' growth of beard and clothes that appeared to have been slept in for a week. Jason watched the bartender refill the glass three times before he took the stool next to him and started up a conversation.

According to what Ozzie told him, his wife had walked out because of his drinking, and had taken his two teenage daughters with her. Instead of it being the wakeup call she later claimed she was hoping for, Ozzie started drinking even more and lost his job. As he explained to Jason over yet another drink, he was behind in his child support and his home was in foreclosure. He was scheduled for court in two weeks on the support case and was scared shitless he was going to end up in jail.

For Jason, he was the perfect candidate. He befriended Ozzie and set out to rescue him much like he would a mangy, stray dog off the street. He loaned Ozzie money to begin bringing his child support up to date, shepherded him to AA meetings and stuck with him while he stopped drinking and his wife put the divorce proceedings on hold. As icing, Jason also loaned Ozzie the money he needed to have the foreclosure action dismissed.

When it came time to call in his chips, Jason didn't hesitate to point out to Ozzie that he had saved his marriage and his home, and that Ozzie would be financially indebted to him for the rest of his life. As Jason explained to Ozzie, he owned him, and he would do whatever was asked of him. When Jason came to him to do the transporting, Ozzie believed he had no choice but to agree even though he had no idea what he would be delivering.

That was two years ago, and all had gone well through several deliveries. It wasn't until Jason called him for this run and Ozzie told him he couldn't do it because his boat was on the fritz that things got fucked up. When Jason pushed him, Ozzie said he would try to borrow a boat. Jason didn't like it but said okay. It all went downhill from there when Ramone drove the girls from the farmhouse, southwest of Cleveland, to Shawnee Falls to turn them over to Ozzie. When he arrived, there was another guy there, a tall, skinny asshole named Spider. And then, two hours later, Ozzie called and told him that, because of the weather, the boat didn't work out, and now who the fuck knew who was transporting the goods or when they would get there.

Jason looked at his watch: 1:05 a.m. Ninety minutes from the time they were originally supposed to arrive at Grant Harbor. Jason had called the purchaser and told him they would be late but not to worry, they would arrive by six, which he made up. He really didn't have a clue when they would get there. Jason started pacing. He had lost control of this transaction, and there was nothing he hated more than not being in control.

Jason pounded his right fist into his left palm as he paced. *Fucking Ozzie, he's going to pay if he screws this up.* Jason had made Ozzie well aware of the fact that he knew where he lived with his wife and daughters, and he wouldn't hesitate to act on that knowledge if he ever crossed him, intentionally or otherwise.

Yeah, either way, maybe Ozzie's time has come.

Chapter Thirteen

When Ellen stepped around the console and continued to glare at Gun Guy, he jabbed the barrel of the gun toward the seat across from the two girls and barked, "Sit down."

Ellen didn't budge. *Oh, shit,* Adam thought.

"I said sit down!"

"Ellen, do as he says." Adam saw her clenched fists. He'd seen her pissed-off before, but never like this. He knew she had been trying hard to contain her anger, but suspected she was close to the end of her ability to do so. "Ellen, please, just—"

"No, I won't sit down," Ellen pointed past Adam at the guy behind him with the gun. "I know who you are and what you're doing…Ozzie…that is your name isn't it? If you want to kill me, go ahead and do it, but there is no way in hell I'm going to help you deliver these two helpless, young girls into a life of slavery."

The gun moved in Ellen's direction.

"No!" Adam screamed just before a loud bang and a

flash of light pierced the night.

The boat lurched hard to starboard when Adam let go of the wheel. He was thrown into Ellen, knocking her back against the seat and collapsing on top of her on the cockpit floor. Sarah and Belle let out shrill screams.

"Ellen, Ellen!" Adam screamed frantically. "You shot her, you fucking shot her!"

As he pushed himself up, he felt Ellen's hands on his chest.

"Adam, I'm okay. Let me up."

He pulled back and looked into her eyes. "Are you...can you—"

"I'm okay. I wasn't hit, at least I don't think I was.

"You only get one of those," Gun Guy shouted. "The next time, I blow your fucking head off."

Adam jumped up and saw that Ozzie had grabbed the wheel. "What the fuck is wrong with you...Ozzie, or whoever the hell you are?" Adam yelled. He took a step toward him with his hands out.

Adam froze when Ozzie jammed the gun into his gut.

"Take it easy, counselor. Just settle down and no one gets hurt."

From behind him, Adam heard a groan and whipped around to see Ellen struggling to push herself up onto the seat with one arm.

He reached out to help her. "You said you weren't hit. What's the—"

"I wasn't, I just smashed my shoulder when I fell."

Ozzie let go of the wheel and the boat lurched again. Adam grabbed it and brought the boat back under control.

Ozzie jammed the gun into Adam's ribs. "That's your last chance. Either of you move or say another fucking word and she dies."

Panting, Adam said, "How about *you* fucking take it easy? I'm taking you where you want to go. There's no reason why anyone has to get hurt."

"As long as you get me there, no one will." Ozzie

reached inside his jacket and pulled out another, smaller gun and pointed it at Ellen. "But if you don't…"

As he caught his breath, Adam glanced at Belle and Sarah. They were sitting with their hands folded in front of them with their heads down and hats pulled low, almost covering their eyes. It wasn't lost on Adam that they likely were no strangers to having men screaming orders at them and threatening to hurt them. His mind went to the multitude of news reports he had read and cases he had seen come through the courts over the past few years involving the exploding problem of human trafficking plaguing not only the U.S. but the world. Young girls were being kidnapped, drugged, beaten, and sold as sex slaves, at an alarming rate. Although many were kids smuggled across the southern border, or addicts, lured off the streets with the promise of more drugs, others were from neighborhoods right out of everyday suburbia, ordinary girls next door. And the age was dropping. It wasn't unusual for girls as young as thirteen or fourteen to be sent out by a pimp to be screwed for money several times a day. The girls were kept in their servitude by drugs or violence—or both. Many died before they were able to get out.

Adam's grip tightened on the wheel. He wiped away the sweat running down his forehead into his eyes. *Ellen is right. There is no way we can sit by and let this happen.*

Chapter Fourteen

The wind and waves that had been beating the hell out of them since they left the shelter of the island were easing up. Adam set the autopilot, then slipped past Ellen to the winch to make an adjustment to the mainsail. When he had it where he wanted it, he came back to the helm and checked the chart plotter. They were a little over twenty miles out from Grant Harbor.

Fuck. Less than four hours to somehow get control of this mess and figure out how to keep us alive. He sat next to Ozzie. His head pounded. *Are we really ready to sacrifice everything, maybe even our lives, for these girls we don't even know?*

He looked at Ellen. She was rubbing her shoulder. "Are you okay?" He half expected Ozzie to scream at him for talking, but he didn't.

Ellen shrugged and mumbled, "I'll be all right."

Adam glanced over his shoulder and saw Ozzie staring back at him. The guns were crossed in his lap, one pointed at him and the other at Ellen. Adam thought about the alternatives. Jump Ozzie and risk getting Ellen killed; jump Ozzie and risk getting himself killed; jump Ozzie and risk getting them both killed. None of those choices sounded appealing. The guns were the issue.

If it weren't for those…

Adam had figured out at an early age that he was never going to be big enough to play football like most of his friends and, instead, started wrestling when he was eleven years old. As it turned out, Adam was good at it, actually more than good at it. His senior year in high school Adam won the state tournament and received a full ride to the University of Michigan where he notched two Big Ten championships. Over the years since then, Adam continued to work-out and stay in shape. He had a thirty-two-inch waist and definition in his shoulders, chest, and arms that put to shame most of the regulars at the gym in their twenties and thirties. He still helped train some of the better high-school wrestlers in the area who made it to the state tournament.

Adam sighed and shook his head. If it weren't for the guns, he surely could handle Ozzie. But there *were* guns, and Ozzie didn't seem ready to put them away any time soon.

Adam looked to the north, out into the seemingly endless darkness and thought about how people seeing the lake for the first time were surprised when they couldn't see to the other side. At one time or another, he had been on every one of the Great Lakes, which, with their connecting waterways, make up the largest freshwater system on the planet. To him, and to anyone who had spent much time on the Great Lakes, they weren't just bodies of water. They were living beings, each having its own unique personality, each a wonder of its own. Even Lake Erie, the fourth largest of the five, at 240 miles in length and over fifty miles across was the eleventh largest lake in the world.

Adam smiled. *Sometimes the lake treats you well and sometimes it doesn't. What's it going to be this time?*

Adam closed his eyes and shook his head as his mind returned to how he was going to keep this night on the lake from turning into an even bigger nightmare than it already was.

It was Ellen who broke the silence. "Okay, Ozzie. By the way, is your name really Ozzie?"

"That'll do." Ozzie grunted.

Adam shifted uneasily in his seat. Although on the surface she appeared calm, the tension in Ellen's voice set off alarms in his head. *Please don't blow up. For now, it would be good if we can just get him talking.*

"Here's the way I see it," Ellen said. "I think you know that we know what's going on here, and I promise you I will do everything I can to keep you from delivering these girls to whomever it is that's waiting for them at the other end...even if I have to die trying. You can kill me if you want, but I'm sure you know that, if you do, there is no way Adam will continue to take you to Grant Harbor. As a matter of fact, you'll probably end up having to kill him too and, if you do that, you'll be on your own to sail this boat and get it where you want to go."

After a long pause, Ellen added, "So, what are we going to do about this?"

Ozzie turned in his seat and raised the guns, keeping one pointed at each of them. "That's easy. You take this boat there, and you live. You don't, you die. Your choice."

"Ozzie, we're not stupid, and I don't think you are either," Adam said. "We just watched you kill someone. Do you really think we don't know that you probably plan to kill us once this delivery is completed? And, by the way, I've seen the kind of folks who engage in this kind of business, and it's pretty obvious that you're traveling in a very nasty crowd. What makes you think the people to whom you are delivering these girls aren't going to kill you once they have what they want?"

Adam waited for a response. When it didn't come, he said, "The bottom line for us is, we're not going to help you turn these girls over to them. And, since we're probably going to die anyway, it doesn't seem like we have much more to lose."

Adam's entire body gave a convulsive shudder. *Fuck, did I just say that? Are we really going to do this?* He looked at Ellen and caught her clear blue eyes staring back at him. She gave a slight nod. Adam looked at the two girls, who continued to sit motionless with their heads down. *Yep...it looks like we are.*

Ellen turned and looked at Ozzie. "Adam's right. So, unless you're prepared to sail this boat yourself, it's time for us to turn back."

"Shut the fuck up, both of you," Ozzie shouted. Then he said, "I didn't kill anyone."

Adam swung around, shocked at what he just heard.

Ellen screamed in frustration, "Screw you, Ozzie. We watched you do it."

Adam jerked forward. "Ellen, don't—"

"I didn't kill him, I shot over his head," Ozzie said.

"Huh...what? You expect us to believe that?" Adam asked. "I watched him go under and not come back up."

"I don't give a rat's ass what you believe. I didn't kill him. He's my friend. I wanted him off the boat."

Adam was still processing what Ozzie had said when Ellen responded, "Well, that was big of you. You didn't shoot him, which I don't believe for a second, you let him drown instead."

"He wasn't going to drown. He's a good swimmer. He could easily make it to the beach on the island."

"How can you be sure of that?" Adam asked.

"I told you, he's my friend. I've known him since we were kids."

Adam felt a moment of relief until Ozzie jammed the gun into his ribs and said, "But that doesn't mean I won't kill the two of you if you don't keep this boat going."

Adam's head was spinning. He looked at Ellen. She started to speak but he put his finger to his lips. He hoped

Ozzie was thinking and wanted to give him time—and himself time.

Adam stood, made some adjustments to their heading, reset the autopilot, and then sat back down. He turned to Ozzie. "Let's say that's true, you didn't kill your friend. I'm sure you know that delivering these girls is still a very serious crime that could put you in prison for a good part of the rest of your life…and killing us will make it infinitely worse. For that, you could get the death penalty. Of course, that is if these people you're working for don't kill you first."

When Ozzie just stared at him, Adam added, "As I told you, I'm a criminal defense lawyer. If we stop all this right now, I can help you."

"No, you can't. No one can."

Adam sensed fear in Ozzie's voice. It surprised him. Needing time to think, he stood and moved forward to reset the mainsail to account for the easing wind. It was still reefed, and he thought about pulling the rest of it out but wasn't sure he wanted to get there any faster. He trimmed the genoa then retook his seat behind the wheel.

Adam looked at Ellen. She didn't say anything but gave a slight nod. He took a breath, exhaled slowly, and said, "There is no way we are going to take these girls to Michigan and turn them over to what's waiting for them. How about we turn around and head back to Shawnee Falls? We'll take care of the girls, and you can take off. As far as we're concerned, we can proceed as if we never saw you and none of this ever happened."

Ozzie didn't respond. Appearing emboldened by his silence, Ellen said. "Listen Ozzie, I don't give a shit if you're a pimp. Well…I do, but that's not what's important now. What's important is that we meant what we said. We are not going to do this anymore. If you want to kill us, you'll have to go ahead and do it, but then you're on your own with this boat. Otherwise, as Adam said, it's time to talk about how you're going to walk away from all this."

There was another long silence. Then Ozzie said, "I'm not a pimp."

Chapter Fifteen

Sarah sat with her head down and her eyes closed, wondering if she heard correctly. *Did these two strangers just say they were willing to die rather than help Ozzie turn them over to whomever it was that Jason had sold them? Was it possible that they really could be rescued?*

When Jason first took her to the farmhouse and she realized what a horrifying mistake she had made, Sarah thought about being rescued all the time. Sometimes she even dreamed about it only to wake up feeling worse than she did when she went to sleep. But, as time went on, she thought about it less and less, the utter hopelessness of her situation making the prospect of being rescued too painful to think about. Even now, after hearing what Adam and Ellen had said, she wanted to have hope that there was a chance it might happen but was having a hard time believing it ever could. She knew Jason all too well and was aware of what he was capable of doing to anyone who crossed him.

When Belle leaned into her, Sarah reached over and

took her hand. Startled by how freezing cold it was, she was relieved when Belle nudged her lightly with her elbow. Had Belle heard it too? What was she thinking? Sarah wished she could talk to Belle. She wished she could talk to anyone.

Sarah's thoughts went to her mother and father. Even though she always felt like she was a disappointment to them, she loved them and knew they loved her. When she decided to run away with Jason it wasn't her intention to just disappear forever. She felt a lump form in her throat at the thought of the pain she'd caused her parents. *How could they ever forgive me?*

Sarah's mind drifted to her grandmother, Sadie, for whom she was named and in whose arms she had always felt more loved than anywhere else in the world. After what she had done, would her grandma still make her tea and her favorite peanut butter cookies when she went to her house to visit? Would she ever again tuck her into bed like she did when she was a kid and continued to do after Sarah was well into her teens whenever she stayed overnight? After what she had done, would anyone in her family ever want to have anything to do with her again?

Sarah thought about going back to her high school and walking the halls with her friends, preparing for her chemistry exam with her study group, stopping for ice cream on the way home from swim practice, going to Friday night football games, and sneaking some hits of weed under the stands at halftime. It all seemed laughable after going out and doing what she had been forced to do for three or four disgusting older men almost every day for the past six months.

No, none of those times with her family and friends she had once taken so much for granted would ever happen again. As Jason constantly reminded her, Sarah was gone, dead to the world. She was now Traci and would always be just another dumb fucking whore. Jason owned her and there was no way he would ever let her go. Even if she and Belle could get away, he would hunt them down and kill them.

Sarah used the sleeve of her fleece to wipe away the tears running down her face.

Chapter Sixteen

"I'm not a pimp."

Not what Adam was expecting to hear. From the expression on Ellen's face, he sensed she was as surprised as he was.

Adam glanced at Ozzie sitting behind him with a gun in each hand crossed in his lap. One was pointed in his direction, the other at Ellen, but down low, not at their heads or even their chests. Keeping his eyes on the guns, Adam decided if either one was raised even the slightest bit, he would go for it.

But Ozzie just sat, silent and still. Finally, he looked at Adam and said, "You can't turn around." His voice was different. It wasn't the usual demand or gruff command.

Ellen opened her mouth to respond but Adam raised his hand in front of her. She acquiesced, and they let the silence grow.

Adam glanced at Sarah and Belle. Their heads were lifted. They had been listening. He turned to Ozzie and said:

"Time is running out. We have to get realistic about what's happening here. Let's say for now that what you've told us is true, you didn't just murder someone before our eyes, and you are not a pimp. The fact remains that you are asking us to help you take these two girls to Grant Harbor to be sold as sex slaves. The problem is, we are not going to help you do that. If you have a need to kill us, so be it. We are both willing to die rather than help you complete this delivery. And, as Ellen said, you should know by now that you can't kill one of us and expect the other to help you sail this boat. If you shoot one of us, the other will come after you and you will have to kill again."

Adam sniffed the air, then added the obvious. "The wind is picking up. Unless you're a pretty experienced sailor, which you said you aren't, it isn't going to be easy for you to get this boat where you need to go on your own."

Adam stopped to let what he said sink in. Appearing to have caught on, Ellen nodded, and they waited. When Ozzie didn't respond, Adam said, "So, you tell me, what are we going to do about this? And, by the way, I do mean, 'We.' It would be a lot better if we could work together to resolve this mess rather than have anybody get hurt."

Again, they waited. After a while, Ozzie looked at Adam and said. "You sound just like a fucking lawyer."

"I told you, I am a fucking lawyer…and I can help you, if you'll let me, before this gets any more out of control than it already is."

Ozzie shook his head and said, "You can't turn around. We have to keep going." His voice was soft, the gruffness gone.

"Okay, tell me why," Adam said.

"First of all, I did not kill Spider. I shot over his head. I wanted him off the boat, for his own good. I've never killed anyone. And, I'm not a pimp, not for these girls or anyone else. I'm just the delivery guy." He hesitated then added, "I don't like this either, but there's nothing I can do about it. I don't want to kill you, but, if I have to, I will. If it's between

71

you two or my wife and daughters, I'll do what I have to do to…" His voice faded off as he turned his head and looked out over the water.

The wind picked up and the autopilot started beeping, the signal the boat had been blown off course. Adam stood, turned the auto off and sat back down to hand steer, thankful that he had left the sails reefed. He turned and looked at Ozzie, who hadn't moved. The guns were still crossed on his lap.

The fear and anxiety Adam felt earlier had given way to anger and his capacity for patience was dwindling. He stifled his growing frustration as best he could and asked, "How about you explain what that means…why it's either us or your family?"

When Ozzie didn't answer, Adam held his tongue and waited but it wasn't easy. If they were going to turn around and head back, it needed to be soon. The wind was continuing to climb and move back around on their nose, which meant if they kept the current course, they were going to get wet again. As much as he loved sailing, he wasn't enjoying being out in the middle of the night in these conditions, and that would have been true even without the guy with two guns threatening to kill them.

"It's a long story," Ozzie finally said.

"Well, it's not like any of us are going anywhere anytime soon," Ellen said harshly.

Ozzie readjusted himself on the seat then looked at Ellen. "I'm delivering these girls to someone at Grant Harbor for a guy from over near Cleveland. My guess is, he's the pimp."

Ellen waved her finger at Ozzie. "So, you think that makes you any better than him? Sorry, not so. You are a full participant in this, no better than the pimp."

"Ellen, please let him talk," Adam said.

"To be honest, I can't say I disagree with you. But…there isn't much I can do about it."

"Why is that?" Adam asked.

Ozzie looked out over the water, then back at Adam. "It was about two years ago. I was in this bar in town. My wife and I had been having some problems and…anyway, this guy, Jason, who'd been sitting next to me started talking. He was a little more clean-cut looking…better dressed, you know, than most of the people in there, and seemed like a nice guy. I guessed him for a banker or an accountant, or something like that. Actually, I'd been there for a while and was pretty fucked up by then. We got to talking about boats and stuff like that, like everyone around here by the lake does. He told me that his boat was out for the season for repairs. I told him that with my divorce and losing my job from coming in drunk so many times, I was going to have to sell my boat."

"That all sounds interesting, Ozzie, but how about getting to the point," Adam said.

Ozzie nodded. "After we talked a while, he said he wanted to help me. It sounded like he'd done that before with people…you know, with drinking problems. Over the next month, we kind of got to be friends. He'd come over to Shawnee Falls, we'd have coffee, or he'd take me somewhere for lunch. He seemed like…well, like he just wanted to give me a hand-up. He got me to go to AA and then helped me with a bunch of other stuff. He even loaned me a shit-load of money to get my house out of foreclosure. Right now, my wife and I are getting back together."

"What does that have to do with any of this?" Ellen asked, her tone softened.

"Once I stopped drinking, he said he needed me to do some work for him. He told me he would make it worth my while, you know, to help me get back on my feet financially. After all he had done for me, like saving my life and my marriage and all, I didn't feel like I could say no." Ozzie stopped, shook his head, and said, "I guess you could say he was pretty fucking good at sucking me in."

"Yeah, he's a real expert at that." It was Belle. "He sucks you in by making you think he's a good person, a nice guy. But then once you trust him, you find out he's nothing but a fucking animal."

For a long second, they all stared at her, speechless. Then Ozzie said, "You got that right. The next time we met, he explained that he needed me to deliver something for him by boat from Shawnee Falls to Grant Harbor. He said it was a delicate matter, and it had to be at night.

"Delivering girls for him?" Adam asked.

"At first, I didn't know what it was. I asked him why I couldn't just drive whatever it was over there, since it was only about an hour by car. He said that was too risky. He said it had to get from Ohio to Michigan by boat. I asked him what it was I'd be delivering, but he said he couldn't tell me. Then he said he'd pay me a thousand bucks, cash, for this one night's work. I'd been out of work for almost a year and, you know, things had gotten pretty tough, money wise. At that point, though, I was getting a little queasy about it all. I'm thinking it must be drugs, I told him I wasn't going to do anything illegal. That's when he reminded me of all the money I owed him. He said until it was paid back, he owned me, and I'd be doing whatever he told me to do."

Ozzie hesitated, looked at Ellen then back at Adam. "I was surprised when he said that. Until then...you know...he seemed like such a nice guy and all, and I was thinking, how bad could it be."

A half laugh and half snorting sound came from Belle. "Oh, yeah, you want to know how fucking bad it can get? With that asshole, beyond your wildest dreams," she said shaking her head.

The wind had continued to build, and the boat was back to bouncing and rolling on the waves. When spray started coming across the bow, Adam stood and changed course enough to settle the boat down.

"So, you went ahead, and did it?" Ellen asked.

"I told him I had an old twenty-seven-foot Baja, and he said that would do. At that point, it all kind of stunk to me, but he had me in a fucking box. I figured I'd do it this once and then—"

"When was all this?" Adam asked.

"The first time was about a year and a half ago. It was spring, early May. I remember because I had just launched. He called me and said he needed me that night, said I should take my boat to the municipal docks at midnight. It was a Tuesday, and no one else was around when this shiny thirty-foot Grady White with two 350s pulls in. I was expecting Jason, but a tall, skinny, dark-haired girl was driving. There was a big Mexican guy with her. He threw me lines, and I helped him tie up. Then the Mexican goes into the cabin and comes out with these two smaller guys…at least I thought they were guys. I was waiting for them to load whatever I was delivering onto the boat, but instead he brings them on and tells me to 'get moving.'

"I didn't know who the fuck they were or what the hell was going on, and was just looking at him, when he pulled a gun out of his belt and put it up to my head, and said, 'You'll be met at the dock at Grant Harbor at 3:00 a.m. Don't be a minute late. If you are, you're dead. And by the way, I know where you live with your wife, Janice, and your daughters, Ellie and Molly. You fuck up, and they're dead too.'"

Adam noticed Ozzie choking up at the mention of his kids.

"Oh, my God," Ellen said.

"Yeah, that was my thought at the time…God, help me," Ozzie said.

"What did you do?" Adam asked.

"I didn't have much choice. I asked about my money, and he said I'd get it after the delivery was complete. He said something about meeting me at the other end, but by then I wasn't listening very well. It wasn't until we headed out and one of my two passengers asked to use the head that I figured out they were girls."

"Did you collect money when you made your drop off?" Ellen asked.

"No. Either the girl or the Mexican drives over there, collects the money, then drives back."

"How many of these deliveries have you made?" Adam inquired.

"This'll be the fourth one. Only this time, when he called yesterday and said we had a run, I had to tell him my boat was down for repairs, and I couldn't do it. He got pretty pissed off, told me to find another boat and to be on time. So, I called Spider and asked him if I could borrow his Whaler. He said okay, but then insisted on coming with me."

"Did you tell him what you were doing?" Ellen asked.

"Just that I had to deliver some stuff for a friend. But when the Mexican brought these two to the boat and started waving a gun around, Spider got pretty spooked."

Ellen shook her head, "Ah...no surprise there."

"Yeah, well I got him settled down, and we headed out, but pretty quick the wind picked up big time. We both knew the boat was too small for the conditions, and it was going to be a damn miserable ride if we made it at all. Spider decided to go around to the north side of Kelleys to get into the lee of the island and out of the wind. That's when we saw your sailboat."

"When they brought these girls to you, was it by boat?" Adam asked.

"No, this time the Mexican drove them over by himself. He did it that way the last couple of times."

Ellen gave an audible sigh and said, "And here we are."

Chapter Seventeen

Spider opened his eyes and sat up. *Fuck, it wasn't all a bad dream. I really am here on the island.* He glanced at his watch. *At least it's still working.* To the best he could tell, he had been out for almost an hour.

He stood, stretched, and started walking down the beach. Foremost in his mind was the question of whether Ozzie had intended to shoot him or just scare him to get him off the boat. While he knew Ozzie had his issues, most of which involved alcohol, he had never known him to be violent. He always had been more the big teddy bear type.

If he wanted to shoot me, how could he miss? I was only a foot away.

Spider replayed in his mind how he had gotten into this fucking mess, how Ozzie had called him around six o'clock and asked if he could borrow his Whaler. To Spider, it wasn't all that big a deal. He had grown up with Ozzie and they remained close friends. As a matter of fact, it was Ozzie who had given him the name Spider. It started the night they took a six pack of Bud Light down to the beach to celebrate their graduation from high school. By the time the beer was gone, they were pretty well smashed and decided to commemorate the occasion by going into town and getting tattoos. Spider went first and picked out a bug with long skinny legs for the back of his neck. When it was Ozzie's turn, he chickened out. As if that wasn't bad enough, because of the tat, Ozzie started calling him Spider. It caught on immediately with all their friends, and he had been Spider ever since.

Spider stopped walking and looked out over the water. He couldn't see it, but he knew the sailboat was out there somewhere heading to the west end of the lake. Chilled by the wind at his back, Spider knew that even though it was peaceful there in the lee of the island with the water lapping gently onto the sand, out on the lake it was pretty lumpy.

He thought about how puzzling it was when Ozzie asked him if he could borrow his Whaler for the night, but then said, "No, you can't come, I just need your boat."

It got even more weird when Spider told him, "No way, either I'm coming or no deal." Ozzie first responded with, "Fuck you, I'll find another boat," but then called back an hour later and said, "Fine, you can come. Bring the boat to the municipal docks at 11:00 p.m."

Spider recalled how shocked he was when that Ramone guy started waving a gun around when he dropped off the two girls. Of course, at the time, Spider didn't know they were girls or that they were what was being delivered. That came later when he engaged in conversation with them and the truth about what they were doing slowly worked its way to the surface. When he finally put it all together, he was shocked and had a hard time believing Ozzie would be involved in that kind of thing. He tried to ask Ozzie about it, but his friend made it clear that it wasn't something he wanted to talk about.

The worst part, though, was when Ozzie called someone before they tied up to the sailboat, told whomever it was at the other end what they were doing, and that they would be late. Ozzie had given their location and the name of the sailboat. When he hung up, Ozzie said, "Fuck, if we run into any cops or the Coast Guard, we're all fucking dead."

"All?" Spider asked.

"Yeah. All of us…and my wife and daughters."

It was pretty obvious to Spider that Ozzie was in way over his head and, potentially, in a shitload of trouble. He turned and walked back to his boat. Unable to think of anything else to do, he pushed the Whaler off the shore and climbed in. Once he was far enough out, he dropped the motor, started it up, and idled out of the bay, toward the west end of the island, in the same direction as the sailboat.

Chapter Eighteen

"So, this guy, this Jason, is the one who's selling these girls?" Ellen asked.

A voice from the other side of the cockpit responded, "Yep." Ellen's head swung around. It was Belle. "And he's meaner than shit, so don't think for a minute he won't carry out a threat to murder his family," she added, pointing at Ozzie.

"Has he threatened the two of you?" Ellen asked.

Sarah gave a grunt. "Threatened us? Oh, yeah, he's—"

"How about every day," Belle interjected. "And when he carries out the threats, he knows how to cause pain in ways that don't leave a lot of marks. He says that's important because we need to look good for his fucking clients."

Sarah sat up, raised her right arm, and formed her hand into a claw. "He does this thing where he grabs you by the shoulder at the bottom of your neck. It hurts so much you think you're going to throw up or even pass out. And then when you're down on the floor, he kicks you in the back, only without shoes so there aren't any bruises, but it still hurts like hell for days."

Ellen shook her head and asked, "And in the middle of all this, he's putting you two out on the street to hustle men for sex?"

"No. He never has us working the streets," Belle said. "It's all by appointment. I think someone, somewhere else does that online, or some kind of shit like that. Jason always says he runs a high-class operation, makes bigger money than anyone else this side of Vegas."

"Yeah, he sure sounds like a high-class guy," Ellen said. She leaned forward and looked at Belle. "How old are you really?"

There was a long hesitation. Adam said, "You can tell the truth. All that's done. We're not going to turn you over to those people for any more of that." Out of the corner of his eye, Adam glanced at Ozzie, expecting a reaction, but there wasn't one, which he took as a hopeful sign.

"Seventeen." Belle pointed at Sarah, "She's sixteen."

"Ah, shit," Adam exclaimed. Then he asked, "Belle isn't your real name, is it?"

"No."

"What is it?"

Another long hesitation. "Elizabeth. I've always gone by Beth, but Jason told me I needed a sexier name. He said Beth was dead...no longer existed."

Ellen stood and stepped around the table to the other side of the cockpit. She sat next to Sarah and put her arm around her. Sarah resisted at first, then leaned her head on Ellen's shoulder. Over the wind, Adam could hear sniffling coming from the direction of the girls but couldn't tell who it was.

Adam looked at Ozzie. Even though he couldn't see his face very clearly in the dark, he appeared to be thinking. Adam gave him a minute, then asked, "How old are your daughters?"

Ozzie sighed deeply then, barely above a whisper, said,

"Thirteen and fifteen."

Ellen pulled away from Sarah and looked at Ozzie. "How about we work together to protect these girls, and your wife and daughters…and to put these assholes away forever?"

"That won't be easy," Sarah said. "Jason is really smart and really mean, and he'll hurt anyone who gets in his way."

"They all will," Beth chimed in.

Ellen turned to Beth. "All…who's the all?"

"He has three people, he calls them his associates, who work for him," Sarah said. "One's a woman, she calls herself Spade. The other two are guys. One is Mexican, his name is Ramone. The other guy goes by Denzel. He's black, says he's going to Hollywood to be a bigtime movie star. I think his real name is Daveed or something like that. They're real assholes, too. But if you saw any of them on the street, you'd think they were just ordinary people, like the kind of person you'd see working in a bank or a doctor's office. Jason makes them dress up like that whenever they leave the house during the day to keep people from getting suspicious. But they're all just as mean as he is."

"Fucking right," Beth said. "We make Jason rich, and they all get to beat us and fuck us any time they want, which is all the time."

Adam saw Ellen's face tighten. He hoped if she reacted it would be tempered. When she didn't, he stood and made some corrections to their course. So far, neither Ellen nor Ozzie seemed to notice that he had been changing direction a little at a time, and they were no longer on their way to the west end of the lake but were still headed away from Shawnee Falls. Adam looked at Beth and saw that she had her head down and her eyes closed. He wondered if she was asleep or maybe feeling seasick. He motioned to Ellen to check on her then looked at Ozzie. He was staring at him, still with a gun in each hand on his lap.

Ellen stood, slipped past Sarah, and sat between the two girls. When she put her arm around Beth, she fell into her.

Ellen held her and rocked her. "It's okay, we're not going to let this happen anymore."

Beth looked up. "He'll find us...he always does. We can never get away."

Sarah spoke up. "I've only been there for six months. Belle, I mean Beth, has been there a year; that in itself can kill you." Sarah hesitated, then said, "Beth has been pretty down for the last month. She said she wanted to kill herself, but I made her stop talking like that."

Ellen sat back, put one arm around each girl, and pulled them close. "Well, that's all over now."

"Not so fast," Ozzie said, pointing a gun at Adam's head. "Nothing has changed. These girls are going to be delivered as planned. If you two would rather be shot right now, that's your business. But I'm not going to put my family at risk for you...or these two girls." When everyone stared at him, he added, "Yeah, okay, I feel bad about it, but that's the way it is."

Any sense of hope Adam had felt began to slip away. He knew he could jump Ozzie and maybe get one of the guns, but there was the other one, which was pointed at Ellen. Even though there was a full moon, it was still dark, and Ozzie might miss, but Adam couldn't take that risk. He was not about to sacrifice Ellen to get to Ozzie and maybe save these girls.

Adam felt a weight descending upon him. His arms and legs felt like they had turned to cement and were too heavy to move. There was a dull pounding in his head, and his body began to twitch. He closed his eyes and sucked as much air into his lungs as he could, then blew it out and did it again two more times. *Clearly, nothing has changed. We're just as fucked as we were a couple of hours ago.*

When he opened his eyes, Ellen was looking at him. He forced a reassuring nod. The thought of what he was putting her through and that she might die because of him made Adam feel queasy, and he feared he might be sick. His mind flashed back to the night at the Stardust Inn when Jon and

Samantha Evans arranged for him to meet Ellen, and how instantaneously they had hit it off. He thought about how patient she had been over the three years since then with his inability to take their relationship to the next level. He felt a chill when he recalled how it had come to a head the previous May.

They were having a Friday night dinner at his house when there was a *quack, quack,* from Ellen's phone. She jumped up from the table and grabbed it off the countertop. "Sorry, Mom's been acting more weird than usual lately, I better see what's up." Ellen broke into a smile and started chuckling as she read the email from her mother.

"What's so funny?"

"Oh…you don't want to know." She laughed harder, as she thumbed a response.

"Another dirty joke? Let's hear it." Grace, Ellen's mother, was known for forwarding off-color jokes that were sent to her by her friends.

Ellen stopped laughing, and her look turned serious. "It's not a joke…at least not to her."

"What is it? Is something wrong?"

"No…not really." Ellen put her phone down and started to clear the table.

"So, what was so funny?"

Ellen plunked the dishes into the sink, turned around, and leaned back against the counter. "Her friend, Dottie, just got engaged to a guy she met online…one of those dating things. Mom sent me the website, wants me to try it."

"Huh…what the—"

Ellen waved her finger at Adam. "I told you, you didn't want to know."

"But your mother…I thought we… I thought she liked me."

"She does like you…or, at least she did," Ellen said.

"Last summer, at the beach…we talked…she seemed so… I don't know…she was so nice to me. When did that change? What did I do to cause her to—"

Ellen looked up at the ceiling. "Adam, don't... I shouldn't have—"

"Has your father turned against me too? And what about your brothers?" Adam threw his hands out in front of him, knocking over his empty beer bottle. "Shit," he said, grabbing it before it rolled onto the floor. He looked up at Ellen.

"She doesn't dislike you, Adam. She's just worried about *me*."

"Worried, what does she think—"

"She remembers the last three-year relationship I was in, the one that ended with me quitting my job and moving to Shawnee Falls, Ohio. I'm sure she expected that, by now, we would be—"

"What...how—" Adam could feel a grapefruit sized hole forming just under his sternum.

Ellen pulled her chair up next to him and sat down. "Don't worry about it, Adam. I probably said some things to her that I shouldn't have."

"What things...what did you say?"

She put her hands on each side of his face and turned it toward her. "Adam, it's okay. You are the kindest and most caring person I have ever known. I love you, and I know you love me. But I also know that you know we can't just go on like this forever."

Adam felt the hole in his chest getting bigger. He raised his right palm to his forehead. His face was red hot. *What the fuck is happening?*

Ellen leaned forward, kissed him lightly on the lips and said, "Look, it's no big deal, just ... just forget it."

And now, here they were, finally married and on the honeymoon cruise from hell with it looking more and more like their wedding night might be their last night alive.

Adam shook off the thought when a big wave hit, causing the boat to roll sharply to starboard. When he got the boat settled down, Ellen stood and stepped past Beth to within two feet of Ozzie. It caught Adam by surprise. Before he could say anything, Ozzie raised the gun and ordered, "That's far enough."

Ellen stopped and, rather than yelling at him, as Adam feared she would, in a soft voice said, "Ozzie, can we at least talk about this?"

When he didn't respond but kept the gun trained on her, she said, "Let's say I believe you that you didn't kill Spider, that you got sucked into all this without knowing what you were getting into, and, once you found out, you were forced to keep doing it because Jason threatened to kill your family if you didn't. The question I have is, if you kill us and deliver these girls as you say you're going to, do you really think you'll ever be able to feel like your wife and daughters are safe? Do you think you'll ever have a normal life as long as this jerk is out there threatening you and forcing you to commit these crimes for him? How confident are you that once this Jason guy has gotten everything he needs from you he won't kill you just to keep you quiet? From what these girls say, he seems to be one crazy son-of-a-bitch."

Adam waited for a reaction but, again, there wasn't one. He decided that was good, maybe Ozzie was at least pondering what Ellen had said. He gave some time for her words to sink in, then said, "Let's think about this, Ozzie. It appears that what Jason wants is the money. We could turn around now and get whatever amount he's expecting to receive to him in the morning. In the meantime, we'll hide your family and these girls until the police bust him."

"I think you may be oversimplifying, Adam," Ellen said. "The guys at the other end are coming to get these girls. They're not going to just walk away when we don't show up."

Adam sighed. "You're probably right. But there has to be a way to—"

"More than probably right," Ozzie said. They all looked at him. "We're talking a lot of money. I can't turn over these girls until Ramone counts out a hundred grand."

"A hundred thousand dollars!" Adam exclaimed. "Are

you shitting me?"

"No, I'm not shitting you…a hundred K," Ozzie said. "I don't imagine you have that kind of cash stuffed under your mattress."

"Are you sure? I can't believe it could be that much," Ellen said.

"It is," Sarah said. "I overheard Jason's telephone conversations about selling us. He told the guy we're his best producers, and it had to be fifty each."

"But, how is that—"

"Easy," Beth said. "The way I figured it, by sending us out together as a high-school sister act, we made him over $200,000 in the past six months."

"That's not possible," Ellen exclaimed.

"Sure it is," Sarah said. "Two or three times a day, five or six days a week, for three weeks out of every month. At $1,000 a pop, it adds up. I heard him tell the guy he can recoup his investment in the first three months, and it would be all gravy after that."

"Holy shit, is that really true?" Adam asked.

"Yep," Beth said. "Before Sarah came to the house, I went alone. When we started going out together, the number of times a week doubled. We were busy all the time, except for our…you know, calendar days each month. We were almost always together, eating, sleeping, and fucking. After a couple of months, we even started having our periods at the same time." She hesitated, then said, "How special is that?"

Adam shook his head. "This is northwest Ohio. I can't believe there's that much—"

"Yeah, well… Cleveland is a big city with a lot of big money people," Beth said.

"Are there other girls at this house, or just you two?" Ellen asked.

"The farmhouse has three bedrooms," Sarah said. "One on the first floor and two on the second. The other second-floor room had two girls in it most of the time since I was there. Every couple of months, one or two girls would disappear, but new ones would come in pretty quick."

"So, he uses girls for a while, makes money off them, then sells them and starts over," Ellen said.

"That's pretty much it," Beth said.

Adam noticed that the wind had eased up again, and the waves and rocking had died down. He knew he could put out more sail but wasn't in a hurry to pick up speed. He hoped Ozzie wouldn't notice. Adam stood, made some slight adjustments to their course, then sat back down and asked Beth and Sarah, "Did you ever try to get away?"

"I did, in the beginning, but never got very far," Beth said. "Jason's pretty fucking smart. He or one of the others always knew where to find me, and when they did, there was hell to pay. After the second time, I decided it wasn't worth it. That's what I told Traci...I mean Sarah, whenever she said we should try it."

Ellen turned to Ozzie. "Are you listening to this? These could be your daughters being sold off as sex slaves."

Ozzie jerked the gun up to within a foot of Ellen's forehead. "You shut the fuck up," he bellowed.

Chapter Nineteen

Ellen froze, her eyes focused on the barrel of the gun, which now appeared to be two inches in diameter.

A chill washed over her. *Is this it...is this the moment my life ends?* Her mind began to race. *Maybe Mom was right when she told me I was crazy to move here. No...no she wasn't. If I hadn't, I never would have met Adam...dear, sweet, love of my life, Adam. But what if we die out here? When they find my body, will Mom and Dad come and take me back to New Hampshire for burial? Will my family even know that Adam and I were married?*

Ellen felt bile in the back of her throat and feared she might throw up. *How can this be happening? This is my wedding night. It wasn't supposed to be this way. This is all crazy. Oh my God, did I really invite this wacko who's holding a gun to my head to go ahead and kill me...and to kill Adam?*

Ellen closed her eyes and clenched her fists, digging her fingernails into the palms of her hands, hoping the pain would wake her from this horrifying nightmare. But when she eased her eyes open, they were all still there…on the boat…on the lake…with a gun pointed at her forehead.

"Sit down…now," Ozzie ordered.

Ellen felt Adam's hand on her shoulder. She looked at him and then back at Ozzie. He had lowered the gun.

Adam gave Ellen a nod, and she sat down between Beth and Sarah. Her heart racing, she glanced at Ozzie. Both guns were back in his lap, and he was looking out over the water, not at either of them. She shot a questioning look at Adam and saw that he had noticed it too.

Ellen sensed a change in the landscape. Ozzie was full of threats but, if he was telling the truth about not shooting Spider, maybe he really wasn't a killer. *If he was, we probably would be dead by now. If that's true, it's two against one, and Adam and I should be able to take him out.*

When Adam looked back in her direction, she pointed at Ozzie and made a fist. She was sure Adam got her message when he nodded in response. But then he followed the nod with a slight shake of his head. Ellen was confused. *If Adam has figured out that Ozzie really isn't going to shoot us, what the hell is he waiting for? We don't have much time left.* Ellen felt her pulse picking up again. *Shit, maybe he thinks it's too risky. But we have to do something, we can't just—*

Ellen's thoughts were interrupted when she felt Beth snuggling in closer to her. Ellen's mind went to her kids, the ones she taught and coached.

Anyone of them could have fallen prey to a predator like this asshole, Jason, and could be sitting here next to me instead of these two girls. If Ozzie really isn't a killer, maybe we can get him to understand that…maybe we could get him to change his mind and get onboard with helping us. Maybe that is what Adam is thinking…try that rather than risk a stray bullet killing someone.

Ellen looked out over the water. *It's worth a try.* She turned to Sarah and asked, "What were you doing before you hooked up with Jason?"

Sarah looked at Ellen for a long moment, shook her head, and then in a low, lifeless tone said, "Jason told me my life before him was dead...gone...and there's no reason to ever even think about it again."

"But you know that's not true, don't you?"

Sarah nodded and sniffed loudly. "I was starting my junior year in high school."

"My guess is you were a good student."

Sarah shrugged. "Yeah...my parents never tolerated anything other than an A."

"Tell me about your parents."

"They're both doctors at the Cleveland Clinic. They're nice... I know they loved me...but they worked all the time. I never saw them very much when I was a kid."

You're still a kid, Ellen thought, but didn't say it. "You said they loved you, past tense. Did something happen to them? Are they still living?"

"Oh, yeah. But Jason always said they had forgotten about me, that I should forget about them, and if I ever went back, they wouldn't have anything to do with me after what I've been doing."

"You don't believe that, do you?"

Sarah shrugged. "I don't know. At first, I didn't want to...but then the more I thought about it, the more I thought...I'm just a whore. Why would they want to have anything to do with me?" As she finished the sentence, Sarah's voice dropped to barely audible.

Ellen reached out and hugged her. She sensed that Sarah didn't like talking about any of this, but she needed Ozzie to hear what she hoped was coming next.

"How did you get hooked up with this guy...this Jason?"

"At first it was on Facebook, IMs, then through email. I knew he was older, but he seemed really nice. He said he was an accountant for some big bank in Cleveland. He sent me some pictures, and I finally agreed to meet him. The first time it was for coffee at Starbucks. He seemed even nicer in person."

"What did your parents think about you meeting up with this older guy?"

"They didn't know about it. As I said, they worked long hours, and I didn't see them very much. When I turned fourteen, I told them I didn't want the nanny any more. They agreed and, from after school on, I usually was pretty much on my own every day until around six o'clock at night."

"So, what happened after your coffee with Jason?"

"For a while, I would see him after school, maybe a couple of times a week. We would have coffee or go for ice cream. He would sit and listen to me like no one else ever did. I felt like I was getting really close to him." She paused. "Later on, he took me out to lunch a couple of times, made me feel like he really cared about me. He told me he…he said he loved me…and that…like he'd never felt that way before. Then he took me to a—" Sarah stopped and dropped her head to her hands.

Ellen waited.

After a while, Sarah raised her head and said, "I was so stupid…so fucking stupid."

"Where did he take you?"

"To a hotel."

"Did he have sex with you?" Ellen asked.

Looking away from Ellen, Sarah nodded. "It's like…after that, I was hooked…couldn't get enough of it…of him. That's when he started talking about my running away with him."

There was another long pause. Ellen wasn't sure Sarah would start up again, but then she did. "A few weeks later I said, "Okay." That's when he took me to the farmhouse. It was after that when…when everything changed. He took my phone and put me in the room with Belle…I mean Beth. I couldn't believe what was happening. I was so scared." Sarah stopped, sniffed loudly, and wiped her nose on her sleeve.

Ellen put her arm around her again. "It's okay. I know it's not easy to talk about it."

"He started making me have sex with the others, Ramone and Spade, and sometimes Denzel. They made me do all kinds of things...like stuff I'd never done before...or ever even heard of. If I objected or cried, they would stomp on me or punch me in different places where it wouldn't show...but it really hurt. Then Jason started making me do it with other people, for money...money for him, not for me. He said he owned me and beyond him and the farmhouse, I was dead."

Sarah stopped talking. The only sound was of the water lapping against the side of the boat. Ellen looked at Ozzie hoping he would say something. He didn't.

Ellen was surprised when Beth spoke up and said, "When Traci, I mean Sarah, got there, Jason started sending us out together. We were supposed to be sisters, a couple of high-school girls for disgusting, older men to play around with and have us do to them what their wives would never do." The building anger was clear in Beth's voice. "I wanted to kill every one of those fucking assholes, but, instead, I had to pretend like I was loving it."

Ellen sniffed, then said, "Well, it's all over now. We're not going to let you go back to that." Ellen looked at Ozzie. Again, he sat silent. *A good sign,* she thought. Ellen turned to Beth. "Where are your parents?" She watched as Beth's chin dropped to her chest.

Without raising her head, Beth said, "I don't have any parents. I never had a father, as far as I know anyway. My mother died when I was six. I lived in foster homes until I ran away a year and a half ago."

Ellen looked at Adam. He was shaking his head when a barely audible grunt came from Ozzie. Ellen thought he might say something, but he didn't.

"Where have you been living since then, or until you hooked up with Jason?" Ellen asked Beth.

"On the streets. I grabbed a bus to Florida to get out of

the cold for the winter. Stayed there until spring, then came back up here. I was working for another guy when Jason found me."

Adam asked, "What about school?"

Ellen thought it was a pretty dumb question and wasn't surprised when Beth didn't answer. Ellen turned to Ozzie and was about to speak when Beth began talking again.

"I was a heroin addict. And yes, I was fucking for money on the street to get it. My pimp didn't beat me that much, he kept his girls in line by giving us just enough drugs to keep us around. It was just a regular fucking night when Jason pulled up in a big old pick-up truck. He motioned me over, and we agreed to terms. Afterwards, he said I was better than the street shit I was doing and that I should come and work for him. He said he'd give me a nice house to live in and a much better life. Sounded good to me, so I figured why not give it a try. Right then and there, he passed Otis a big wad of cash and took me to the farmhouse.

"When was that?" Ellen asked.

"A little over a year ago. At first, the house seemed great, at least as good as any of the other shitholes I had been living in. But it didn't take long to figure out it was nothing more than a prison. The worst part was, the first thing he did was make me get off the drugs cold turkey, right there in the farmhouse. I thought I was going to die. He took care of me through it, though. Said I was too valuable to let go. When I asked him why I had to do it, he said he wanted me looking good...and keeping me on drugs was too fucking expensive. Like Sarah said, for a while I actually thought he was a good guy.

"Once I was feeling better, the fucking honeymoon was over. It was like I was locked in a jail with nothing to look forward to but the next time he or one of the others fucked me in some new weird way and then beat the shit out of me if I objected to any of it. After a few weeks of what they called my training, he started taking me out to his fucking clients. Shit...clients...you'd think he was a fucking lawyer or something." Beth stopped talking, and her chin dropped back down to her chest. To Ellen, it was as if she had run out of gas.

CHAPTER TWENTY

The wind had died down, and the bouncing and rolling the boat had been doing most of the night finally stopped. Adam stood and checked the chart plotter. They were nineteen miles from Grant Harbor. As he sat back down, he wondered how long it would take Ozzie to figure out they no longer were headed there or that, in the abated wind, he could pull out the rest of the sails, power up the engine, and increase his speed by several knots.

Not very long. Time is running out. I have to make a move...have to find out if there's any chance he'll work with us. Adam, too, had decided that it was not likely that Ozzie would follow through on his threat to shoot them. His concern was wrestling him for a gun and having it go off and kill someone. And now there was the matter of Ozzie's wife and daughters. *Do I want to be responsible for them getting killed? Shit, this is getting more complicated by the second.*

Adam turned and looked at Ozzie. "You haven't said anything. I know you heard what these girls said." Adam waited for a response but got nothing. *This is getting old,* he thought, his frustration building. "You told us you're not a murderer...and not a pimp. You can turn this into something positive and help us get these girls out of all this and take them someplace safe. Or you can murder us and get yourself into more trouble than you can possibly imagine...and still end up getting yourself and your family killed by these thugs you're working for." Adam hesitated then said, "We don't have much time left. What are we going to do?"

Ozzie didn't flinch. His head faced straight ahead, not at any of them. Adam looked at Ellen and saw that she was about to say something. He raised his hand and shook his head.

After a long pause, Ozzie looked at Adam and said, "I'm listening. But you gotta know, there is no way in hell I'll put my wife and daughters at risk."

"I get that," Adam said. "First of all, I suggest you call your wife right now and tell her to get herself and your kids out of the house to someplace safe, and to stay there until you tell her it's okay to come out."

Ozzie shook his head. "Can't do that. When I called Jason to tell him we were changing boats, he was pissed as hell. He said I better not fuck up because he'd have someone watching my house, and, if anything looked out of the ordinary, they'd all be gone when I got back. For all I know, there's someone there now." He shook his head. "If my wife tries to leave in the middle of the night, he'll know something's up. I sure as hell don't think they'd get very far."

Adam slammed his hand into the wheel. "Shit! You're right, can't do that. Okay then, plan B."

"What's that?" Ellen asked.

Adam shrugged. "I fucking wish I knew."

After a while Ellen asked, "If we keep going as planned, what exactly is likely to happen when we get to Grant Harbor?"

"We were supposed to get there in Spider's boat

between 2:00 and 3:00, well before daylight," Ozzie replied. "But then we had to switch to your boat. Just before that, I called Jason and told him what we were doing, that we were changing boats, and we'd be a lot later. Part of what he was so pissed about was that we might arrive in daylight. I'm supposed to call him when we're an hour out so he can let the pick-up guys know when to come."

"Sounds like he doesn't want them hanging around the marina before we get there," Adam said.

"That's for sure. Especially if it's daylight."

"Tell me the specifics of the plan for the drop off," Adam said.

"The girls stay in the boat 'til the Mexican gets the money and counts it. Once he says it's all there, I can turn over the girls. The first time I did this, I asked Jason what would stop them from killing us and taking the money back after they have the girls."

"What did he say?" Adam asked.

"He said he and this guy have a business relationship…that he wouldn't be dumb enough to start a fucking war by pulling that kind of shit."

Ellen spoke up. "And you believed him? That's putting a lot of trust in the word of someone who's a lying piece of shit."

"At that point, it wasn't like I had a lot of choices," Ozzie said.

"So, this time, what are you supposed to do once they have the girls and Jason's guy has the money?"

"Take off in Spider's boat and return to Shawnee Falls. I'd call Jason when I'm thirty minutes away. I get my money after he has his and knows the girls were safely delivered…and that I didn't fuck anything up."

"How does the money get back to him?"

"The Mexican takes it to him."

"Does Jason himself meet you when you get back?"

"No, I've never seen him in the past, but I always had the feeling he might be around somewhere, watching. Either the Mexican or the girl meets me at the dock and gives me my money."

the Mexican or the girl meets me at the dock and giving me her money."

Chapter Twenty-One

"Get up!"

Spade's eyes shot open. Jason was standing over her with his hands on his hips and a grim look on his face.

"Go to Ozzie's house. Call me when you get there."

"And good morning to you, too," Spade retorted, looking up at him.

"Don't be a smart ass. I need you to go there and watch the place."

Spade looked at her watch: 2:32 a.m. She wanted to say *fuck you* and go back to sleep but, instead, stood and stretched then shuffled into the bathroom where she splashed cold water on her face. She took a quick look in the mirror then closed her eyes and shook her head, clearly not liking what she saw staring back at her. When she came out of the bathroom, Jason tossed her a backpack. She opened it and pulled out a black hoody, a stocking cap, a pair of black leather gloves, a roll of duct tape, a handful of zip-ties, and a switchblade knife. She flipped open the six-inch blade, touched the point with her finger then closed it and dropped it back into the pack. From a separate zippered compartment, Spade pulled out a 9-mm Glock. She checked to make sure the clip was full and tucked the gun into her belt. Without a word, she re-stuffed the backpack, walked out of the farmhouse, climbed into Jason's black, F-150 pickup truck, and headed up to Rt. 2 for the drive to Shawnee Falls.

When she hit the highway, traffic was light, and she wished she had made herself a coffee for the road. Her mind flashed through a half dozen subjects before, as always, settling on Jason. Spade had known of him since they were in middle school together. He was the acknowledged smartest kid in the class while she, Amy Dankworth, was the invisible, classic under-achiever. He lived in a middle-class, Cleveland suburb with both his parents. She resided with her alcoholic mother in what she knew her classmates referred to as the Dogpatch area of the school district, which was, literally, on the other side of the railroad tracks.

By the time Spade turned thirteen, she was a tall, black-haired, blue-eyed beauty. She knew the boys were always looking at her and, out of boredom more than anything else, began experimenting with sex. As it turned out, she loved it and, by the time she got to high school, realized she must be pretty good at it because the boys were all over her. That is, all except the cripplingly shy, smart kid named Jason Walker.

As the occasional headlights sped past her, Spade recalled how fascinated she had been by the weird, brainy kid who wandered the halls, rarely speaking to anyone, and never receiving anything but a perfect score on any test he took. His refusal to acknowledge her existence, no matter how much she flirted and tried to get his attention, frustrated her almost to the point of pissing her off.

At the beginning of her junior year, Spade decided to try using her mind instead of her body to impress Jason. Knowing she was fully capable of getting straight A's, she began to take her Adderall pills instead of selling them in the school hallways. She spent that entire school year doing everything she could to get his attention. Finally, as exams approached that spring, she got Jason to agree to come to her house to help her study for their upcoming chemistry exam.

It was a warm night, and Spade greeted him at the door wearing a light-green sundress with tiny pink flowers that barely covered her perfectly rounded butt. He was wearing dark-blue athletic shorts that hung to his knees and an orange Cleveland Browns T-shirt. Spade stifled a laugh as she directed him to the couch and sat next to him. Jason seemed oblivious to her until their knees touched. Although, he wouldn't look at her, she was sure he started breathing more heavily. And then, a few minutes later, he seemed to stop breathing altogether when she rested her hand on the four inches of skin that was visible between the bottom of his shorts and his knee cap.

Spade laughed to herself when she recalled the loud gasp he emitted when she moved her hand slowly up his leg, and then how quickly things progressed from there. Although Jason clearly was a virgin, he was an unbelievably quick study. Bottom line, he loved having sex just as much as she did and was eager to learn whatever she was willing to teach him. In the months that followed, he wanted it as often as she was available and could go over and over again, non-stop until she was totally worn out.

What puzzled Spade the most about him during that time was how different he was from all the other guys she had screwed who became instantly infatuated and claimed to be in love with her. For Jason, sex was more like a science project. No expressions of affection, just fucking and sucking in whatever new way she introduced to him. She kept hoping that would change but it never did. By the summer after their graduation from high school, she had stopped seeing other guys and truly cared about him.

Spade recalled how disappointed she was when the time came for Jason to head off to college. Instead of telling her how much he would miss her, his only concern was with whom he would have sex when she wasn't around. Spade responded that, considering how well she had taught him, he shouldn't worry because he probably would have girls chasing him all over campus.

For the next seven years, Spade didn't hear a peep from him, but never stopped wondering where he was and what he was doing. And then, on a cold, January evening, she was at a Friday happy hour in a bar in downtown Cleveland when she looked down the way and saw Jason sweet talking an underage looking girl. When he turned his head to take a sip from his drink, their eyes met, and he did a doubletake that made Spade laugh out loud. Without another word to the woman he was talking to, Jason picked up his drink, walked down the bar and gave Spade a hug. Thirty minutes later, they were at her apartment fucking their brains out and, except for a couple of food breaks, didn't stop until early Monday morning.

Whenever Spade reflected on that night, three things stood out. First, Jason's prowess as a sexual athlete had grown exponentially since she was last with him. Second, his shyness was gone, replaced by an inexplicable ability to be charming. Third, what had not changed was his inability, or refusal, to express feelings of affection. While she may never have stopped loving him, their marathon sex appeared to have been nothing more than sport to him.

With half the distance to Ozzie's house still to go, Spade pulled into an all-night gas station/minimart to grab a large coffee and a medium-sized bag of peanut M & M's. Back on the road, her mind went to how, over the next two years, her relationship with Jason was based entirely on sex. Although he talked more than he used to and could be very charming when he wanted to be, Jason avoided conversing about anything personal and was always elusive when she raised the subject of how he made a living. There were those occasions, though, when every now and then she could get him to talk about his childhood, albeit never anything specific. To the best she could glean from what little he did say, mostly when he was drinking his expensive scotch, Jason had grown up in a home with an abusive mother who constantly demeaned and belittled him, and occasionally even beat him. If that was true, Spade guessed that might explain why he hated women so much.

It had been four years since Jason gave her the name Spade and talked her into quitting her job and coming to work for him. At first, she was shocked when she saw what he was doing and threatened to leave or even report him to the police. But he was a master at manipulation and, using the feelings he obviously knew she had for him, was able to convince her that it really wasn't all that bad. No matter how disgusting and wrong she knew what she was participating in to be, she was under Jason's spell and couldn't get herself to say no to him. The longer it went on, the easier it all became even though, from deep inside of her, a voice kept screaming that she had become just as big a monster as she knew he was.

Now she was on her way to Ozzie's house and had no idea what Jason might ask her to do once she got there. On two other occasions when Ozzie was late with a delivery, Jason had sent her to stakeout the house, but nothing ever came of either one. She knew Ozzie lived with his wife and two teenage daughters and figured that she could handle scaring them or even hurting them a little bit if she had to. That actually was something she had become rather good at with Jason's girls. But what if he ordered her to really hurt them, or even kill them? She felt her entire body shudder at the thought of it as she pulled off the highway onto Rt. 6 and headed into town.

Ozzie's house was easy to find. It was on a cul-de-sac in an ordinary looking subdivision of 1960's two-story homes that repeated themselves every fourth house. She pulled to the curb a half a block away and cut the engine. She snatched her phone off the passenger seat and called Jason.

"I'm here."

"How's it look?"

"Normal...dark."

"Stay put. Watch for movement. I'll call when I know what the fuck's going on."

Spade popped a few M&M's into her mouth then sat back and waited.

Chapter Twenty-Two

Adam's mind plowed through every conceivable alternative. The more dubious they were the more exasperated he became. *There has to be a way to protect these girls and Ozzie's family...and ourselves. But, how...how the hell do we do that?* The headache that began in the back of his neck was migrating up his skull. *Not much time left to figure it out. This is so fucking crazy.*

Adam turned to Ozzie. "Tell me again why we can't call the police, tell them when and where we're coming in, and have them meet us there."

Ozzie responded with biting sarcasm, "How about because as soon as one of those assholes gets a text off to Jason, my family is dead. No cops. That's an absolute."

"Right...okay, I get it. Before we involve the police, the guys at that end have to communicate to Jason that they have the girls, and Ramone has to let him know he has the money."

"Close, but not quite. I have to know my family is out

of the house and safe before any cops are called."

"In that case, we have a problem," Ellen declared, "a really big problem. Because, as long as I'm alive, they are not getting their hands on these girls." She looked out toward the horizon and then back at Adam and Ozzie. "So…it looks like we're all pretty well screwed."

The tension was palpable. Adam scanned the faces of each of his passengers, then stood and said, "Ellen, can you take the wheel? I need to go down and get something."

Ellen stood and worked her way past Beth. Adam went around the other way. He expected Ozzie to object but was relieved when he didn't. When he got to the steps, Adam paused in front of Sarah. "You look cold, why don't you come down and warm up for a few minutes?"

Sarah shrugged and said, "Okay."

Adam went down ahead of Sarah. When they were standing face to face in the salon, Adam saw that, as he suspected, he and Sarah were eye to eye, which meant she was his height, about 5'6". He guessed his shoulders were much wider than hers, but it was hard to tell with the bulky fleece jacket she was wearing.

He turned on the cabin lights then asked Sarah if she needed to use the toilet.

"Uh, huh."

"You can use this one." He pointed to a door to her left. "I'll wait here for you."

When she came back out into the salon, Adam was sitting on the bench seat in front of the nav station. He took off his yellow foul-weather jacket and held it out to Sarah. "Let's switch coats…and hats."

Sarah looked puzzled.

"I would like to try something. I'll give them back to you."

"Okay." She took off her fleece jacket and knit hat and handed them to Adam. He gave her the old sailing hat he was wearing. He put on Sarah's jacket and pulled her hat down over his forehead. She put on Adam's jacket and hat.

Adam turned to switch off the cabin lights but stopped when he heard the sound of a drawer in the galley being pulled open. He looked back at Sarah. She was standing in front of him holding a large butcher knife out in front of her.

Adam jumped back hitting his head on the wall behind him.

"Whoa... Sarah...what are you doing?" Adam lifted his hands out in front of him. "Let's not..."

"Oh, no—"

"...do anything—"

"No...this isn't—"

"Please, just put the knife down."

"This isn't for you. I was thinking I could use it to get Ozzie. He would never suspect—"

Adam let out a huge sigh. "Sarah...we're not going to do that." Adam reached out his hand. "Please, give me the knife."

Sarah hung her head and lowered the knife to her side. "I'm sorry, I just thought—"

"We have to think of Ozzie's family. Anyway, I have an idea that I'm hoping might work."

Sarah sighed and put the knife back in the drawer.

When she turned back around, there was a tear running down her cheek. "I didn't mean to frighten you, I just thought, you know, I could—"

"It's okay, Sarah. Don't worry about it, I understand." Adam pointed to the steps. "Let's go back up." He switched off the cabin lights and said, "Let me go first."

When Adam got to the top, he paused with his head down.

Ellen looked at him and asked, "Sarah, are you okay? Are you feeling sick from being down below?"

Adam shook his head but didn't say anything.

Keeping one hand on the wheel, Ellen reached out and motioned with her other hand to the seat next to her, "Come and sit down here."

When Adam slid into the seat, she put her hand on his

shoulder and did a double-take. "What the fuck, Adam."

"Do you think it could work?"

"Sure, for about five seconds. Actually, I doubt it'll even take that long for whomever it is to figure out you aren't one of the two teenage girls he was expecting to see. As soon as he does, he'll let Jason know and we're all—"

"Hold on a second, I know that, but just listen...here's what I'm thinking." Adam looked at Ozzie. "You're supposed to call Jason when we're an hour away, right?" Ozzie nodded. "Instead, you call when we're a half-hour out so we can get there ahead of everyone else and get the lay of the land. When Ramone and the pickup guys arrive, I can be up on deck as one of the girls. We say the other one is seasick and lying down. If they want to look, we can have a blanket covering up some pillows. Ellen and the girls will be off the boat hiding somewhere. They give Ramone the money, he counts it, and takes off."

Ozzie was shaking his head. "That's fucking crazy. There's still the—"

"Just wait, let me finish. You have two guns. Between us, we should be able to take care of the rest of them before they figure it out. If it works, Jason will never know we still have the girls, and we can head back and make sure your family is safe before we contact the police." Adam hesitated, then said, "We'll need a car, though, taking the boat back will take too long."

"Are you fucking nuts?" Ozzie snarled. "This isn't a God damn fantasy video game." He waved a gun at Adam. "You don't get it. This guy threatened to kill my wife and daughters. Do you really think the assholes at the other end are any different...that whoever the fuck they are won't be armed? Why the fuck do you think I brought my guns? These assholes would probably kill you as soon as look at you."

"I know all that, but we have to, at least—"

Beep, beep. The alarm on the autopilot signaled they were off course.

"Adam, take the wheel," Ellen said.

Adam traded places with Ellen and reset their course.

"He's right," Ellen said. "No offense, but this isn't a Disney movie. With that kind of money at stake, nobody is going to just roll over, and they're probably going to want to see what they're buying before they pass over the cash."

"I'm not saying it's a sure thing, but if we play it—"

"There may be a way that'll give us a better shot at making it work." Ellen paused, collected her thoughts, then said, "As long as you keep your head down and don't take off your hat, you could pass for Sarah. If they want a closer look, I can be out front, as Beth. They'd have no reason to think I'm not one of the—"

"Are you crazy? There's no way you're going to do that."

"Why not? As soon as Ramone gets the money and takes off, the three of us will have a better chance of taking care of the pickup people." Ellen looked at Ozzie, "You're going to have to give us one of your guns."

Adam shook his head and pounded the wheel with his hand. "No, that's nuts. I've never fired a gun. I don't even know how to—"

"I do."

Adam stared at Ellen. "You do?"

"Yes, I do. My dad grew up on a farm. They had all kinds of guns. He used to hunt with his father all the time. He taught both my brothers and me to shoot when we were kids whenever we went to the farm to visit my grandparents."

Adam knew Ellen's parents. He had visited them with her at their home in Manchester, New Hampshire, and the previous Labor Day weekend at their summer house at the shore on Cape Cod. Ellen's father, Arthur, was a plastic surgeon. He was a little staid, compared to her mother, Grace, but still very welcoming. He taught Adam how to catch bluefish off the beach, which they took home for Grace to dump into a giant cast-iron pot of her famous seafood chowder as it simmered over a wood fire in the back yard.

Ellen had warned Adam that her mom was a little unique, which proved to be true. With long, graying hair, and her usual bright colored, tie-dyed smock hanging loosely over blue jeans with holes in the knees, and glittery flip-flops on her feet, she looked like a real-life, leftover sixties flower child.

According to Ellen, after twenty years as a surgical nurse, Grace had branched out and refashioned herself as a *Wholistic Spiritual Life Coach.* Ellen's two older brothers, Art, Jr. and David, were both docs, as well. Adam had enjoyed playing a round of golf with them. They both were married, and David had two young sons. Adam recalled how much he liked all of them and thinking at the time that someday becoming part of Ellen's family wouldn't be a bad way to go.

But now, depending on what happens over the next few hours, that may never happen.

"Before I moved to Ohio, Dave bought me a gun and took me to the range," Ellen said.

Adam was stunned. "Do you...do you still have it?"

"Of course. It's in a lockbox in the top of my closet."

"Were you planning on bringing it to my house?"

"Yes, but don't worry, I have a concealed carry permit."

"You do?"

"Yes, I do."

"How come you never told me about this?"

"You made it pretty clear, right off, how you felt about guns."

Adam shook his head. His bride, the love of his life, was a gunslinger and he never even knew it. He looked at Ellen. "Okay, but still, there is no way I'm going to let you do that. You could get yourself killed."

"Oh, so, it's okay for you to risk getting killed for these girls, but not me. Why is that...because you're a boy and

I'm a girl?"

"No...ah, it's not that...I just think—"

"Don't even try that one."

"I never said—"

"Listen, I know you can handle yourself hand-to-hand with just about anyone. You didn't spend your whole life wrestling and working out for nothing. And whether you believe it or not, I can handle a handgun."

"No! There is no way you're going to—"

"Ozzie, can you let go of one of those guns...preferably the smaller one? It looks like the same size as mine." Ozzie didn't respond.

Adam opened his mouth to voice another objection, but stopped. There were no good answers. He couldn't let Ellen do this, but he also couldn't allow these girls to be turned over to whomever was at the other end. The only positive development was that he no longer believed Ozzie really would shoot them if he turned the boat around but doing that could result in Ozzie's family being killed.

How the fuck can this be happening? I'm a lawyer from Shawnee Falls, Ohio. All I did was get married and head out for a weekend honeymoon sail. And now this. How the hell did it all get so fucked up in so short a time? He closed his eyes, hoping that, when he opened them, Ozzie, the two girls and everything about this fucking nightmare would be gone.

He felt someone take hold of his arm. It was Ellen. He opened his eyes and looked at her.

"Adam, if we aren't going to turn this boat around—"

"And that's not going to happen," Ozzie said.

"...what choice do we have?"

"Ozzie's right." They all looked at Beth. "Jason is one mean fucker. He probably would kill his family if he doesn't go through with this. In the year I've been at the house, he would have killed me in a second if I stopped bringing in cash. My guess is the guy he sold us to is just as nasty as he is. I'm not saying I don't want you to do this, but you have to know...you all could end up dead at the end of it...even if you do turn us over to them."

A chill went up Adam's spine and his stomach started to do a slow roll.

Sarah said, "She's right. Beth and I are the only ones who are of value to them. They could care less about any of you."

Ellen looked at Sarah. "Do you think Jason is capable of murder? That he would kill—"

"Yeah, I do," Sarah said. "About a month after I got there, the two girls in the other room started getting weird. They had been big producers and knew it. One night I heard them telling Jason that they wanted some of the cash they were bringing in for themselves or they wouldn't go out anymore."

"What did he say?" Ellen asked.

"Not much, which surprised me," Sarah said. "He went back downstairs but a few minutes later I heard Denzell...Daveed...come up and go into their room. From the sounds coming out of there it was pretty clear he was beating the shit out of them."

"Yeah, and probably flashing that fucking shiny, toothy smile the whole time," Beth said. "The next morning both girls were gone...never saw either one of them again. Later that day, we came back to the farmhouse and saw Daveed scrubbing out the back of Jason's pickup truck. He had a bucket of soapy water, a long-handled brush, and a hose. We'd never seen him doing anything like that before. We figured he killed them, used the truck to get rid of the bodies, and was making sure there weren't any traces of blood left in the truck."

The boat was consumed by an eerie silence. Then Sarah said, "She's right. Jason would kill any of us without thinking twice about it."

Beth added, "I appreciate what you're trying to do for us but...I think it would be better if you just drop us off and let it go down as planned. I sure as hell can't say I'm worth you risking your lives over."

"I agree," Sarah said.

Ellen wiped her eyes, then reached over and pulled Beth to her. "Yes, you are…both of you are. You're worth just as much as any of us. We're not going to turn you over to these assholes."

Chapter Twenty-Three

Adam noticed the wind had eased up even more and the waves were down to less than a foot when Ozzie leaned forward in his seat and squinted at the knot meter. "We're only going four knots, it's time to power up this thing."

Then he looked at the chart plotter. Adam waited for his reaction.

"You're not headed in the right direction. You're way north. What the fuck's wrong with you? Do you really want to die?"

When Adam felt the barrel of the gun touch the back of his head, he turned and pushed it away. "Stop threatening to kill me, Ozzie. And stop pointing those guns at us! If you want to shoot me, then go ahead and do it...but I don't think you do. So, unless I'm wrong about that, it's time to put those damn guns away. We've all had enough of this shit."

Other than a loud gasp from Ellen, there was no sound for what seemed like a full minute. Adam hoped he hadn't miscalculated and screwed up bigtime. He sat back down.

"Listen Ozzie, you said you've never killed anyone. If that's true, I don't believe you want to start now."

Adam waited for Ozzie to say something. When he didn't, Adam said, "We have to protect these girls, and we have to protect your wife and daughters. It's time we work together to do that."

Ozzie remained silent, his head turned toward the water. Finally, he looked at Adam and said, "Believe it or not, I don't like this any more than you do. If I'd known what it was about back when it all started, I never would have gotten into it."

"I believe you," Adam said. "So, how about it? Will you work with us?" Adam looked at his watch. It was just past 3:00 a.m. "With the wind down, I can pull out the rest of the sails, power up, and get us there well before daylight, which I think would be better for us."

Ozzie looked at Adam, then Ellen, then back at Adam. "I'll give it a try, but you have to know, my family comes first. If it ends up being you or them getting hurt, it's going to be you."

"I understand...and we'll take that," Adam said, "So how about putting the guns away?"

Ozzie's shoulders slumped, and he slowly stuffed the small gun in an inside pocket of his jacket and the other in his belt.

Adam had just let out a sigh of relief when his ears picked up the sound of a motor in the distance. It became obvious he wasn't the only one who heard it when the others turned and looked off toward the northeast. Adam squinted to make out the lights of a boat coming in their direction.

"Who the fuck is that?" Ozzie asked.

"It's coming pretty fast," Adam said, just before a powerful spotlight swept across the water in their direction.

"It's the Coast Guard," Ozzie said. "Fuck...damn it...we can't—"

"They can help us," Ellen said.

"No, they can't. We can't let them—"

Ellen stood. "They can get the girls to safety."

"No, it'll fuck up everything, you're not getting it," Ozzie screamed. "We have to deliver these girls and get Jason his money. If we don't, he'll kill—"

"Ellen, he may be right. We shouldn't—"

"For God's sake, Adam, continuing on could get us all killed. I thought we wanted to help these girls."

The boat drew closer, the spotlight intermittently lighting up the sailboat's cockpit. They were running out of decision time. Adam felt perspiration forming on his forehead. *The Coast Guard won't know we aren't part of this trafficking scheme. The boat will be impounded, and Ellen and I will be hauled off to the nearest jail until it gets sorted out. If that happens, the girls will be safe but what about Ozzie's family? They could be killed. But Ellen's right, if we keep going, we all could end up dead.*

"Ozzie, maybe Ellen's right. With their help, we could have the police at your house in minutes."

"Not good enough. Jason may have already taken them away somewhere. You heard what the girls said. If he knows we've called the cops, he'll kill them. I told you, I'll do what I can to help, but you can't let them stop this boat…we have to keep going."

Adam hesitated for a second then said, "Beth, Sarah, go down below now, before their light is back on us. Go to the forward bunk. Get under the covers but only have one of your heads outside the blanket. Don't come out until I tell you to."

Ellen grabbed Adam's arm. "Adam, no. What are you doing? This is their chance to get away."

The boat was closing in on them.

"Ozzie's right, if Jason already has his family—"

"But we don't know that, and if we keep going, we could be—"

"No!" Ozzie was on his feet. "We have to—"

"We're out of time," Adam said firmly. The spotlight was now fully on them. "I'm making the call. Follow my lead…let me do the talking."

The boat, which Adam now saw wasn't the Coast Guard but Customs and Border Protection, stopped about twenty feet away. The amplified voice was crisp and clear. "Drop your sails and shut off your engine."

Shit, we're out here in the middle of the night with no lights. They must think we're drug smugglers…or worse. Fuck…we are…this is fucking insane.

Once the sails were down, the CBP boat pulled alongside and dropped a line over the sailboat's midship cleat. The four officers wearing life jackets with CBP printed in yellow letters on the back did not look like anyone you would want to mess with. Two of them stood motionless with their hands covering their holstered weapons. The one who seemed to be in charge spoke. "Everyone stand as you are and keep all hands where we can see them. What is your destination?"

Adam said, "Grant Harbor."

"What is your port of call?"

"Shawnee Falls Yacht Club."

"How many people onboard?"

"The three of us plus one more in bed down below."

"Are you the captain of this vessel?"

"I am," Adam said.

"Care to tell me why you are running without lights?"

"I didn't realize I was until you were approaching. Whoever went down to use the head the last time must have hit those switches when they turned off the cabin lights before coming back up."

"We're coming aboard," the one who had been doing the talking said. She and one other officer climbed onto the sailboat. Her name tag read A. Turner. "I need to see some identification and the boat registration."

"Sure." Adam pointed to the companionway. "I'll have to go below to get them."

She nodded to the other officer, who pulled out a flashlight and climbed down the steps into the cabin.

"You can go down and get your documents."

While Adam was retrieving his wallet and the boat registration from the desk at the nav station, the officer who had preceded him down the steps was shining his light into the forward cabin. He let it linger on the blonde head that was poking out from under the blanket on the bunk. Adam's heart raced.

If he lifts the blanket, we're fucked.

Finally, the officer turned and began a cursory look around the salon. When the officer gave him a nod, Adam switched on the navigation lights then climbed back up into the cockpit where Turner was finishing up getting Ozzie and Ellen's personal information. As Adam handed Turner the boat registration and his driver's license, he noticed Ozzie sitting with his arms wrapped around his body, an apparent unconscious effort to protect his guns. Ellen was sitting behind the wheel, stone-faced, with her arms crossed tightly across her chest.

I don't think she's very happy, Adam thought.

"Why are you running at night?" A. Turner asked.

"We're supposed to meet someone at Grant Harbor first thing in the morning. Thought we would try a night sail."

"You come directly from Shawnee Falls?"

"No, we spent the evening at Kelleys Island…anchored in the North Bay."

"Seems to me you should have stayed there."

"You're right, it wasn't the best idea."

Turner was holding the registration up to the light. "Looks like you just bought this boat."

"Yes, this was our first trip with it."

The other officer came back up into the cockpit. According to his tag, his name was: R. Jackson. Adam noticed him looking at him intently.

"Any firearms onboard?" Turner asked.

It was the question Adam had been dreading. The last thing he wanted was to be caught lying to a Customs Officer. He swallowed hard and opened his mouth to speak but before any sound came out, R. Jackson said, "I know you. Aren't you a lawyer?"

Adam exhaled. "Yes, I am."

"Isn't your name Kennedy?"

"Yes, Adam Kennedy."

"I was at the courthouse a month ago on a personal matter. You were in the middle of a hearing on what everyone was calling the crime-of-the-century for the county. A murder or something. I stopped in and watched for a while. You're pretty famous around there."

"The Cummings case," Adam said."

"You're the one representing that guy?" Turner asked.

"Yep."

"Whatever happened? Was he found guilty?"

"Not yet. The trial is in November." Adam looked at Jackson. "What you saw was a hearing on the Motion to Suppress."

"How did that go?" From the grin on her face, Adam guessed that Turner already knew the answer.

"Not very well for my client."

Turner's grin broadened into a full smile. "Actually, I recognized you, too," she said.

Adam gave the officer a curious look. She was about his age and did look vaguely familiar, but he couldn't recall ever meeting her.

"When I was in high school, I raced against you, Jon Evans, and Nick Cromwell at the Sailing Club in Sandusky."

Adam's eyes popped. "Wait a minute... Turner...you're Annie Turner. You had the all-girl team that beat the shit out of all the boys for years."

"That was us. Actually, you guys were the only ones we never beat."

"I can't believe it. You're a...wow, it's good to see you...well, kind of... I guess...other than, you know..." Adam stammered.

"Yeah, I understand. Sorry about giving you such a hard time...you being so famous and all."

Adam actually felt his face turning red. "Okay, I deserve that. Anyway…I'm the one who screwed up."

She passed the ID and registration back to Adam. "I won't hold you up any longer…just make sure you keep your lights on. We'll cast off, and you can get going."

"That was lucky," Ozzie said as they watched the CBP boat pull away.

"I think I'll wait to see if any of us are still alive when the sun comes up to call that lucky," Ellen snapped in response.

Rather than try to respond to that one, Adam asked, "Would you go and tell the girls they can come out?"

Chapter Twenty-Four

For the first time since she woke up to the strange sounds of something bumping against the back of the boat, Ellen allowed herself to sit back with a modest sigh of relief. When Beth leaned into her, Ellen felt her shaking. Although the wind was down, the temperature had been dropping all night, and Ellen realized she too felt chilled. She slipped her arm around Beth and pulled her closer.

How screwed up is this? This is my wedding night. I should be snuggling up to my new husband to keep warm. Instead, I'm out here on the lake heading to who knows what and don't have a clue if I'll still be alive this time tomorrow. Ellen's whole body gave a shudder. *I can't believe this is happening.*

When she brought the girls up from down below, Ellen wondered if Adam had seen her wince from the pain in her shoulder, or felt her exhaustion, or if he too hurt all over.

She looked at Adam standing behind the wheel. "How much longer?"

"We're 14 miles out...a little more than two hours."

"So, that's how long we have to figure out how we're going to pull off this plan of yours?"

"Unless someone can come up with a better idea, yep...that's what it looks like."

Ellen stood. "Beth is shivering, I'm sure Sarah is cold too. I'm going to take them down for a while to warm up."

"Okay...for a while...but then we need to talk."

Ellen stepped up to the companionway and motioned for Sarah and Beth to follow her. Before going down, she turned toward Adam and Ozzie and asked, "Can I get either of you anything?"

"Not for me," Adam responded.

"Nope," Ozzie said. "But I think I'm going to take a leak off the back of the boat if you all don't mind."

Ellen watched him climb down onto the swim platform and thought about jumping back there and pushing him off—which a few hours earlier would have been a no-brainer. Adam was looking at her and shaking his head as if reading her mind. She knew he was right. At this point, they needed Ozzie, and there was no way she wanted to be responsible for anything happening to his family. She turned and climbed down the companionway steps with Sarah and Beth following close behind her.

As she stepped off the bottom step, she heard Ozzie say, "Thanks for not pushing me off when I was down there." To the best she could tell, Adam didn't respond.

Ellen turned on the lights, pointed to the table and said, "You two have a seat. You're freezing. I'm going to make some tea." Ellen lit the stove and put a kettle of water on to boil. "Will you both have some?"

Sarah answered, "Yes, please."

Beth, at the table with her head resting on her forearms, mumbled, "Okay."

"How about something to eat?" Ellen added, setting a couple of granola bars on the table. "Or I have some fresh bread. I could make up some peanut butter and jelly sandwiches."

"No, thank you," Sarah said.

Beth didn't respond.

Ellen began to step back to the stove but saw Beth crying. More than crying, she sobbed. Ellen wrapped her arms around her. "This is all going to be over soon. Trust me, we're going to do everything we can to get you safely home."

Beth raised her head, wiped her nose on her sleeve and, barely above a whisper said, "I don't have a home."

Ellen wanted to kick herself. Beth had mentioned earlier that she was an orphan. Fighting back her own tears, she patted Beth on the back.

"When I turned fifteen, I decided I'd rather live on the street than have one more asshole sneaking around outside my door trying to get a peak every time I got undressed."

"That actually happened?"

"Oh, that's nothing…those were the good guys. I could tell you some shit you wouldn't—" She stopped and looked at Ellen. "I'm sorry, I don't want to gross you out." She dropped her head back down onto her forearms.

Ellen stroked the back of her neck. "Don't worry about that, Beth. If it would help to talk about it, I can take it."

The kettle started whistling. Ellen wiped her eyes as she got up to make the tea. "How old were you when all that started?"

"I was twelve and hardly had tits when the first jerk tried to feel me up while he tucked me in at night." Beth paused then said, "Don't get me wrong, most of the foster parents out there are really nice people. I just had some bad luck with a couple of them. Some of the ones I had were pretty good, really tried to give me a nice home." She shrugged. "Actually, the problems I had with the good ones were probably my fault. I wasn't exactly the easiest to…you know, get along with."

Ellen felt a wave of nausea wash over her as an image of a frightened little girl fighting off a loathsome, deranged older man with stained teeth and foul-smelling breath swirled in her head. She shook it off as she poured three steaming mugs of tea, brought them to the table, and sat next to Beth. "So, you were living on the street from the time you were fifteen?"

"Only for a month or so. When I went to Florida, I stayed at a shelter in Jacksonville for four months, till they kicked me out for doing drugs. When I came back north, Otis picked me up. Right off, he started giving me drugs and food if I'd fuck him and anyone else who'd pay him to do me. He let me sleep in a stinking, fucking flop house. After a couple months of that, Jason found me. He said he had a nice house I could live in, and he'd take care of me and help me get off the drugs. He actually told me he loved me...and I was fucking dumb enough to believe him."

Beth stopped, picked up one of the napkins Ellen had placed on the table and blew her nose. "The fucking asshole...at first, I really did like him. He helped me get off the drugs, one of the worst things I've ever done in my life. Once I was clean, everything changed. He started sending me out to his fucking clients. When Sarah got there, he took us out together—a real sister act. He said we were his biggest producers...that we better not screw it up because he could get a lot of money for us."

"Where did he get the other girls...where did they come from?"

"We didn't interact with them much, mostly just when we were in the kitchen at the same time. When I was with Otis, some of the girls were out of the foster system, like me, or runaways. Most of them were druggies when he picked them up. But Jason always said he preferred classier girls."

"I know that two of the girls at the house while I was there were from regular homes, like mine." Sarah said. "He sucked them in and got them to run away...just like—" Sarah stopped, and her bottom lip began to tremble.

Ellen put her arm around her. "Don't worry, sweetheart. All that is done."

"I wish I could believe that," Beth said.

"You can, and I promise I will do everything in my power to see to it that you have a good place to live when this is over."

Sarah reached across the table and took Beth's hand. Beth pulled it to her face and said, "Sarah is the only person who's been nice to me for as far back as I can remember."

Chapter-Twenty-Five

Adam glanced at his watch—3:16 a.m. According to the chart plotter, they were eleven miles out.

Less than two hours to figure out how the hell we're going to make this happen. Fuck...there's only about a thousand ways it could all go wrong.

Adam recalled what Ozzie had said about everyone else having guns. A knot formed in his gut. *Shit, what if they figure we're not the girls they're buying before we want them to? What if someone starts shooting?*

Over the years, Adam had seen countless photos of GSWs—gunshot wounds—as they were passed around for jurors to examine during trials: the face half blown off, the disgusting bloody cavity opened by a shotgun blast to the abdomen, the fine hole in the forehead caused by the low caliber execution style shot delivered from pointblank range. The images flashing through his brain paused on one of the bodies. It was a woman, and she was turning her head slowly in his direction. As his mind focused on the tortured, bloody visage, the face he saw was Ellen's. There was terror in her eyes and her mouth was open in an agonizingly silent call for help. He felt the knot in his stomach expand and work its way to the surface. He tried to erase the vision, but it hung on, refusing to be banished. *Oh, God, what if Ellen gets shot? If she dies, it will be my fault...I will have killed her. What the fuck am I doing?* A cold sweat descended upon him like a thick, dark cloud. He grabbed for the lifeline, leaned over the side of the boat and emptied the contents of his gut into the lake. When the retching finally stopped, he continued to hang there, watching the water pass under him, wishing that he and Ellen were anywhere but here.

The sound of a strange tune Adam didn't recognize brought him back. He straightened and turned around in time to see Ozzie reach into his jacket pocket and pull out his phone. "Yeah?" He looked at Adam. "How much longer?"

Adam hesitated, then, deciding to give them some leeway, said, "At least two...maybe two-and-a-half hours."

Ozzie repeated what Adam told him into his phone, listened, then said, "You wanted me to call when I'm an hour out, I'm going to do that."

Adam heard a voice at the other end but couldn't make out what was being said.

Ozzie responded, "Okay, I'll—"

Adam watched as Ozzie's face twitched.

"Yes, I told you, I get it. There's nothing to worry about. Okay...okay, I will."

Ozzie pressed off and then slipped the phone back into his pocket. He looked at Adam. "He's definitely not happy."

Spade grabbed the vibrating phone off the seat beside her. It was Jason. She hoped to hell he was calling to say everything was fine and she could come back to the farmhouse.

She leaned her head back against the seat and answered. "Hello."

"What's it look like?"

Fuck, he can't even say hello.

"The same."

"Make sure they're there"

"Everything's dark. How do I do that?"

"Figure it out," Jason said, and then he was gone.

Spade pulled the black stocking cap out of the backpack and put it on, then snatched a small flashlight from the glovebox. When she climbed out of the truck, a streetlight at the corner allowed her to see the outline of Ozzie's house a few doors down. It was a modest two-story, painted a dull blue with white trim. The attached, two-car garage was on the right, facing the street. She approached the garage first but the small windows at the top of the door were too high for her to see in.

She walked around to the side, found a service door, turned the knob, and eased it open. Directly in front of her was a dark gray Honda minivan that blocked the view to the rest of the garage. She closed the door and walked around to the back of the house onto a cement patio. She stepped past the rusted gas grill and the round umbrella table surrounded by four molded plastic chairs. Using the flashlight, she could see tiny weeds sprouting out of a multitude of cracks in the cement.

Spade stopped and surveyed the area. To her right was a large backyard with grass a couple of inches higher than it should have been. She was relieved to see that on the other side of the split-rail fence that bordered the property was a long row of unruly, overgrown bushes blocking the view to the house behind Ozzie's on the next street over.

To her left was a door into the house, and next to it was a pair of side-by-side, double hung windows. Spade approached the windows and peered inside, but it was too dark to see much of anything.

Crouching below the windowsill, she flicked on the flashlight and shined it through the glass. Immediately in front of her was a rectangular wood table with four ladderback chairs. In front of each chair was a blue and yellow plaid placemat. Spade pictured Ozzie, his wife, and their two daughters sitting at the table eating dinner and talking about how everyone's day had been.

She shined the light through a doorway into what appeared to be a dining room with an archway on the right into what looked like a darkened living room. Spade shuddered when she envisioned what she would have seen if it had been her home when she was a kid. The woman with scraggly, salt and pepper hair slouched to one side on a worn, brown Naugahyde recliner with her mouth open, appearing to be asleep, would have been her mother. A pile of empty beer bottles lying on the floor next to the chair would grow until the woman ordered her young daughter to pick them up and haul them to the trash.

Spade swung the light back to the table. She envisioned a very young Amy sitting there, with her long black hair falling over her shoulders, writing on a sheet of lined paper with a yellow pencil, a math book opened in front of her. Spade's hand unconsciously moved to her abdomen as she recalled how hungry that little girl would have been. Unpleasant memories continued to flood Spade's brain until she finally looked away from the empty kitchen table. *Fuck. This is not what I'm here for. Do your fucking job.*

Spade raised the beam and scanned the rest of the kitchen. To the right was all the usual stuff: refrigerator, stove with microwave mounted above it and next to it, the sink with a window over it, facing what she assumed was the house next door. Directly across from the table was a built-in desk and a chair that matched the ones around the table. A woman's purse hung from the back of the chair. What looked like a ring of car keys lay on the desk.

To Spade it all looked remarkably normal, or at least what she had always envisioned a normal home would look like in the middle of the night, when everyone inside was asleep. She turned off the flashlight and walked around the other side of the house, peering through the windows into dark rooms, unable to see much of anything. When she got back to the front yard, she took one more look then returned to the truck and called Jason.

"Well?"

"It all looks fine. No reason to think they aren't in there."

"Stay and watch. Call me if anything seems off. I'll let you know if you need to go in."

Spade responded, "Okay," but he had already hung up.

CHAPTER TWENTY-SIX

After taking a few minutes to allow his stomach to settle and swish some gulps of water, Adam turned to Ozzie and said, "So, you're supposed to let him know when we're an hour away?"

"Yeah. He doesn't want those guys hanging around the marina waiting for us."

"We definitely want to get there before they do. As I said before, I think you should call when we're thirty minutes out, but tell him we'll be there in an hour."

"You know this whole plan of yours is fucking crazy, don't you?"

"Yes, I think I do."

"And you know that if it all goes south, I may have to shoot you two myself to make sure it doesn't look like I was in on it."

"I understand that."

"So why are you doing this? You don't even know these girls."

Adam wished he could come up with some profound statement in response but had nothing to offer. He stood and again checked the chart plotter, which indicated they were on course to arrive around 5:30. When he sat back down, his mind went to his mother and father. His dad, Sam, had been gone for over twenty years, dying of lung cancer when Adam was a junior in college. His mother, Rose Marie, had lived another seventeen years, spending her final two in a memory care facility where Adam visited and spent time with her almost every day. They were older when they adopted Adam, but even though they often seemed to be from a different era than the mothers and fathers of the kids he grew up with, to him they were the best parents anyone ever had.

Adam wondered if his mother would have approved of him risking his life, and Ellen's life, to save Sarah and Beth. But then it wasn't just these two girls. The lives of Ozzie's wife and daughters were on the line too, not to mention the other young girls at that house and who knew how many others this guy Jason would abuse in the future.

Adam looked out over the water into the endless darkness. As if she were sitting next to him, he could hear his mother saying: *When you do the right thing, God will protect you.* It was one of those sayings she repeated often throughout his childhood. While he no longer bought into the *God will protect you* part, it had instilled in him a need to always strive to do what was right.

So, is that what this is about...doing the right thing? But, at what cost? This could end very badly...and without anyone being saved.

Ozzie had spoken, but Adam hadn't heard what he said. "Huh...did you say something?"

"What the fuck are you going to do if they pull your hat off and start shooting?"

"I'm going to hope that doesn't happen."

"And, what if there are three or four of them, and they all have guns?"

"I'm hoping that's not going to happen, either."

"What are you going to do when I have to turn over the girls and say you forced me to do this shit?"

"Ozzie, stop this! It's not helping."

Realizing that the wind had died down so much that the lake was nearly flat, Adam kicked up the engine to 2200 rpms. "I think it's time to get there as fast as we can...well before daylight."

"I agree. When I talked to Jason, it sounded like he was getting more pissed off by the second."

"You are going to give Ellen one of your guns, aren't you?"

"I will. But, if I have to, I'm going to tell them you used it to force me into this stupid fucking scheme of yours."

"Ozzie, I told you, I get it. As I said, I'm hoping it won't come to that."

Adam took a minute to check their course and reset the autopilot. "I have to go below and talk to Ellen...and the girls. The auto is on. You shouldn't need to do anything, it'll let you know if we slip off course."

"I know how it works."

"Good, then just stand watch."

Adam noticed Ozzie looking at him and suspected he was surprised that he had asked him to take the wheel. "It's okay, Ozzie. We're in this together now, at least until...as you said...something goes wrong."

Ozzie slid over behind the wheel as Adam stepped around the pedestal to the companionway. When Adam climbed down the steps, he was surprised to see Ellen sitting at the table with her arm around Beth who appeared to have been crying. Sarah sat across from Beth, holding her hand. When Ellen looked his way, he saw her eyes were red.

"Is everything okay?"

Ellen smiled. "Hopefully, it will be soon."

Adam sat on the bench seat at the end of the table, across from Ellen and the girls. He looked Ellen in the eye. "You do understand, don't you, that there are a hundred variables over which we have no control that could turn this into a complete and total disaster?"

Ellen reached across and took Adam's hand. "Yes, I do. But, if you heard what I just heard, you'd feel even more strongly that we have to do this."

"Sounds like you're saying I shouldn't even think about trying to talk you out of this."

Ellen shook her head. "Don't waste your energy."

As much as Adam dreaded the thought of putting Ellen in the kind of danger that was most likely waiting for them, he knew it was useless to try to convince her otherwise. He had learned very early on in their time together that there was no future in ever suggesting to Ellen that there was something she couldn't do. While her determination—or what some would very appropriately perceive as stubbornness—had always been part of what he loved about her, the thought of that now costing Ellen her life was enough to make him ill again. He was endeavoring to force that thought from his fried brain when Ellen got a weird look on her face.

"Did you leave Ozzie up there alone at the wheel?"

Adam shrugged. "Yes. We're going to have to have some level of trust if this is going to work."

Ellen frowned. "If you say so."

Adam stood. "Okay, then. It's time to get ready for this."

"Yep, it is."

"Why don't you get some clothes for Beth to change into? You two are about the same size, anything of yours should fit her. I'll stay in these." Adam motioned with his hands to Sarah's fleece jacket and knit hat that he still wore.

Ellen went into the forward cabin. Adam heard drawers opening and closing. She came out with a pair of her jeans, a sweatshirt, and a pair of dry socks, and put them on the table in front of Beth. "You can go into the back cabin and change, and then bring out the clothes you're wearing."

Sarah stood and put her hand on Beth's shoulder.

"Come on, let's do this."

"Oh, wait, take this." Ellen took off her hat and passed it to Beth.

A few minutes later, the door opened and both girls came out into the salon. They had their hair tucked up under their hats with the bills pulled down low over their foreheads. Ellen's clothes fit Beth perfectly. To Adam, there was no reason why, in the dark, anyone would think that either one of them was a young girl.

Ellen took the sweatpants and flannel shirt that Beth had been wearing and pulled them on over her own clothes. She then put on the quilted, black jacket that Beth had worn onto the boat. When Beth handed Ellen her stocking cap, she put it on and pulled it down low over her forehead leaving her blonde hair hanging out the sides.

Ellen turned to face Adam. "How do I look?"

Adam grinned. "As I've always said, you look good in anything."

Ellen returned a tentative smile. "It's not a matter of looking good. If Ramone, or whatever his name is, sees us, he needs to believe that we're Sarah and Beth."

"Right." He pulled Sarah's knit hat down to his eyebrows. "Can I pass for a girl?"

"Not with that stubble on your face. Get in there and give yourself the closest shave of your life."

"Good idea."

Adam stepped through the door to the forward cabin and into the head. He looked in the mirror. He was the same height as Sarah but much bigger across the shoulders. Even though her fleece pullover was bulky and too big for her, he was squeezed in, but it would have to do. He took off the fleece and his shirt, turned the water on to warm up, and reached for a brand-new razor.

CHAPTER TWENTY-SEVEN

Jason was pacing from room to room around the first floor of the farmhouse when his phone went off. It was Ramone. "Where are you?"

"Toledo, in a parking lot off 475 and 75, about twenty minutes from the marina. Where the fuck are they?"

"I just talked to Ozzie. From what he said, they should get there around 6:00, before daylight. He'll call when they're an hour out."

"I don't like this shit, Boss."

"You think I fucking like it?"

"We got his family covered?"

"Spade is outside the house."

"They there?"

"She says so."

There was a long silence, then Ramone said, "Boss, maybe it's time to…you know, clean things up."

"Yeah…maybe."

"Just say the word. Once the transfer's made, I can end

it for that asshole and whoever else is on that sailboat."

"We'll see…stay put for now. I'll let you know when I hear from him."

"Whatever you say, Boss."

Ellen and the two girls were still sitting around the table when Adam emerged from the forward cabin. They looked up at him.

"What do you think?"

"Better," Ellen said, working hard to keep the quiver out of her voice. She had been playing different scenarios in her head and felt her courage waning as each one concluded with a more wretched outcome than the one before. "So…how do you see this playing out?" she asked apprehensively.

Adam didn't answer. Instead, he turned to the companionway steps and hollered up, "Heh, Ozzie, everything okay up there?"

"Yep. The wind is light, the auto's holding fine. It says we have eight and a half miles to go."

"Okay, I'll be up in a few minutes." Adam turned back to Ellen. "We can be at the dock by 5:30. It'll still be dark when we do the exchange. I'm thinking that's best."

That Adam was avoiding answering her question, wasn't making Ellen feel any better. She slid her trembling hands off the table and dropped them to her lap, out of Adam's sight. When he sat down across from her, Ellen hoped he couldn't hear the thumping in her chest.

Adam opened his mouth to speak but no sound came out. On his second try, he said, "I have no idea how this will play out. Almost everything about it is unknown and out of our control." Adam looked around the salon then settled his gaze back on Ellen. "We don't know if there will be one guy or four guys…or if they'll have guns, but we have to assume they will. We also don't know to what extent they'll want to examine the merchandise before they hand over the money."

"Am I correct that, for this to work, we need to have that Ramone guy get the money, count it, and take off with it before the others figure out we're not the girls they came for?"

"That's the way I see it."

"And then you, me, and Ozzie will have to deal with...with these guys who'll be planning to haul us off as their newest sex slaves?"

Adam nodded. "Yes."

Ellen lifted her hands, held them up in front of her, then slapped them down onto the table. "Adam, this whole thing is crazy. You could end up dead, and I could wind up being some big, ugly asshole's bitch for whatever life I have left."

"You're right, that's a real possibility. But, as you well know, we don't have to do this. We can let Ramone get the cash, let the assholes have the girls, and take Ozzie back to Shawnee Falls on the boat. He can get his money, go home, and live happily ever after with his family...at least for as long as his luck holds out and Jason doesn't kill him. From what Ozzie said, he can't do it, but when it's over we can call the police and do whatever we can to help them chase this Jason guy down."

Ellen poked her figure at Adam. "You never should have let those CBP people leave without telling them what was going on. They could have helped us. You shouldn't have done that, Adam. Now we're all going to—"

"Ellen, as I just said, we don't have to—"

"He's right," Sarah said. "You don't have to do this. As a matter of fact, I don't want you to. There's no reason for you two to risk getting killed because of us."

Ellen reached out and grabbed Adam's arm "Wait a minute. Ozzie can't make us do this. There's one of him and four of us. We can jump him, get his guns."

"Yes, we could," Adam said. "And to be honest, that would be the smartest thing we could do if we really want to save these girls...and ourselves. But then—"

Ellen sat back. "You're going to say, but then there's Ozzie's family."

"Yes, we don't know for sure what the story is with them, but if his daughters end up being killed because we didn't keep going, how would we ever..." Adam's voice trailed off.

"Of course... I know that." Ellen raised her hands to the sides of her head. "I'm sorry... I must sound like I'm losing it."

Adam put his hand on Ellen's shoulder. "There's nothing to be sorry for. You're not losing it. You're just—"

Ellen drew her hands into fists in front of her. She could feel her terror being squeezed aside by building anger. "You're right, we can't sit back and let Ozzie's family get killed, and we're not going to turn these girls over to those guys, at least not without a fight. All of this is wrong, and we can't just do nothing and let it happen." Ellen looked Adam in the eye. "So, how do we plan for all these...these unknowns?"

Adam raised his eyebrows and said, "That's a good question. Unfortunately, I don't have a good answer." He leaned forward, resting his forearms on the table. "Let's say they handover the money, and Ramone counts it and takes off before they realize we're not the girls they bought, which is what we want. The problem is, as soon as he leaves, they're going to want to shove us into a car and head back to who knows where, and, once that happens, we're screwed."

"So, we have to take out however many of them there are as soon as Ramone leaves, but before they notice we're not the girls they paid for."

"That's the way I see it."

"But at some point, if they look closely, they are going to know you're not a girl."

Adam hesitated for a long second, then said: "For this to work, we have to do everything we can to control when that happens. I don't think I have to tell you what we'll be facing if they figure that out before we want them to."

"So, where does Ozzie fit into all of this? Can we trust him not to turn on us?"

"I'd like to think so...at least until it all starts to fall apart, which, hopefully, won't happen."

The cabin went silent. It was Beth who finally spoke. "You both have been very good to us, and we appreciate it, but I can't let you do this. I really want you to...to just turn us over, let Ramone get his money, and take Ozzie and get the fuck out of there. We know what we're in for...we'll manage."

Ellen looked at Beth, then Adam, then down at the table, and shook her head slowly. "No, we're not going to do that."

After a while, she raised her head and said to Adam, "You're right. There are a hundred different things that could go wrong."

"And that's why I don't want you participating in this. Once we dock, I think you should take the girls and get the hell out of there."

Ellen knew Adam was right. They weren't cops or bad guys who knew how to deal with these kinds of people. She was a high-school teacher and tennis coach. Adam was a criminal defense lawyer. They would be in so far over their heads that the odds of ever reaching the surface were pretty much nonexistent.

Ellen felt a pit in her stomach as she recalled the stories the girls had told her about what their lives had been like with Jason. How would she deal with it if she got dragged into that kind of existence? Maybe she would just kill herself. But was this how she wanted her life to end? Was it worth risking everything on the off chance they could get these two girls, whom they just met, to safety? And none of it would work if the guys at the other end pulled Adam's hat off to inspect the merchandise before handing over the money.

Ellen looked at Sarah and Beth.

Just sixteen and seventeen-year-old kids who should be home studying for a chemistry exam, or arguing with their mothers over the crisis of the day, or texting friends on their way to soccer practice.

She turned to Adam. "We have no choice. If we give these kids to these assholes, it will be like we put a gun to their heads and pulled the trigger. We have to do this."

CHAPTER TWENTY-EIGHT

Adam knew Ellen was right. Ozzie was no longer the threat. They could handle him if they wanted to. The wildcard was whatever the hell they would face when they docked at Grant Harbor. Despite the scenarios flashing through his mind, none of which had a happy ending, Adam also knew there was no way he could live with himself if they didn't, at least, try to rescue these girls and do everything they could to keep Ozzie's family safe. He looked at Ellen. "You said you know how to handle a gun."

"I do."

"Are you prepared to shoot and kill someone if you have to...because that may be the only way you can avoid getting killed or being hauled off to God knows where by these jerks?"

Ellen sighed. "I don't know if I can answer that right now."

"I think you're going to have to before we get much further into this."

"What about you? Do you think you could kill—"

"To protect you from what will happen if they get a hold of you…yes, I think I could."

Ellen hesitated, then said, "I guess I'll have to cross that bridge when I get there. As you said, we need to keep them fooled long enough for Ramone to get the money, count it, and get out of there." Ellen looked up and then back at Adam. "I suppose that's when I'll have to decide whether I can shoot—"

"Not just shoot, we're talking about killing another human being. Can you say that you could—"

"But if there's only one of them and he doesn't have a gun, you can handle anybody hand-to-hand. You never know, maybe—"

"Yeah, well, don't count on that happening. We're going to need a lot of luck to pull this off, and I'd say that's asking a little too much." Adam reached out and took Ellen's hand. He loved her more than he ever dreamed he could love anyone, and he couldn't believe he was even considering what they were about to do. He already knew the answer but had to ask the question. "Is there any way I can talk you out of this?"

She shook her head. "No. We have to do this."

"Okay then. I think I'd better get back up there and relieve Ozzie."

As he headed up the steps, Ellen said, "I'll be right up."

Ellen looked at the girls. Beth had her head down on her arms that were folded on the table. Sarah's eyes appeared glazed over. It was obvious that both of them were exhausted. "I need to head up. Why don't you two go and stretch out on the bunk in the forward cabin?"

Sarah reached out and grabbed Ellen's hand. "I can't believe you're doing this for us."

Beth raised her head and said, "You should let me help.

I sure as hell wouldn't have a problem killing any of those assholes."

Ellen smiled and stood. The girls slid out from behind the table and, one at a time, gave Ellen a hug.

Beth said, "I mean it, I've shot a gun before. I could easily—"

"Let's not talk about that now. You two could use some rest. Go in there and lie down for a while." Ellen watched Beth and Sarah go into the forward cabin then turned and climbed up the companionway steps.

CHAPTER TWENTY-NINE

Adam watched Ellen step into the cockpit. "How are they doing?"

"Okay…they're exhausted. I told them to lie down and rest for a while." Ellen took the seat next to Adam. "How much longer?"

"A little more than an hour."

Adam looked at Ozzie. "Tell me how you see this going down when we get there."

"No way to tell for sure. It's never the same."

"What about the pickup guys, will they be someone you know, someone you've seen before?"

"Hard to say. It's been the same, and it's been different. I never really knew if they were the actual buyers or just runners."

"What do you mean?"

"Like I told you about Jason, he stays totally away from any exchanges, money or people. If anything goes wrong, he doesn't want to be anywhere near it."

"That's why you do the delivery, and Ramone picks up the money," Adam said.

"Yeah, except Ramone is always in contact with Jason by phone. Like, when he brought these girls to us, as soon as they were on Spider's boat, he called Jason. The guys we're meeting may be the same, just delivery people. They could be on the phone reporting to someone else if it doesn't go down like it's supposed to."

"Okay, so we're going to have to watch for that," Adam said. "Can't let them call anyone and say they didn't get the girls."

"That's for sure."

"In the past, how many guys were there for the pickup?"

"Once there was just one, but that time I only delivered one girl. Every other time there were two."

"What were they like?"

"What the fuck...I don't know. It's not like we sat down and had a beer together."

"Take it easy, Ozzie," Ellen said. "What Adam means is, were they like...say professional mob people, or more like street pimps?"

Ozzie shrugged. "How the fuck do I know? I don't think they were fucking Sunday school teachers." Ozzie paused for a moment, then said, "They didn't look like the Sopranos, if that's what you mean. They were just, you know, regular, cocky assholes who think their shit doesn't stink."

"What about guns?" Ellen asked.

"Ramone's always flashing a gun around, so my guess is the others have them too, even though I never saw any. But in the past, everything always went smooth, like it was supposed to."

"We have to assume they'll be armed," Adam said.

"Where will Sarah and Beth be during all of this?" Ellen asked.

"I've been thinking about that," Adam said. "I see two

ways to do this. They could be visible, dressed as us, or we can hide them away somewhere until it's over."

"I say we have them as far away as possible," Ellen responded. "If anything goes wrong, I don't want them caught in a crossfire."

"I agree. We should have them—"

"Not so fast," Ozzie said. "Jason knows you two are here. If you're dressed as the girls, what the fuck do I tell Ramone when he asks where you are?"

"Shit…you're probably right," Adam said. "They need to be visible too, dressed as us, but in the background, away from any lights."

"Don't forget, Ramone knows these girls. If he sees you two up close, he'll know you're not them," Ozzie said.

"Good point." Adam looked at Ellen. "You and I could be out front but, somehow, try and stay in the shadows. Our having their clothes on should help. We may have to wait and figure out where everyone is going to be after we dock the boat and see what the light is like."

"Yeah, well…as you said, there are only about a hundred ways this can go south," Ellen said.

"I also said we don't have to—"

"Stop saying that. Yes, we do have to do this." Ellen stood. "Ozzie, could you give me that gun? I'd like to check it out."

Ozzie pulled the smaller of the two guns out of his jacket pocket. He looked at it, then at Ellen. "You sure you know how to handle this?"

"I'm sure."

"It's a Glock 26, 9mm, small and lightweight…it's actually my wife's." Ozzie shook his head. "But she doesn't know about it. I bought it for her last year. She was working nights for a while, and I wanted her to have it for safety reasons. But she hates guns, and I never got around to giving it to her. I'm still hoping someday she'll learn how to use it and get her own permit. You're about the same size as her. It should work for you."

Adam watched as Ellen took the gun and turned it in her hand to get the feel of it. "I'm going to go below and take a look at it in the light."

As she disappeared from view, Ozzie asked, "You think she really knows how to use it?"

"I have no idea. But we're probably going to find out pretty soon."

Ozzie pulled the bigger gun out of his belt and held it out to Adam. "Maybe you should have this one."

Adam didn't have to think about it very long. "Thanks, but you should keep it. You know how to use it. I don't. Depending on what happens, it'll be a lot better if you—"

"Whatever you say. I'll do my best to cover you." Ozzie then added, "I've never shot a person. I mean I've done a lot of target practice and some hunting, but I never shot a…a human being."

"Can you do it if you have to?"

"To save our lives…I think I can."

"By the way, at some point we're going to have contact with the police. Do you have a permit for these guns?"

"Yes, I do. I'm legal."

Adam sat and listened to the hum of the engine as he tried to picture how it all might go down. He recalled what Ellen had said about his being able to handle anyone hand-to-hand. His thoughts went to his junior year in high school when he won districts and headed to the state wrestling championships for the first time. For everyone else, the season was over, but his coach had kept several of his teammates coming to practice to help him workout and prepare for the tournament. Although he was a one-hundred-twenty pounder, the coach had him working with some of the bigger guys. By the time they headed to Columbus, size no longer mattered. Regardless of how big they were, he was faster and could out move any of them.

In the years since then, Adam never stopped working out. He had been lifting weights, running or swimming three to five days a week for years. Now, at age forty, he only weighed ten pounds more than his one-hundred-thirty-three-pound college wrestling weight and almost none of it was fat. He hoped Ellen was correct, that he could handle just about anyone who would come at him, regardless of how big he is.

But what if he's a six-five, 240-pound ex-marine and martial arts specialist? Can I handle that? And what if he has a gun...or a knife...and how many of them will there be? Whatever the number, I have to assume they'll be armed. Fuck. This could get screwed up so fucking fast.

Adam broke into another cold sweat when grizzly images began to invade the periphery of his consciousness. *No! Can't think like that, it's not productive.* Adam summoned every ounce of energy he possessed to fend off the jarring visuals. *Have to keep my shit together...and think clearly.*

He checked to make sure they were still on course and the auto was holding, then turned and opened the locker under the seat on the port side of the cockpit. From a bin on the shelf, he pulled out his old boy scout pocketknife, the one that had two blades, a bottle opener, and a small scissors. *Not much, but better than nothing,* he thought, as he slipped it into a jacket pocket. After rummaging around in another bin, he pulled out a roll of duct tape and four, three-foot-long, quarter inch lines that he used to hang fenders, and stuffed it all into another pocket.

"What's that for?"

It was Ellen. Startled by her presence, he said, "Oh...ah...in case we need to tie someone up. I'm trying to think of everything."

"Good." She tapped the pocket on the right side of her jacket. "The gun seems fine to me, fits right in here."

Ozzie said, "By the way, if you really want to stop someone with that, you'll want to be up close, and keep shooting."

Adam felt a chill go up his back.

"I know that," Ellen said. "Are you keeping the other

one?"

"He offered it to me," Adam said. "I told him to keep it since he knows how to use it."

"Good decision."

Chapter Thirty

Jason had no idea how long he'd been pacing, stopping every now and then to peer out a window at nothing in particular. The whole thing with Ozzie changing boats and bringing in other people was making him crazy. He pulled out his phone and scrolled through his contacts.

After several rings, a groggy voice answered, "What the fuck, it's the middle of the night."

"Get up, Daveed. I need you at the house."

"It's Denzell, boss."

"I don't give a fuck what you call yourself, just get your ass over here."

"What's going on?"

"I may have to leave. If I do, I'll need you to babysit…and maybe do some cleanup."

"Got it, boss, on my way."

Jason went back to pacing. After two more turns around the living room, he stopped and scrolled through his contacts again.

Spade saw the phone vibrating on the passenger seat next to her. Again, she hoped Jason was calling to tell her to come home. Slowly, she reached for it.

"Hello."

"What's going on?"

Spade could tell from the sound of Jason's voice that he was agitated. *Not good.* "Nothing. I'm just sitting here watching the house."

"What's it look like?"

"Same as it looked the last time you asked."

"Don't be a smartass, I need you to make sure you can get in the house without being noticed."

"How am I supposed to do that?"

"I'm sure you can figure that out. You may have to get inside in a hurry, so—"

"Jason, I don't like this. I don't want to go breaking into someone's house in the middle of the night. What if they have an alarm, or what if—"

"Did I fucking ask you what you want? Just do what I tell you to do. This is not going as planned and I might have to—"

"But, Jason, this isn't what I—"

"I'll let you know when I need you inside. Make sure you don't wake anyone until I tell you to."

"Why do we have to do this?"

"Because I fucking said so."

Spade heard Jason breathing into the phone. "What's going on that's so—"

"I have a bad feeling about this delivery. Just do what I said."

He clicked off.

He's such a fucking asshole.

Chapter Thirty-One

From the corner of his eye, Adam could see Ozzie sitting behind him, to his left, with his arms folded across his lap, pretty much the same as before only without the guns. It suddenly struck Adam that he and Ellen were entrusting their lives to this guy who, just hours before, had threatened to kill them. Aware that any attempt to make sense of the insanity of it all would be a waste of energy, Adam gazed out over the water for a few minutes then turned to Ozzie and asked, "So…where do you live?"

"Shawnee Falls, about a half mile from the lake. We bought the house five years ago. Been fixing it up."

Adam noticed the change in Ozzie's tone and concluded he must have been putting on the gruff act to scare them.

Ellen asked, "What kind of work were you doing, you know, before—"

"I was the manager at Bennett's, over in Huron."

Adam knew the place. It was a very successful, locally

owned supermarket.

"I started working there when I was fourteen as a bagger and stock boy, ended up the manager ten years later when Arty Bennett had a mild stroke. It was a good deal for me, and Arty, until he died fifteen years later, and his kid came back to town and took over the business. Junior said they didn't need me anymore, and that was after I'd given it over twenty-five years of my life. That was three years ago. Didn't leave me with much in the way of skills to get another job since that was the only thing I'd ever done. Those big box stores want you to have a college degree before they hire you as a manager."

"How's your family been living since then?" Ellen asked.

"My wife, Janice, is a nurse, but only with a two-year degree, not the kind that makes a lot of money. For a while, she worked in the hospital, but they said she'd have to go back and get her RN if she wanted to advance anywhere working for them. We had two young kids and I was working long hours, sometimes six and seven days a week. There wasn't time for her to take care of them, work, and go back to school. Now she does home healthcare stuff. Works for this company that sends her into people's homes to help them take care of themselves instead of going to a nursing home. She loves it except the company makes a ton of money while they only pay her eighteen bucks an hour." There was a long silence. Then: "Do you see why the money Jason offered me for one night's work seemed pretty attractive?"

Adam was thinking about how to respond when Ellen asked, "Was losing your job what caused you to start drinking?"

"It'd be nice if I could blame it on that, but I'd been drinking too much for most of my life. Not working just made it worse."

"You said you stopped drinking. What are you doing now? Do you have a job?"

"Been working at Jake's Hardware. It's good but doesn't pay very much. I've been looking for something better, but it hasn't been easy."

"Are you back living with your wife?" Ellen asked.

"Yeah, for four months now." Ozzie shrugged. "It's going pretty good."

"You're away overnight. Does she know what you're doing with Jason?"

"Hell no. She'd go nuts if she ever found out. She knows I do some overnight deliveries for extra money every now and then, but nothing about what it is."

Ozzie stopped, looked at Adam, and said: "Your last name is Kennedy, isn't it?"

Before Adam could respond, Ozzie said, "When you went below, I saw you in the light. After what those cops said, I recognized you from the news back a couple years ago. You were representing a guy in some big murder case."

"Yep, that was me."

"What happened? I don't remember."

"He's on death row."

"No shit?"

"Yeah...no shit."

"I hope you'll be able to do better for me if we ever get out of this mess."

"So do I, Ozzie...so do I."

Adam looked around and saw that Ellen was staring straight ahead into the darkness that seemed to go on forever. He wondered what she was thinking but wasn't about to ask. He felt a momentary warm glow as he thought about how lucky he was to have her in his life. His mind flashed through the three years they had been together and how the more he learned about her the more he grew to love her. He thought about how her endless energy and sense of adventure never ceased to amaze him, and how her kind and caring nature continually challenged him to be a better person.

He recalled seeing her with the kids she coached and

how she related to them, and the remarkable way they responded to her no matter how demanding she was. He also had watched her interact with the children of friends of theirs and had seen how much they all loved her. Adam knew, if they someday had a family, she would be an incredible mother.

On top of all that, Adam felt satisfied that Ellen *got* him, which often was more than he could say for himself. She was sensitive to his idiosyncrasies and mood swings, and always gave him space when he needed it. Considering everything he had come to know about Ellen, Adam could not say that he was surprised that she would do whatever she had to do, including risking her own life, to keep Sarah and Beth from being sold off to more human traffickers.

But are we going to live to tell about it? A deep tremor ran through his entire body. *I can't fucking believe this is happening.*

After a few more minutes, Adam checked the chart plotter again.

"We're three miles out. Let's get the sails down."

"Why so soon?" Ellen asked.

"They may be watching. We'll be less visible from the shore without the sails…and I think we should turn off the lights."

"That's crazy, Adam," Ellen said. "We were just stopped for not—"

"It's risky, I know, but I'd rather have them off."

Ellen raised her hands out in front of her. "I don't think that's a good idea…but you're the captain. I'll go turn them off."

"Thank you."

Ozzie asked, "What does that mean for timing?"

"About forty minutes. As soon as we have the sails in, you should call Jason."

When Ellen returned, Adam stood and said to Ozzie, "I need you to move forward so I can bring in the sail." Once Ozzie was out of the way, Adam reached over and wrapped the furling line around the winch. "Okay," he said to Ellen.

On the other side of the cockpit, she unwrapped the jib sheet partway then slowly eased it out as Adam turned the boat until it was almost into the wind. When the sail began to luff, he furled it in. "Do you want to get the main or should I?"

"I'll do it," Ellen offered. She grabbed a winch handle then stood and wrapped the inhaul for the mainsail around the winch. When Adam turned into the wind and the sail started flapping, Ellen released the outhaul and rolled the sail into the mast.

Adam pushed the throttle forward and reset their course for the harbor entrance. "Okay, Ozzie, we'll be there in thirty minutes. It's time to call Jason."

Ozzie pulled his phone out of his jacket pocket. "Here goes," he said, as he lifted the phone to his ear.

Adam heard a ringing sound. When it stopped, Ozzie said, "It's me. We'll be there in an hour."

Adam could hear a voice on the other end but couldn't make out what was being said.

"Everything's good…no, they'll be fine," Ozzie said. He looked at Adam. "They don't know anything. They understood we needed help because our boat was undersized for the weather conditions." Ozzie shook his head. "No, they're good people, it's not going to be a problem."

The voice at the other end got louder, but Adam still couldn't discern any words.

"No, they're down below, they can't hear me. Like I told you, they won't be a—" Ozzie closed his eyes and grimaced. "Yes, I get it, nothing's going to—" Ozzie pulled the phone from his ear, looked at it and pressed end, then put it back in his pocket. "He's royally pissed."

"I'm not surprised," Adam said.

Ozzie shifted in his seat and sighed. "I never should have gotten you involved in this."

"Yeah, well, you did, so we're going to have to deal with it."

"I sure hope—"

"How about giving our phones back?" Ellen said.

"Uh…oh, yeah." Ozzie reached into an inside pocket of his jacket and pulled them out. He started to hand the phones to Adam then pulled them back. "No calling anybody until I say so."

"We understand," Adam responded.

"Okay…here they are." Adam took both phones and passed the one with the red case to Ellen.

"We there yet?"

They all turned and saw Sarah's head pop up through the companionway.

"We'll be at the dock in a half hour," Adam said.

As they watched Beth follow Sarah up into the cockpit, Ellen asked, "How are you two doing?"

"We're okay," Beth said as she took the seat next to Ellen.

Sarah scanned the horizon ahead of them then sat on the seat across from Ellen and Beth. "We've been talking. Like we said before, we really don't want you to do this," she said, looking from Ellen to Adam and back to Ellen.

"I've known people who do this kind of shit, and I don't mean just Jason," Beth said. "I knew others before him. These are really bad people. They'll kill you just as soon as look at you. And believe me, Ellen, you're good looking…if they get their hands on you…I mean, you could end up making money for them and wishing they had killed you."

"No," Ellen said, "we're not going to let you—"

"We've decided," Sarah said firmly. "We want you to let Ramone get his money, then give us to them and get the hell out. We're already ruined. You're a really nice person, Ellen. We don't want what happened to us to happen to you."

"I told you, we're not going to do that," Ellen said. "And don't worry about me, I can take care of myself." Ellen brushed her hand over the pocket with the gun.

"I'm with them," Ozzie said pointing to Ellen and

Adam. "I know I really fucked up here, but I'm going to do everything I can to make this better. They're right, you two could be my own daughters. We're not going to turn you over to those guys."

"And here I thought you were just as big an asshole as the rest of them," Beth said.

"Yeah, well, I don't blame you for that."

"Fuck," Adam exclaimed. "We won't have a car there. What if we need to get back in a hurry?"

"True," Ellen said. "That's why we have to let Ramone get the money and leave, and then deal with the pickup guys before anyone makes any phone calls. If we can pull that off, we can take the boat back, and Ozzie can tell Jason he'll see him tonight to get his money."

"He knows we're on a sailboat, and it'll take much longer to get back," Ozzie said. "Shit, under the original plan, I would have been back by now." Ozzie paused then said, "I'd say the most important thing is that you two don't get into a car with those guys."

"Well, there is no way I'm going to do that," Ellen declared. Adam saw the tension building on Ellen's face. "But what if they, you know, try to force us to..." Ellen stopped and looked up at Adam, "... we really may have to shoot someone before this is over."

Adam reached out and placed his hand on Ellen's back. "Yes, that's very possible...that's why I asked if you could do that if you had to."

Ellen shook her head then gave Adam a punch on shoulder. "Nice honeymoon you brought me on."

"Huh...what do you mean, honeymoon?" Ozzie asked.

"We got married this afternoon...actually, yesterday afternoon," Ellen said. "This was supposed to be our honeymoon cruise."

"No shit!"

"Yep, no shit," Adam said. "Pretty romantic, don't you think?"

"Oh, my God," Sarah said. "That makes it even worse."

"Not really…but definitely memorable," Ellen said.

Ramone answered on the first ring. "Hey, Boss."

"He just called. They'll be there in an hour. You still in Toledo?"

"Haven't moved…except to get out and take a piss in some bushes."

"Wait a half hour then head up to the marina."

"Got it. What about, you know…do I take care of—"

"Yes, do it, I've had enough of Ozzie's shit."

"All of them, right?"

"No loose ends. Make sure you leave it clean."

"Will do, boss."

"Let me know when you're heading back."

As Jason hung up the phone, he heard the back door open. "What the fuck took you so long?" Jason said as Daveed sauntered through the hallway into the living room.

"Hey, man, chill, I came direct," Daveed said with a grin. "You got some coffee? It's still the middle of the fucking night."

"In the kitchen. Get some, I need you awake. I may have to leave."

As Daveed headed into the kitchen, Jason pulled up Spade on his phone. It took her a while to answer, which pissed him off.

"What the fuck's going on?"

"Nothing, I'm just sitting here watching the house."

"Can you get in?"

"Yes. The service door into the garage and the door from the garage into the house are unlocked."

"I might be coming over there."

"Jason, no, I thought I was just watching to see if they left."

"Go inside now, but don't do anything until I—"

"What for? What do you want me to do?"

"Keep your phone on vibrate. I'll call back with instructions."

"Why are we doing this?"

"Ozzie fucked up. We have to make sure he hasn't talked."

"But how do we—"

"Stop. No more questions. Just do what I fucking tell you to do."

Jason was pocketing his phone as Daveed came back into the living room with a steaming cup of black coffee. "What the fuck is going on, Boss?"

"Ozzie screwed up the delivery. If I have to go to see how bad, I'll need you to cover the house." Jason motioned toward the ceiling with his thumb. "The other two are down for the rest of the night. Depending on what happens, I could need you to clean things up here."

Daveed broke into a big toothy smile. "You saying like a total cleanup?"

"Depending on what happens…yeah, like they never existed."

"Sure thing, Boss, whatever you need. Just say the word."

"I'll know more the next time I hear from Ramone."

Chapter Thirty-Two

Adam slowed the boat to an idle as they approached the red and green lights marking the entrance to the harbor. "Sarah, Beth, go down below and stay there until we tell you to come up." As the two girls descended the companionway steps, Adam turned to Ellen and said, "The only place in here that's deep enough for this boat is the fuel dock. We'll go there. It'll be a starboard tie." Ellen nodded and climbed onto the deck to hang fenders and set dock lines.

The wind had subsided, and there was an eerie stillness to the small trees and shrubs growing out of the rocks on either side of the channel into the harbor. Ahead of him, in the light from a single bulb over the door of the marina office, Adam could see that the wide dock in front of it was empty. When he eased the boat alongside, Ellen jumped off with the bow and midship lines. While she tied those down, Adam looped a stern line around a post, secured it to a cleat on the boat, and then cut the engine.

When Ellen came back onboard, she, Adam and Ozzie stood and looked out across the marina property. Directly in front of them was a small building with peeling, gray paint and a sign on the door that read "Office Closed." The wood dock they were tied to was well worn and covered with the remnants of seagull droppings. There was a slight odor of dead fish in the air.

To their left was a gas pump and two boat launch ramps; beyond those were a small beach and a grassy lawn with several picnic tables and a kids' climbing gym with four swings. All that was bordered by a dense wooded area. Behind the marina office was a large gravel parking lot and past that were two big buildings where boats could be worked on and stored during the winter. Each of those buildings had a single light over a large overhead door. The road into the marina ran behind the two storage buildings.

When Ellen's hand brushed up against Adam's, he noticed it was freezing cold.

"Are we really going to do this?" she asked.

"Unless you've changed your mind."

"No…I haven't."

"Then I'd say we are."

"Looks like no one's around," Ozzie said.

Adam looked at Ozzie, then at Ellen. "Stay here, I'm going to check it out."

"Make it fast. You two need to be out of sight before any of them get here."

Adam jumped off the boat and walked to his right, back toward the boat docks. The Grant Harbor marina was shallow, limiting what could be docked there to smaller motorboats, almost all of which were under twenty-six feet. Although it wasn't very likely, he wanted to make sure no people were there sleeping on their boats in case things got out of hand and guns started going off. After walking briskly up and down the docks and then back through the empty parking lots, Adam crossed over the launch ramps and went toward the playground area. He had just turned to head back to the boat when he heard a twig crack in the woods behind him.

He froze. *Fuck! They're out there.* His heart pounded as he stood perfectly still and listened. Nothing. *They could be watching me through night vision scopes.* He slowly turned around and looked down at his chest for a red dot. *Nothing there. But it could be on my forehead.* Adam wondered briefly if he would hear the kill shot or if his world would just cease to exist. He exhaled slowly, picturing whomever it was seeing him all in green. Adam's pulse raced and sweat stung his eyes. He heard footsteps to his left and swung around. There was a strange guttural sound, then he saw the white tails of two deer bouncing off through the trees. Feeling lightheaded, Adam bent over at the waist and sucked air into his lungs.

This just gets fucking crazier by the second.

Adam looked at his watch. *Shit...almost six o'clock. By seven, fisherman will be piling in here. We need to have all this shit over with before then...one way or another. Looks like there's no one else around. Better get back to the boat...they could be here any minute.*

When Adam approached the boat, Sarah and Beth were standing in the cockpit with Ozzie and Ellen.

As he climbed aboard, Ellen asked, "Are you okay? You look a little weird."

"I'm fine," he snapped in response.

"Ramone will be expecting to see you two when he gets here," Ozzie said. He pointed at Sarah and Beth. "Since they are, you know, disguised as you, I'm thinking they should be out here."

"I agree." Adam looked at the girls who were standing next to each other, motionless in front of the companionway. "But since he knows both of them, they'll need to be in the shadows somewhere." Adam looked around and said, "Wait a minute." He grabbed the boathook from the deck, jumped off and ran to the marina office. With one swipe he smashed the light over the door, sending glass flying in all directions. "That should help," Adam said as he climbed back on the boat.

They all stood silently surveying the area for an extended moment before Adam slowly turned his head in Ozzie's direction. "Is Ozzie your real name?"

Ozzie shook his head. "I was named after my grandfather, Oswald Jacob Buttinger. My mother wanted me to be Jake, but when I got to school the kids started calling me Ozzie…it stuck. Why'd you want to know that?"

"Just curious." Adam felt his heart thumping in his chest as his gaze swept the darkness in search of approaching headlights. *Maybe they'll come lights off…if they do, we should be able to hear them before we see them.*

Adam turned to Beth and Sarah. "You two go and sit up on the deck, in front of the mast. It's pretty dark up there." To Ozzie he said, "You wait here in the cockpit. Ellen and I'll be down below."

"They could be pulling up any time now. If that's what you're doing, you better get down there."

"Right…we should," Adam said. "You going to be okay up here?"

Ozzie shrugged. "It's gonna be what it's gonna be. Whatever it is, I'll give it my best shot."

To Sarah and Beth, Adam said, "Make sure you keep your heads down so he can't see your faces."

Adam opened the locker under the seat on the starboard side of the cockpit. He dug around for a while then pulled out a small flashlight. "I'm sure the buyer is going to want to see us before he hands over the money. The cabin lights will be too bright, we'll keep them off. Use this if he wants to look down there."

Ozzie took the flashlight. "Yeah…okay."

Adam looked at Ellen and indicated that she should go first. He watched her climb down the steps and take a seat at the table, then followed her down and slipped in beside her. They sat for a while listening for the sound of a car pulling up. When Adam took Ellen's hand and leaned over to give her a kiss on the cheek, she turned her head to him, wrapped her right hand around his neck, and pulled him to her. The kiss was long and deep, and he didn't want it to end. When they finally parted, Adam felt breathless.

"I'm so sorry about this," he whispered.

"Don't be, none of it is your fault. It was my choice to do this. Hopefully, it will all work out like we planned."

"Yes, that's the hope." He looked into Ellen's eyes and asked, "Do you think you'll be able to shoot someone if it comes to that?"

Ellen raised her eyebrows. "I think we're about to find out."

Spade stood in the middle of the dark kitchen clutching her phone, hoping it wouldn't start vibrating. She wanted nothing to do with whatever Jason was likely going to ask of her but, as always with him, felt powerless to say no. There had been times when she hated Jason for the things he made her do, but always hated herself even more for doing them. Instead of standing in the home of these strangers listening to the refrigerator hum, if she could have, she would have said *fuck you* and been on her way home, her own home, not that fucking farmhouse.

Her hand felt the vibration. *A text.* She turned her phone over and scanned the message:

R u inside

Yes

Anyone awake

No

How do I get in

Side door into garage

I'll get back soon - stay where u r.

Chapter Thirty-Three

Through the window across from the table, on the other side of the salon, Adam saw the trees along the road into the marina light up. "Someone's coming."

As the vehicle turned toward the water, the lights went out. Adam got up from the table and moved to the seat under the window. A dark SUV pulled up near the launch ramps and stopped.

"What's going on?" Ellen whispered.

Adam put his finger to his lips as he watched a big, brawny looking figure climb out of the Explorer and look around. He wore a black leather jacket that hung down over his hips creating a giant square.

A few minutes later a second set of lights lit up the road then swung toward the fuel dock. A full-size black sedan came to a hard stop twenty feet behind the SUV. When the door opened, the big guy from the first car yelled, "Turn off the fucking lights, asshole."

The lights went out. A tall skinny guy emerged slowly

from the driver's seat. "Be cool, man, no need for that kind of talk."

It was too dark for Adam to see anything other than the tall guy's black skin, dark clothing, and what appeared to be dreadlocks cascading over his shoulders.

Adam was thinking, *Good, there's only one of them,* when a very large figure exited the passenger side and strutted around the front of the sedan. He was the opposite of the first guy. With his light hair and pale complexion, Adam thought he looked like a caricature of the Eastern European gangster regularly portrayed in the movies.

"Looks like there are two of them for the pickup," Adam whispered.

The guy who had yelled about the lights turned and pointed toward the bow of the sailboat. "Who are they?" Adam guessed he was Ramone.

"It's their boat," Ozzie responded.

"Where are the whores?" Again, it was Ramone.

"Down there," Ozzie pointed to the companionway steps.

"Bring them up," the tall guy from the sedan said. "I want to see what I'm buying."

Adam waited for Ozzie to say something, but he didn't.

"Now, asshole," Ramone barked.

"Yeah…sure," Ozzie stammered. "You two, come on up here," he called down to Adam and Ellen.

Adam pulled Sarah's hat down over his eyebrows and stood up. "Here we go," he whispered.

He had his foot on the first step when Ellen grabbed his arm. "No, I should go first. We want them focused on me, not you."

Adam stepped back. He watched Ellen climb the steps then followed her up to the cockpit. In the dim glow from the lights on the outside of the back buildings, Adam saw Ramone standing halfway between his Explorer and the office, about twenty feet from the boat. To Ramone's left, about ten feet away, the other two were standing next to each other. The taller one took a step forward and motioned with his hand toward Adam and Ellen. "Get on down here."

"Not so fast, Jerome," Ramone said. "Money first."

"Fuck you, I need to inspect the merchandise."

"You can inspect all you fucking want after I count the money, not before."

The big guy next to Jerome put his right hand inside his jacket and took a step forward.

Ellen let out a gasp. Adam edged sideways halfway in front of her and watched as Jerome put his hand on the guy's shoulder. "It's okay, Mace. We'll let him count his fucking money. Either way, he ain't going nowhere 'til we approve the goods." Mace gave a grunt then went back to the car and pulled out a dark duffle bag. He tossed it at Ramone who took a step back and watched it land at his feet.

"Nobody fucking move. I'll be right back." Ramone bent and picked up the bag then turned and headed back to the SUV.

Adam looked to his right. Beth and Sarah were still huddled next to each other on the deck, up near the bow. He felt Ellen's hand brush against his and wished he could wrap his arms around her and hold her.

"I think I'll have the shorter one first," Mace mumbled then snorted a stupid laugh.

"Shut the fuck up," Jerome ordered.

A vision of the monster guy in front of him touching Ellen flashed in Adam's mind. His hand brushed over the knife in his pocket.

The driver's door to the SUV opened. Ramone stuck one foot on the ground but stopped. From the interior light, Adam could see him raise a phone to his ear. It was a short conversation. He clicked off, got out and closed the door. "They're all yours. Take them and get the fuck out of here."

Jerome gave a thumb up. "Sure thing, Ramone, as soon as I know we're getting what we were promised." He turned to Adam and Ellen. "You two, get your asses down here."

Adam felt paralyzed. This wasn't how it was supposed

to go. Ramone was supposed to leave first, as soon as he got the money. But he wasn't leaving. He was just standing there waiting for the others to take them away.

"You fucking sluts, I told you to get down here. Move it, now," Jerome yelled.

Adam looked at Ellen. She gave a slight nod. He stepped around the front of the console and up onto the seat. He felt Ellen's hand on his back as he took a tentative step over the side and onto the dock. He kept his head down and hoped Ellen would do the same as she followed him off the boat.

"What's wrong with that one?" Jerome asked. He was pointing at Adam.

"It was rough out there, she got seasick," Ozzie said.

Jerome moved toward Adam with his hand reaching out toward his hat. Ellen slid in front of him and said, "She's not feeling so good, sweetie. You better be careful. She might puke all over you."

Jerome stopped and pulled Ellen's hat off instead. He looked at her for a few seconds. "A little older than I was expecting, but good. Yeah…real good." He reached out and stroked Ellen's face with his right hand then gave it a light slap.

Adam fought like hell to keep his fists at his side. That's when Mace stepped forward. "We got to see this one too." Before Adam could react, the hat was pulled off his head.

"What the fuck!" Jerome screamed at Ramone. "You lookin' to die, mother-fucker?" Jerome grabbed Adam by the hair and yanked his head back so hard he fell over backward. For a second, he felt stunned when his head hit the wood planks of the dock. He started to flip over but froze when he looked up and saw the barrel of a gun three inches from his forehead.

"No!" Ellen screamed.

She took a step toward Adam, but Jerome blocked her with his arm. "Shut the fuck up, bitch." He kicked Adam in the ribs. "And you stay the fuck where you are."

Adam looked up at Mace and saw that he had a gun pointed at Ramone.

"Heh, take it easy, put the fucking guns down," Ramone yelled. His hands were palms up, out in front of him. He motioned with his head toward Ozzie. "He did this, not me. I'm just as surprised as you are. You think I didn't know you'd want to see the merchandise. He's fucking with all of us." Ramone pointed at Sarah and Beth up on the deck. "I'd say, those are your girls, up there."

Adam started to stand, but Jerome gave him another kick and pushed him down with his foot. "I said stay where you are, fuckhead. I'll tell you when you can move." When Ellen let out a yelp, he grabbed her around the neck and shoved her to the ground on top of Adam. "If you want to live, bitch, don't fucking move."

Adam pushed himself up to sitting. Ellen was next to him with her legs pulled up in front of her. A small line of blood ran down her face from a cut above her left eye.

"Mace, get up there, bring those two down," Jerome yelled.

Ozzie stood motionless in the cockpit as Mace climbed onto the boat and called to Sarah and Beth, "You two, get your asses down here, now. And keep your fucking hands where I can see them."

The two girls made their way back to the cockpit. When they were standing in front of Mace, he reached out and yanked their hats off. He broke into a big smile. "Okay, this is more like it."

"Bring them down here, let me take a look," Jerome said.

As Beth stepped off the boat, Mace gave her a shove. She tripped and ended up on all fours in front of Jerome. When Ellen made a move to help her, Adam grabbed her arm and pulled her back.

Beth let out a scream when Jerome snatched her by the hair and yanked her to her feet.

When Sarah climbed off the boat, Mace took hold of

the back of her jacket and pushed her over in front of Jerome. "I'd say these are the ones," Mace said.

Sarah and Jerome were nose to nose when he put his hand around the back of her neck and planted a kiss on her mouth. "Mmm, not bad," he said, "I think I'm going to like this one." He let go of Sarah and pointed his gun at Adam and Ellen, "Get down there with those two, both of you."

Beth and Sarah sat down next to Ellen.

"You got what you came for, now get the fuck out of here," Ramone said. He was standing to Adam's left about fifteen feet away.

"Sorry, asshole, not so fast. After all this shit with you trying to cheat us, I get a discount. Half that cash comes back to me. Then we go." Both Jerome and Mace had their guns pointed at Ramone.

"No fucking way." Ramone pointed at Ozzie. "He did this shit, not me. He was fucking with all of us."

"I don't give two shits who's responsible, you dumb fuck. You all fucked with me, and I get a discount...or I can just shoot your fucking brown ass right now."

"You do that, and you won't live twenty-four hours, either one of you. You want to fuck someone up for your trouble," Ramone pointed at Ozzie, "shoot him, it'll save me having to doing it."

Jerome shook his head and took a large step forward, stopping when the barrel of his gun was five feet from Ramone's forehead. "You're not listening, shithead. You tried to fuck me, and you're giving half my money back." Keeping the gun on Ramone, he motioned with his left thumb and smiled. "And as a bonus, I'll be happy to off that asshole for you."

Adam half expected Ozzie to turn on them right then, but, instead, he just stood there, stone cold silent, appearing frozen in place.

"Now here is what you're going to do," Jerome said. "First you're going to slowly reach under your jacket and take out your piece."

Adam was surprised when Ramone just stood, unmoving, with a smirk on his face.

"Now, you stupid fuck!" Jerome screamed. "Or I'll blow your fucking head off and take the whores and all the money."

Ramone slowly reached inside his jacket and pulled out a large handgun.

"Now, slowly bend over and put it on the ground," Jerome ordered.

Ramone bent over, set the gun down, then stood up.

"Now, keep your hands where I can see them and take five steps backward."

Ramone did what he was told, and Jerome bent over, picked up the gun, and jammed it into his belt. "Now, lift up your pantlegs. When Ramone didn't move, Jerome screamed, "Do it!"

Ramone slowly pulled up both his pantlegs. Another gun was strapped to his right calf. "Take it out and slide it over to me." When it was on the ground in front of him, Jerome kicked it off to the side. "Pick it up, Mace."

Adam watched as Mace sidestepped past Ellen and the girls, picked up the gun, and stuffed it into his belt. By Adam's count, there were at least six guns among them, four of which were now in Jerome and Mace's control. *Shit, this is getting more fucked up by the second.*

Keeping his gun pointed at Ramone, Jerome said, "I'm done fucking around with you. Either you get me half the money, or I blow your fucking brains out and get it myself. Your choice but, as I said, if I get it, I'm taking all of it." He broke into a big smile. "Yeah, I know, that might screw up a good business relationship for the future, but so be it."

Ramone pointed at Ozzie, "And you'll kill him?"

"Be happy to do that for you."

"No, wait a minute!" Ozzie screamed. "It's not my fault, they made me do it."

"Oh, yeah, how the fuck did they do that?" Ramone sneered.

Ozzie pointed at Ellen. "In her jacket pocket, on the right side, she has a gun. They said they'd kill me if I didn't go along with it."

Adam looked at Ellen. She rolled her eyes. *Good while it lasted.*

Mace was back standing over Ellen with his gun pointed at her head. "Take it out, slowly."

Ellen stuck her hand into the jacket pocket and pulled out the 9mm Glock Ozzie had given her. Mace took it.

Okay, now they have five out of the six guns.

"See, I told you, I never wanted to do this," Ozzie said. "They forced me, it's not my fault."

"Get your ass down here," Jerome ordered.

Ozzie climbed out of the cockpit and onto the dock.

"On the ground, with them," Jerome ordered.

Ozzie eased himself down next to Adam. "Sorry," he whispered. "I just—"

"Shut the fuck up, asshole," Mace screamed.

"What's it going to be?" Jerome said to Ramone.

"I'll get it," Ramone said. He turned, walked slowly to the Explorer and opened the back door. Adam saw him lean in and reach for something, then straighten back up. As Ramone came out from behind the door, there was a blast of light and the deafening sound of rapid gunfire. Ellen and the girls screamed as wooden splinters and glass from the office building rained down on them. Jerome and Mace looked like ragdolls, their limbs being thrown wildly in all directions. The blasting ended as abruptly as it began, but the smell of burnt sulfur hung in the air. Adam's heart pounded through his chest as he surveyed the scene. Jerome and Mace's bullet-riddled, contorted bodies lay in front of them in pools of blood. Ellen rocked back and forth clutching the sides of her head as she gasped for air. Sarah and Beth were wrapped in each other's arms crying.

"Quiet, all of you," Ramone yelled as he walked toward them. "None of you move." The automatic rifle was in his right hand, pointed at them. He stopped a few feet away.

"You…bitches, get up." When Sarah and Beth continued to sit clutching each other, Ramone screamed, "Move…now." The girls slowly unwrapped themselves. Beth got to her feet first and helped Sarah up. "Search their bodies. Go through all their pockets, get everything that's on them. Make sure you get their phones." He looked back at Adam, Ellen, and Ozzie. "If any of you move a muscle, I'll blow your fucking heads off."

On shaky legs, Sarah and Beth walked over to the two men on the ground. Beth bent down and started to go through Mace's jacket pockets. "Fuck, there's blood everywhere," she said, lifting her hands in the air.

"Your blood will be everywhere if you don't shut the fuck up and do what you're told. Make sure you get everything out of their pants' pockets. Roll them over if you have to."

Sarah was on her knees next to Jerome. Adam saw her entire body shaking as she searched for his belongings.

"What do we do with this shit?" Beth asked as she stood up with what looked like a wallet and phone in one hand and a long silver chain with a bunch of keys in the other.

"Put it on the floor on the front passenger side of my car." Sarah stood with a few things in each of her hands that Adam couldn't identify. They both walked over to the SUV and threw the stuff inside. As they were walking back, Ramone ordered, "Now the guns, the ones on the ground and in their belts. Pick them up and put them in the car."

The guns that Jerome and Mace had in their hands when they were shot were on the ground. Sarah picked one up, and Beth grabbed the other. When the girls hesitated, Ramone yelled, "I said get all of them."

Sarah got down on her knees and pulled the gun out of Jerome's belt. Beth was bent over Mace with her back to Ramone. When she stood up, Adam saw she was holding two guns against her body with her left hand. The third was in her right hand down at her side, with her finger on the trigger. Adam let out a gasp when she raised the gun as she turned around.

"Stop!" Ramone yelled, his automatic rifle pointed at her.

Beth froze, the gun halfway out in front of her.

"Beth, no!" screamed Ellen. "Don't—"

"Raise that any further and you're dead." Ramone said.

"Please do what he says," Adam said.

"And then I'll kill all your friends."

When Beth didn't move, Sarah walked slowly up to her and took the gun from her hand.

"Smart move," Ramone said. "Now, put them all in the car with the other shit."

Sarah nudged Beth, and they carried the guns to Ramone's SUV.

Adam did the math. *One gun left on our side...or maybe not on our side. Fuck, Ozzie did just rat us out.*

"Now, come back here and sit down with them," Ramone ordered, once the girls had dumped the guns in his car.

When the girls sat back down, Sarah was next to Ellen. Her face fell to her hands, and she started sobbing. Ellen put her arms around her and pulled her close.

Ramone kept the rifle pointed at them as he walked backward to the Explorer. He leaned against the driver-side door and pulled his phone out of his pocket.

Chapter Thirty-Four

Jason glanced at his watch as he waited for the water to finish dripping through the K-Cup into his mug. *Fuck, Ramone should have called by now.*

The beeps, boings, and pops from the stupid fucking game Daveed was playing on one of the computers were making Jason even edgier than he already was. He grabbed the full mug and headed back into the living room.

"Shut that fucking thing off."

Daveed looked up and smiled. "Hey, be cool, I got it." He closed the computer. "So, what's up? I take it we got a significant issue?"

"You could say that."

"What's the deal…how bad is it?"

"Not sure yet, but this whole fucking thing should have been over a long time—" Jason stopped and pulled his vibrating phone out of his pocket. It was Ramone. "What the fuck's going on?"

"We got a problem, Boss."

"How bad?"

"Real bad."

Jason listened while Ramone went through the story.

"So, you have the girls and the money?"

"Uh huh. I'll bring them—"

"Just the money."

"You want me to—"

"Yeah, do it."

"All of them, even the sailboat people?"

"Yes, no loose ends."

"Sure thing, Boss."

"Make it look like a...a business deal gone bad that ended in a shootout."

"Got it."

"Get going. The sun will be up soon."

Spade jumped when she felt her phone vibrating in her left hand. She turned it over and stared at Jason's name on the screen. Slowly, she lifted it to her ear and whispered, "I'm here."

"Leaving now, I'll be there in an hour," Jason said.

"Why, what's going on?"

"Ozzie fucked up. It's being taken care of, but he might have talked. Can't take the chance his wife knows something."

"Jason, no, I don't want to—"

"Shut the fuck up, and do what I tell you. Have everyone in the house secured by the time I get there."

"But why can't we just—"

He was gone. Spade felt nauseous. She thought about what Jason was asking her to do, and how it might end up. Could she participate in this? What if he decides to kill Ozzie's wife? There were bicycles in the garage. Ozzie has kids. What if he wants to kill them too? It sounded like he was having Ramone take care of Ozzie.

What if I just head out of here and never come back? Can I do that? Can I live with never seeing him again? It would never work. I know Jason, he would find me. But maybe I can stay and keep him from killing these people. Yeah, maybe I can do that.

Spade sighed deeply and slid the phone into her pocket.

Chapter Thirty-Five

The sky slowly changed from midnight blue to deep gray.

Any time now, a parade of fishermen will be pulling in here, Adam thought. He looked at the two bodies on the ground in front of them and then at Ramone, still leaning against his SUV with his phone to his ear and his gun trained on the five of them huddled together on the ground. Ramone stopped talking and appeared to be listening.

Sarah sniffed loudly and whispered, "He's going to kill us, isn't he?"

"I don't think so. If he was, he probably would have done it when he shot those two," Adam said, not really believing it.

"He's asking Jason what to do with us," Beth said.

"I'm...I'm worried about you guys," Sarah said. "At least we have value to him. He can sell us again."

Adam turned to Ozzie. "You still have your gun on you?"

"Uh huh."

"You're going to have to use it…soon."

"You think I don't know that. I'm waiting for the right time. I'm hoping for a second or two when he's not pointing that thing right at us."

"Yep, he's getting instructions from Jason," Ellen said.

Ramone nodded, said something, then slipped the phone back into his pocket.

"We're about to find out." Adam said.

Ramone kept the gun pointed at them as he slowly approached to within fifteen feet of where they were sitting and stopped.

"You, Ozzie, keep your hands where I can see them, and stand up. You so much as flinch and you're fucking dead."

Ozzie used one hand at a time to push himself up to standing.

"Take three steps toward me and stop."

As ordered, Ozzie took the three steps.

"Now stretch your right arm up as high as you can get it." When Ozzie had his arm raised, Ramone said, "Now use your left hand to unzip your jacket."

When Ozzie hesitated, Ramone screamed, "Now, asshole. And keep your other hand up high."

As Ozzie pulled the zipper down, his jacket fell open.

Ramone broke into a smile. "Well, well, will you look at what we found?" The smile disappeared. "Now, you're going to use only your thumb and one finger of your left hand to lift it out. You try anything else, and I'll turn you into Swiss cheese."

Adam felt like he had been punched in the gut as he watched Ozzie lift the gun from his belt. *Fuck, now he has all of them*.

"Very slowly, bend over and place it on the ground."

Ozzie did as he was instructed.

"Now back up and sit your ass down with them."

Once Ozzie was on the ground next to Adam, Ramone picked up the gun and shoved it into his belt.

"Listen carefully, assholes, because here is what's going to happen next," Ramone said. "You do anything other than exactly what I tell you and you're fucking dead. Now…you're all going to stand up, very slowly."

Adam stood first, and the rest followed. Adam held his hands in the air in front of him and took one hesitant step forward. "There is no reason for anyone else to get hurt," he said. "You have your money, which is what you came for. We'll get in our boat and take off, and no one will ever hear anything from any of us about what happened here."

Ramone let out a half grunt, half laugh. "Oh, yeah, and next you're going to tell me you can make pigs fly out of your ass. Do you really think I'm that stupid?

"No, we don't, but I'm sure you'll know where to find us…that should be good enough," Ellen said.

"We'll see. You do what I tell you, and I'll think about it." Ramone pointed at the bodies. "Grab those two assholes and drag them over to the edge of the dock."

When nobody moved, Ramone screamed, "Do it, now."

Adam walked over to where Mace was face down with his legs splayed and twisted. "I'll do this one. You take that one," he said to Ozzie.

Adam grabbed Mace's shoulders and pulled but couldn't budge him. He was a big guy, and moving his dead weight was much harder than Adam thought it would be.

"You…bitches, help them," Ramone yelled.

Ellen reached for Mace's feet. The girls went to help Ozzie with Jerome. Adam and Ellen struggled but finally got Mace's body to the edge of the dock.

"Now help them," Ramone ordered.

Adam helped Ozzie and the girls drag Jerome the last few feet and drop him behind Mace.

"Now push them in," Ramone directed.

"What?" Ellen exclaimed.

"You heard me. Do it now, or you'll be going in with them."

As they bent over Mace's body, Ellen leaned toward

Adam and whispered, "I can't believe we're doing this."

"No shit...are you okay?"

"Oh, yeah, I'm real okay. Can't you tell?"

Unable to move him, Adam got down on his knees and slid his arms under Mace's torso. Ellen hesitated, then did the same with his legs.

Adam whispered, "I am so sorry about all this."

"Stop talking and do what you're fucking told," Ramone yelled.

"Okay, okay," Adam said. He looked at Ellen, "Ready?" She nodded. "Go."

Together, Adam and Ellen lifted and rolled Mace into the water. Ozzie and the girls did the same with Jerome. Adam watched as the lifeless bodies were swallowed up by the dark water. He turned toward Ramone. It was now light enough to see his large round face. He wasn't smiling. "We did what you asked, can we go now?"

"I don't think so."

Ellen took a step forward with her hands up in front of her. "Please don't do this. I mean it, we won't say—"

"Shut the fuck up, bitch."

"Wait a minute," Ozzie said. "These are good people. They didn't have any part in this. They just helped me out when I needed a bigger boat. You got the money and the girls. I fucked up, and I know you're going to kill me...there's nothing I can do about that, but please, let them go."

"You have us, Ramone, please don't hurt them," Beth blurted out. "I'll do anything you want, just...just take us and the money back to Jason."

"No," Ellen yelped. "Let us all go. We'll never tell anyone about any—"

"That's right, Ramone," Adam said. "Just let us get on the boat and leave, and it will be like this never happened."

Ramone broke into a perverse grin. "What the fuck. Yeah, sure, you can go. And you can take the fucking whores with you."

When they all just looked at him, he shouted, "Do you fucking want to leave or not? All of you, get the fuck up on the boat, now."

Shocked, Adam turned to the others and indicated with his hand that they should go first. Then he heard a clicking sound behind him. He swung his head around in time to see Ramone load a new clip into the rifle and raise it toward them.

Adam threw his arms in the air and screamed "No!" just as a dark figure came flying around the corner of the office and dove at Ramone, hitting him in the back and throwing him off balance onto the dock. There was a flash of light, three rat, tat, tats from the automatic rifle and more wood splinters flying off the office building. Adam watched in horror as Ramone jumped to his feet and turned the gun toward the tall male figure lying on the ground.

From behind him, Adam heard the crack of another gun firing. He jerked around and saw Beth, arms outstretched, with both hands on a handgun, pull the trigger two more times. He turned back to see Ramone stand straight up, stiffen, then fall like a large tree trunk and land with a loud thud. The person on the ground who had charged Ramone, reached over, grabbed the automatic rifle, and threw it aside.

Open mouthed, Adam turned back to Beth. Her arms were still out in front of her, and she appeared to be in a daze. Still looking straight ahead, in a quivering voice she said, "When we picked them up, I kept this one."

Then her hands started shaking. Adam reached out and took the gun from her. As she began to crumble to the ground, Ellen ran up, threw her arms around her, eased her down and held her. "Oh…oh, my God, I killed him. Fuck, I just killed—"

"It's okay, Beth, you saved our lives," Ellen said. "He was going to kill all of us."

When Beth started sobbing, Sarah wrapped her arms around her and Ellen. "Don't worry, Beth. After what he did to you…to us, he deserved to die."

"But I murdered—"

"Fuckin-A...see, I told you he was alive," Ozzie exclaimed. He helped Spider up and threw his arms around him.

"Holy shit, it's you," Adam said.

"How the fuck did you get here?" Ozzie asked.

"My boat is over there, a few docks down. I figured you'd gotten yourself into some pretty deep shit and might need some help. So, I came over and...fuck, I never dreamed it'd be anything like this."

"You saved our lives," Ozzie said hugging his friend again.

Adam stooped down next to Ramone. He was sprawled halfway on his side with blood running out of his mouth and pooling under his chest. Adam slowly reached under Ramone's jacket collar and felt for a pulse. "He's dead." *I can't believe it. This fucking nightmare just keeps getting worse.*

Adam felt a hand on his shoulder. It was Ozzie. "Better him than us."

When Adam got to his feet, Ozzie pointed at Ramone's body. "I hope you know this doesn't end it. He just talked to Jason. That fucker told Ramone to kill all of us, and I bet he's expecting a call back saying it's done." Ozzie jabbed a finger past Adam. "And that asshole is probably on his way to my house right now, if he isn't there already."

"Shit. You're right."

"I need to get there...take him the money." Ozzie threw his hands in the air. "How the fuck am I going to—"

"You can take Ramone's car," Adam said.

"How long do you think it'll take?"

"A little over an hour. I'll go with you, but I have to call the police first." Adam looked around. "Fuck...there's a body here and two in the water." He raised his hands to the sides of his head. "I can't just walk away from all this."

"Yes, you can," Ellen said. "We all can. Call whomever you need to call and make a report. You can explain later."

"What about Sarah and Beth?" Adam said.

Ozzie pointed at Spider. "He can take them back to Shawnee Falls in his boat."

"Okay," Adam said. "Ellen, you go with them. I'll go with Ozzie. But we need to report this and get moving. We're not going to be alone here much longer."

"No way. I'm going with you," Ellen responded. "You don't even know how to use one of those guns. And the girls are coming with us. Now that we've come this far, I'm not letting them out of my sight."

Adam paced in a circle. "Yeah, okay. I get that."

"Spider can stay and explain what happened to the police," Ellen said.

Adam shook his head. "Not a good idea. Spider doesn't know the whole story. They'd lock him up for God knows how long while they figure it out."

"I agree," Ozzie said.

Adam turned to Spider. "You need to get the hell out of here now, before somebody comes. But stay available, the police will want to talk to you."

Ozzie gave Spider another quick hug. "Thanks again, Buddy. We all owe you bigtime."

"That's for sure," Ellen said slapping him on the back as he walked past her. When she turned around, Adam was going through Ramone's pockets. "What are you looking for?"

"His keys...and phone." Adam popped up. "Got them."

When Adam pulled out his own phone and started scrolling, Ellen said, "Not now, you can call on the road, we need to get going."

"Yeah, right." Adam pointed at Ramone's Explorer. "Sarah, Beth, get in the back with Ellen."

When Ozzie started to walk around to the passenger door, Adam yelled, "You drive, so I can make some calls."

Ozzie stopped dead in his tracks, pointed at Adam and said, "You can report this but nothing about me and my family. If Jason gets wind of cops being called, he'll kill them for sure. Our only chance is to—"

"I get it, Ozzie. I don't agree with you, but I gave you my word, and I'll keep it. But we have to get moving, now."

As Ozzie spun the car around, Adam dialed 911. "Hello, my name is Adam Kennedy. I'm an attorney from Shawnee Falls, Ohio. I want to report a…" He proceeded to give a bare bones version of why the responding officers would find three dead bodies at the Grant Harbor Marina, and why he and every witness to what had happened was leaving the scene. "I assure you, we will all be available in a few hours to talk to whomever wants to interview us. But, for now, we have to make sure no one else gets killed."

"Where are you going?" the voice on the other end asked. "We'll have a crew—"

"I can't tell you that. I'll explain everything later when—"

"Mr. Kennedy, tell me where you are headed," the voice demanded.

"You have my number. I will get back to you later."

"No, do not hang up. Tell me where—"

When Adam hung up the phone, Ellen asked, "How long do you think it'll take for someone to call you back?"

"Not long. That's why I'm turning off the ringer."

"How much trouble are we in for leaving?"

"A lot, but we have no choice." Adam felt Ramone's phone vibrating in his pocket. He pulled it out and looked at the screen where the word "Boss" appeared.

"Fuck, it's Jason calling him."

"Are you going to answer it?" Ellen asked.

"No." Adam pulled his knife out of his pocket and opened it.

"What are you doing?" Ozzie said.

"Taking the battery out so Jason can't track it." The car fishtailed when Ozzie made the turn off the road out of the marina onto the entrance ramp to I-75 south. "Take it easy, Ozzie. I know we need to get there, but it'll take a lot longer if we get stopped."

"Yeah, sure, whatever…" Ozzie said without letting up on the gas.

When Adam started scrolling on his phone again, Ellen asked, "Who are you calling now?"

"Sam, we're going to need her help."

Samantha Evans, the same Sam Evans who with her husband Jon had introduced Adam to Ellen, was an Assistant Wendall County Prosecutor. After several rings, a groggy Jon answered. "Adam, it's 6:30 in the morning…is something wrong?

"I need to talk to Sam."

"Are you okay? You don't sound—"

"Please, is Sam there? I need—"

"Sure, here she is."

"What's going on? It's six—"

"He wants to talk to you."

"What about?"

"How the hell do I know?"

"Adam. What's up?" Sam asked.

Adam ran through the entire story, from the hijacking to the murders. When he finished, he said, "We're going to need someone to affirm that we reported this as soon as it was possible to do so. So far, I've only been able to talk to the dispatcher over in Monroe County. If you have any suggestions as to anyone else I should talk to, I think I—"

"Yeah, well, with three dead bodies, I agree with that. I know the prosecutor over there. I'll call him."

"Thank you very much."

"What's this guy's address…where you're going now? I'll get someone there right away."

"I can't tell you that. We promised Ozzie there would be no police until his family is safe."

"Adam, that's crazy. I've prosecuted guys who do this kind of thing. They're bad, very bad. They kill people. You can't go in there alone and try to—"

"Believe me, from what these girls told us, I get it. But we gave Ozzie our word."

"No, you can't do that. You have to—"

"Thanks again for your help. I'll get back to you."

Chapter Thirty-Six

Spade stood motionless in a shadowy corner of the kitchen. The gray dawn light spilling through the window lent the room a haunted air. She looked around. Clearly, Ozzie's wife was a meticulous housekeeper. There were no dirty dishes in the sink, and the countertops were cleared of everything except what was supposed to be there: the coffeemaker with a sugar bowl sitting next to it, an earthenware crock filled with cooking utensils, a wire cookbook holder, and a toaster. A few papers and what looked like bills were stacked neatly on the built-in desk.

A dozen or so photographs were stuck on the refrigerator with magnets adorned with a variety of tiny, colorful flowers. Most of the pictures were of a pair of dark-haired, teenage girls. By their looks, they could have been twins except one was almost a head taller than the other. In several of the photos, the girls were playing soccer or tennis. In others, they were either at the beach or on a boat. In one, they were huddled on either side of a woman who looked like an older version of themselves, standing arm-in-arm with her, wearing matching smiles.

Nothing like any house I ever lived in.

She felt her phone vibrating and pulled it out.

"Where are you?"

"In the kitchen," she whispered.

"They up yet?"

"No, I was waiting for them to come down on their own."

"I'm a half-hour away. Give it fifteen minutes. If no one is up, wake them one at a time. Start with the mother. I want them all secured before I get there. Let me know when they are."

Before she could respond, he hung up.

Isn't that special? I do the dirty work before he gets here. If anything goes wrong, he drives on by and leaves me to go down with the fucking ship. Asshole!

Traffic was picking up on Rt. 2, but it wasn't holding Ozzie back any. Adam looked down at Sarah's too-small-for-him clothing and pictured being stopped for speeding and asked to step out of the car. Once the cop took a look at him and Ozzie in the front seats, and Ellen and the two girls in the back, he doubted it would take more than two seconds for backup to be called in. Add to that their being in a car registered to who-the-fuck-knows and all the guns, and they wouldn't be going anywhere for a very long time. Adam envisioned his license to practice law flying right out the window.

He was about to implore Ozzie to slow down when a phone went off. It was Ozzie's. He pulled it out of his pocket and looked at it. "It's Jason."

"Are you going to answer it?"

"I think...I have to." He lifted the phone to his ear but held it so Adam could hear both sides of the conversation.

"Hello."

"Where the fuck are you?"

"On the way back. We had a problem."

There was a long hesitation then, "Where's Ramone?"

"He…he's…those guys shot him. I mean…he shot them, but he was hit too. It was a big fucking shootout. Bullets were flying everywhere. They're all…it was a real—"

"Are you telling me Ramone is dead?"

"Ah, yeah…I had to get the fuck out of there, so I took his car. You don't have to worry. I'm bringing you the money and the girls."

"What about Jerome? What did you do with—"

"He and the other guy, the one who was with him, their bodies are back there."

Adam noticed that Ozzie's hand shook, and sweat was dripping down his face. Adam knew Ozzie was trying hard, but also knew that what he was saying would not be making sense to Jason. Ramone had called Jason after he killed Jerome and Mace. *Shit, this hole is getting deeper by the second.*

"Did you just leave Ramone there?"

"Uh…yes…I didn't know what else to do."

"What about the sailboat people? What happened to them?"

"When it was over, they got in their boat and took off."

Adam heard a loud, "Fuck!" on the other end before Jason said, "Bring the girls and the money to your house, I'll meet you there. And you better have every fucking penny of—"

"No, please, leave my family out of this. They don't know—"

"Call me when you're ten minutes away, I'll give you instructions. If you fail to do exactly as I say, or if I get the slightest hint that you've called the police or anyone else, they're all dead. Do you understand?"

"Jason, no, please don't—"

The line went dead. "Fuck!" Ozzie screamed. He pressed down harder on the accelerator.

"Ozzie, don't do that, slow down," Adam said. "We're in a car that isn't ours with a shitload of guns. For all we know, they and this vehicle were stolen. If we get stopped, we're screwed. It's not worth the risk just to save a few minutes."

Adam saw Ozzie's white-knuckled grip on the wheel and was afraid he wasn't hearing him. He was relieved when a few seconds later he felt Ozzie ease off the gas pedal and slow down to five miles over the speed limit.

Adam noticed Ellen's hand reach between the seats and rest on Ozzie's shoulder. "Thank you...the most important thing is that we get there. And thank you for trying to save us back there. I promise you we're going to do everything we can to see that your family isn't harmed."

Chapter Thirty-Seven

Spade's ears perked up when a toilet flushed somewhere above her. Light footsteps overhead were followed by a squeak on the stairs. She waited, hoping it was the mother. She wanted her under control before the daughters came down. Spade pulled the knife out of her pocket and switched it open.

The woman with mussed dark hair, wearing a faded blue robe and furry slippers, didn't appear to be aware of Spade standing in the corner as she switched on a light and shuffled across the kitchen to the coffee maker.

For a moment, Spade wished she could blink her eyes and transport herself to some other time and place. Instead, she took three quick steps forward and, in one fluid movement, clamped her left hand tightly around the woman's mouth and pressed the point of the knife against her neck.

In a low voice, she said, "Do not make a sound. Follow my instructions and you and your daughters will not be harmed. If you don't, you all will be hurt very badly. Do you understand?"

The woman arched her back but wasn't fighting.

"I said, do you understand? If you do, nod your head."

The woman moved her head up and down.

Keeping her hand over the woman's mouth and the knife in place, Spade said, "We are going to back up slowly." She stepped backwards, leading the woman to the table. "Pull out a chair and lower yourself onto the seat."

Once the woman was seated, Spade said, "I am going to take my hand away from your mouth. If you scream, this knife will go right through your neck, and, when your daughters come running in here, they will die too. Do you understand?" She pressed the knife a little harder, enough for a small trickle of blood to seep out from under the point.

The woman nodded. Spade let go of her mouth and said, "Drop your arms and let them hang down to the back legs of the chair."

When the woman's hands were lowered, Spade pulled a handful of zip ties out of her pocket. As she secured each of the woman's wrists to a leg of the chair, Spade experienced a sick feeling in her stomach. She recalled the early days and how Jason had taught her to do this when the girls he brought to the farmhouse didn't obey as he thought they should. "It's all part of their training," was his usual response whenever Spade objected to doing it.

Fuck, I've become just as big a monster as he is. But if I don't do this, he'll kill this woman...and her daughters...and maybe me. I don't have a choice...at least for now.

Spade swung around in front of the woman and tied each of her ankles to a leg of the chair. When it was done, she stood up and pocketed the knife.

"Please don't hurt my daughters," the woman pleaded in a throaty whisper. "I don't know who you are or why you're doing this, but..." she choked up as tears streamed down her face. "...you can kill me if you have to, but please don't hurt them. They're wonderful kids. They've done nothing to deserve…" she started gasping.

Spade stepped behind the woman so she wouldn't have to look at her face. Hearing footsteps behind her, Spade spun around and saw a young girl wearing pink and green striped boxer shorts and a gray T-shirt coming through the doorway with a phone in her hand.

"Mom!" she screamed.

Spade pulled the gun out of her belt and pointed it at the girl's forehead. "Do not say another word."

"Who…who are you? Why are you—"

"Molly, please, just be quiet."

Spade took a step closer, keeping the gun pointed at the girl's head. "Do as I say, and no one will get hurt."

The girl looked at her mother and then back at Spade. Her hands began to tremble.

"The first thing you're going to do is put your phone on the floor and slide it over to me," Spade said in as soft but firm a tone as she could muster. Since she was a little taller than her mother, Spade guessed that this was the older of Ozzie's two daughters, probably around fifteen. She wanted her tied up before the other one woke up and came downstairs, but the girl just stood there with her mouth open, staring at her. "Don't make me hurt you or your mother."

"Do it, Molly. Just do what she says, and everything will be okay."

The girl put her phone on the floor and slid it toward Spade with her foot.

"Now, pull out a chair and put it in front of your mother, facing her." When the chair was in place, Spade said, "That's a good girl. Now sit down." Once she was seated, Spade went through the same process of tying down Molly's arms and legs. When she was finished, she stood and asked, "Is your sister still asleep?"

The mother responded, "She isn't here. She spent the night at a friend's house."

"When will she be back?"

"Not until later. She's spending the day there."

Spade retreated to a dark corner of the kitchen, pulled out her phone, and texted: Mom & 1 kid secure – other kid not here.

There was an immediate response: B there in 10

As Jason drove into Shawnee Falls, the sky was getting darker instead of lighter, and the lightning that had been flashing in the distance grew closer.

Good, let it storm. At least nobody will be out walking their dog.

He had no trouble finding Ozzie's house; he had checked it out back when he was thinking about hiring him for the delivery job. He drove past it to the next block and pulled his midnight-blue Mustang convertible to the curb and cut the engine. Out of the duffle bag on the seat next to him, Jason pulled a Smith & Wesson M&P 9, which was his favorite because it could accommodate a laser sight if he needed it. He stuck the gun in his belt then took a small can of brown spray paint out of the glove box. He climbed out of the car and sprayed a quick shot of paint on the license plate, obliterating half the numbers. As light rain began to fall, he tossed the can into the back seat and ran to the house.

As Spade had said, the side service door into the garage wasn't locked. Jason eased it open and slipped inside. Immediately in front of him was a Honda Odyssey van just like the ones half the people in the country who had kids owned. When he stepped around the rear of the van, there was enough dull light coming through the row of windows at the top of the overhead door to make out the lineup of bicycles hanging from the ceiling. Underneath them, along the side wall, were a lawnmower, all the usual yard equipment, and a heavy-duty workbench with tools hanging from a pegboard on the wall behind it.

At the far end of the garage were shelves piled high

with all kinds of sports paraphernalia. Next to the shelves was a door, which Jason guessed was the entry into the house. He stepped up to it, slowly turned the knob, and gently pushed it open. Before him was a long narrow space that had a built-in bench running along one side with hooks above it filled with a variety of outdoor clothing and a couple of backpacks. On the other side were a washer and dryer.

Through an open doorway at the other end, Jason saw Spade standing with her arms folded across her chest, leaning back against a countertop. In front of her were two women tied to a pair of kitchen chairs. When he entered the room, the older woman exclaimed, "Oh, my God, Jason, is that you? How did you get here? Thank God...please help us. This woman is—"

"Hello, Janice." Jason had met Ozzie's wife back when he was helping him with his drinking problem.

The woman's eyes widened. "Wait...Ja...Jason, why are you here?"

"Are they behaving themselves?" he asked Spade.

"Oh, no...is she...oh, my God. You're not going to help us. She's with you? But why...why are you—"

"Mom, who is that? Do you know him?"

"Where is your husband?"

Tears streamed down Janice's face. "Why are you doing this? Please don't hurt us. Please don't hurt Molly. She didn't do anything to—"

"Stop the fucking blubbering. I asked you where Ozzie is."

"I don't know. He was doing some night job...a delivery thing...to make extra money."

"Who is he working for when he does that?"

"I don't know, he would never tell me. Please, I don't know anything. Just let us—"

"Mom, why is this happening? Is Dad in trouble?"

"Molly, be quiet, don't—"

"Listen to your mother, kid. Not another word."

Molly swung her head around. "Fuck you, asshole, I

don't have to do what you—"

Jason whipped out his Smith & Wesson and jammed it up against Janice's left temple. "Oh, you don't think you have to do what I say? How the fuck would you like to see your mother's brains splattered all over that refrigerator?"

"Jason, no!" Spade screamed.

"And you shut the fuck up too!" The gun was now pointed at Spade.

"No, please, don't. I promise, I'll be quiet," Molly exclaimed.

"Just do what he says, Molly," Janice pleaded. "Don't say another word. If we do what he says, they won't hurt us."

"You don't know that," Molly said, a little above a whisper.

Jason felt his phone vibrating in his pocket.

Chapter Thirty-Eight

The sky had darkened again, and a light drizzle was falling as Ozzie pulled to the curb.

"Which house is it?" Adam asked.

"You can't see it from here, it's in the next block." Ozzie grabbed his phone out of his pocket. "I have to call him." As he lifted the phone to his ear, Adam leaned closer, hoping to hear both sides of the conversation.

"Where the fuck are you?"

"About ten minutes away. But I want to meet somewhere else, not at my house. I don't want my wife and kids to see—"

"Did I ask for your opinion?"

"Please, leave my family out of this. They've done nothing to—"

"Shut up and listen. If you want to see Janice and your daughter alive again, you'll do exactly as I say."

From the expression on Ozzie's face, Adam sensed that hearing his wife's name cross Jason's lips hit him like a sucker punch to the gut. "Okay, okay. Just don't—"

"When you get here, pull in the driveway, up close to the overhead door. Turn off the engine and the lights, then call me for further instructions. Do not get out of the car until I tell you to. I'm here in your house with Janice and Molly. I don't think I have to tell you what will happen to them if you fail to follow my instructions. Do you understand?"

"Yes, I hear you. Just don't—"

"The two whores are with you, right?"

"Yes."

"And the money?"

"Yes. It's all here."

The line went dead.

"Fuck, fuck, fuck," Ozzie screamed as he pounded his fists against the steering wheel. "He's in my house. He has my wife and daughter."

"Yes, I heard most of it," Adam said. He put his hand on Ozzie's shoulder. "Are you sure you don't want to call the police?"

"No, we can't do that. If I do and he finds out, he'll kill them. I have to do what he says."

"He always listened to police calls at the house," Beth said from the back seat. "He had a radio or a scanner thing that could pick up—"

"See, that's what I mean. If he's listening, he'll know…he could kill them and be gone before the cops get here," Ozzie said.

"But he wouldn't carry that kind of thing around with him," Ellen said. "There's no way he'd be able to—"

"No, but he has a phone," Adam said. "Someone else could be listening and call him. Ozzie's right, we can't risk it."

"I have to do what he says. I know it's not what you want, but I have to give him the money and the girls, and pray he doesn't hurt my family."

"I wouldn't count on that," Beth said. "Like I told you before, he's one mean son-of-a-bitch."

A heavy silence hung in the enclosed air of the SUV. The windows were beginning to fog up when Adam asked, "Tell me the layout of your home."

Ozzie described the first floor of his house. "My guess is he has them in the kitchen. That's where Janice—my wife—would have gone first when she came downstairs."

"Is there a door from the outside into the kitchen?" Adam asked.

"Yes, from the patio, in the back of the house. There's also a service door into the garage. It's around the side, to the right from the street. And there's a door from the garage into the house."

Ellen said, "Adam, you and I could go around to the back to try and see what's going on inside."

"That's what I'm thinking."

"I'm really sorry about this," Ozzie said. "I know this isn't how you wanted this to go, but... I have to give him the money and the girls."

"It's okay, Ozzie," Ellen said. "We understand. Your family comes first." She turned to Beth and Sarah and took their hands. "This isn't what we wanted or hoped for, but we have no choice, for now anyway. But I promise you, we will not let him take you back to that farmhouse."

Sarah sniffed and wiped her eyes.

Beth said, "I don't want you to get killed because of me. I think you should just leave now while you—"

"I agree," Sarah said. "Don't do this. Just leave us, and get out of here."

"Listen to me, both of you. This, obviously, isn't what any of us wanted. But it is what it is, and we're going to have to deal with it. Unfortunately, you two may to have to play along with Jason for a little while longer, just until we can—"

"Whatever you're going to do, you have to get on with it," Ozzie said. "He's expecting me to pull up in a few minutes."

"Okay, but wait...Adam, here, take this." Ellen reached

between the seats and offered Adam one of the handguns Beth and Sarah had picked up after the shootout with Jerome and Mace.

"No thanks, I'm breaking enough laws already. I'm not going to add carrying a stolen gun that I'm not licensed to have…and don't know how to use."

"I'll show you how to use it. You're probably going to need—"

"No, I'm not—"

"I'll take it," Ozzie said.

Adam laid his hand on Ozzie's arm. "I don't think that's a good idea. It'll provoke him even more if he sees you're armed." Ozzie didn't respond. "And I think you should leave your own gun in the car when you go inside."

"He's right," Ellen said. "But if it's okay, I'm taking the one you gave me on the boat."

Ozzie hesitated then took his gun out of his waistband and shoved it under the seat.

"We should get out here," Adam said. "How will we know which house is yours?"

"The fourth house from the corner, on the right, it's blue with white trim. You should start walking. I'll wait a couple of minutes to give you a chance to get there."

Adam looked at Ellen. "Ready?"

"Yep. Let's go."

They slipped out of the Explorer and started walking briskly down the sidewalk. The sky had continued to darken, and thunder rumbled in the distance. Adam noticed Ellen looking at him. "What?"

"I was thinking it's a good thing it's dark and stormy. Considering what we look like, if anyone saw us, they'd probably call the police."

"True, but I'd say, at this point, that might be the best thing that could happen."

"I know. That Ramone guy was about to kill us all when Beth shot him, wasn't he?"

"That's my guess."

"Jason probably told him to do that."

"Yep."

"He's probably planning to kill Ozzie and his family, and maybe the girls."

"That's the way I see it."

"We may have to kill Jason to save their lives...and our lives."

"Yep. Do you think you can do that?"

"I don't know. Can you?"

"I'm afraid I'm about to find out."

"I can't believe this is happening. Wasn't it just twelve hours ago that we were finishing our wedding night dinner on our new boat and watching a beautiful sunset over the island?"

"Uh huh. It feels like that was weeks ago."

"Yes, it does."

When they got to the corner, a flash of lightning lit up the block. "There it is. Let's go," Adam said.

"After you."

Adam took off at a run, leading the way across the yards to Ozzie's house. They slipped past the service door into the garage and ducked behind some shrubs that ran along the side of the house. They crouched close to the ground and peeked around the corner. The patio with the door into the kitchen was exactly as Ozzie had described it. On the other side of the door was a pair of double hung windows.

Adam felt Ellen tapping him on the arm. He turned and looked at her. "I have a feeling this isn't going to end well," she whispered. "I want you to know that I...that I love you...very much."

Adam kissed her on the forehead. "I love you, Ellen, and I don't want to lose you." He looked away and then looked back into her eyes. "Please, get out of here now, and let me take care of this mess."

Ellen put her hand up to his lips and shook her head. "No way. We're in this together."

"I can't deal with the thought of anything happening to

you."

"Either we both go, or we both stay."

Adam sighed and shook his head. "I can't leave."

"I can't either."

"It's the right thing to do."

They both turned when they heard the Explorer pull into the driveway.

When Jason felt his phone vibrating in his pocket, he turned to Molly and Janice, and said, "If either of you moves a muscle, I'll blow your fucking brains out." He looked at Spade and motioned for her to follow him to the garage.

"Speak," he said into his phone.

"I'm outside," Ozzie said.

"Nobody moves until I tell you to, got it?"

"Yes, I do, but just don't—"

Jason pressed the phone to his chest, as he walked to the middle of the garage and pulled the handle to release the lever for the automatic door opener. Then he grabbed a rake off the wall and used it to yank the plug out of the ceiling causing the motion sensor light to go out. "Lift it by hand, and bring the bitches in," he said to Spade. He pointed to the workbench. "Cuff them to the legs of that thing."

Spade let out a grunt as she hefted the door up over her head.

To Ozzie, Jason said, "You stay in the car. The girls will come in first."

Spade hurried out into the now pouring rain and opened the passenger side rear door. She pulled Sarah and Beth out and directed them into the garage.

"On the floor, right there, hands behind your back," Jason ordered.

When they dropped down onto the cement floor, Spade knelt and zip-tied each girl's wrists to a leg of the workbench.

Once they were secured, Jason said into his phone, "Now it's your turn. Get out of the car and slowly come in here with your hands over your head. Leave the keys in the car."

Jason kept his gun pointed at Ozzie as he walked into the garage. "Stop and turn around," Jason said when Ozzie was within ten feet of him. "Put your hands together behind your back."

When Spade had zip-tied Ozzie's wrists together, Jason asked, "Where's the money?"

"In a duffle bag on the floor, front passenger side. It's all there."

"It fucking better be." Jason motioned for Spade to retrieve the bag. She got it from the car and brought it in. "Pull the door back down."

"You have everything, Jason. I want to see my wife and daughters."

"Shut the fuck up until I say you can talk." Jason looked at Spade. "Count it."

She unzipped the bag and peered inside. "It's too dark out here, I can't see it."

"Take it inside." Spade walked past Jason and into the house. "Follow her," he said to Ozzie.

When they paraded into the kitchen, Molly screamed, "Dad!"

"Ozzie," Janice said breathlessly. "Please give them what they want...whatever it is...please just give it to them."

"I will, Janice, I will." He looked at Jason. "You have it all. If you feel like you have to kill me, go ahead and do it, but they—"

"No!" Janice screamed.

"They know nothing. Please let them go," Ozzie begged.

"Shut up, all of you." Jason's gun was at Janice's head. "One more word out of anyone and she's first."

"Can you see anything?" Ellen whispered.

Adam had crept along the back wall of the house to the windows hoping to get a glimpse of what was going on inside. He put his finger to his lips then crawled back to where Ellen was crouched. "Ozzie's wife and a daughter are tied to chairs. Ozzie's standing by the counter. It looks like his hands are tied behind his back."

"What do we do?"

"I want to see if that side door into the garage is unlocked."

"Okay, I'll follow you."

"Oh, shit, wait a minute." He reached into his pocket and pulled out his phone. "Make sure your ringer is off."

When Adam got to the door, he turned the handle slowly and gave it a gentle nudge. "It's open. Wait here, I'm going in." Adam stepped slowly around the back of the van. He was just gaining his focus when he heard someone say his name. In the dim light, he was able to make out the outlines of Sarah and Beth on the floor across from him.

"Be careful, they're right inside," Sarah whispered.

Adam felt Ellen brush past him and scoot over to the girls. "Are you hurt?" she asked laying a hand on each of them.

"No, but we're tied to this thing," Beth said.

Adam pulled out his knife, opened it, and cut them loose.

"Jason took Ozzie inside," Beth said. "He has his wife and daughter in there."

"I know, I saw them," Adam whispered.

"Spade is with him," Sarah said. "He had her tie Ozzie's hands before he took him in. They both have guns. Knowing that asshole, he's probably going to kill all of them."

Adam looked at Ellen. "You should take these two and get out of here."

"Oh, yeah, and what are you going to do without a gun, sweet talk them into letting everybody go? Sorry, I'm not going anywhere."

"Okay, but they should get out of here," Adam said pointing to the two girls.

"Be quiet," Ellen whispered. "Someone's yelling in there."

Adam pointed to the door at the far end of the garage that was slightly ajar. "Does that go into the house?"

"Yes," Sarah said. "That's the way they went in."

Adam walked slowly over and put his ear to the narrow opening.

"It's all there."

It was a woman's voice he didn't recognize. *Must be Spade.* He felt Ellen below him pressing her head against the door.

"I told you," Ozzie said. "You have everything, Jason, so please, just let them go."

"Sorry, not that easy," Jason responded. "You fucked up, and you're going to have to—"

"Okay, I get that," Ozzie said. "But they didn't have anything to do with any of it. Do what you have to do to me, but please, leave them alone."

"I don't think so."

"Dad, what's he saying, why is he doing this?"

"Please, Jason, she's just a child, don't hurt her," a different woman's voice pleaded.

Ozzie's wife, Janice.

"You, shut the fuck up," Jason ordered.

"Janice, be quiet," Ozzie said. "Jason, can't we talk about this? I promise you, none of us will tell anyone anything."

"You want to talk? Fine, sit down, we'll talk." There was a brief hesitation, then, "I said sit the fuck down," Jason screamed.

"Okay, okay, take it easy, I'll sit." There was the sound of a chair scraping on a wood floor.

"You want to talk, go ahead," Jason said, "tell me what the hell happened out there, why you're here and Ramone is dead because of your fuckup. While we're at it, let's talk about who the fuck killed him, seeing as I talked to Ramone after he shot Jerome and Mace. Would you like to tell me all about that?"

The venomous tone of Jason's voice sent a shiver up the back of Adam's neck.

"I didn't kill him. Those other guys…they shot up the whole place, I had nothing to do with—"

"Enough!" Jason screamed.

"Ozzie, what the hell's going on?" Janice cried. She turned to Jason. "What are you going to do to us?"

Jason's face contorted into an evil sneer. "I haven't decided yet. Maybe it's time to have a nice little murder suicide right here in your kitchen."

"No!" Janice screamed. "You can't do that. Not my daughter. She's done nothing to—"

"Jason, please don't do this," Ozzie begged. "Okay, you're right, I fucked up. Kill me if you have to, but let them go. They know nothing about any of it. They'll never say—"

"You're repeating yourself, Ozzie," Jason said.

"If you're trying to scare us, Jason, you've succeeded," Janice said, her voice quivering. "There's no need for this to go any further. Ozzie's right, we will never say a word about this to anyone."

"Oh, is that right?" Jason snarled. "Do you think I'm stupid? The first thing you'll do after I leave is call the fucking police." He pointed at Ozzie. "You can thank your husband for this. He's the one who fucked it all up."

Jason turned his gun toward Ozzie. "No!" Molly screeched.

"Jason, stop!" Spade screamed.

Adam pushed the door halfway open. Directly in front of him stood Spade, dressed in black and pointing a gun at someone across the room out of Adam's sight.

"Are you threatening me, little girl?" Jason growled. He gave a sick laugh. "What the fuck are you going to do with that? You think you're going to shoot me?"

"Yes, if I have to. This has gone far enough. Let them go!"

"Not very well played," Jason said. "Sorry about this."

There was a loud pop, a flash of light and a chorus of screams. As Spade fell to the floor, Ellen smashed through the door, past Adam, with her gun out in front of her. Adam grabbed for her but missed, then followed on her heels. As he cleared the doorway into the kitchen, Adam saw a hand with a gun swinging toward Ellen. He screamed, "No!" and dove over her, at the figure holding the gun.

Adam's shoulder connected with Jason waist high, and another shot fired as they crashed to the floor. More screams echoed through the room. Adam was on top, driving his shoulder into Jason's rib cage when he looked up and saw the gun moving in his direction. He lifted his left arm and reached for it. As his hand closed around Jason's wrist, there was another blast. For a split-second Adam's mind flashed to Ellen, and whether she had been hit by either of the two shots. He pushed the gun away, smashing it into a cupboard. There was another gun blast and the sound of glass shattering, but Jason was still holding onto the gun and his free arm was now around Adam's neck, choking him. Adam smashed the gun into the cupboard again, this time hitting a pull handle. There was a grunt from Jason, and the gun fell to the floor. Adam grabbed the arm that was around his neck and, with brute strength, pulled it away and flipped over on top of Jason. In his head, Adam was back on the mats as his wrestling instincts kicked in. He sunk his right arm around Jason's waist, drove his shoulder under his rib cage and pulled his left arm behind his back. If he held Jason in this position, there was no way in hell he was going anywhere.

Adam looked up and saw Ellen pick up Jason's gun. Blood was running down the side of her face. "You're bleeding. Were you hit? Are you okay?"

"Only by you when you jumped over me. I hit my head on the corner of the cabinet."

Jason reared up, but Adam jammed his head into the floor.

"You fucking asshole, I'm going to kill you," Jason yelled.

"I don't think so," Adam responded. To Ellen he said, "I've got him, check on her."

Keeping the gun pointed at Jason, Ellen scooted across to where Spade was sprawled face up on the floor. "I'm not sure about her. She's conscious, but she's bleeding a lot."

When Adam lifted his head to look in Spade's direction, Jason threw his head upward, smashing it into Adam's nose. Adam's grip loosened, and Jason flipped over and drove his fist into the side of Adam's jaw.

"Fuck," Adam screamed as Jason slipped out from under him. Adam swung his head back around and saw Jason backhand Ellen across the face. When the gun went flying out of her hand, Adam dove for it but missed, slamming his head into the edge of the countertop and falling to the floor. Blurry eyed, he looked up and saw Jason standing over him, lowering the gun toward his head. Adam froze, a vision of his own death flashing through his brain.

He heard the shot but felt nothing. Then he saw the gun drop from Jason's hand as he collapsed to the floor with a dark red spot in the middle of his forehead.

Adam looked at Ellen, the side of her face a bright red and her eyes bugging out of her head. Next to her, Spade slowly lowered her outstretched arm, dropped the gun to the floor, and grabbed her side. With blood seeping between her fingers, she let out a long, low groan, lay back down and closed her eyes.

Chapter Thirty-Nine

Ozzie was on his feet leaning into Molly who was sobbing uncontrollably. "It's okay, Molly. It's over. Everything's going to be okay."

"No, it isn't!" she screamed. "They're going to kill us!"

"No, Molly, they're not going to hurt us, they're here to help us." Ozzie looked around. "Will somebody cut me loose?"

Adam crawled over Jason's legs, pulled out his knife and cut the zip ties that bound Ozzie's wrists, then handed him the knife.

Adam looked at Ellen. She was shaking and staring off into space. "Ellen," he exclaimed. As he slid in her direction, she blinked several times before her eyes focused on him. He placed a hand on each of her shoulders. "Are you okay?"

"I think so," she said, "but I don't know about her." Ellen pulled away from Adam and crawled over to where Spade lay sprawled on the floor.

"Is she alive?" Adam asked.

Spade let out another groan when Ellen put her hand on her neck to check for a pulse. "Yes, she is," Ellen said. "But she's bleeding a lot."

Adam could see blood seeping around the edges of Spade's fingers on the left side of her abdomen. "Put pressure on the wound."

"I'll try," Ellen said.

Adam checked for a pulse on Jason who was lying half on his side with blood pooling under the back of his head. "This one is gone."

Adam grabbed his phone from his pocket and hit 911. After three rings, the dispatcher answered. "We have two GSWs, one dead, one still alive, but barely." He looked at Ozzie. "What's the address?"

"1992 Maple Street"

Adam recited what Ozzie had told him. "No...no more active shooters. But we need help fast for the injured one."

Adam glanced up. Ozzie had cut Janice and Molly loose. They were holding on to each other. Janice pulled back and looked at Ellen kneeling beside Spade. "I'm a nurse, let me do that." She stepped over Jason's body.

Ellen lifted her blood-soaked hands, and Janice took over. Ellen scooted backwards on her butt and leaned against the wall. Her face was a chalky white except for the big red blotch where Jason had smacked her. Adam slid over to her and cupped her head with his hands. Her eyes were glazed over again. "Ellen, look at me. Are you okay?"

It took a while, but she finally refocused her eyes on his. Adam feared she was going into shock. He stood up. "Ozzie, can I get some water?"

"Sure." Ozzie pointed to the cupboard above the counter to the right of the sink. "Glasses are in there."

Adam filled a glass and took it to Ellen. He held it up to her lips. "Try and drink some of this." She wrapped both hands around it, took several small sips, then gulped down what was left.

Next to her, Janice was pushing down on Spade's

wound. She looked up at Ozzie. Her face was bright red. "So, are you going to tell me what the fuck this is all about?" She turned to her daughter and said, "Oh... I'm sorry, Molly, I shouldn't have used that—"

"Mom, do you really think I haven't heard that before?"

"And who are these people?" Janice demanded. "Are you sure they aren't going to kill us?"

Ozzie shook his head. "No, they're not going to kill us. They're good people who just saved our lives."

"Adam, are you okay? We heard gunshots." Adam turned and saw Beth stepping cautiously through the door from the garage. Sarah was right behind her. "We were afraid you were—"

"Who the hell are they?" Molly screeched.

"It's a long story," Ozzie said.

Adam took out his phone again and started scrolling through his contacts.

"Who are you calling now?" Ellen asked, her voice so weak that Adam barely heard her.

"Detective Smiley. We need her to be here...for the girls."

Joan Smiley was the only woman detective on the Shawnee Falls Police Department. Over the years, Adam had worked with her on several domestic violence cases and matters involving juveniles. Although she could be tough as nails if you crossed her, he always admired her sensitive touch in her interactions with victims, particularly kids. In one of the last cases he had with her, she gave him her cell number. She answered on the third ring.

"Hi, Joan, it's Adam Kennedy. Sorry to bother you, and I don't mean to interfere with police business, but I'm sure you'll be called in on this one anyway, and I think it would be best if you get involved sooner rather than later."

"Well, you probably are interfering, so, how about you tell me what is so urgent that you called me on my day off?"

After giving her a condensed version of the past twelve hours, Adam said, "I'm thinking you'll know better than anyone the best way to take care of these two young girls."

"What's the address?"

Adam gave it to her, then hung up and dialed Jon and Samantha Evan's number. Sam answered immediately. "What's going on? Are you okay?"

"Yes, we're fine." Adam glanced at Ellen. Her head was down, her eyes were closed, and she was as white as a ghost. "At least I think we are. Ellen's a little—"

"Where are you?"

Adam brought Sam up to date on what had happened since he last talked to her.

"Adam, you're both lucky as hell to be alive."

"You're right...but we are...it was—"

"By the way, you've got a shitload of cops in Michigan who are falling all over themselves to talk to you and everyone else involved in this thing. They've been trying to call you, but you haven't—"

"Oh, yeah...sorry, my ringer's been off since we last talked."

"Cops never like it when perps take off and leave three dead bodies in their wake."

"We're witnesses, not perps."

"I know that, but you're still going to have to convince all of them. I told everyone I'd let them know when you'll be available if I got ahold of you."

"I'm sure we'll be tied up here for a while, but any time after that...probably later this afternoon would work."

"I'll give them a call and see what I can arrange. I'll get back to you about the time and place."

"Oh, and I just called Detective Smiley. I wanted her to be here from the beginning, because of these girls. I thought she'd know the best way to deal with them."

"Good idea. Tell her I'd like her to call me when she's done there."

"Will do."

"Is there anything you and Ellen need right now?"

"No, we're fine. Thanks, though." Adam clicked off.

The sound of approaching sirens pierced the air.

Adam looked at Sarah and Beth, then at Ozzie and his family. "A lot of people are going to be asking all of you a whole lot of questions. While the choice is yours, I would recommend that the most important thing you can do is be completely and totally honest with your answers." To Ozzie he said, "Because I'm a witness to all of it, I can't be your lawyer, but if you like, I can suggest a couple of attorneys who would be good for this kind of situation. For now, I think it would be best if you hold off on any substantive discussion with the police until after you've consulted with whomever you are going to use. If that's what you want to do, you can just say that you prefer to talk to your lawyer before answering any questions about how you got involved in all this."

"What is he talking about?" Janice asked.

Ozzie gave a weak shrug. "Sure, thanks, I would appreciate that."

Chapter Forty

Adam and Ellen were sitting on lawn chairs in the garage when the paramedics wheeled Spade out on a stretcher. She had an oxygen mask covering her face and an IV in her arm.

"She saved our lives," Adam said. "I hope she makes it."

"I'm not quite there yet," Ellen responded. "After what she did to those girls..."

"I understand, but she—"

A while later, the door into the house opened again. This time it was a couple of guys from the coroner's office bringing Jason out in a bag.

Ellen shook her head in disgust. "Him, I don't feel badly about at all." Adam nodded but didn't say anything. "How much longer are we going to have to sit here?" Ellen asked.

It had been almost thirty minutes since Smiley left them sitting alone in the garage and went inside. The paramedics had cleaned up the wound on Ellen's forehead and given her an icepack for the right side of her face. Adam was relieved when, after checking over his bruised nose and face, they determined nothing was broken.

Ellen slid her chair so it touched Adam's and leaned her head on his shoulder. "So, how long has it been since we last slept?" she asked.

Adam reached over and patted her knee. "Seems like forever, doesn't it?"

"Actually, I don't know that I could sleep if I wanted to. My stomach feels kind of weird."

"I know what you mean. It's been even longer since we've eaten anything."

"You're right, but, after all the blood and dead bodies, I'm not sure I have much of an appetite." Ellen lifted her hands and stared at her palms. "At least they let me wash the blood off my hands before they sent us out here."

"Your color seems to be returning. You're not quite as pale as you were a while ago. How are you feeling?"

"I'm okay. I think I was dehydrated." Ellen sighed. "At least Sarah and Beth are safe."

"I bet Sarah can't wait to see her parents. I can't imagine how happy they'll be to have her back home."

Ellen lifted her head and looked at Adam. "I'm sure you know that none of what comes next is going to be easy for those girls."

"Yeah...no, I understand, I just—"

"After the trauma they've been through, they're going to need a lot of help before they can—"

"Adam." It was Detective Smiley coming through the door from the kitchen. "I need to talk to you...actually, both of you."

Trim with broad shoulders, Smiley was a striking figure with her blonde hair pulled back into a ponytail and tight blue jeans that showed off her long, athletic legs. She was a couple of years younger than Adam but still looked like the state champion swimmer she had been at Shawnee Falls High School. She grabbed another lawn chair off the wall, set it up in front of Adam and Ellen, and sat down.

"You were right to call me, Adam. These two girls are a mess." She looked down at the floor and seemed to be gathering herself. Then she looked up and said, "I'm going to need both of you to help me convince Beth and Sarah to let me take them to the hospital, especially Beth. She seems to have an extreme dislike for the police and every other kind of authority figure."

"I'm not surprised," Ellen said. "She told us she grew up in the foster system, and a lot of it wasn't very pleasant."

"Yes, well, she hasn't talked very much about her past, but I kind of gathered it was something like that. She wants me to let her just walk away. When I explained to her that, since she's a minor, I can't do that, she started getting aggressive, which I fully understand considering what she's been through."

"Of course, we'll do anything we can to help," Ellen said. "What about Sarah, how is she doing?"

"She's been crying a lot but sticking close to Beth."

"Where will you take them? The County Hospital?"

"No, Mercy Hospital over in Sandusky. They're much better equipped to handle this kind of case. I've already contacted the forensic nurse they have on staff and their psychologist who has had a lot of experience with this kind of thing. I know them, and they're both very good at what they do."

"Have you contacted Sarah's parents?" Adam asked.

"Not yet. I want to get them both to the hospital first. The problem I'm having right now is they both are very firm that the only people they want to talk to are the two of you. I think you're the only ones they trust at all at this point. It's pretty obvious they don't trust me." Smiley shook her head. "So, do you think you could help me talk to them? The last thing either of them needs is to be thrown into the back of a police car and taken to the hospital against her will."

"Of course," Ellen said. "Whatever we can do to help them."

"That's great." Smiley leaned forward and placed her hands on her knees. "You have to know, though, it's going to take some delicate handling, especially with Beth."

"We understand," Ellen responded.

"Okay, then, I'm ready if you are."

They were about to stand up when the door from the kitchen opened, and Ozzie stepped through it with his hands cuffed behind his back. A uniformed officer was on each arm. Detective Ramirez, whom Adam knew was SFPD's lead homicide detective, was right behind them. As Ozzie walked past, he looked first at Adam, then at Ellen.

"Thank you for your help, Ozzie," Adam said.

Ozzie nodded as one the officers nudged him forward.

When Detective Ramirez stopped in front of them, Ellen said, "You do know that, in the end, he helped save all our lives don't you?"

The detective just stared back at her. Adam reached over and took Ellen's hand. "There will be plenty of time to talk about all of that."

"You going to be representing him?" Ramirez asked.

"I don't know if he would want me to…and even if he does, I don't think that would be a good idea since I'm a witness to so much of what has happened."

Ramirez gave a grunt. "I'll finish up in there," he said to Smiley as he turned and walked back into the house.

"Don't mind him, he's just pissed because he was supposed to be off the whole weekend," Smiley said.

Adam rolled his eyes. "Oh, really? How about, we were supposed to be on our honeymoon?" He shrugged and shook his head. "No problem. I'm too tired to worry about things like that."

"I get it," Smiley said. "You ready to do this?"

"Sure."

Chapter Forty-One

"Don't touch anything, only step where I step," Detective Smiley instructed. She led the way back inside and through the kitchen.

A guy with a camera stood and let them pass. A uniformed sergeant, Detective Ramirez and someone Adam assumed was a forensic tech were tagging plastic bags of evidence. Smiley pointed through an archway. "They're in the dining room."

Adam watched Ellen avoid looking at the blood on the floor, as they followed Smiley into a fairly large dining room. In front of them, a rectangular table surrounded by six chairs was centered on a multicolored, faux oriental rug. Beyond the table, a bay window provided a view of the front yard and the street. The rain had stopped, but the dark gray sky seemed to go well with the mood in the room. Beth and Sarah were seated at the side of the table nearest them. In front of the two girls were empty coffee mugs and a plate sprinkled with remnants of toast someone had prepared for them

Ellen seemed a little taken aback when Sarah jumped up, threw her arms around her, and started sobbing.

"I can't...I can't believe it...you...you saved us," she said between sobs.

Ellen held her, whispering over and over again, "It's okay...it's okay. It's all over now."

Adam looked down at Beth. She had her arms wrapped tightly across her chest and a dour look on her face. The body language couldn't have been more obvious. His first inclination was to put his hand on her shoulder to comfort her, but reconsidered figuring the last thing she likely wanted was some guy putting his hands on her. Instead, he pulled out the chair next to her and sat down. Within a few minutes, Sarah stopped crying and sat back down next to Beth. Ellen took the chair next to Sarah.

Ellen was right, this isn't going to be easy.

Detective Smiley, who had been standing in the entryway from the kitchen, walked around the table, pulled out a chair across from them, and sat down. "I've been explaining to Beth and Sarah why it's so important that they go to the hospital," she said in a soft, gentle tone.

Beth exploded. "Yeah, and from there some children services asshole is going to haul me away and try to dump me into some hellhole of a foster home. No fucking way that's going to happen. I want out of here...now!"

Ellen leaned forward with her elbows on the table. "Considering what you've been through, Beth, that's certainly understandable."

"Tell her that," Beth exclaimed pointing at Smiley.

"I don't think I have to. My guess is she gets it."

"I do, Beth," Smiley said. "I really do."

"Then why won't you just let me go?"

"My first concern right now is for your health. With what you've been...you know...what you've been forced to do, it's very important that you allow a doctor to examine you to make sure you aren't carrying any diseases which, if left untreated, could affect you adversely for the rest of your life."

Beth sat and glared at the detective.

Ellen reached out and placed her hands palms down on the table. "I know it's not what you want, Beth, but she's right. Without being examined by a doctor, there is no way to tell what you might have picked up from God-knows-who you encountered over the last year. Now is not the time to make a mistake that you could end up regretting later."

Beth's faced tightened, but Adam thought he detected a slight nod.

"I understand that you're scared to death of falling back into the same kind of awful conditions that you ran away from," Ellen said. "Believe me, I get that, at least as much as anyone who hasn't lived it can. But I'm asking you to trust Adam and me...and trust that we will not let that happen to you." Ellen waited for a response, but Beth remained stone-faced. "Please, Beth, all we're talking about is allowing a doctor to examine you. If they find you're okay, then that will be the end of it."

"No, it won't." Beth pointed her finger at Detective Smiley. "Let's say I go with you, get examined, and they say nothing's wrong with me. You're not going to let me just walk out of the hospital, are you?"

Detective Smiley folded her hands and lifted them up to her chin. "I won't lie to you, Beth. No, since you're a juvenile, I can't let you leave on your own. But I've heard you, and I will do everything within my power to see that nothing happens to you that isn't of your choosing."

Beth shook her head and rolled her eyes. "Care to hear how many hundreds of times I've heard that line of shit?"

"I'm sure you have, and I understand that you have no reason to believe that this time will be any different. All I can do is give you my word that—"

"This time will be different, Beth," Ellen interjected. "This time Adam and I will be there for you...to help you...to make sure that doesn't happen."

When Ellen glanced his way, Adam suspected she saw his eyes widen slightly, but he didn't say anything.

"I don't need anybody's help. I've been on my own for two years. I'm not going to go back to having some fucking social worker telling me what to do with my life."

"Beth," Sarah said hesitantly, "I know you probably don't want to hear this, but I think we should, at least, go to the hospital and get checked out. Both of my parents are doctors, and I know they would say to do that."

"That's fine for you, you have a home and family to go back to. After the hospital, they're going to try and put me somewhere that's—"

"I promise you, Beth, we will not let that happen," Ellen said.

"Oh, yeah, how are you going to do that? There's no way you'll be able to stop them."

"Adam is a lawyer. He will go to court if he has to; he'll make sure that your rights and your wishes are protected."

"Yeah, well, I've heard that one before, too."

"I get that you don't feel like you can trust anyone right now, and I fully understand that," Ellen said. "But I'm asking you to trust us now. We're not going to abandon you. We'll be with you every step of the way. Won't we Adam?" Ellen shot him a, *you-better-give-the-right-answer-buddy,* look.

"Yes, absolutely."

Ellen reached over and put her hand on Beth's shoulder. "Let's just take this one step at a time, starting with the medical exam."

"Please, Beth, I think we should do it," Sarah said.

Beth nodded slowly. "Okay, but if I don't like what's happening, I'm out of there."

Ellen looked at Detective Smiley. "Can we take them?"

Adam spoke up. "Ellen, we don't have a way to do that. My car is at the marina."

"That's okay, I have to do the transporting," Smiley said. "But I can have an officer take you to get your car when you leave here."

"Thank you, we'll meet you at the hospital," Ellen said.

"They will be pretty tied up for the rest of the day and will probably be kept overnight to wait for test results," Detective Smiley said. "I suggest you wait and come by this evening. Otherwise, you'll just be sitting and waiting around in a hallway by yourselves."

It was another half hour before they were allowed to leave. As they walked out, Adam told Detective Smiley, "Samantha Evans, from the Prosecutor's Office, wants you to call her when you're done here." Smiley looked at him quizzically. "When we left Grant Harbor, I called Sam. She contacted the authorities in Michigan to let them know what was going on…you know…with all the bodies lying around over there and no one lingering to explain."

"I'll call her." Smiley turned and walked Beth and Sarah to her car.

Chapter Forty-Two

Adam had purchased his three-bedroom, split-level home on Jefferson Avenue two years before he met Ellen. The bedrooms and one full bathroom were on the upper level, an eat-in kitchen, living room, and half bath were on the middle level, and a family room and another full bathroom were on the lower level, which could be entered from the garage.

As he pulled into the driveway, Adam's phone started vibrating. He pulled it out and looked at it. Samantha Evans. "Hi, Sam, what's going on?"

"As expected, you have a bunch of people who want to talk to you. I was able to put them off until three o'clock this afternoon at the Shawnee Falls Police Station. They'll talk to the girls and then interview Ozzie at the jail first. Detective Smiley would like you both at the station a little before then."

"Thanks, Sam. We'll be there."

"How are you guys doing?"

"We're okay. I think it's all just starting to sink in."

Adam looked at Ellen. Her head was leaning back against the headrest, and her eyes were closed. "A little tired...not exactly how we planned to spend our wedding night."

"No kidding. Do you need anything? Is there anything we can do for you?"

"No, we're fine, but thanks for asking. I do appreciate all you've done."

"No problem. Take care of yourselves."

Adam put his phone back in his pocket and unclipped his seatbelt. "We have to be at the police station at—"

"Yes, I heard, three o'clock. What time is it now?"

Adam looked at his watch. "Ten fifteen...a.m....but it feels more like it should be p.m."

Adam wondered if Ellen's feet felt as heavy as his did as they trudged up the steps to the front door of his house. When they entered the foyer, Ellen glanced down at herself. "I can't wait to take a shower and get into my own clothes."

"I agree."

"Can we sleep for a couple hours before we go to the police station?"

"That would be my first choice."

"Good, I was hoping you'd say that."

"We need to get going, we're supposed to be there in twenty minutes," Adam said. He cleared the table of the dishes from the fried egg sandwiches he had prepared for them. When he closed the dishwasher and turned around, he saw that Ellen hadn't budged from her chair. "Are you okay?"

"I'm fine. The couple hours of sleep helped. So, what's going to happen when we get there? Who will we be seeing...what kind of questions will they be asking?"

"Same kind of questions that Smiley asked. There'll probably be Detectives from the Monroe County Sheriff's Department. Because of Sarah and Beth, they may have gotten the FBI involved. They could be there too."

"Should we have a lawyer with us?"

"I'm a lawyer."

"I know that, but maybe we should have someone—"

"No...there's no need for that. We're witnesses, not suspects."

"Can I just let you do the talking?"

"I don't think that will work. They'll probably separate us."

"Why would they do that?"

"To make sure our stories are the same." Adam noticed that Ellen was wringing her hands. "Listen, it'll be easy. Just answer whatever questions they ask you. Don't embellish, leave out the adjectives, and tell it exactly as you remember it. As I always tell my clients, if you're honest they can't trip you up."

"Are they going to try to trip me up...like with trick questions?"

"Probably not...well, maybe a little. But, as I said, just be honest and you'll have no problem."

"What if I don't like the kind of questions they're asking?"

"Then say you're done answering questions. But that shouldn't happen. They just want to hear our version of everything that happened out there."

As they walked out the door, Ellen asked, "We are going to the hospital when we're done there, aren't we?"

"That's the plan."

Adam drove past his storefront office on Market Street where he had spent his entire legal career as a sole practitioner and found a parking spot on Perry Avenue in front of the Wendell County Courthouse. The Shawnee Falls Police Station was across the street from the courthouse next door to the Wendell County Jail.

"How long do you think this will take?" Ellen asked.

"I have no idea. Depends on how many questions they have."

Ellen sighed and opened the passenger side door. "Let's get this over with."

"Shit," Adam exclaimed as he climbed out of the car.

"What's the matter?"

"Look." Adam pointed at two vans parked down the block from the Police Station. One had WKYC Cleveland plastered across the side, the other said Channel 11, Toledo. Two local newspaper reporters whom Adam knew were standing on the corner.

"Word sure travels fast," Ellen said. "What do we do?"

"Keep our heads down and walk past them without saying a word." Adam grabbed Ellen's hand. "Let's go."

They were in the middle of the street when one of the reporters on the corner shouted, "There he is, that's Kennedy." The doors of both vans flew open.

"Mr. Kennedy, can we have a word with you?" A woman jogged toward them with a microphone in her outstretched hand. A short guy with a camera was close on her heels. The crew from the other van was right behind them.

"Mr. Kennedy, will you answer a few questions about the murders?" a male voice shouted.

They all converged as Adam and Ellen arrived at the entrance to the police station. Adam pulled open the heavy glass door, let Ellen in, then slipped inside and pulled it shut behind him. The gaggle of reporters jostled each other on the other side of the glass for a moment, then hung their heads and grumbled to each other as they turned and walked away.

Ellen looked around, surprised at how vulnerable she felt in this unfamiliar territory. *Maybe even more than when Ozzie was pointing a gun at my head on the boat. Probably because I didn't have time to stop and think about it then.*

Chapter Forty-Three

Silence prevailed during the twenty-minute drive from the Shawnee Falls Police Department to Mercy Hospital in Sandusky. The weather from the night before had cleared, and the sun was shining with the temperature pushing seventy degrees. Adam pulled into a guest parking spot. When he looked at Ellen, he could see the tension in her face. "Are you okay?" he asked.

"You have to stop asking me that. No, I'm not okay…whatever the hell that means. That whole thing with the police was awful."

"I'm sure you did just fine. After what we went through, who wouldn't be—"

"Oh, yeah, I don't suppose you broke down and cried or almost passed out when you were talking about…you know, people getting shot up and blood all over the place."

"Don't be so hard on yourself. I found it plenty hard to talk about."

"Yeah, right." Ellen shook her head. "Screw it. It is

what it is, and now we have to see what we can do for these girls, especially Beth. Sarah has her parents and family, Beth has no one. I'm afraid she's going to want to take off, and, if she does, she'll end up back on the street."

When Ellen turned toward him, Adam saw a tear fighting to escape from the corner of her left eye. He leaned over, put his arm around her and kissed the top of her head. "Then let's go and see what we can do to help."

By the time they were walking into the hospital, it was close to six o'clock. The small lobby area was empty, and the air was filled with the fragrance of whatever institutional food was being served to the patients for dinner. Adam's stomach let out a low groan. They approached the reception desk realizing for the first time that they didn't know either of the girl's last names. They were in the midst of describing whom they were looking for when they heard an elevator door ding and saw Detective Smiley come around the corner.

"Adam, Ellen, I'm glad you're here."

"How are they? Can we see them?" Ellen asked.

"They're okay…I think, but it's a little complicated. I'd like you to talk to the psychologist first."

Ellen frowned. "Why can't we just—"

"Trust me, you need to do this." She pointed in the direction from which she had come. "Follow me. Let's find a room where we can talk."

Smiley led them to the elevator. When the doors opened on the second floor, immediately across from them was a small glassed-in room in the center of which was a rectangular, oak table surrounded by six chairs with dark-blue upholstered seats and arms.

"Why don't you grab that room before someone else does? I'll go find her," Smiley said as she headed off down the hall.

As Adam opened the door for Ellen, he noticed a large picture of waves breaking onto a shell-covered beach under a pink and purple sky hanging on the opposite wall. It reminded Adam of how beautifully their weekend had begun and how quickly it had disintegrated from there.

As they pulled out chairs on the far side of the table and sat down, Ellen said, "I feel like I'm a player in one of those scenes where the doctor is about to come in and give the bad news to family members that someone has died. I don't like this."

Adam reached out and took her hand. "I don't either, but I trust Smiley, and—"

The door opened. A tall woman wearing a black, knee length skirt and a white blouse that set off her dark-brown complexion and close cropped, deep red hair, stepped in ahead of Detective Smiley. When Adam stood to greet her, she towered over him. Lean and athletic, his first reaction was that, although she looked to be in her mid-forties, she still could be playing in the WNBA.

She smiled and stretched out her hand. "Hi, I'm Cherice Collins." After shaking hands with Adam and Ellen, she pulled out the chair across from them, sat down, and dropped the large, black leather bag that had been slung over her shoulder to the floor.

Still standing in the doorway, Smiley said, "I was on my way out when I saw you come in. I'm going to take off. Let me know if you need me for anything." She gave a wave and closed the door behind her.

Cherice Collins looked first at Adam then at Ellen. "Thank you for being here. This is a very complicated situation, and I'm hoping you can help."

"Of course, that's why we're here," Ellen said. "How are Beth and Sarah? Are they okay?"

"It's going to be a long time before either one of them is okay. But hopefully, we can begin to move them in that direction." Cherice reached into her bag, pulled out a business card, and set it on the table in front of Adam and Ellen. It indicated that she was a PhD in Clinical Psychology. "I'm on staff here at the hospital parttime, I also have a private practice." She leaned forward and folded her hands on the table. "Over the last ten years, I have worked with many of these kinds of cases, here and across the northern half of the state. What we've learned is that if we are going to be effective in treating victims of human trafficking, it requires a very individualized approach."

Adam noticed Ellen cringe at the sound of the words—human trafficking.

"As I'm sure you know, both girls are very fragile right now. I've read the police reports, at least what's available so far, and from what I've been able to put together it appears their backgrounds are very different, which definitely will be a factor in their respective responses to their current situation."

"We're aware of that," Ellen said. "Have you contacted Sarah's parents?"

"Yes, it took a while, but Detective Ramirez finally got ahold of them. They're in California at a medical meeting. They're getting an early flight back in the morning."

"Has Sarah talked to them?" Ellen asked.

"Yes, she has. It was a tough conversation for her." Dr. Collins paused. "Actually, at this point, the only people either of them wants to talk to are the two of you."

Adam and Ellen looked at each other. Ellen frowned. "Oh, no. That's not good."

"No, it isn't, but not surprising, either. It's going to take a long time for them to trust anyone, including those who want to help them. That will be even more so for Beth. From what she told Detective Smiley and the officers from Michigan, she has a history of a lack of familial support and overall stability in her life." Dr. Collins looked down at her hands and then back up at Adam and Ellen. "And that's where you two come in."

"We'll do anything we can to help. Can we go talk to them?" Ellen asked.

"Yes, but first it's important that you understand what they're dealing with as a result of what they've been through."

"I think I get it," Ellen said.

"I'm sure you do, but if you'll bear with me for a few minutes, I would like to explain a little more fully what I mean before you talk to them."

"Of course," Adam said.

When Ellen began to fidget in her seat, Adam knew she was getting impatient. He wasn't surprised when she blurted out, "Could you just get on with whatever it is you have to say so we can see them?"

"Ah...sure." Cherice smiled and continued. "Speaking hypothetically, when young girls, or anyone for that matter, suffer the kind of persistent violence and threats of violence that they have, it's almost impossible for them to meaningfully return to any sense of normal living without extensive treatment."

Ellen sighed. "Trust me, we fully understand that Sarah can't just go back home and return to school as if none of this ever happened."

Dr. Collins nodded. "The stigma and shame, particularly if anyone found out, would be more than anyone in her situation could bear. But that's only a small part of it. It's not unusual for young girls who have experienced what they have to exhibit symptoms of PTSD—post traumatic stress disorder—and everything that goes along with that, which in itself can cause prolonged problems with otherwise normal daily functioning.

"Victims can also experience difficulty controlling their emotions, exhibit serious anger issues, and often suffer from depression with suicidal tendencies. And even those problems can be just the tip of the iceberg. Many also suffer extreme anxiety, panic disorder, and a multitude of other symptoms. A huge issue in their recovery is rebuilding self-esteem and getting to a point where they can see themselves as valued and responsible members of society. For young girls in Sarah's situation, it's compounded further by the guilt they feel over having run away and hurting their parents and other family members. And for those like Beth, who have a history of repeated victimizations throughout their childhood and adolescence, often accompanied by drug abuse, the symptoms and treatment can be even more complicated."

"None of that surprises me," Ellen said.

"That's good. Then, I'm sure it also will not surprise you that, as victims of this kind of violence, it will take a long time for these girls to get past being afraid for their lives and being unable to trust anyone, even those who want to help them."

"Just tell us what you want us to do," Adam said.

"So far, they're sticking together like glue, refusing to be in separate rooms even while they were being examined. They both talked to Detective Smiley, the detectives from Michigan and the FBI agent, but Beth sees me as a threat and refuses to say anything other than she wants to 'Get the fuck out of here.' But since she only just turned seventeen, we can't let her do that. And even if we could, that would lead to disaster for her."

"She'd be right back on the street," Ellen said.

"Exactly."

"So, if you could make it happen, what would be the optimum treatment plan for them?" Ellen asked.

"It would be something that would evolve, depending on how they respond at each stage, but, ideally, it would begin with both girls going to a kind of shelter, for lack of a better word. The one I'm thinking about just happens to have two beds available now. It's in a home in the country, about fifty miles from here in the southeast corner of the county. It has exceptional staff, all of whom I have worked with in the past. It was started by a psychiatric nurse whose daughter ran away and ended up much like Beth and Sarah. She ultimately was rescued but six months later took her own life. A year after that, her mother opened Julie's House, named for her daughter."

"That's terrible," Ellen said.

"Yes, it was. But this is a way for the mother to try to

make something good out of something awful."

"How long would they stay at this house?" Ellen asked.

"The program is for ninety days. It provides the opportunity for them to get stabilized to a point where they can begin to rebuild the trust that is needed for them to meaningfully participate in a treatment plan that would be designed to meet their individual needs. While there, they can begin to get back to school, online of course, and have the support of peers who have had experiences like theirs, which can be very helpful."

"It sounds like a good program," Ellen said.

"Actually, it's the best I've ever seen, when it comes to this type of crisis intervention. To be honest, though, those first ninety days are just the beginning. It's still a long haul from there."

"So, you would like us to try and talk them into that?" Ellen said. "Well, at least Beth, we wouldn't want to interfere with what's going on between Sarah and her parents."

"Yes…but it's a little more complicated than that. There's a cost involved, and it isn't cheap. For Sarah, a lot of it should be covered by insurance. It would be up to her parents to cover the rest."

Ellen said, "But Beth doesn't have any insurance."

"Actually, while she was in the foster system, she was in the custody of Children Services and probably still is. So, we should be able to get the county to cover some of it. Even if we do, though, it wouldn't come close to covering the cost of this program. But you asked what the optimum treatment plan would be. There are other alternatives which would be fully covered."

"What would happen to Beth if she can't go there?" Adam asked.

"Unless something appears in her test results, she won't be able to stay here past tomorrow. I will work with Children Services to find a temporary, emergency placement for her."

"Well, I can guarantee you that's not going to work,"

Ellen said. "She'll be out of there in a second."

"I have that concern, too," Dr. Collins said. She looked from Adam to Ellen, and then added, "But before anything can happen, I need her to talk to me."

"Why don't we see if we can help with that?" Adam said.

"Do either of you have any questions?"

"I probably have a lot of questions…but they can wait," Ellen said.

"Okay then…let's go see them."

Chapter Forty-Four

Ellen had an unsettled feeling in her gut, as Dr. Collins escorted them down a long hall and stopped outside the last room on the right. There was a card inserted into a holder on the door with two names handwritten on it: Sarah Sanderson, Elizabeth Hardy.

Dr. Collins stepped back. "You two go on in, I'll be in my office. When you're done, ask the nurse to call me."

Ellen looked at Adam, knocked, then slowly pushed the door open. There were two beds in the room, but the girls were curled up together on the one closest to the far wall. As Ellen crossed the room to their bedside. Sarah jumped up and threw her arms around her. Over Sarah's shoulder, Ellen saw Beth sitting on the edge of the bed and it appeared that she had been crying. When Sarah finally let go, Ellen sat down next to Beth and put her arm around her. She rested her head on Ellen's shoulder as Sarah cuddled up on the other side of Ellen.

"You saved our lives," Sarah said. "You almost got

killed…and…and we never had a chance to thank you."

"There's no need for thanks. We just wanted to make sure you were safe."

Beth lifted her head and looked at Adam still standing in the doorway. "Thank you, Adam," she whispered.

He smiled, "You're very welcome."

"So, how are they treating you?" Ellen asked. "Have you had anything to eat?"

Beth stood and moved to the other bed. "Uh huh, they just took the trays away. Some meatloaf stuff with mashed potatoes and gravy. I only ate it because I was starving."

"That's what you say about everything you eat." Sarah said.

Beth shrugged. "Yeah, whatever."

"Have you had a chance to get any rest? After being up all night, you must be exhausted."

Sarah responded, "Not really, people have been in and out the whole time we've been here. A doctor examined us. She was okay, but it was—"

"It was pretty fucking disgusting." Beth interjected. "I'm sorry, I shouldn't have said that."

Ellen smiled. "Don't worry about it." She turned to Sarah. "I heard you talked to your mother and father."

Sarah nodded but didn't say anything.

Ellen put her arm around her. "Tell me what you're thinking."

"I'm afraid that…after what I've done…when they get here tomorrow, they won't want to…I don't know…see me." When Sarah let out a big sniff, Ellen pulled some tissues out of a box on the tray table and handed them to her.

"It sounds like you're feeling a lot of guilt," Ellen said.

"If I hadn't run away, none of this would have happened. If I hadn't been so stupid and believed Jason when he said he—"

"I keep telling her it wasn't her fault," Beth said. "That asshole stalked her, preyed on her for months. He was a master at that shit."

Ellen rubbed her hand over Sarah's back. "She has a point, Sarah."

"I know...he did do that. But still, I'm the one who chose to—"

"That's bullshit. He sucked you in, turned you against your parents," Beth said.

"Do you really think your mother and father aren't thrilled that you're alive and safe, and out of their minds excited and happy to have you back?" Ellen asked.

"Yes, they are, I know that. But after what I've done...I feel so ashamed. How can I ever explain to them why I—"

"You don't have to tell them anything you don't want to tell them," Beth said.

"You know they love you, don't you?" Ellen asked.

"Yes, I know that. And I love them." Sarah hung her head and covered her face with her hands. "I do want to see them. I'm just...really afraid of how it will..."

When Sarah stopped, Ellen put her arm around her and pulled her close. Sarah looked at Ellen and said, "I think I'm glad it won't be until tomorrow. Every time I close my eyes, I feel like Jason is going to come through the door and beat the shit out of us all over again."

"I understand."

"I hate to ask this but, could you be here? I mean...what if they don't believe me...you know, about what happened?"

"I will be here for as long as you want, for whatever you want."

"Will you tell that shrink to let me out of here?" They all turned to Beth. Her jaw was set, and her expression had turned hard.

"Can we talk about what that would look like?" Ellen asked.

"What do you mean?"

"Where would you go?"

"I have friends. I can manage on my own. I've done it before, and I can do it again."

"Oh, yeah, and how did that work out?" Sarah asked. Beth glared at her. "You can come home with me. I'll ask my parents if—"

"No way. You're going to have enough on your hands just dealing with them. I'm not getting in the middle of that."

Feeling lost as to where to go next, Ellen looked across the room at Adam. He gave a reassuring nod. "May I make a suggestion?" she asked.

Beth shrugged. "Sure, but I'll tell you right now there's no way I'm going to let them stick me in another foster home."

"I fully understand how you feel about that, and I don't blame you. I do think, though, that you should at least hear what Dr. Collins has to say about some other alternatives that may be of interest to you."

Instead of responding, Beth looked at Adam. "You're a lawyer? Can you please help me get out of here?" she pleaded.

Adam stepped over to the green vinyl chair that was at the foot of the two beds and sat down. They all watched as he made a finger tent with his hands and touched it to his lips then lowered his hands to his lap. "I promise I'll do everything I can to help you, Beth," he said. "But, since you're still a juvenile and don't have any parents, we will have to work with Children Services, which technically has custody of you. It's going to be up to them to—"

"I've been that route before. All those assholes ever did was stick me in another shithole foster home."

Adam looked at Ellen. There was a definite frown taking shape on her face. He sighed and said, "I'm sorry, Beth. I know that wasn't what you wanted to hear. What I would say, though, is that there may be a number of alternatives available to you for where to go from here, and I think you should explore all of them."

"Oh, yeah, like what?"

"Well, I think Dr. Collins has some ideas, and I believe it would be good for both of you to keep an open mind and hear what she has to say."

With Beth's eyes locked on Adam's, Ellen added, "I hope you trust us, Beth, and I want you to know that Adam and I are here for you. We will do everything in our power to see to it that you aren't forced to do anything that you don't want to do."

Ellen thought she detected a softening of her features, as Beth turned her face away from Adam. Sarah got up and moved over to the other bed and sat down next to Beth. "I think we should, at least, hear her out."

"That's easy for you to say, you have a home to go to."

"I'm not going anywhere without you. I never would have made it at that house on my own. If it hadn't been for you, I'd probably be dead by now."

"That's bullshit. Toward the end, you were keeping me alive. I probably would have killed myself if you hadn't stopped me."

"Okay, so let's just say we kept each other going. That's why we need to stick together now. I think we should listen to her."

Beth shrugged. "I'll listen, but that doesn't mean I don't want out of here."

Ellen smiled. "Good decision, Beth." Ellen turned to Adam. "Would you go find someone to call Dr. Collins?"

Chapter Forty-Five

Adam was heading down the hall to the nurses' station when he spotted a tall, trim, young-looking guy sporting a crew cut, a dark suit, white dress shirt and dark tie, pointing his finger at Dr. Collins, almost touching her nose. It was Special Agent Lafferty from the FBI who had interviewed them at the Shawnee Falls Police Station. He didn't look happy.

When Collins shook her head emphatically, Lafferty threw his hands in the air and stomped away. She still had a grim look on her face when Adam approached her.

"What was that about?" he asked.

"They haven't been able to find the farmhouse where the girls were kept. He wanted me to release Sarah and Beth for a few hours so he could take them over there to help him locate it."

"Now?"

"Yes. And, as you saw, he didn't like it very much when I told him there was no way I could permit that. After the trauma they've suffered, going back there right now is the last thing they need. I told him he could check back with me tomorrow."

"Good, thank you for doing that."

"Sure. So, how did it go? Will they talk to me?"

"I think so, at least they said they would. As I'm sure you know, Beth is on the edge. She's pretty determined, and I think she'll definitely run away again before she'll go back into a foster home."

"That doesn't surprise me." Dr. Collins motioned with her hand back toward the girls' room. "Shall we go?"

As they approached, Adam could hear Ellen and the two girls talking. The conversation stopped the instant he and Dr. Collins appeared in the doorway. He followed her in as she greeted Beth and Sarah.

"How are you two doing?" she asked in a soft, soothing tone.

Sarah said, "Okay." Beth didn't respond.

Adam wasn't disappointed when Dr. Collins suggested that it had been a long day for them and that he and Ellen should go home and come back in the morning. With Dr. Collins' blessing, Ellen wrote down her cell number on a napkin and handed it to Beth. "I want you both to know that you can call me any time." She gave each of the girls a hug and followed Adam out the door.

"Are you hungry?" Adam asked as they walked out of the hospital. "We could pick something up on the way home."

"Not really...but I know I should eat something. Has it really been only twenty-fours since you were grilling that delicious salmon for our wedding night dinner?"

"Yep, seems more like a month, doesn't it?"

"At least."

"How about Chinese?"

"Sure, but I need to stop by my apartment and pick up

a few things first."

Although their courthouse wedding had been in the works since Ellen gave her thirty-day notice to her landlord three weeks earlier, most of her things were still at her apartment.

Adam opened the passenger door to his SUV for Ellen, then walked around to the other side and climbed in. "We're going to have to arrange for you to get moved out of there."

"Yeah, I know, we're down to a week. I'll get the rest packed up over the next few days."

As Adam hauled two suitcases filled with clothing upstairs to the bedroom, Ellen unloaded white cartons of fried rice and almond chicken onto the kitchen table.

"Smelling that made me realize how hungry I am," Adam said as he came into the kitchen and opened the refrigerator. "I'm having a beer. Would you like one?"

"Sure. I don't think I'll need it, but it wouldn't hurt to have one to help me sleep tonight."

They had been eating in silence for a few minutes when Adam looked up and saw Ellen staring at him. "What?"

"I love you."

Adam reached out and took Ellen's hand. "Even after all I put you through over the last twenty-four hours?"

"You didn't do that. It just happened...wrong place, wrong time."

Adam started eating again but after a couple of bites noticed Ellen still sitting there looking at him. He put down his fork and waited.

Finally, she said, "About Beth."

"I agree."

"Agree with what?"

"We should help her."

"But, according to Dr. Collins, even this initial ninety-day program could get very expensive."

"I know. But…it's the right thing to do."

Ellen took a couple of bites then looked at Adam and said, "What do you think about letting her live here?"

"You mean here in the house in which we haven't even spent one night as husband and wife?"

Ellen smiled and nodded. "Yep, that one."

"Well…if she'll do the program at Julie's House, it'll give us time to turn the lower level into a living space for her."

"Are you sure you would be okay with that?"

Adam sat back and opened his hands out in front of him. "I don't know about you, but I didn't just almost get us both killed saving her life so she could go back to living on the streets." Adam hesitated then said, "Until she turns eighteen, it would need approval from Children Services…we'd probably have to get licensed as foster parents.

"Do you think we can make that happen?"

"Sure, but that'll be the easy part."

"What do you mean?"

"From what she told you on the boat, Beth has never lived in the kind of home environment that either of us has. I've represented dozens of young people with backgrounds like hers over the years, and I think you need to know that, if we do this, it won't be easy. We'll have to keep our expectations in line with the realities of her past."

"You think I don't know that?"

"Well…no…I'm sure you do, but I'm just saying that it's important to—"

"Before I came here, I taught for five years at an inner-city school in Cincinnati. I've probably had more contact with marginalized kids than you have. So, please, don't start lecturing me about—"

Adam put his hands up in front of him. "Okay, I get it. I just wanted to make sure you know what we'd be getting into, and that it won't be easy."

"Trust me, I get it. I just feel like we have to do

whatever we can to help her, so she doesn't fall right back into the same shit all over again."

"So do I, but first we may need to nudge her a little more to go to Julie's House."

"I agree but, hopefully, that won't be necessary. It would be great if, by the time we get there in the morning, she'll have made that decision on her own." Adam took a few more bites then said, "Actually, I was hoping to go pick up the boat tomorrow."

"I was thinking about that too, but I really want to be available to Beth if she needs me for anything. Plus, I promised Sarah I would be there tomorrow when her parents arrive."

"I think you should be. I'll see if I can get Jon to drive me over there. I can sail it back myself."

"Are you sure you don't mind doing that?"

"No, as long as you don't mind."

"Not at all. Go for it."

Chapter Forty-Six

Seven Months Later

"I can't believe it. Look what it's doing out there," Adam said. He was sitting at the kitchen table in his usual Saturday work clothes: khaki pants, blue button-down collar shirt, and navy, V-neck sweater, sipping coffee and watching oversized, white snowflakes pile up on the grass in the front yard.

"You ought to be used to it by now," Ellen said as she stuffed sliced bagels into the toaster on the counter. "You're the one who chose to live your entire life in northwest Ohio. For us New Hampshire folks, April snow is a necessary rite of passage before we get to appreciate real spring."

"I am used to it, but that doesn't mean I have to like it." Adam took another sip of his coffee. "I got a call from Ozzie this morning."

"How is he doing?"

"Seems okay. He said he thinks his lawyer is close to getting him a plea deal with the prosecutor."

"What kind of plea deal?"

"Minimal time and a few years of community control."

"What did you tell him?"

"The same thing I always tell him, follow your attorney's advice."

"He did help us rescue the girls."

"I know, and I'm sure it's the only reason an offer like that would be on the table. That and the fact that Jason threatened to kill his wife and kids if he didn't follow his orders."

"Whatever happened to the other guy, Daveed, or whatever his name was? Did they ever find him?"

"The last I heard, no. When they finally found the house, he was gone. Fortunately, the other two girls were there, locked in an upstairs bedroom. They were hungry and had been beaten pretty badly, but otherwise were okay."

They both turned to see Beth shuffle into the kitchen with her head down and thumbs tapping on her phone, seemingly oblivious to their presence. She looked like she did every morning in her thick pink socks, yellow boxers, and graying, white sweatshirt. Beth did her own laundry and Ellen wondered if those items of clothing had been included in a load anytime in the last several months. She thought about mentioning it but instead asked, "Would you like a bagel?"

"No, just some coffee. I have to get dressed for work."

"Good morning, Beth," Adam said.

Ellen smiled, knowing Adam was hoping for a similar greeting in response, but not really expecting one. *There are only so many things you can work on at a time.*

Beth responded with a "Huh, yeah." She poured herself a coffee and started for the door but then stopped, turned around, and took a seat at the table. "I'm worried about Sarah."

"Why, what's going on?" Ellen asked as she carried the plate of bagels and a jar of raspberry jam to the table.

"She called me at four this morning. She's having

nightmares again. This time it was about Spade. Sarah dreamed she had gotten out of jail and was coming after her. I got her calmed down, but just now she asked me to go home with her after our group session this afternoon and stay over with her tonight."

"How do you feel about that?" Adam asked. He and Ellen were aware that Sarah's mother and father were not in favor of her having an ongoing relationship with Beth.

"It's okay." She blew on her coffee and took a sip. "Her parents never seem very excited about having me around. Whenever I walk in the door, they all but frisk me to make sure I'm not bringing drugs into their monster house." Beth took another sip of coffee. "Actually, I think they see her being with me as holding her back from getting past all the other shit, which is total fucking crap." She shook her head. "Like that's ever going to happen."

Ellen wanted to say something reassuring but instead asked, "Anything we can do?"

"No. It's just that…I think she needs me."

Ellen sensed that what Beth was really saying was that they needed each other.

"For what it's worth, I think you should do whatever you feel is best for Sarah…and for you."

Beth looked up at the clock that hung on the wall behind Adam. "I have to get going." She stood. "Oh, and I decided I don't want to spend the rest of my life passing greasy fucking hamburgers out a drive-through window. I think I want to sign-up to get my GED. Could you guys give me a hand with that?"

"Of course, we will," Ellen said.

Beth shuffled toward the door then stopped and over her shoulder said, "Good morning, Adam," then disappeared.

Adam smiled at Ellen. "Small steps."

CPSIA information can be obtained
at www.ICGtesting.com
Printed in the USA
BVHW071005050622
638947BV00025BB/339

9 781633 635760